Blacks of the Land

Originally published in Portuguese in 1994 as *Negros da Terra*, this field-defining work by the late historian John M. Monteiro has been translated into English by Professors James Woodard and Barbara Weinstein. Monteiro's work established ethnohistory as a field in colonial Brazilian studies and made indigenous history a vital part of how scholars understand Brazil's colonial past. Drawing on over two dozen collections on both sides of the Atlantic, Monteiro rescued Indians from invisibility, documenting their roles as both objects and actors in Brazil's colonial past and, most importantly, providing the first history of Indian slavery in Brazil. Monteiro demonstrates how Indian enslavement, not exploration or the search for mineral wealth, was the driving force behind expansion out of São Paulo and through the South American backcountry. This book makes a groundbreaking contribution not only to Latin American history, but to the history of indigenous slavery in the Americas generally.

John M. Monteiro was a professor in the department of anthropology of the Universidade Estadual de Campinas and the director of the same university's Instituto de Filosofia e Ciências Humanas. He also held visiting positions at the University of North Carolina at Chapel Hill, the University of Michigan, and Harvard University.

James Woodard is Professor of History at Montclair State University. He is the author of *A Place in Politics: São Paulo, Brazil, from Seigneurial Republicanism to Regionalist Revolt* (2009).

Barbara Weinstein is Silver Professor of History at New York University and Past President of the American Historical Association. She is the author of *The Color of Modernity: São Paulo and the Making of Race and Nation in Brazil* (2015), *For Social Peace in Brazil: Industrialists and the Remaking of the Working Class in São Paulo, 1920–1964* (1996), and *The Amazon Rubber Boom, 1850–1920* (1983).

CAMBRIDGE LATIN AMERICAN STUDIES

Other Books in the Series

111. *The Street is Ours: Community, the Car, and the Nature of Public Space in Rio de Janeiro*, Shawn William Miller
110. *Laywomen and the Making of Colonial Catholicism in New Spain, 1630–1790*, Jessica L. Delgado
109. *Urban Slavery in Colonial Mexico: Puebla de los Ángeles, 1531–1706*, Pablo Miguel Sierra Silva
108. *The Mexican Revolution's Wake: The Making of a Political System, 1920–1929*, Sarah Osten
107. *Latin America's Radical Left: Rebellion and Cold War in the Global 1960s*, Aldo Marchesi
106. *Liberalism as Utopia: The Rise and Fall of Legal Rule in Post-Colonial Mexico, 1820–1900*, Timo H. Schaefer
105. *Before Mestizaje: The Frontiers of Race and Caste in Colonial Mexico*, Ben Vinson III
104. *The Lords of Tetzcoco: The Transformation of Indigenous Rule in Postconquest Central Mexico*, Bradley Benton
103. *Theater of a Thousand Wonders: A History of Miraculous Images and Shrines in New Spain*, William B. Taylor
102. *Indian and Slave Royalists in the Age of Revolution*, Marcela Echeverri
101. *Indigenous Elites and Creole Identity in Colonial Mexico, 1500–1800*, Peter Villella
100. *Asian Slaves in Colonial Mexico: From Chinos to Indians*, Tatiana Seijas
99. *Black Saint of the Americas: The Life and Afterlife of Martín de Porres*, Celia Cussen
98. *The Economic History of Latin America since Independence*, Third Edition, Victor Bulmer-Thomas
97. *The British Textile Trade in South America in the Nineteenth Century*, Manuel Llorca-Jaña

(*Continued after the index*)

Blacks of the Land

Indian Slavery, Settler Society, and the Portuguese Colonial Enterprise in South America

JOHN M. MONTEIRO

Edited and Translated by

JAMES WOODARD

Montclair State University

BARBARA WEINSTEIN

New York University

CAMBRIDGE
UNIVERSITY PRESS

University Printing House, Cambridge CB2 8BS, United Kingdom

One Liberty Plaza, 20th Floor, New York, NY 10006, USA

477 Williamstown Road, Port Melbourne, VIC 3207, Australia

314–321, 3rd Floor, Plot 3, Splendor Forum, Jasola District Centre, New Delhi – 110025, India

79 Anson Road, #06–04/06, Singapore 079906

Cambridge University Press is part of the University of Cambridge.

It furthers the University's mission by disseminating knowledge in the pursuit of education, learning, and research at the highest international levels of excellence.

www.cambridge.org
Information on this title: www.cambridge.org/9781107114678
DOI: 10.1017/9781316335406

The text translated here was first published in Portuguese as *Negros da terra: índios e bandeirantes nas origens de São Paulo* by John M. Monteiro (São Paulo: Companhia das Letras, 1994).

First published in English by Cambridge University Press 2018 as *Blacks of the Land: Indian Slavery, Settler Society, and the Portuguese Colonial Enterprise in South America*; translation by James Woodard and Barbara Weinstein.

Printed in the United states of America by Sheridan Books, Inc.

A catalogue record for this publication is available from the British Library.

Library of Congress Cataloging-in-Publication Data
NAMES: Monteiro, John M. (John Manuel), 1956– author. | Weinstein, Barbara, translator, editor. | Woodard, James P., 1975– translator, editor.
TITLE: Blacks of the land : Indian slavery and the origins of colonial Sao Paulo / John M. Monteiro ; translated and edited by Barbara Weinstein, James Woodard.
DESCRIPTION: Cambridge, United Kingdom ; New York, NY : Cambridge University Press, [2018] | Series: Cambridge Latin American studies | Includes bibliographical references.
IDENTIFIERS: LCCN 2018012563 | ISBN 9781107114678 (hardback) | ISBN 9781107535183 (paperback)
SUBJECTS: LCSH: Indians of South America – Brazil – São Paulo (State) – History. | Indian slaves – Brazil – São Paulo (State) | Slavery – Brazil – São Paulo (State) | Bandeiras – Brazil – São Paulo (State) | São Paulo (Brazil : State) – Economic conditions.
CLASSIFICATION: LCC F2519.1.S2 M65 2018 | DDC 981/.61–dc23
LC record available at https://lccn.loc.gov/2018012563

ISBN 978-1-107-11467-8 Hardback
ISBN 978-1-107-53518-3 Paperback

Contents

Foreword

James Woodard

Beginning in the 1490s in the Caribbean, and through the slow demise of native slavery in North and South America over the eighteenth and nineteenth centuries, millions of Amerindians were subjected to enslavement, captivity, and forced labor. Indian slavery was practiced across the Americas, at one point in time or another, in jurisdictions claimed by every European power that engaged in New World colonialism. Spanish, Portuguese, Dutch, English, Scottish, French, and Russian colonists held native Americans as slaves, exerting their mastery over them and dealing in them as chattel. In parts of the United States, Mexico, and Brazil, native slavery survived the ending of European colonial claims and the formation of independent nation-states, lasting well into the nineteenth century. By that point, however, the numbers of Amerindians held as slaves in Brazil and the United States were tiny compared to the masses of African and Afro-American captives that made up the absolute majority of the populations of the two countries' plantation zones. Indian slavery thus seemed a small thing – economically, socially, demographically – when set alongside African and Afro-American slavery, on the ascent through the first half of the new century in Brazil and the southern United States alike.

Until recently – and for many good reasons – scholarly attention to Indian slavery has been similarly dwarfed by the volume of care and attention paid to African and Afro-American slavery in the Americas. Over the last fifteen years, however, the study of native slavery has undergone a remarkable boom among North American historians. Indeed, some of the most exciting recent work on the history of colonial and borderlands North America has focused on Amerindian captivity and Indian slavery. The year 2002 is the key one here, marked by the appearance of two prizewinning books – Alan Gallay's *The Indian Slave Trade* and James F. Brooks's *Captives and Cousins* – though 2007, 2010, and 2012 are noteworthy also, for the publication of Juliana Barr's *Peace Came in the Form of a Woman*, Christina Snyder's *Slavery in Indian Country*, and Brett Rushforth's *Bonds of Alliance*, respectively. In different ways, applying varied methodologies to arrays of distinct source materials, these books examine native and colonial models of captivity, explicating their significance in specific local and regional contexts while also documenting their place in the making of larger imperial structures and practices. The original contributions presented in these books have been complemented by synthetic essays by Gallay and Snyder that provide overviews of the history and historiography of Indian slavery in North America, while placing that historical experience and scholarship in a larger hemispheric context, in Gallay's case including extended considerations of forms of unfree (but non-slave) native labor that arose in Spain's New World colonies.

Looking north from Brazil – the American antipode to Gallay's and Snyder's area of study – the underrepresentation of Portuguese America in this series of works is striking. It was in Brazil, after all, that Indian slavery developed furthest and lasted longest, in the process shaping Portuguese colonialism while wreaking havoc on native societies. Indeed, it was in Brazil that the plantation-slavery complex was first implanted on the American mainland, and where nearly half of all African captives to survive the Middle Passage would be landed, though in its cane fields, sugar mills, and slave quarters, Indians would outnumber Africans through the close of the sixteenth century. In the seventeenth century and after, as Africans replaced Amerindians on the sugar-growing coast, Indian slavery acquired increased importance elsewhere, from the southeastern interior of Portuguese America to its Amazonian north. But only in Rushforth's *Bonds of Alliance* is Brazilian priority in the development of indigenous slavery acknowledged, and in Gallay's summary statement on Indian slavery in the Americas, non-slave varieties of forced native labor adopted in Spanish America receive greater coverage than the enslavement of Indians in Portuguese America, a pattern followed in Andrés Reséndez's recent overview.

The major obstacle to greater attention to Brazilian experiences of Indian slavery has been the Portuguese language. This language barrier has been doubly unfortunate, for it has meant that Brazilian historical literature has not received its due recognition in the Anglo-American academy, while English-speaking historians have been deprived of access to scholarship that might inform their own work, as well as their students' perspectives on the history of the Americas. As far as Indian slavery is concerned, the renewed attention to the topic that one may date to 2002 in this country was in some ways anticipated by Brazilian historical scholarship of the early 1990s. Indeed, by the time Gallay's and Brooks's books received Columbia University's Bancroft Prize in 2003, in some sense the analogous historiographical moment in Brazil had passed. Today, Indian slavery and its place in the making of colonial Brazil is an established, well-explored field among Brazilian scholars and has been for over two decades. Indeed, in the last twenty years some of the most exciting work on the Portuguese colonial experience in the New World – which began in 1500 with the accidental landfall of an India-bound fleet on the Atlantic coast of South America and ended in 1822 with the declaration of Brazilian independence by a Portuguese-born prince – has dealt with the hitherto neglected history of native peoples' roles across these three centuries.

The key work here, now available in English for the first time, is John M. Monteiro's *Negros da terra: índios e bandeirantes nas origens de São Paulo*, the title of which translates literally as "Blacks of the Land" (one of many terms the Portuguese used for Amerindians), the subtitle referring to the origins of the southeastern Portuguese American colony of São Paulo and two of the principal protagonists in its early history: Indians and *bandeirantes*, the latter a term invented in the eighteenth century to refer to the European settlers of the region who had organized expeditions (*bandeiras*) into the interior beginning in the late sixteenth century. To the so-called *bandeirantes* were attributed gritty entrepreneurialism, heroic wanderlust, civilizing dynamism, and the aggrandizement of Portugal's territorial claims in South America, and thus the future geographic immensity of the independent nation-state of Brazil.

The term *bandeirante* – though meaningless to non-Portuguese speakers – is an important, even emblematic one in Brazil, and in São Paulo has been used in contexts as incommensurate as nineteenth-century political discourse and more recent product placement. Its appearance in the subtitle of *Negros da terra* is closer to the latter than the former, likely added to a book that scarcely uses the term at the insistence of the publisher, Companhia das Letras, since the 1980s Brazil's most important commercial publishing house, due in part to the savvy of its marketeers. The latter paid off handsomely in the case of *Negros da terra*, for the book became a scholarly best-seller in Brazil. Originally published in 1994, the first edition sold out within a year, prompting reprint editions in 1995, 1999, 2000, 2005, 2009, and 2013. Among the book's eager buyers were no doubt many local history buffs, adherents of what the book's preface calls "the potent myth of the *bandeirante*," in which the grizzled, suspect-originned backwoodsman of history was recast as an enterprising, patriotic explorer, the totemic embodiment of modern São Paulo's progressiveness and predominance.

Rather than a celebration of the early Paulistas – as residents of the region and later of the state of São Paulo are called – *Negros da terra* offered a serious, finely grained history of the society and economy of São Paulo between the 1500s and the early 1700s that centered on the hunting of Indian captives by Paulistas and these captives' subsequent exploitation on colonial estates. Revisionist in the best sense of the word, it restored indigenous people and the institution of forced labor to which they were subjected to their rightful places in the history of colonial Portuguese America. For this reason, as we shall see later, the book won accolades and academic laurels for its author, who helped lead the development of colonial Brazilian ethnohistory as a significant field of study, in Brazil and abroad.

*

This remarkable set of outcomes was richly deserved and to the great benefit of Brazilian history as a field of scholarly endeavor. Such is the consensus among historians and allied social-scientific stakeholders, in Brazil and abroad, but even among this specialist audience, the history of *Negros da terra* – a history that in some ways makes its success all the more remarkable – is underappreciated.

In its earliest incarnation, *Negros da terra* was a doctoral dissertation submitted to the University of Chicago in 1985, based on research in Portugal, Brazil, and Rome, and emerging – in a deeper sense – from a childhood and adolescence split between the United States, where John was born and where he attended college, and Brazil, specifically Campinas, one of a number of the state of São Paulo's secondary cities, some sixty miles north of the state capital. The title of the dissertation, "São Paulo in the Seventeenth Century: Economy and Society," captures some of the best of the dominant tendency in the English-language historiography of the period: materialist, monographically focused social history pursued with austere rigor. That the society and economy in question were based on a dogged, regionally specific mode of exploiting the labor of native peoples, as the dissertation exhaustively documents, and that this exploitation could be taken to explain patterns of poverty, waste, and inequality, past and present, reflected abiding concerns among historians of Latin America in the United States and their counterparts in Brazil.

After defending the dissertation, John took a visiting position at the University of North Carolina at Chapel Hill. Married by that point to the Brazilian historian Maria Helena Pereira Toledo Machado, he spent two semesters at Chapel Hill, where their son Thomas was born. John might have remained at Chapel Hill for another year, but Brazil beckoned and so in 1986 they returned to São Paulo. Thereafter, John experienced a South American variant of what William Sewell has called the "occupational picaresque" of the modern academic, which came to an end in the year of *Negros da terras*'s publication, with his appointment to a permanent position in the Department of Anthropology at the University of Campinas. Along the way, he published articles, in Portuguese and English, in Brazil and abroad, related to his dissertation and to additional research in Paulista archives. Amid the work of reading, revision, and reflection, between dissertation and manuscript, his interests and approach shifted. Indian men, women, and children and their exploitation had been central to the dissertation and remained central to the book, but their agency – to employ a term very much of that moment, though not one over-used in John's work – had not been so emphasized, nor had the culture, practice, and worldviews of indigenous peoples loomed as large as they now did. Where the first chapter of the dissertation had begun with early European descriptions of Brazil's native inhabitants, the first chapter of the book now began with the sixteenth-century indigenous leader Martim Afonso Tibiriçá, who led his people into an alliance with the Portuguese, a decision very much in keeping with the dynamics of their society, culture, and worldview, which thus exercised a preponderant influence upon the encounter between Amerindian and European worlds. How indigenous peoples saw and experienced that encounter and subsequent transformations was now central. In other words, John had become an ethnohistorian.

From the *bandeirante* myth through materialist social history and on to ethnohistory: here were three traditions, each with its own literatures and approaches, each of which John engaged in turn. The traditional historiography of São Paulo had roots going back to the genealogists and chroniclers of the eighteenth century, but it was not yet dead in the early 1980s, when John began his research in São Paulo. At that point, ideas of regional exceptionalism manifest in the notion that the early Paulistas were a "race of giants" – a nineteenth-century expression revived in the twentieth by the odious racist Alfredo Ellis Júnior, to whom John dedicated a sharply penned article published at the same time as *Negros da terra* – still had some currency at the University of São Paulo (USP), where Myriam Ellis had long held a chair in history, as her father had before her, and was the director of the Institute of Brazilian Studies. In her own work, Myriam Ellis – who was a university-trained historian, unlike her father – updated and provided a professional imprimatur to the hagiographic account of regional history he first laid out in the 1920s, most importantly in the chapter she contributed to the *História geral da civilização brasileira* (1960–1984), never out of print over the half-century since its initial publication in the premiere volume of the first serious attempt at a comprehensive, collaborative accounting of Brazilian history from its origins into the twentieth century. In the making of *Negros da terra*, Myriam Ellis's work represents the quintessence of traditional Paulista historiography. According to this tradition, as refined by Ellis, carrying on her father's work while also displaying the influence of the Portuguese historian Jaime Simões, one of her professors at USP during his long exile, the hunting of Indian slaves had constituted a stage in *bandeirantismo*, a movement that began as a matter of settler self-defense and became a proto-patriotic crusade that aimed at territorial expansion. During the slaving stage, this view further held, most of the captives sought by the Paulistas were brought to market on the coast, to serve as slaves on vast sugar plantations, particularly in northeastern Brazil, while the society of the southeastern interior – the *planalto paulista*, or Paulista plateau – remained Spartan, egalitarian, and striving. *Negros da terra* demolished this set of constatations, showing instead that the pursuit of indigenous peoples to enslave was the driving force behind the Paulistas' expeditions into the interior as long as those expeditions lasted, that the captives brought back from the interior were overwhelmingly bound for slavery in and around São Paulo, and that the settler society that was raised on their labor was characterized by profound inequalities that deepened over time as wealthier colonists cornered the essential resources of land, local office-holding, and labor, of which the most essential of all was labor.

These rejoinders to the traditional scholarship were very much in keeping with the materialist scholarship in which the dissertation was conceived. Here the most important tradition was Marxism, but it was in important ways a plural tradition. For Brazilian Marxist historians, starting with Caio Prado Júnior through Jacob Gorender and Fernando A. Novais, the essential problematic was twofold: to explain how Brazil's colonial past and the African and Afro-American slavery that characterized it fit within Marxian stages of the development of modes of production, and how the two characteristic institutions of Portuguese colonialism in South America (slavery and the latifundium) produced Brazilian underdevelopment. The influence of this tradition is apparent in *Negros da terra*, from the respectful nods to the authorities just named to the desolate vision provided in the book's closing lines. Academic Marxism in the United States at that point had different concerns (though their imprint was apparent too in the coda of *Negros da terra*). To be sure, there had been a loud, if generally unenlightening debate in the United States regarding allegedly feudal aspects of southern slavery, but it was only a memory by the early 1980s. By that point, the central concern of Marxist historians in the Anglo-American academy was the history of class society and the interrelationships between the economic, the social, the political, and even the cultural elements of human life, a problem that had been outlined most famously by the British Marxist historian Eric J. Hobsbawm and developed furthest in Eugene D. Genovese's studies of the antebellum South as a class society. The problem of "economy and society," of course, appeared in the very subtitle of John's dissertation, and there are obvious reasons why a US-born historian of Indian slavery in Brazil would be interested in Afro-American slavery in the United States, but there is an additional explanation for the depth of his interest. The dissertation refers obliquely to "brilliant young graduate students at the Universidade de São Paulo" who were taking on "the difficult topic of slave crime." Among these students – though unnamed in the dissertation – was Maria Helena Machado, who spent much of the year they were in Chapel Hill together reading the work of Genovese and other historians of the slave South. Helena's first book, published in 1987, made her one of the principal Brazilian figures in the bridging of the Brazilian and Anglo-American traditions in Marxian historical writing.

The sources of John's ethnohistorical turn are less easily summarized. Some of the best of the Marxian history coming out of the US academy in the 1980s was in some sense ethnohistorical. John expressed a great admiration for Steve J. Stern's work on the native peoples of Andean South America under Spanish rule and applied Stern's concept of "resistant adaptation" in *Negros da terra*. At the time of John's writing, however, Stern would have identified himself as a historian in the Marxist tradition long before proclaiming any allegiance to ethnohistorical study as an end to itself. John, by that point, would have identified with the latter tradition. Although the relevant works of European ethnographers of South America are duly cited in *Negros da terra*, alongside pioneering work carried out by the Paulista sociologist Florestan Fernandes beginning in the 1940s, John's turn to ethnohistory seems to be explicable by disciplinary divisions in Brazil in the 1980s and early 1990s that in some ways drew him closer to Brazilian anthropologists than to Brazilian historians (or sociologists, for that matter). In his telling of it, when he returned to Brazil in 1982 as a doctoral student and visited the University of São Paulo, the history faculty directed him to the anthropology department. Indians, it would seem, even long-dead ones enslaved by figures of generally acknowledged historical importance, were the province of anthropology rather than history. The upside of this disciplinary prejudice was John's convergence with Brazilian anthropologists involved in a historical turn of their own: by the mid-1980s they were engaged with a newly visible movement for indigenous rights in Brazil that would influence their scholarship, and his. The leading figure here was the University of São Paulo anthropologist Manuela Carneiro da Cunha, who at that point was engaged in ethnohistorical work on Brazil's indigenous peoples as well as on West African communities descended from slaves who had returned from Brazilian captivity. In 1990, Cunha founded the Núcleo de História Indigena e do Indigenismo (Center for Indigenous History and the History of the Study of Indigenous Peoples), in which John was an active participant. Two years later, she published the landmark edited volume *História dos índios no Brasil* ("History of the Indians in Brazil"), to which John contributed an important study of Guarani history. In the quincentennial of the Columbian encounter, Brazilian ethnohistory was coming into being.

*

The place of *Negros da terra* in that nascent field, and John's roles in the field's growth and development, are addressed in the Afterword. The book's architecture, rather than its impact or the career of its author, is more immediately relevant at this point.

Negros da terra's first chapter opens, as we have indicated, with the indigenous headman Martim Afonso Tibiriçá. Tibiriçá's death, on Christmas Day, 1562, is the occasion Monteiro uses to provide a retrospective of this most important of indigenous actors in the making of Portugal's colonial presence in South America, from his succoring the Portuguese castaway João Ramalho at some point in the early 1510s to his conversion to Catholicism by Jesuit missionaries. Rather than portray Tibiriçá as a dupe or, worse yet, a knowing collaborator in the disasters that would follow, Monteiro insists, rightly, that his actions had a logic rooted in the internal dynamics of the Tupi-speaking societies of Atlantic South America. These dynamics – which likewise oriented the actions of other indigenous actors, individual and collective – are the subject of the chapter's longest section. The rest of the chapter takes the reader through what Monteiro calls "the first cycle of Luso–indigenous relations" (that is, of relations between the Portuguese and Amerindians of the region through the late sixteenth century), which saw the founding of the Jesuit College of São Paulo near Tibiriçá's village, the expansion of European settlement from the littoral onto the plateau, and the emergence of rival formulas for colonial rule over the native population: missionary resettlement and colonial slavery. Along the way, the latter helped to spark a sustained rebellion, the War of the Tamoio (1540s–1567), which even as it expressed anticolonial aims continued to obey the characteristic dynamics of Tupi-speaking peoples. This is, as is no doubt apparent, a tremendous amount of ground to cover, which Monteiro does ably while drawing on an array of sources, from sixteenth-century accounts to modern ethnographic works.

Chapter 2, "Backcountry Incursions and the Expansion of the Labor Force," scrutinizes the pursuit of native captives that characterized Luso–indigenous relations through the seventeenth century, as the settlers of São Paulo ranged increasingly through the wilderness and backlands (*sertão* and *sertões*) of South America in search of their human prey. The high point of this activity, such as it was, came between the late 1620s and the early 1630s, when Paulistas and Amerindian auxiliaries numbering in the thousands ravaged the Carijó (Guarani) of Guairá, located a forty-to-sixty-day march to the west of the town of São Paulo and populated by independent villagers and by Guarani settled in Jesuit missions, long prized by colonists for their agricultural skills. This predatory activity yielded thousands of slaves (most of whom, this chapter shows, ended their days on agricultural properties on the plateau rather than on the coast), but it also had serious consequences for the future pursuit of captives. The destruction of Guairá – which was technically Spanish territory – meant that Paulistas would now have to range even further in their pursuit of the coveted Guarani and that when they encountered other missions administered by Spanish Jesuits, the mission villagers would be ready, as they were at Mbororé in 1641, when Jesuit-trained and -armed catechumens destroyed one of the last large-scale slaving expeditions out of São Paulo. (As we shall see, 1640–1641 was an important moment for other reasons as well; worthy of mention at this point is that it also marked the reconsolidation of Portuguese independence from Spain under the first Braganza monarch, rule over Portugal having fallen to Philip II after the deaths of the last Avis kings in 1578–1580.) After the Mbororé debacle, smaller expeditions set out to points north and east rather than south and west, often in at least token service to the desiderata of royal officials, but obtaining indigenous captives to be brought back to the Paulista plateau remained the fundamental motive for these campaigns.

The economy of the plateau is the subject of the book's third chapter. In the seventeenth century, the labor of Indian slaves made São Paulo "The Granary of Brazil," as captive agriculturalists cultivated wheat and enslaved porters carried flour to the coast, to be brought to market in Santos or in other port cities further up the coast. Nested within this account of production and transport is key detail on territorial expansion and the creation of new settlements on the plateau, for which some explication of terms may be in order. Under Portuguese colonial rule, the smallest multi-household population clusters were *bairros rurais*. The term *bairro rural* – often translated as "rural neighborhood," just as often shortened to *bairro* – may refer to a tiny hamlet, a more substantive settlement, or a rural district encompassing a patchwork of properties, including large estates and their individual teams of resident workers. In colonial São Paulo, rural *bairros* generally shared at least two features: a chapel raised by local settlers of means, and the civil power the latter claimed for themselves or had bestowed upon them by the town council (*câmara municipal*), authority that brought with it the title "captain," and militia duties as often as not neglected. Prosperous, demographically significant *bairros* would aspire to become towns (*vilas*). This aspiration was not merely, or even chiefly, as this chapter shows, a matter of local or civic pride. Rather, the raising of a rural *bairro* to the status of town brought with it the creation of administrative structures that provided leading settlers with access to land, local power, capital, and, in some cases, Indian labor.

As early as 1570, Indian slavery had been declared illegal by the Portuguese Crown, save in one or two limited sets of circumstances. Most of the Indian laborers of the plateau were nonetheless slaves in all but name, and native peoples would continue to be treated as partible property in São Paulo well into the eighteenth century. Chapter 4 details some of the processes through which this system developed, while providing some of the book's most important considerations of the parallels between African slavery and the Paulista version of Indian slavery. The richness of this chapter makes summary particularly difficult, but the key processes at work were: the development of pro-slavery arguments so powerful that they became a regional and in some cases a colonial commonsense; the assertion, by settlers, of a historical prerogative to the personal service of indigenous peoples, accompanied by the elaboration of paternalistic discourse and practice; the vanquishing of the threat to this prerogative represented by the Jesuits, who were expelled from the region in 1640 and only allowed to return thirteen years later, after having surrendered to local settlers; and the winning of formal Crown recognition of settlers' rights to the "administration" of the local Indian population in 1696.

While Chapter 4 examines ideological and institutional struggles within and between powerful colonial interests over a hundred-year period, Chapter 5 looks at the local processes through which settlers sought to impose order on their subalterns, even as the latter sought to resist or at least attenuate their subjection. Amerindian captives who survived the forced march back to São Paulo, the waves of Old World disease, and the unfamiliar labor regime that was forced upon new arrivals became colonial subjects and slaves. They were baptized and initiated into the world of ritual coparentage (*compadrio*); old identities were, if not erased, at least obscured by the generic ethnonym the settlers imposed on their slaves, that of *Carijó*, which no longer referred to anything about the Guarani, but rather to servile status. Their family organization and material life underwent dramatic changes, though some captives adapted well enough to the latter to engage in the petty theft and furtive marketeering of non-indigenous goods, including wheat, hides, and meat. Unambiguous resistance peaked in 1660, as new, non-Guarani captives rose up in isolated revolts against particular masters. Meanwhile, fugitive Indians were a near-constant complaint of individual masters of Indian slaves, but flight typically occurred within colonial society and probably strengthened the slave system. In any case, it scarcely undermined it. Throughout, as the harrowing anecdote that ends the chapter shows, violence was the essential means by which Amerindians and others – in this case, a free *bastarda*, the unrecognized daughter of a settler and an Indian woman – were reduced to slavery.

Chapter 6 is in many ways the most straightforward, pivoting back to where Chapter 3 left off and using tax assessments levied between 1679 and 1682 to provide a measure of the distribution of wealth among the slave-owning colonists of rural São Paulo. Very unequal from the beginning, colonial *bairros* only became less unequal when the wealthy moved on to new riches elsewhere, leaving their country cousins sunk in poverty. Along with the tax rolls of 1679–1682 and the minutes of the town council of São Paulo, this chapter makes able use of colonial wills and estate inventories while tracing these processes.

Wills and inventories are similarly well-mined in the book's final chapter. While royal recognition of settlers' prerogatives in 1696 was a victory for Paulista slaveowners, it was something of a hollow one as far as the existence of Indian slavery on the plateau was concerned. In the 1690s, strikes of gold in unsettled areas to the north of São Paulo, which was made the separate jurisdiction of Minas Gerais in 1720, drew settlers and their Indians from the plateau, exacerbating the constant long-term population loss that began in the second half of the seventeenth century, if not sooner. To population movement and mortality were added manumission and suits for freedom, the subjects of the middle sections of this chapter. Manumission, most often granted in wills going back to the early seventeenth century, was rarely obtained in fact, and even when it was it often produced new kinds of dependence and precariousness. The law, in the early eighteenth century, might represent a surer path to freedom, but it too had its hazards for indigenous supplicants. This chapter's final section weighs the question of transition, dispensing with the idea of a transition to African slavery at this point in São Paulo's history (the rise of African slavery in the region would occur a century later, under different stimuli), while making much of the transition to cattle raising and the production of sugar-cane brandy, commercial activities appropriate to a land that had been denuded of so much humus and so many human beings. For colonists who could not manage this transition – and most could not – there was indigence, and so "an impoverished peasantry" was left behind as Indian slavery disappeared.

*

The final section of the book not only outlines this transition of sorts, it also underlines the degree to which *Negros da terra* was itself a transitional work, a bridge between the traditions in social and economic history in which John had been trained in the United States and the ethnohistorical field then in formation in Brazil. This latter aspect of the book is likewise highlighted by the parts of it that have already been published in English. Parts of Chapters 2, 4, and 5 appear in "From Indian to Slave: Forced Native Labour and Colonial Society in São Paulo During the Seventeenth Century," published in *Slavery & Abolition* in 1988, whereas much of the first section of Chapter 1 was incorporated into "The Crises and Transformations of Invaded Societies: Coastal Brazil in the Sixteenth Century," the greater of John's two significant contributions to the South American volume of *The Cambridge History of the Native Peoples of the Americas* (1999).

The existence of the latter two texts, as well as of the dissertation from which the book emerged, presented the translators with problems and opportunities. On the one hand, these texts offer a guide to how John translated certain portions of his work back and forth from English to Portuguese, together with valuable suggestions as to how he might have rendered into English the significant passages of the book that have no parallel in the dissertation or his other English-language work. On the other, a dozen years separate the completion of the dissertation (1985) and the final revisions of the chapter in the *Cambridge History* (the most recent works cited in which date from 1997). John's authorial voice developed over those years, in English and in Portuguese, and the terminology used by historians of native peoples shifted considerably, particularly in the Anglo-American academy. How to draw on these different sources and signposts without producing cacophony or anachronism, while remaining true to John's vision for his work?

In answering this question, and in facing other problems related to translation, we have endeavored to keep our audience foremost in mind. Contemporary English-language readers interested in the history of New World colonial societies generally and of Indian slavery specifically – including specialists and their students – deserve an edition of this critically important work that is consistent, comprehensible, and up to date. With the latter aim in mind, we have felt free to choose from among the texts available to us and to update or otherwise alter them for readability. At certain points this meant restoring background material from the dissertation – on South American geography, for example – or adding a line or two of new explanation designed to help along readers who are unfamiliar with Brazil. At others, it meant suppressing extraneous information that would only distract or confuse such readers, as when *Negros da terra* refers to modern-day place names that would be meaningless even to many Brazilians. The ways in which we refer to native peoples and their societies have been informed by the flexible criteria outlined in Frank Salomon and Stuart B. Schwartz's introduction to the South American volume of *The Cambridge History of the Native Peoples of the Americas*. Thus, we avoid the term "Indian" when referring to independent native peoples, while employing it as the description of a colonial social grouping and in cases where the text describes European perceptions of or desires for such peoples. We likewise avoid the noun "tribe" and the adjective "tribal," despite their use by Brazilian authorities going back at least as far as Florestan Fernandes. Editorial decisions like these were adjudged not only on the noble enough criterion of cultural sensitivity; they also sought to avoid historical misapprehension on the part of readers. As Salomon and Schwartz rightly point out, the North American connotations of "tribe," in particular, are unhelpful in most South American contexts. Hewing to these conventions had the happy additional effect of more closely approximating John's published and unpublished English writings of the early twenty-first century, in which the word "Amerindian" increasingly replaced "Indian" as a portmanteau term for non-colonial native peoples.

Whereas liberties like these were taken with the text of *Negros da terra* in order to make this book as accessible as possible to non-specialist readers, some of the anachronistic "sense" of quotations from sixteenth-, seventeenth-, and eighteenth-century sources was preserved through more literal translations. This desire to preserve the pastness of colonial voices also led to the verbatim translation of *negros da terra* as "blacks of the land." At the same time, we have inserted commas and periods into some quotations, particularly longer ones in which colonial scribes scarcely deigned to employ punctuation, to make these passages more readily decipherable for readers, as is conventional among colonial historians in this country. The result is a new edition of a classic only a generation old, one designed to bring John's pioneering study to the widest possible audience beyond Brazil. Readers of Portuguese may decide that they prefer *Negros da terra*; we would be inclined to agree.

*

Preparing his work for a Brazilian audience freed John from having to deal with some of the more nettlesome aspects of Portuguese American history. To begin with, certain details of administrative organization and high politics, ancillary to his contributions to the social history of Luso–indigenous relations and the development of the economy and society of colonial São Paulo, could be left aside, sufficiently understood, if only implicitly, by enough of his audience to be bypassed without causing the kind of confusion that might arrest readers' progress. The same was true, of course, of a good number of Portuguese words that have no exact English equivalent, as well as of archaic currencies and units of measure, among other terms.

More than three decades elapsed between the first Portuguese landfall in South America in 1500 and the beginning of effective settlement, following which Portuguese claims continued to be subject to challenge by Spain, France, and the Dutch West India Company. In 1534, the Crown sought to encourage colonization by dividing its territorial claims among a dozen grantees, who were to administer, settle, and develop these vast territories for their own benefit and for their lineage in perpetuity, while respecting certain monopolies and other royal privileges. The grantees, called *donatários*, also received the old Portuguese military title of *capitão-môr*, and their jurisdictions were called *capitânias*, most often rendered in English as "donatary captaincies" (the term *proprietário* was sometimes used as a synonym for *donatário*, yielding the translation "proprietary colony," perhaps worthwhile for its drawing a parallel with later British experiments in the Caribbean and North America). One of the few donatary captaincies to achieve any appreciable measure of success was the southeastern one granted to Martim Afonso de Sousa. It was centered on and was named after the town of São Vicente, which Martim Afonso had founded in 1532 while reconnoitering the Atlantic coast of South America for the Portuguese Crown. Despite Martim Afonso's inattention (he never returned to Brazil, leaving the title of *capitão-môr* – the governorship of the territory – to subordinates, as his heirs would), the captaincy of São Vicente witnessed the early development of some sugar-cane agriculture on the humid littoral, accompanied by the building of sugar mills (*engenhos*) for processing. By the mid-1550s, settlement had proceeded inland and up the coastal escarpment known as the Serra do Mar to include the site where the town of São Paulo would be raised in 1560. Although this modest prosperity and somewhat timid territorial expansion paled in comparison with the fortunes of the northeastern captaincy of Pernambuco, these results were a far sight better than what the experiment in proprietary colonization yielded in much of the rest of Portuguese America, at least from the perspective of the Crown. The generally disappointing results of the donatary system led the Portuguese Crown to name the first Governor-General of Brazil, Tomé de Sousa, who received his standing orders in late 1548. Arriving in the colony in April 1549 with a retinue numbering several hundred, Tomé de Sousa founded the first capital of Brazil, the city of Salvador, on the shore of the Bay of All Saints.

Beyond background – for Tomé de Sousa and some of his retinue will appear in the first chapter of this book, as will scattered references to the proprietor of the captaincy of São Vicente throughout – this short narrative is relevant because it allows us to clarify one area of potential confusion regarding Portuguese colonial administration and to outline how we dealt with it in English translation. Taking these issues in order, there is the fact that the establishment of royal government in Salvador did not immediately replace donatarial rule in large parts of Portuguese America. In certain regions, including the captaincy of São Vicente, the proprietors and their heirs continued to hold some of the powers they were originally vested with into the eighteenth century, through competing claims between rival heirs and other jurisdictional contretemps that we may thankfully leave aside. Importantly, for our purposes, the proprietor continued to name the governor of the captaincy of São Vicente for much of the period covered by *Negros da terra*, even as the Crown and its agents – foremost among them, the Governor-General of Brazil – sought greater power and authority. As if to create further potential for confusion, at different points in the history of colonial Brazil, the Governor-Generalship of the colony was split between the "North" and the "South." What all of this means is that at points in the documentation and in the secondary literature – including *Negros da terra* – there are multiple governors with sometimes-overlapping, sometimes-exclusive jurisdictions, an easier issue to finesse in Portuguese than in English. In preparing the chapters that follow, we have used the term or title "Governor-General" when referring to the authority charged by the Crown with administering all of Portugal's colonial holdings in Atlantic South America, from the northeastern "bulge" of Brazil through the far south. At two key points at which royal administration was split between north and south, we refer to Governors-General of the southern captaincies by the title "Governor of the South." When the word "governor" appears unmodified, it refers to the administrator of the captaincy of São Vicente, who served at the behest of the proprietor for much of this period.

In comparison with the labyrinth of administrative history, sorting out measures, money, and other terminology is straightforward. Throughout the book, including in this introduction, we have included spot translations of Portuguese language terms – *sertão*, *sertões*, *planalto* – when first introduced; in cases where such terms are used more than once, they are also collected in the glossary that follows the text. For measures used in quotes from colonial documents (*arrobas*, *alqueires*, *braças*), readers should refer to the glossary. Money, in Portuguese America, was generally measured in *réis*, most often tallied as *milréis* for sums of 1,000 réis or more (as 1$000). One thousand milréis (or one million réis) was also called a *conto de réis* or simply a *conto* (1:000$000). Where other denominations appear in the text – *maravedis*, *patacas*, *cruzados* – their equivalent in réis or milréis is provided.

*

The debts we rang up in preparing this volume came in other tenders. Most will be impossible to repay in kind, but we would like to record them here. Debbie Gershenowitz, our editor at Cambridge, was an enthusiastic sponsor of this project from the beginning, as was Herb Klein, who was editor of Cambridge's Latin American Studies series when we first proposed an English-language edition of *Negros da terra*. We are also grateful to the Press's editorial and production staff, including Kristina Deusch and especially Ian McIver, for their help in the final phases of readying the text for publication as *Blacks of the Land*. Preliminary versions of the tables and bibliography were prepared by Cos Tollerson, who also assisted in the preparation of the book's endnotes. Bibliographical detail was also provided through the work of Kevin Prendergast, Siobhan McCarthy, and Arthur Hudson, of the inter-library loan office at Harry A. Sprague library. And we thank Emma Young for her excellent work on the index, and Jeff Strickland for his assistance in preparing reference maps, available to readers online at www.cambridge.org/monteiro.

In August 2016, *Negros da terra* and our draft translation were the subject of a workshop hosted by the John Carter Brown Library. We were much impressed by the organizational acumen of Neil Safier and Brenda de Santiago, and thank them for having put together a unique event in an inspiring setting. Each of the workshop's participants brought unique insights into John's scholarship and the work of translation, and so we would like to express our gratitude to Maria Regina Celestino de Almeida, Marcela Echeverri, Rebecca Goetz, Hal Langfur, Brett Rushforth, and, once again, Neil Safier, for their many individual contributions to this edition. Hal Langfur generously followed up with further suggestions, for which we remain very grateful. Needless to say, any mistakes or missteps are our own.

As readers will see, John dedicated the final words of the acknowledgements of *Negros da terra* to his wife, Maria Helena, and to their sons, Álvaro and Thomas. We dedicate our work on this book to them as well.

Bibliography

Barr, Juliana. *Peace Came in the Form of a Woman: Indians and Spaniards in the Texas Borderlands*. Chapel Hill: University of North Carolina Press, 2007.

Brooks, James F. *Captives and Cousins: Slavery, Kinship, and Community in the Southwest Borderlands*. Chapel Hill: University of North Carolina Press, 2002.

Cunha, Manuela Carneiro da. *Negros, estrangeiros: os escravos libertos e sua volta à África*. São Paulo: Brasiliense, 1985.

(ed.). *História dos índios no Brasil*. São Paulo: Companhia das Letras, 1992.

Ellis, Myriam. "As bandeiras na expansão geográfica do Brasil." In Sérgio Buarque de Holanda (ed.), *História geral da civilização brasileira*, t. 1: *A época colonial*, vol. 1, 273–296. São Paulo: Difusão Européia do Livro, 1960.

Ellis Júnior, Alfredo. *Raça de gigantes: a civilisação no planalto paulista. Estudo da evolução racial anthroposocial e psychicologica do paulista dos séculos XVI, XVII, XVIII e XIX, e das mesologias physica e social do planalto paulista*. São Paulo: Helios, 1926.

Fernandes, Florestan. "A economia tupinambá: ensaio de interpretação sociológica do sistema econômico de uma sociedade tribal." *Revista do Arquivo Municipal* 122 (February 1949): 7–77.

Gallay, Alan. *The Indian Slave Trade: The Rise of the English Empire in the American South, 1670–1717*. Cambridge, MA: Harvard University Press, 2002.

"Indian Slavery." In Robert L. Paquette and Mark H. Smith (eds.), *The Oxford Handbook of Slavery in the Americas*, 312–335. Oxford University Press, 2010.

"Indian Slavery in the Americas." *History Now*. 2010. Online. Accessed April 19, 2016.

Genovese, Eugene D. *The Political Economy of Slavery: Studies in the Economy and Society of the Slave South*. New York: Pantheon, 1965.

Roll, Jordan, Roll: The World the Slaves Made. New York: Pantheon, 1974.

The World the Slaveholders Made: Two Essays in Interpretation. New York: Pantheon, 1969.

Gorender, Jacob. *O escravismo colonial*. São Paulo: Ática, 1978.

Hobsbawm, Eric J. "From Social History to the History of Society." *Daedalus* 100/1 (1971): 20–45.

Machado, Maria Helena P. T. *Crime e escravidão: trabalho, luta e resistência nas lavouras paulistas, 1830–1888*. São Paulo: Brasiliense, 1987.

Monteiro, John M. "Caçando com gato: raça, mestiçagem e identidade paulista na obra de Alfredo Ellis Júnior." *Novos Estudos CEBRAP* 38 (1994): 79–88.

"The Crises and Transformations of Invaded Societies: Coastal Brazil in the Sixteenth Century." In Frank Salomon and Stuart B. Schwartz (eds.), *The Cambridge History of the Native Peoples of the Americas*, vol. 3: *South America*, pt. 1, 973–1023. Cambridge University Press, 1999.

"Os guarani e a história do Brasil meridional, séculos XVI–XVII." In Manuela Carneiro da Cunha (ed.), *História dos índios no Brasil*, 475–498. São Paulo: Companhia das Letras, 1992.

"From Indian to Slave: Forced Native Labour and Colonial Society in São Paulo during the Seventeenth Century." *Slavery & Abolition* 9/2 (1988): 105–127.

"The Heathen Castes of Sixteenth-Century Portuguese America: Unity, Diversity, and the Invention of the Brazilian Indians." *Hispanic American Historical Review* 80/4 (November 2000): 697–719.

"Rethinking Amerindian Resistance and Persistence in Colonial Portuguese America." In John Gledhill and Patience A. Schell (eds.), *New Approaches to Resistance in Brazil and Mexico*, 25–43. Durham, NC: Duke University Press, 2012.

"São Paulo in the Seventeenth Century: Economy and Society." Ph.D. dissertation, University of Chicago, 1985.

Untitled presentation to the Brazilian Studies Committee of the Conference on Latin American History. Chicago, January 6, 2012.

"Vida e morte do índio: São Paulo colonial." In John Manuel Monteiro, Lúcia Helena Rangel, Mara L. Manzoni Luz, Marco Antonio Barbosa, Maria Inês Ladeira, and Silvia Helena Simões Borelli, *Índios no estado de São Paulo: resistência e transfiguração*, by 21–44. São Paulo: Comissão Pró-Índio de São Paulo, 1984.

Novais, Fernando A. *Estrutura e dinâmica do antigo sistema colonial*. São Paulo: CEBRAP, 1974.

Prado Júnior, Caio. *Formação do Brasil contemporâneo*. São Paulo: Martins, 1942.

Reséndez, Andrés. *The Other Slavery: The Uncovered History of Indian Enslavement in America*. Boston: Houghton Mifflin, 2016.

Rushforth, Brett. *Bonds of Alliance: Indigenous and Atlantic Slaveries in New France*. Chapel Hill: University of North Carolina Press, 2012.

Salomon, Frank, and Stuart B. Schwartz. "Introduction." In Frank Salomon and Stuart B. Schwartz (eds.), *The Cambridge History of the Native Peoples of the Americas*, vol. 3: *South America*, pt. 1, 1–18. Cambridge University Press, 1999.

Sewell, William H., Jr. *Logics of History: Social Theory and Social Transformation*. University of Chicago Press, 2005.

Simões, Jaime. *Raposo Tavares e a formação territorial do Brasil*. Rio de Janeiro: Ministério de Educação e Cultura, 1958.

Snyder, Christina. "Indian Slavery." Oxford Research Encyclopedias. American History. First published online, December 2014. Accessed April 14, 2016.

Slavery in Indian Country: The Changing Face of Captivity in Early America. Cambridge, MA: Harvard University Press, 2010.

Stern, Steve J. *Peru's Indian Peoples and the Challenge of Spanish Conquest: Huamanga to 1640*. Madison: University of Wisconsin Press, 1982.

(ed.). *Resistance, Rebellion, and Consciousness in the Andean Peasant World, 18th to 20th Centuries*. Madison: University of Wisconsin Press, 1987.

Chronology

1500	Fleet captained by Pedro Álvares Cabral makes landfall on what will become the Brazilian coast, territory which he claims for Portugal as the Island of the True Cross.
1501–1502	Portuguese voyage to Island of the True Cross, of which Amerigo Vespucci, who serves as pilot, leaves an account. The voyage reaches the coast of what will become southeastern Brazil, ascertains that the landmass is not an island, and discovers the presence of dyewood similar to varieties found in Asia, referred to generically by the Portuguese as *pau brasil.* Rechristened the Land of the True Cross, the Portuguese-claimed territory is increasingly identified with its major commodity, as the Land of Brazil Wood, Land of Brazil, etc.
early 1510s (?)	The Portuguese sailor João Ramalho is shipwrecked on the coast of Atlantic South America, near where the town of São Vicente will be founded; he is subsequently adopted into the Tupinikin group led by Tibiriçá, marrying one of the powerful chief's daughters and becoming an influential leader in his own right on the inland plateau where the town of São Paulo will later be founded.
1530s	Portuguese colonists begin settlement of the region, make contact with João Ramalho and another Portuguese castaway, and found the town of São Vicente; Tupinikin headman Tibiriçá agrees to ally his people with the Portuguese.
1537	Pope Paul III issues Sublimus Deus, a bull proclaiming the liberty of the native inhabitants of the Americas.
1540s	Initial outbreak of the War of the Tamoios, as the Tupinambá-led struggle against the Portuguese presence in southeastern Brazil will be called; the war will last into the 1560s.
1549	Arrival in Salvador da Bahia of the first Governor-General of Brazil, Tomé de Sousa, accompanied by first Jesuit missionaries.

1553	Founding of the inland town of Santo André da Borda do Campo, the first official Portuguese settlement on the Paulista plateau.
1554	Father Manuel da Nóbrega's founding of the Jesuit College at Piratininga, with the assistance of João Ramalho and Tibiriçá, who takes the Christian given names Martim Afonso at his baptism.
1557–1558	Evidence of fragmentation of Tupinikin villages of Inhapuambuçu and Jerubatuba; abandonment of the town of Santo André under pressure stemming from War of the Tamoios.
1560	Founding of the town of São Paulo alongside the Jesuit College at Piratininga.
1560s	Founding of Jesuit mission villages in the immediate orbit of the town of São Paulo, including São Miguel and Nossa Senhora dos Pinheiros; large-scale smallpox epidemic results in thousands of deaths, including, in 1562, that of Martim Afonso Tibiriçá; War of the Tamoios brought to an end.
1570	Crown law states that only Indians taken in so-called Just Wars may be subjected to slavery.
1580–1640	The "Iberian Union" of the kingdoms of Portugal and Spain under Spain's Habsburg monarchs.
1591–1601	Governor-Generalship of Dom Francisco de Sousa; during his mandate, Dom Francisco visits São Paulo for the first time, in 1599.
1592	Arrival of new governor of the captaincy of São Vicente, Jorge Correia.
1596	Royal decree formalizes the mission-village project, placing mission-village Indians under Jesuit tutelage and limiting their availability as laborers outside of their villages.
1608–1611	Dom Francisco de Sousa, having returned to Brazil from Portugal, serves as Governor-General of the South (the captaincies of Espírito Santo, Rio de Janeiro, and São Vicente) while inspiring a program of colonial development in the São Paulo region.
1609	Jesuits establish first missions of Guairá, an area technically under Spanish jurisdiction but forty to sixty days' march from São Paulo.
1611	Founding of the town of Mogi das Cruzes, to the east of São Paulo.
1620s	Founding of the town of Santana de Parnaíba, to the northwest of São Paulo; spread of wheat farming throughout the São Paulo region.

1624–1625	Dutch occupation of Salvador.
1628–1630	Paulista "invasion" of the Jesuit missions of Guairá, beginning with the expedition led by Antonio Raposo Tavares and ending with the destruction of nearly all of the missions of the region.
1630–1654	Dutch occupation of Pernambuco, as New Holland, at its peak covering much of northeastern Brazil.
1631	Relocation of the two surviving Guairá missions of Loreto and San Ignacio
1633–1634	Founding of the Jesuit missions of Tape.
1635–1641	Paulista attacks on the Tape missions.
1639	Pope Urbano VIII restates the principle of Indian liberty outlined in the papal Bull of 1537.
1640	Restoration of the Portuguese crown, under the first Braganza monarch, King João IV; settlers' expulsion of the Jesuits from São Paulo.
1641	Defeat of the expedition led by Jerônimo Pedroso de Moraes at Mbororé at the hands of Jesuit-trained and -armed Indians; marks the end of large-scale raiding of the missions and the beginning of the end of such raiding as a satisfactory response to the Paulistas' labor requirements.
1641–1648	Dutch occupation of Portuguese Angolan ports of Luanda and Benguela.
1640s–1650s	Founding of the Paraíba Valley towns of Taubaté, Guaratinguetá, and Jacareí.
1652	Isolated uprisings by Indian slaves in the *bairro* of Juqueri and near the mission village of Conceição dos Guarulhos.
1653	Jesuits permitted to return to São Paulo following agreement mediated by Crown officials.
1654	Dutch surrender of Pernambuco, following a decade-long war of reconquest.
1655	Founding of the town of Jundiaí; agreement puts an end to the Pires–Camargo conflict.
1650s	So-called Wars of the Barbarous in northeastern Brazil, in which Paulistas serve as Crown mercenaries.
1660	Isolated uprising of Indian slaves in Mogi das Cruzes; four such uprisings in the *bairro* of Juqueri.
1660s	Founding of the town of Sorocaba west of Santana de Paraíba; effective settlement of the area to the north of São Paulo between the Juqueri and Atibaia rivers.
1670s	Settler conflicts with ecclesiastical and royal officials in Rio de Janeiro.
1685	Another settler attempt at expelling the Jesuits from São Paulo.

1692 Settlers of São Paulo present their "sixteen doubts" in response to real and imagined interference in their system of personal service.

1694 Local agreement between settlers of São Paulo and Jesuits of the region leaves "administered" Indians under settler control.

1695 Destruction of the northeastern escaped-slave redoubt of Palmares by Paulista mercenaries led by Domingos Jorge Velho.

1696 Royal decree recognizes the settlers' rights to the "administration" of Indians, thus legitimizing their regime of personal service, which was slavery in all but name.

1690s Major gold strikes in the unsettled northern reaches of the captaincy of São Paulo, which come to be called Minas do Ouro and, later, Minas Gerais, amid the ensuing gold rush.

1709 The captaincy of São Paulo and Minas do Ouro is created.

1710 Tithe contract of the mining districts separated from the rest of the captaincy, increasingly poor in both relative and absolute terms.

1711 The town (*vila*) of São Paulo is raised to the status of city (*cidade*).

1720 The captaincies of São Paulo and Minas Gerais are created by dividing the captaincy that had encompassed both territories into a declining, mostly subsistence-farming zone and an area of recent settlement characterized by booming output of mineral wealth.

1758 "Administration" as a legal category of personal service is abolished, though dwindling numbers of Indians and Indian-descended people are listed as "administered ones" (i.e., as slaves) in local civil and ecclesiastical records produced through the late eighteenth century.

Glossary

alqueire:	Unit of dry measure equivalent to approx. 13.8 litres; also used as equivalent of planted land, theoretically equivalent to the amount of grain a given plot could yield.
arroba:	Unit of weight, variable but usually equivalent to 32 lbs.
bairro rural:	Often translated as "rural neighborhood," just as often shortened to *bairro*; may refer to tiny hamlet, substantive settlement, or rural district encompassing several properties, including large estates and their individual teams of resident workers.
bandeira:	Literally, flag; by extension, militia company; used in reference to some seventeenth-century expeditions to the wilderness at the time and more generally since then.
bandeirante:	Invented eighteenth-century term for participants in so-called *bandeiras*.
bastardo (fem. bastarda):	Offspring of white father and Indian mother, considered closer to Indian population.
braça:	Unit of linear measure equivalent to 2.2 meters.
compadrio:	Ritual coparentage established through baptismal rite.
crioulo:	Literally "creole"; used most often in Brazil's colonial and early national eras to describe a slave (African or Indian) born in captivity.
ladino:	Used to refer to a slave (African or Indian) who had been "seasoned."

lingua geral:	Tupi-Guarani lingua franca, developed largely by Jesuits, used in colonial-era relations with Tupian peoples.
mamaluco (fem. mamaluca; variation, mameluco, mameluca):	Offspring of white father and Indian mother, considered closer to white population.
mestiço:	Refers to person or persons of mixed ancestry.
Paulista:	Refers to person or persons of the settler society of the São Paulo region.
planalto:	Plateau, tableland; in southeastern Brazil during colonial era, inland region of township of São Paulo and points north and west, excluding Paraíba River valley region to east.
roça:	Agricultural plot planted in subsistence crops, especially maize and manioc.
sertão (plural sertões):	Wilderness, backlands, distinct from *povoado* (area of established settlement).
sesmaria:	Land grant, from Crown, proprietary governor, or representatives thereof; may refer to grant itself as well as land so bestowed.

Abbreviations Used in Notes

ACDS	Arquivo da Cúria Diocesana, Sorocaba
ACMRJ	Arquivo da Cúria Metropolitana, Rio de Janeiro
AESP	Arquivo do Estado de São Paulo
AESP-AC	AESP, Autos Civeis
AESP-IE	AESP, Inventários Estragados
AESP-INP	AESP, Inventários Não Publicados
AESP-IPO	AESP, Inventários do Primeiro Ofício
AESP-Mogi	AESP, Inventários do Segundo Ofício de Mogi das Cruzes
AESP-Notas	AESP, Livros de Notas de Tabelião
AHMSP	Arquivo Histórico Municipal Washington Luís, São Paulo
AHU	Arquivo Histórico Ultramarino, Lisbon
AHU-Bahia	AHU, Catalogados da Bahia
AHU-Rio de Janeiro	AHU, Catalogados do Rio de Janeiro
AHU-SP	AHU, Catalogados de São Paulo
Ajuda	Biblioteca do Palácio da Ajuda, Lisbon
AMDDLS	Arquivo Metropolitano Dom Duarte Leopoldo e Silva, Cúria Metropolitana, São Paulo
AMP	*Annaes do Museu Paulista*, 1922–1938; *Anais do Museu Paulista*, 1938–
ARSI	Archivum Romanum Societatus Iesu, Rome
ARSI Brasilia	ARSI, Brasilia Codices
ARSI-FG	ARSI, Fondo Gesuìtico
BNL	Biblioteca Nacional, Lisbon
BNRJ	Biblioteca Nacional, Rio de Janeiro
BNRJ-DH	*Documentos históricos*, 110 vols. (Rio de Janeiro: Biblioteca Nacional, 1928–55)
BNVE-FG	Biblioteca Nazionale Centrale Vittorio Emanuele, Rome, Fondo Gesuìtico
CMSP-Atas	*Actas da Câmara da villa de S. Paulo*, 7 vols. (São Paulo: Archivo Municipal, 1914–15)

CMSP-Registro	*Registro geral da Câmara Municipal de S. Paulo*, 20 vols. (São Paulo: Archivo Municipal, 1917–23)
DHA	*Documentos para a história do açúcar*, 3 vols. (Rio de Janeiro: Instituto do Açúcar e do Âlcool, 1954–63)
DI	*Publicação official de documentos interessantes para a historia e costumes de S. Paulo*, 54 vols. (São Paulo: Archivo do Estado, 1894–1932)
IEB	Instituto de Estudos Brasileiros, Universidade de São Paulo
IHGB	Instituto Histórico e Geográfico Brasileiro, Rio de Janeiro
IT	*Inventários e testamentos*, 44 vols. (São Paulo: Archivo/Arquivo do Estado, 1920–77)
MB	*Monumenta brasiliae*, ed. Serafim Leite, 5 vols. (Rome: Monumenta Historica Societatis Iesu, 1956–60)
Mss. de Angelis	*Manuscritos da coleção de Angelis*, ed. Jaime Cortesão and Hélio Viana, 7 vols. (Rio de Janeiro: Biblioteca Nacional, 1951–70)
RIHGB	*Revista*, IHGB (slight variations in title), 1839–.
RIHGSP	*Revista do Instituto Historico e Geographico de São Paulo*, 1894–1938; *Revista do Instituto Histórico e Geográfico de São Paulo*, 1938–.
Sesmarias	*Sesmarias*, 3 vols. (São Paulo: Archivo/Arquivo do Estado, 1921–40)

Blacks of the Land

Indian Slavery, Settler Society, and the Portuguese Colonial Enterprise in South America

John M. Monteiro

Preface and Acknowledgements

In 1651, following a prolonged march through the wilds of South America, a few surviving members of the once grand expedition led by the master backwoodsman Antonio Raposo Tavares reached Belém do Pará so stricken by illness, hunger, and wounds suffered in Indian attacks that, according to the Jesuit missionary and renowned orator Father Antonio Vieira, "those who remained looked more dead than alive." Nonetheless, the same priest added, their journey "truly was one of the most notable that has been carried out in the world to this day": for three years and two months the members of the company had completed a "great walkabout" through the interior of the continent, though after a certain point they scarcely knew where they were or where they were going. Lost in the immensity of America, they only learned that they had traveled down the great Amazon River when their precarious, improvised crafts reached the military outpost of Gurupá, on the falls of the Xingu River, and the fort's astonished soldiers told them where they were.

However, what most shocked Vieira was the evident contrast between such extraordinary efforts and the prosaic objectives that had led these Portuguese colonists to travel so many leagues and suffer such privation. For the single motive that had impelled their undertaking was to uproot "either by force or by will [Indians] from their lands and take them to São Paulo and then have them there as their servants as they are accustomed to doing."

To a certain extent, the expedition led by Raposo Tavares was emblematic of seventeenth-century expansionism in Portuguese America. Although many historians, following Jaime Cortesão, have emphasized the geopolitical dimension of the undertaking, Raposo Tavares's expedition and so many other slaving parties that set out from São Paulo were not motivated by territorial expansion, nor did their efforts result in more expansive settlement. Quite the contrary: rather than contributing directly to the occupation of the interior by the colonizing power, these incursions – like the heavily armed canoe flotillas that plied the Amazon basin, and the forcible resettlements carried out by missionaries in both regions – contributed to the devastation of innumerable native peoples. To paraphrase Capistrano de Abreu, the activities of these "colonizers" were profoundly tragic in their effects, depopulating rather than settling vast stretches of the continent.

In their day, the Paulistas – settlers of the colonial nucleus of São Paulo and founders of its satellite towns – came to be known in the Americas and Europe as great backwoodsmen, peerless in their knowledge of the vast wilderness, in their perseverance, and in their courage. Much later, historians would christen them *bandeirantes* while building them up to epic proportions, emphasizing their role in the geographic expansion of Portuguese America. But while their expeditions came to occupy a prominent place in Brazilian historiography, the society that these ventures created remains little understood.

Indeed, tales of the legendary feats of brave explorers have obscured the gripping history of the thousands of Indians – the *negros da terra*, or "blacks of the land" – captured by the backwoodsmen of São Paulo. Thus, a sizeable body of scholarship has recounted the dramatic adventures of the *bandeirantes*, but in this literature a "cycle of Indian hunting" appears as a preliminary, relatively unimportant phase of their activities, in which the Paulistas furnished Indian slaves for the plantations of the sugar-producing northeast. At the same time, the immense bibliography on the colonial economy and society of Portuguese America has paid scant attention to indigenous labor. Although a few recent contributions have shed some light on this neglected subject, the major trends in the study of colonial Brazil remain bounded by a theoretical framework in which the organization of labor is subordinate to the logic of the expansion of mercantile capitalism. In this perspective, the Indian – when mentioned at all – is described as having played the ephemeral, secondary role of precursor to the millions of African slaves whose fundamental place in the history of colonial Brazil and the broader Atlantic world is unassailable.

Blacks of the Land returns to the seventeenth-century history of São Paulo, while seeking to re-evaluate the historical context of the *bandeirante* phenomenon. Its starting point is the simple claim that the frequent incursions into the interior, rather than provisioning a supposed market for Indian slaves on the coast, sustained the growth of an indigenous labor force on the plateau, thus enabling the production and transport of an agricultural surplus; in this way, the São Paulo region was linked to other parts of the Portuguese colony and even to the commercial circuits of the South Atlantic. But the dimensions and significance of Indian slavery in the region went far beyond this commercial nexus. In fact, virtually every aspect of the formation of São Paulo during its first two centuries was tied in some fundamental way to the expropriation, exploitation, and destruction of indigenous populations.

In this new critical interpretation of the social history of São Paulo between the sixteenth and eighteenth centuries, native peoples play a central role. By focusing on the origins, development, and decline of Indian slavery, the chapters that follow seek to demonstrate that the principal structures of colonial society in the region emerged from a specific historical process in which several distinct indigenous societies came to be subordinated to an elaborate structure designed to control and exploit Indian labor.

Though it focuses most specifically on the structure and dynamic of Indian slavery, this book seeks to engage with three central problems in the history of Brazil: the role of the Indian in colonial economic and social history; the potent myth of the *bandeirante*; and the importance of non-export economies in the making of the country. Far from settling these issues, the material presented here seeks instead to contribute new elements to a broader and more critical discussion of the internal dynamic that developed in the interstices of an economy and a society oriented above all to the Atlantic world.

This book was born of a doctoral dissertation defended at the University of Chicago in 1985. Although much of the original material of the dissertation remains, it was expanded and enriched over the last six years by additional research and by revisions undertaken in response to criticism. I am greatly indebted to John Coatsworth, Bentley Duncan, Friedrich Katz, and Stuart Schwartz, the members of the doctoral committee, for their precise comments and suggestions, many of which were incorporated into this book.

I am grateful to the following institutions, which funded research in Portuguese, Italian, and Brazilian archives: the Center for Latin American Studies of the University of Chicago, the Social Science Research Council, the Fulbright/Hays Commission, and the Conselho Nacional de Desenvolvimento Científico e Tecnológico (CNPq). I also benefited from the institutional support of the Centro Brasileiro de Análise e Planejamento (CEBRAP), which generously hosted me as a visiting researcher in 1991–1992, enabling the completion of the final draft of this book in a rich interdisciplinary environment, a rare privilege for someone accustomed to the intellectual austerity of the academy.

Parts of this book previously appeared in several scholarly publications: *Slavery & Abolition, Estudos Econômicos, História* (Universidade Estadual Paulista), *Revista de Antropologia, Ler História, Ciências Sociais Hoje*, and *Revista de História*. I am grateful to the anonymous referees of these journals for their important critiques.

Innumerable people offered helpful collaboration at various stages of this trajectory. During my stays in Portugal, I enjoyed the valuable assistance and intellectual company of Albino Marques, L. M. Andrade,

Patrick Menget, Bill Donovan, and Ivan Alves, the last two of whom also hosted me in Rio de Janeiro. Among my American colleagues, I am grateful to Martin Gonzalez, Cliff Welch, Joel Wolfe, Herb Klein, Alida Metcalf, Mary Karasch, Muriel Nazzari, and Kathy Higgins, who read and commented on parts of the work. My parents, Manuel and Madelyn Monteiro, as well as my brother Willy, offered several kinds of support on many occasions.

In São Paulo, the interdisciplinary Núcleo de História Indígena e do Indigenismo provided a fertile environment for discussion of this book. I am particularly grateful to Marta Rosa Amoroso, Beatriz Perrone-Moisés, Nádia Farage, Robin Wright, the late Miguel Menéndez, Paulo Santilli, Dominique Gallois, and Manuela Carneiro da Cunha. Among my colleagues at the Universidade Estadual Paulista (UNESP), I must recognize the commentaries and support of Luiz Koshiba, Sonia Irene do Carmo, Ana Maria Martinez Corrêa, Manoel Lelo Bellotto, Teresa Maria Malatian, Kátia Abud, Ida Lewkowicz, Jacy Barletta, and Angélica Resende. For their readings of earlier versions of this work, I am especially grateful to Francisco "Pancho" Moscoso, Carlos Eugênio Marcondes de Moura, Jacob Gorender, André Amaral de Toral, Luiz Felipe de Alencastro, and Lilia Moritz Schwarcz, each of whom offered valuable suggestions. I also counted on the encouragement of Horácio Gutiérrez, José Roberto do Amaral Lapa, Bob Slenes, Lúcia Helena Rangel, Sílvia Helena Simões Borelli, Mara Luz, Maria Odila Leite da Silva Dias, Luiz and Dida Toledo Machado, and especially Maria Cristina Cortez Wissenbach.

Finally, my greatest debt is to Maria Helena P. T. Machado, for her companionship and indispensable intellectual support, to say nothing of the assistance she provided in the translation of this book. Our sons, Álvaro and Thomas, also contributed, since without them the work would have been completed earlier, but the experience would have been poorer.

I

The Transformation of Indigenous São Paulo in the Sixteenth Century

On Christmas Day, 1562, Martim Afonso Tibiriçá lost his final battle, succumbing to one of the infectious diseases that ran rampant among the indigenous inhabitants of Brazil at the time. In a way, the life and death of this important Tupinikin warrior and chief mirrored the very march of European expansion in the captaincy of São Vicente in the sixteenth century. Many years earlier, he had brought the first white man into his community – as a son-in-law – and witnessed the newcomer's speedy rise as an influential leader of Indians and Portuguese. In the 1530s, Tibiriçá agreed to enter into an alliance with the outsiders, undoubtedly thinking of the advantage over his traditional enemies that this alliance would provide. With the arrival of the first Jesuits at mid-century, he authorized the raising of a rustic chapel in his village and allowed the priests to convert his people, he himself becoming the first to be baptized. The Jesuits, for their part, expressed their reverence for an Indian they considered to be an exemplary Christian leader and a valued ally, interring his body in the modest church of São Paulo de Piratininga.

Although his collaborative role in the establishment of European dominion over the region tends to be emphasized in the sparse biographical data on Tibiriçá, this material can also be read in such a way as to provide another perspective. Indeed, while Tibiriçá's actions were greatly influenced by European demands, they responded first and foremost to the logic and internal dynamics of indigenous social organization. Moreover, even as he figured as a protagonist in the making of Luso–indigenous relations in the region, Tibiriçá, alongside the other members of his society, endured the profound crises and transformations unleashed by European expansion. What appeared at first to be an inoffensive and even beneficial alliance soon proved to be very harmful to the Indians. Changes in patterns of warfare and grave crises of authority, punctuated by waves of epidemic disease, conspired to debilitate, disorganize, and, ultimately, destroy the Tupinikin.

Although the internal dynamics of indigenous Brazil have been largely ignored in the existing historiography, they were sufficiently profound and historically dense to influence the formation of the colony in a significant way. The importance of these dynamics lay not only in the social and economic configurations of native societies, but also in the various ways that they constituted the historical memory of aboriginal peoples. In this sense, it was often the consciousness of an indigenous past that provided the bases for action in the face of the historically novel situation of the conquest. Strong expressions of this disposition emerged in native social movements throughout the sixteenth century, whether in messianism or armed resistance, some cases of which involved the participation of multiple villages, as in the case of the Confederation of the Tamoios (1555–1567), which brought together Tupinambá communities in a long-lasting armed movement that aimed to destroy Portuguese colonialism.

Taking into consideration the internal dynamics of Tupi-speaking groups – including the Tupinambá and the Tupinikin – and these groups' clashes with the process of Portuguese expansion, this chapter aims to evaluate the history of Luso–indigenous relations in southern Brazil in the sixteenth century. During this period, indigenous actions and reactions ran contrary to Portuguese expectations and, as such, proved significant in shaping the structures of domination that emerged in the colony. In their relations with the Indians, the Portuguese attempted to impose diverse modes of labor organization and, in turn, were faced with shifting stances that oscillated between collaboration and resistance. While none of the various forms of exploitation that were attempted proved satisfactory, all had the negative impact of hastening the demographic decline and social disintegration of indigenous populations. As a result, the colonizers increasingly turned to forced labor in their attempt to establish an economic basis for colonial society. In this sense, one may locate the origins of slavery in Brazil – African as well as Indian – in this initial phase of Portuguese–indigenous relations.

The Tupi in the Age of Conquest

What formed the "internal dynamics" of Tupi societies? At the risk of oversimplifying the enormous complexity of the social structures of sixteenth-century Brazil, we may identify some of the constitutive elements of the dynamics that animated them: the process of fragmentation and reconstitution of local groups, the leadership roles played by chiefs and shamans, and finally the fundamental importance of the warrior complex in the affirmation of these groups' historical identity. Taken together, these elements were of particular relevance to turning points in the subsequent development of relations with the Europeans. In this sense, they help to explain not only the historical bases on which patterns of indigenous resistance and adaptation rested, but also the means by which Portuguese domination became possible.

Upon arriving in Brazil, the European invaders soon discovered that much of the coast as well as the more accessible parts of the interior were occupied by societies that shared certain basic characteristics, common to what came to be called Tupi-Guarani culture. Despite this apparent homogeneity, however, any attempt at providing a synthesis of the ethnographic situation of sixteenth-century Brazil immediately runs into two problems. In the first place, Tupi society remained radically segmented, and relations between segments and even between local units most often were associated in one way or another with internecine warfare. Referring to the relationship between the Tupinambá and Tupinikin groups of southern Brazil, Gabriel Soares de Sousa observed, in his rich descriptive treatise on early colonial Brazil, considered by many to be the most important sixteenth-century account: "And even though the Tupinikin and Tupinambá are enemies, between them there is no greater difference in language and customs than between the residents of Lisbon and those of Beira."[1] Second, large parts of Brazil were also inhabited by non-Tupi peoples, representing dozens of unrelated language groups.[2]

To deal with these problems, sixteenth-century Europeans sought to reduce the vast ethnographic panorama to two generic categories: Tupi and Tapuia. The Tupi side of this dichotomy encompassed the coastal societies, including the Guarani, that were in direct contact with the Portuguese, French, and Spanish. While these groups exhibited similar traditions and cultural patterns, the same cannot be said of the so-called Tapuia. Indeed, the term "Tapuia" was often applied to groups that not only differed socially from the Tupi pattern, but were little known to Europeans. In the *Tratado descritivo*, Gabriel Soares de Sousa acknowledged the precarious state of European knowledge: "As the Tapuia are so many and are so divided by group, custom, and language, in order to say much of them, it would be necessary to take careful and deliberate notice of their divisions, life, and customs; but, up to the present this has been impossible. . ."[3] At around the same time, the Jesuit Fernão Cardim classified seventy-six non-Tupi groups as "Tapuia."[4] It would seem that for these early observers the denomination represented little more than the antithesis of Tupi society, and that the groups so described were thus defined in purely negative terms.

In any case, the emergence of the Tupi–Tapuia dichotomy had some basis, to the degree that it identified different historical trajectories and distinct forms of social organization, something emphasized in virtually all sixteenth-century sources.[5] Laying out his first impressions of the Indians of Brazil, the Jesuit missionary Father Manuel da Nóbrega portrayed the Tapuia in vague terms: "There is in these lands a sort of people who do not live in houses, but in the hills, and they are at war with all and by all are feared."[6] Gabriel Soares de Sousa, referring to the Gê-speaking Guaianá of

São Paulo, emphasized in a more detailed fashion the apparent backwardness of these Indians relative to the Tupi:

> They are people of little work, much leisure, they do not work the land, they live from the game they kill and the fish they take from the rivers, and from the wild fruits that the forest provides; they are great archers and enemies of human flesh... These heathens do not live in villages with fixed homes, like their neighbors the Tamoio [Tupinambá], but in caves in the countryside, beneath the ground, where they keep fires night and day and make their beds of branches and the skins of the animals they kill.[7]

These superficial and incomplete images of Tapuia groups contrast with more elaborate descriptions of Tupi societies. As we shall see in greater detail, these differences – real or imagined – played an important role in Euro-indigenous relations as they unfolded with the arrival of the whites. Whether manifested peacefully or contentiously, the coexistence of radically divergent forms of social organization was apparent in every part of Brazil in the sixteenth century. The region encompassed by the captaincy of São Vicente was no exception, though the identity of the original inhabitants of the place where the town of São Paulo was founded has aroused some controversy. There, alongside one another, lived Tupinikin and Guaianá, the former Tupi-speaking and the latter Gê-speaking, thus neatly fitting the dichotomous Tupi–Tapuia scheme. We have already invoked Gabriel Soares de Sousa's observations of the Guaianá; to these we can add the comments of one of the most direct observers of the situation, Hans Staden, a German adventurer who was held captive by a Tupi-speaking group. He clearly distinguished the Guaianá from the Tupinikin, describing them as inhabitants of the coastal escarpment, who "do not have permanent homes, like the other savages," and identifying hunting and gathering as their basic source of sustenance.[8]

In fact, most sixteenth-century reports make it clear that the Tupinikin constituted the principal inhabitants of the captaincy of São Vicente, at least until the last decade of the century.[9] While present on the coast, the Tupinikin – "whose region extends eighty miles into the interior and forty along the coast," according to Staden[10] – maintained an important network of villages above the coastal escarpment that the Portuguese would call the Serra do Mar, around the site of what would become the town of São Paulo.

Early sources use ethnic terms to identify what may be considered tribal agglomerations, but the basic unit of social and political organization among Tupi groups was the multi-family village. Different communities could have very close relations, bound by alliances or kinship ties, without these relations involving the development of larger political or territorial units.[11] In effect, connections between local units were subject to constant changes stemming from historical circumstances, as frequent shifts in the makeup of alliances affected the nature and extent of multi-village bonds. This mutability escaped the attention of colonial-era chroniclers, who described groups of villages as if they formed larger, more stable political groupings.

Unfortunately, contemporary accounts tell us little about the number and size of sixteenth-century Tupinikin villages.[12] It would seem, however, that the principal Tupinikin settlement at the time of the arrival of the Europeans was the one headed by the chief Tibiriçá, certainly the most influential indigenous leader of the region. In the 1550s, this village – known as Inhapuambuçu and, perhaps, as Piratininga as well[13] – would be host to the chapel and precarious College of São Paulo de Piratininga, installed by the Jesuits on January 25, 1554. Another important village of the period was Jerubatuba, under the chieftainship of Caiubi, supposedly Tibiriçá's brother. It was located about 12 kilometers south of Inhapuambuçu, near the future settlement of Santo Amaro. In 1553, the German adventurer Ulrich Schmidl, having spent a few days in the village, described it as "a very large place."[14] Finally, a third village that stood out in sixteenth-century reports, Ururaí, also had as its chief a brother of Tibiriçá, named Piquerobi. Located 6 kilometers to the east of Inhapuambuçu, this settlement became the site of the Jesuit mission village of São Miguel.

We have little information about the size of these precolonial units, but from what can be ascertained from post-contact accounts, Tupinikin villages may have been smaller than their Tupinambá counterparts in Rio de Janeiro, Bahia, and Maranhão, according to the detailed descriptions of French and Portuguese chroniclers and missionaries. Referring to the interior of the captaincy of São Vicente, Father Diogo Jacomé mentioned the existence of some villages with four hundred souls each.[15] His fellow Jesuit, Brother José de Anchieta, affirmed that each village "consists just of six or seven homes," which for Hans Staden would be a "small village."[16] These observations contrast with the population size frequently attributed to Tupinambá villages, estimated at around 800 to 1,000 inhabitants, though some awestruck chroniclers arrived at figures in the thousands.[17]

In any case, what is known for certain is that these villages did not constitute permanent, fixed settlements, for after a few years groups tended to move to a new locale. In the plateau region, the first Jesuits alleged that migrations occurred every three or four years, while other accounts suggest longer spans of time between moves, of twelve or even twenty years. Already in the initial period of Jesuit influence, in 1557, Inhapuambuçu and Jerubatuba were experiencing a process of fragmentation. "What is worse," commented Father Luís da Grã, "is that they do not go together."[18]

These moves were stimulated by various possible factors, including soil exhaustion, shrinking game reserves, the emergence of a charismatic new leader, internal factional disputes, or the death of a headman. Whatever the precise motive, the recurrent creation of new units of settlement constituted important events involving the reproduction of the principal bases of indigenous social organization. In this sense, it is important to recognize the fundamental role played by the chief in the original composition and proliferation of each village, as the community's identity – both historical and political – corresponded to the personal trajectory of its leader.[19]

The formation of independent villages occurred when an emergent political leader managed to mobilize a significant following of relatives and friends. Although the headman's principal source of authority came from his role as wartime leader, his responsibilities also had much to do with the organization of material and social life. According to Gabriel Soares de Sousa, once a headman determined that his group should move, he would pick the site of the new village, supervise the construction of *malocas* (multi-family residential lodges), and select the ideal location for the garden plot that was to provide the community's subsistence. He not only worked alongside his followers, he also set the example: "when he prepares the plot of land with the help of his relatives and friends, he is the first to begin work."[20] This detail is revealing, for it shows that despite the headman's greater responsibility and prestige, he remained essentially equal to his followers in the productive sphere. In other words, political leadership rarely brought with it economic privilege or distinct social position.[21]

Similarly, the authority of headmen always remained subject to the consent of his followers. In describing leadership in Tupinambá and Tupinikin communities, Staden commented: "Each one obeys the headman of his hut. What the headman orders is done, not by force or out of fear, but out of goodwill."[22] The first Jesuits, for their part, frequently lamented the lack of a "King" among the Tupi, recognizing that political fragmentation served as an obstacle to their work. Writing from São Vicente, Pedro Correia reported that the conversion of the Indians would be a very difficult task "because they have no King, rather each Village and house has its Headman."[23]

The latter observation reflects the difficulty the Europeans had in identifying the sources of political authority in indigenous societies. The sixteenth-century literature projected three distinct levels of political leadership, designating the term *principal* for each type of leader. The term was applied to *maloca* headmen, to village headmen, and to pan-village leaders. This last category appears only rarely, in general only in times of war, when distinct groups formed alliances in the face of a common enemy.

For example, on various occasions in the sixteenth century, the Tupinikin headman Tibiriçá and the Tupinambá headman Cunhambebe led warriors from several villages in battle, each earning widespread fame as a brave, well-respected leader.[24]

While the principal source of authority lay in the headman's ability to mobilize warriors, he also possessed other significant attributes. One notes, for example, oratorical skills, which figured in the making of a great leader among the Tupi. Anchieta, himself an excellent public speaker, gave an admiring account of Tibiriçá's speech on the occasion of the death of the Jesuit Pedro Correia.[25] According to Fernão Cardim, before dawn every day the headman "for a half an hour preaches to them, and admonishes them that they will work as their ancestors did, and assigns them their tasks, telling them the things that they must do."[26] In a similar account, the Jesuit Manuel da Nóbrega, writing from São Vicente, provided further description of the content of such speeches: "every day before dawn, from a high place he tells each house what they must do that day, and he tells them that they must live as a community."[27]

In addition to describing the headman's coordinating role, Cardim's and Nóbrega's comments indicate another of the figure's non-military attributes. Headmen acted as guardians of tradition, expressing and organizing the tasks of daily life in terms of what had been set down in the past. The preservation of tradition was a fundamental element in defining a collective identity. The Tupinambá headman Jap-açu, who submitted to French pressures to eradicate prisoner sacrifice and cannibalism only to have his will vetoed in a meeting of village elders, explained how tradition dictated practice:

> I well know that the custom is bad and contrary to nature, and because of this I sought many times to extinguish it. But all of us, elders, we are almost equals and with identical powers; and if it should happen that one of us presents a proposal, even if it is approved by a majority of votes, one unfavorable opinion is enough for it to fail; it is enough for someone to say that the custom is ancient and that it is improper to change that which we learned from our fathers.[28]

The role of guardian of tradition was shared by shamans, or *pajés*, who sometimes wielded political authority as well.[29] According to the Capuchin missionary Yves d'Évreux's description of the Tupinambá of Maranhão, the shamans "occupy among the savages the position of mediators between the spirits and the rest of the people."[30] As intermediaries between the supernatural and everyday life, the shamans exercised multiple functions, such as healing the sick, interpreting dreams, and warding off the many outside threats to local society, including evil spirits and demons. Their authority derived primarily from the esoteric knowledge they possessed, resulting from long years of apprenticeship with experienced shamans. Referring to the Tupinikin, Nóbrega wrote: "there are among them some who make themselves holy men and promise health and victory against enemies."[31] The importance and prestige of the shamans were also emphasized by the Tupinambá headman Porta Grande, who told the Jesuits that "they gave them the good things, that is, supplies of food."[32]

In addition to the shamans, who lived in the villages, the spiritual life of Tupi-Guarani peoples was marked by the occasional presence of wandering prophets, known as *caraíbas*. Although outsiders to community life, the caraíbas exerted considerable influence over the inhabitants of the villages. According to Nóbrega, "every few years, sorcerers come from distant lands, feigning holiness; and at the time of their arrival they order the Indians to clear the paths and receive them with dancing and festivities as is their custom."[33]

Gifted speakers, these prophets traveled from village to village, spreading messianic revelations. Nóbrega offered a suggestive description of their apocalyptic message:

> The sorcerer tells them not to worry about work, nor to go out to the fields, that the crops will grow by themselves, and that they will never lack food, which will come to their houses on its own; and that the digging sticks will break the earth, and the arrows will go into the forest to hunt for their master, and that they will kill many of their enemies, and capture many for their feasts.[34]

Messages like this one persuaded entire villages to embark on long voyages in search of an earthly paradise, a "land without evil," where abundance, eternal youth, and the taking of captives prevailed. Although many authors have explained these migrations as either messianic responses to the conquest or manifestations of inherent conflict between different types of indigenous authority (between headmen and caraíbas), it is important to recognize their historic dimension.[35] According to Carlos Fausto, along with the spatial orientation of these movements, which resulted in migrations (generally to the East), the search for the "land without evil" had a temporal basis as well. The land of valiant ancestors also figured as the future destination of brave warriors who killed and ate many enemies.[36] In effect, the prophet's message addressed the basic elements that placed the Tupi within a historical dimension: spatial movements, headmanship, shamanism, and, above all, warfare and prisoner sacrifice.

Among the Tupinikin, political and spiritual leadership was most significant in wartime. Headmen prepared battle plans and led warriors; shamans, through the interpretation of dreams and other omens, determined when attacks would be most advantageous; and the caraíbas exalted the warrior ideal in their speeches. In his lengthy description of indigenous social organization, Soares de Sousa ably summarized the central role of war in Tupi society: "As the Tupinambá are very warlike, all of their fundamental principles have to do with making war on their enemies."[37]

Early colonial accounts, despite their differences, highlight three significant features that played crucial roles in internecine and, subsequently, Euro–indigenous warfare: the vengeance motive, the practice of prisoner sacrifice, and the complex configuration of inter-village alliances and rivalries.

On the plateau, the Tupinikin and their enemies – particularly the Tupinambá of the coast – provide consummate examples of internecine warfare. Through the early sixteenth century, the Tupinikin and Tupinambá engaged in frequent skirmishes, in an unending cycle of armed conflicts. These ongoing conflicts assumed gigantic proportions by mid-century, mainly because of the colonial implications of the so-called War of the Tamoios. Eyewitness accounts describe battles involving hundreds and even thousands of combatants on land and at sea. In his description of the Tupinambá, the sixteenth-century historian Pero de Magalhães Gândavo declared: "and it thus seems a strange thing to see two, three thousand naked men on one side and the other with great whistling and howling, launching arrows at one another."[38] For his part, Anchieta, as a hostage of the Tupinambá, witnessed the preparation of two hundred canoes for war against the Portuguese, each capable of carrying twenty to thirty warriors, along with weapons and provisions.[39]

Although the circumstances of the War of the Tamoios were exceptional, the observations of the Jesuits, Hans Staden, and the French missionary Jean de Léry, all of whom lived for substantial stretches of time among Tupi peoples during this period, do reveal significant aspects of indigenous warfare that must have existed before the arrival of the Europeans. All accounts agree that the principal motivation for the constant fighting between local groups lay in the thirst for revenge. "These people have the feeling of vengeance deeply rooted in their hearts," wrote Jean de Léry.[40] Nóbrega, shortly after his arrival in Brazil, observed, "And there is no war of covetousness, because no one has any more than what they fish and hunt, and the fruit that all the land yields: but only for hatred and vengeance."[41] And Staden, explaining "why they devour their enemies," reported various provocative statements called out in the heat of battle, such as: "I am here to take vengeance on you for the death of my friends."[42]

Despite the skepticism of many modern authors, the revenge motive explains a great deal. In defining traditional enemies and reaffirming social roles within local groups, vengeance, in particular, and warfare, more generally, played important parts in situating Tupi peoples within a spatial and temporal dimension. During his time among the Tupinambá, Jean de Léry recorded an interesting series of indigenous orations that are suggestive of the significance of warfare in preserving the collective memory of the local group. According to Léry, Tupinambá elders constantly reminded the other Indians of their traditional duties with respect to warfare:

Our ancestors, they say speaking uninterruptedly, one after the other, not only fought valiantly but also subjugated, killed, and ate many enemies, leaving us honorable examples; how can we thus remain in our homes like cowards and weaklings? Must our enemies come find us in our homes, to our shame and confusion, when before our nation was so feared and respected by others that no one resisted it? Will our cowardice allow the Margaiá [Tememinó] and the Peró-angiapá [heartless Portuguese], who are worthless, attack us?

This orator would then answer his own exhortations, exclaiming, "No, no people of my nation, powerful and unyielding young men, it is not thus that we should proceed; we should go seek out the enemy even if we all die and are devoured, but we must avenge our fathers!"[43]

Thus, it would appear that indigenous warfare, fueled by a universally perceived need to avenge past injuries, provided an essential link between the past and future of local groups.[44] Revenge itself was to be consummated in one of two traditional ways: through the killing of enemies in battle or through their capture and subsequent ritual sacrifice. Enemies spared on the battlefield would endure long captivity in their enemies' village, culminating in a great feast, when captives were killed and eaten. The taking of prisoners was directed solely toward these events, though colonial observers, for obvious reasons, sought to equate captives with slaves.

The role of prisoner sacrifice and cannibalism has stirred considerably controversy since the sixteenth century. However, an exaggerated focus on cannibalism, naturally abhorrent to Western sensibilities, has led to a distorted view of the warfare-sacrifice complex. It is interesting to note, for example, that despite the success of some Jesuits and Capuchins in persuading particular groups to give up cannibalism, the missionaries did not find it so easy to curtail ritual sacrifice. This suggests, once again, that the consummation of vengeance – with or without cannibalism – constituted the driving force behind indigenous warfare in coastal Brazil.[45]

The importance of the sacrificial rite also extended to the sphere of inter-village relations. The ritual feast marking the end of captivity often brought together allies and kinfolk from various villages. According to Nóbrega, it was the killing "that drew everyone from the district together to watch the festivities."[46] Even when the influence of the Jesuits was beginning to be felt among the Tupinikin, one group refused to suspend "a great slaughter of slaves," despite the insistent appeals of the priests. "The Indians excused themselves by saying that it could not be [halted] because all of the guests were already assembled and all of the expenses already made on wines and other things."[47]

Warfare, the taking of captives, and prisoner sacrifice thus provided one of the bases for relations among Tupi villages in precolonial Brazil. Battles often brought together warriors from various villages; in Piratininga, for example, even in the presence of Jesuits, the Tupinikin hosted other local groups in preparation for attacks on the Tupinambá.[48] And, in the aftermath of victories and defeats, allies and kinfolk gathered in host villages: in victory, to savor the consummation of vengeance; in defeat, to rebuild villages that had been destroyed and to renew their decimated populations. The dynamics of inter-village relations, whether expressed in terms of conflict or alliance, in turn provided one of the keys to European success – or failure – in gaining control over the native population.

Contact, Alliance, and Conflict

Upon arriving in São Vicente, the first Portuguese immediately recognized the fundamental importance of warfare in inter-village relations. Seeking to explain the phenomenon, they convinced themselves that the unending conflicts represented little more than meaningless vendettas; at the same time, they saw that they could achieve a great deal by becoming involved in them. Considering the state of political fragmentation that existed in indigenous Brazil, the prospect of conquest, domination, and exploitation of the native population depended on the involvement of the Portuguese in these internal wars through sporadic alliances. Moreover, at least in the eyes of the invaders, the presence of a considerable number of prisoners of war offered a potential mechanism for supplying captive labor to colonial enterprises.

Native peoples, for their part, certainly perceived immediate advantages of their own in the formation of alliances with the Europeans, particularly in making war against their mortal enemies. However, they soon discovered the harmful effects of such alliances. The consequent transformation of warfare, aggravated by frequent outbreaks of infectious disease, brought serious ruptures in the internal organization of indigenous societies. Even more important, the insatiable appetite of their new allies for captives, who would now be used for their labor, threatened to subvert the principal end of indigenous warfare: ritual sacrifice.

The Tupinikin began to confront these problems in the captaincy of São Vicente in the first half of the sixteenth century. When the Portuguese arrived in 1531–1532, the Tupinikin had accepted the European presence precisely because it did not present a direct threat to indigenous well-being. After all, the main Tupinikin villages were located above the coastal escarpment, along the Tietê River. In addition, among their principal "warriors" was one João Ramalho, a Portuguese who had joined the local group led by Tibiriçá years earlier. Wedded to a daughter of this chief, Ramalho ended up establishing another village, which would serve as the base for the future Portuguese town of Santo André da Borda do Campo.

Without a doubt, the alliance between the Tupinikin and the Portuguese owed a great deal to the presence of João Ramalho. According to the Jesuit Nóbrega, who had arrived in São Vicente recently and was thus writing on the basis of secondhand information, Ramalho was a completely indigenized Portuguese. Nóbrega wrote: "his whole way of life and that of his children follow the way of the Indians . . . He and his sons have many women, they go with their sisters and have children with them, father and sons alike. His sons go off to war with the Indians, and their celebrations are those of the Indians and thus they live going about naked like the same Indians."[49]

Despite his initial disgust at Ramalho's heathenish ways, Nóbrega immediately recognized the fundamental importance of his presence in the colony. In fact, on its first visit to the villages of the plateau, the Jesuit mission led by Nóbrega counted on the support of Ramalho's eldest son, André, "to lend more authority to our ministry, because [João Ramalho] is very well known and venerated among the heathen, and has daughters married to the principal men of this captaincy, and all these sons and daughters are from an Indian woman, daughter to one of the greatest and most prominent ones of this land."[50] Later, when the Portuguese resolved to settle the plateau, the principal Luso-Tupi settlement grew up around the village of João Ramalho.

However, even before the formal settlement of the plateau by the Portuguese in the 1550s, the alliance was put to serious test. The development of colonial enterprises on the coast had increased the demand for supplies of basic foodstuffs and Indian labor, particularly in the 1540s. Although some larger units, like that of the Schetz family of Antwerp, had gone so far as to import slaves from West Africa, most turned exclusively to the local Indian population. In 1548, according to a contemporary account, the captaincy already had six sugar mills and a slave population of more than 3,000 captives.[51]

Early on, the settlers attempted to obtain indigenous workers in two ways: through barter or the purchase of captives. In the first mode of recruitment, the Portuguese offered tools, mirrors, and trinkets to Tupinikin headmen, who would send work crews to the fields of the Europeans. Though useful in the initial phase of clearing lands to be planted, this mode of labor acquisition soon proved inadequate as it came up against the apparent inconstancy of native peoples. In the second mode of recruitment, the Portuguese sought to encourage indigenous warfare in order to produce a steady stream of captives, who instead of being sacrificed would be traded to the Europeans as slaves.

Neither process was very efficient, due especially to the refusal of native peoples to meet the expectations of the Portuguese, which provoked fundamental changes in the balance of inter-group relations that had existed before the arrival of the Europeans. The negative impact of European products on native societies was underscored in the 1550s by the Jesuit Pedro Correia:

> If the Indians of Brazil are now more warlike and evil than they should be, it is because they have no need for the objects of the Christians, and they have their houses filled with tools, because the Christians go from place to place and from port to port giving them all that they want. And the Indian who in other times was nobody and always dying of hunger, because he did not have an axe with which to clear a plot of land, now they have as many tools and plots as they like, they eat and they drink continuously and are always going about the villages drinking wines, making wars and doing much evil, as everyone who is much given to drink does in all parts of the world.[52]

Beneath this moralistic discourse lies a hint of the deep process of change and disintegration that had taken hold of indigenous villages as a result of contact with the Portuguese. As time went on, the Tupi response began to undermine the Europeans' plans, precisely because the transformation of native societies did not occur in the manner envisioned by the Portuguese.

An immediate problem emerged with the failure of the barter system as a mechanism for obtaining what the colonizers needed, particularly in the provisioning of foodstuffs. Tupi-Guarani cultivators easily produced surpluses and it seemed possible to increase this output with the use of iron tools. Sixteenth-century accounts, for example, contain numerous references to indigenous villages that maintained abundant stocks of corn and manioc flour. Vicente Rodrigues, a Jesuit based in Pernambuco, wrote that "the heathens came from six and seven leagues away [drawn] by the fame of the Fathers, carrying corn [manioc] and whatever else they had to offer them..." A colleague of Rodrigues, also in Pernambuco, Antonio Pires stated that at one point there arrived at the mission "a headman from another village, who came laden with corn, along with six or eight blacks." At the same time, in the south, the Guarani were known for the abundant quantities of foodstuffs they provided the Europeans. "Oftentimes, many Indians came with great presents of venison and fowl, fish, beeswax and honey," wrote the Jesuit Leonardo Nunes in a summary description of the Carijó.[53]

To the dismay of the colonists, however, Amerindians only provided provisions sporadically and in limited amounts, even as the Portuguese came to depend more and more on indigenous production and labor for their own sustenance. It is true that in the mid-sixteenth century barter relations flourished for a time, but each side attributed radically different meanings to these exchanges. The supply of foodstuffs by native peoples was not – as Alexander Marchant and subsequent authors have asserted – simply an economic response to market conditions.[54] Rather, both the acquisition and supply of goods had more to do with their symbolic value than their commercial significance. Taken out of context, the observations of the Jesuits cited above may lead to a mistaken idea of indigenous production at this crucial conjuncture. For example, Father Pires thus explained the offer of foodstuffs by an indigenous headman: "His understanding is that we will give him a long life and good health and means of sustenance without working as his sorcerers promise him." Similarly, Leonardo Nunes revealed that the Guarani brought their "great presents" in the expectation of spiritual compensation on the part of the Jesuits.[55]

Hence, it is worth emphasizing that barter only made sense to the degree that it responded to the internal dynamics of indigenous societies. Far from conforming to the context of a market economy in formation, the terms of exchange were linked intrinsically to the forging of alliances with the Europeans. Therefore, native peoples accepted and even promoted such relations as long as they advanced traditional objectives. Ironically, it was through this ostensibly conservative response that Tupi groups contributed to the increasingly rapid transformation of inter-group and Luso–indigenous relations.

Since barter proved an unreliable way to obtain basic foodstuffs, the Portuguese turned to the direct appropriation of Indian labor, mainly through outright slavery. At the outset, the acquisition of slaves was subordinated to the patterns of inter-group relations that existed in the area. However, with the increased presence of Europeans, these inter-group wars became *saltos* ("raids") carried out for the express purpose of capturing slaves for colonial enterprises. In this respect, as suggested by Father Correia in the above-quoted passage, the most important result of shifting barter relations was the intensification of warfare between traditional enemies, such as the Tupinikin and Tupinambá, with disastrous consequences for the indigenous groups in question.

The Portuguese believed that the resulting increase in the numbers of war prisoners would result in a large market in slaves, and colonial legislation ended up encouraging this form of labor recruitment.[56] But war captives were not transformed into chattel slaves so easily. The Europeans soon faced resistance to the sale of prisoners not only among their captors but also among the captives themselves. For example, when the Jesuit João de Azpilcueta Navarro offered to purchase a Tupinambá prisoner about to be sacrificed, it was the victim who prevented the transaction from occurring: "he said not to sell him, because for him to endure such a death as a valiant captain was to fulfill his honor."[57]

Little by little, it became clear to the Portuguese that the transformation of prisoners into slaves would require the social and ritual redefinition of human sacrifice. Although most local Tupi groups struggled to preserve their traditions, Euro–indigenous relations ended up provoking significant changes. For example, after the arrival of the Jesuits some Tupinikin groups gave up cannibalism and provided their enemies with Christian burials. Anchieta, commenting upon the difficulty of eliminating the sacrifice of prisoners, wrote that, "among such a multitude of infidels, at least some few sheep abstain from eating their fellows."[58]

In the captaincy of São Vicente, the Portuguese sought to increase the supply of Indian labor through their alliance with the Tupinikin, which they transformed from a relationship of relative equality to one of subordination. The exact details of this transformation are unknown, but it seems clear that by the 1540s the Portuguese controlled some Tupinikin villages directly or indirectly. The role of Tibiriçá's son-in-law, João Ramalho, was fundamental to the expansion of the influence and authority of the colonizers. According to Ulrich Schmidl, a German who visited a Luso-Tupinikin village in 1553, Ramalho "can assemble five thousand Indians in a single day."[59] Having thus taken on the attributes of a Tupi headman, Ramalho made the perfect intermediary, assisting greatly in the shaping of Luso–indigenous relations in favor of the Portuguese.

Likewise, the specific case of João Ramalho and his relationship with Tibiriçá illustrates another crucial element in the process of Portuguese domination. In the sixteenth century, marriage and concubinage became important means by which the Portuguese established themselves among the indigenous peoples of South America. According to Father Nóbrega: "In this land there is a great sin, which is that almost all the men have their slave-women as concubines, and other free Indians whom they demand as wives for their male slaves, according to the custom of the land, which is to have many women."[60] In São Vicente, concubinage took on such alarming proportions, at least in the eyes of the Jesuits, that Pedro Correia observed in disgust: "Not so long ago, I remember that [when] one asked a *mamaluca* [the daughter of a European father and an Amerindian mother, raised in settler society] what Indian women and female slaves are these that you bring with you; she would respond by saying that they were the women of her husband, whom she always brought along with her and watched over them like an abbess with her nuns."[61] However, this was not simply the adoption of native habits by Portuguese men in the absence of white women. More importantly, polygamy and concubinage reflected the alliances entered into by Portuguese and Amerindians, conferring prestige on colonists within the structure of indigenous society.[62]

While the Portuguese achieved the support of some local headmen through these alliances, such strategies for consolidating power were not always successful. As we shall see shortly, the resistance of other Tupinikin elements to Portuguese advances provoked serious crises of authority among local groups, leading to intense factionalism. Even Tibiriçá, considered by the Jesuits to be an exemplary case of conversion, shocked and disgusted Anchieta when he insisted on sacrificing a Guaianá prisoner "in the heathenish fashion." Even more disconcerting, at least from Anchieta's point of view, was the enthusiastic response of the other Indians present, "even the catechized ones themselves, since it was exactly what they desired, and they shouted as one that he should kill."[63]

In spite of the difficulties they faced in establishing dominion over the Tupinikin, the Portuguese of São Vicente were successful in inciting their allies to intensify their conflicts with the Tupinambá. This escalation led various Tupinambá groups along the coast from Cabo Frio to São Vicente to enter into an alliance, which created a powerful movement of anti-Portuguese resistance. Between the 1540s and the 1560s, the entire coast and many parts of the area above the coastal escarpment were immersed in the War of the Tamoios.

The war reflected important changes in the structure of inter-group conflict in southern Brazil. While the initial outbreak of the war was rooted in the logic of precolonial relations and rivalries, warfare increasingly came to respond to the pressures and demands of early colonialism. These transformations, in turn, would have profound effects on the internal structures of indigenous societies. Jean de Léry, in recounting a French attempt to buy some Tememinó captives from the Tupinambá, sheds light on this issue:

> As hard as we tried, however, our interpreters only were able to ransom some of the prisoners. I saw that [even] this was disagreeable to the victors when I bought a woman with her two-year-old son, which cost me nearly three francs worth of goods. The vendor told me then: "I do not know what will happen in the future, ever since Father Colá [Nicholas Villegaignon] arrived here we have not eaten even half of our prisoners."[64]

Furthermore, it became clear to the Portuguese authorities that Indian insubordination and rebellion were directly proportional to European provocation, to the extent that the unchecked exploitation of indigenous labor led to armed resistance and demographic decline. Recognition of this connection between European demands and indigenous conduct contributed to a radical shift in Portuguese policy toward Brazil, in which the Crown became directly involved for the first time. In drawing up the standing orders (*regimento*) of Tomé de Sousa, the first Governor-General of Brazil, in 1548 the Crown not only established the foundations of colonial government, it also outlined the first formal statement of Indian policy, inaugurating a long series of laws, decrees, orders, and regulations that would yield an often ambiguous and contradictory body of legislation.[65] The new stance laid out in the *regimento* openly admitted that the failure of most captaincies was rooted in the illegitimate and violent processes of enslavement practiced by settlers. At the same time, it also implicitly recognized that the success of the colony ultimately depended on the subordination and exploitation of the indigenous population.[66]

Jesuits and Settlers in the Occupation of the Plateau

The fleet that brought Tomé de Sousa to Brazil in 1549 carried among its passengers a handful of Jesuits who would represent the key to early Indian policy. In spite of their relative independence, since they answered to the head of their order in Rome to a greater extent than to the King of Portugal, and in spite of their subsequent economic power within Brazil, during these years the Jesuits served the interests of the Crown as instruments of its policy of colonial development. As a counterpoint to the settlers' destructive practice of unrestrained enslavement, the Jesuits attempted to control and preserve "useful" Indians through a civilizing process that would transform them into productive workers. By establishing *aldeamentos*, or mission villages, the Jesuits offered an alternative method of conquest and assimilation. This project backfired, as we shall see below, and had the grave result of creating a bitter, conflictual relationship between Jesuits and settlers.

However, these conflicts only became heated years later. In the immediate context of the War of the Tamoios, despite serious differences of opinion, Jesuits and colonists collaborated in the formal settlement of the plateau in the 1550s. Frequent Tamoio raids on the fringes of Portuguese settlement curtailed the output of subsistence crops that supplied the sugar plantations, threatening the continued development of the coast. Father Manuel da Nóbrega, recognizing the need for complementary centers on the coast and in the interior, commented that the inhabitants of the coast, "while they have fish in abundance, do not have lands for subsistence crops nor for livestock, and above all they live in great unease because they are each day persecuted by their enemies and the foodstuffs they eat come from the Campo, ten, twelve leagues up the way. . ."[67] The Municipal Council of São Paulo, for its part, also highlighted this complementarity in a formal request made to the Crown appointee Estácio de Sá:

> . . . we remind Your Lordship of how this town of São Paulo that was built up a few years ago a dozen leagues inland and formed with much effort far from the sea and

> the towns of Santos and São Vicente inasmuch as they could not be sustained at the present just as in times to come given that along the sea they could not supply the foodstuffs for the sustenance of said towns and plantations nor were there pastures in which to graze the many head of cattle that there are in said town and captaincy...[68]

Along with creating a subsidiary economy, the formal settlement of the plateau aimed to provide new sources of captive labor. The Tamoio uprising made the enslavement of the Tupinambá an increasingly uncertain and costly business. Given this situation, the Portuguese turned their attention to another rival of their Tupinikin allies, the Carijó, who in many ways became the main reason for the presence of Jesuits as well as settlers in southern Brazil. It is worth pointing out that even before the founding of São Vicente there existed a modest trade in slaves along the southern coast, and so many Carijó slaves were to be found on the plantations of Santos and São Vicente at mid-century.[69]

In effect, the consolidation of European settlement in the São Paulo region beginning in 1553 established a gateway to the *sertão*, a wilderness that offered settlers an attractive source of wealth in the form of Indians. Two almost simultaneous developments, the raising of the town of Santo André da Borda do Campo and the founding of the Jesuit college of São Paulo de Piratininga, laid the foundation for subsequent conflict between settlers and Jesuits over the Indians. On the one side, a group of settlers led by João Ramalho and their Tupinikin followers founded the town of Santo André, officially authorized by the proprietor of the captaincy in 1553, when a charter was granted and a Municipal Council installed to handle administrative matters. Santo André became the third town chartered in the captaincy, following São Vicente, founded in 1532, and Santos, established in 1545. The site for the new town, atop the coastal escarpment near the main trail that the Tupinikin used to reach the coast, afforded access to the vast expanses to the south and west of the captaincy, as the title Borda do Campo ("edge of the countryside") suggests.[70] The settlers wasted no time in exploring those expanses, as shown by the voyage of one Francisco Vidal, who in 1553 journeyed to Paraguay, returning in a matter of months with twenty Guarani slaves. Although such commerce was frowned upon by the Crown, the records of the Municipal Council of Santo André point to constant contact with the Spanish of Paraguay.[71]

At about the same time, the Jesuits of São Vicente prepared to scale the coastal escarpment, as Father Nóbrega planned the consolidation of three Indian villages at the site of Tibiriçá's village, between the Tamanduateí and Anhangabaú rivers, today the center of metropolitan São Paulo.[72] The Jesuits, particularly Nóbrega, had high hopes for the expansion of Portuguese influence in São Vicente, in part due to the failure of most of the other captaincies, but especially because of the favorable reports they received regarding the indigenous population of southern Brazil. In 1553, the largest group of Jesuits in all of Brazil was to be found in São Vicente "as it is the land better suited to the conversion of the heathen than any of the others, because they never warred with the Christians, and through here is the gateway and the most certain and secure pathway to the peoples of the *sertão* of which we have reliable information."[73]

In keeping with Nóbrega's plan, thirteen fathers and brothers of the Company of Jesus, many of them recently arrived on the fleet of 1553, scaled the Serra do Mar and founded the College of São Paulo de Piratininga on January 25, 1554. The college, at the same time as it sheltered the priests working among the local Indians, was to serve as an outpost from which to project the faith into the remote wilderness. However, as the Jesuits began to direct their energies toward the Carijó, they ended up on a collision course with the settlers, who sought these very same Carijó as a source of involuntary labor for their embryonic economic enterprises.

This inevitable conflict developed slowly, as settlers and Jesuits were forced to collaborate in the face of indigenous resistance. Throughout the 1550s, the Tamoio maintained the coast in a state of siege and occasionally launched attacks on the plateau, threatening the fledgling town of Santo André.[74] This situation became even more serious in that the permanent settlement of the plateau by the Portuguese provoked conflict among their Tupinikin allies. This factionalism had serious consequences: in 1557, the Jesuit Luís da Grã reported that the main Tupinikin villages were in the process of disintegration.[75]

The resulting insecurity led Governor-General Mem de Sá to order the extinction of Santo André in 1558, instructing residents to move to the safer location of the College, where the town of São Paulo was formally established in 1560. The move was completed by 1562, and both settlers and Jesuits began to prepare for an onslaught of the Indians in revolt. Over the next three years, São Paulo was repeatedly threatened with extinction by the Tupinikin, led by Piquerobi and Jaguaranho, Tibiriçá's brother and nephew, respectively, who encircled the new town.[76] The war caused heavy losses on both sides, with the Indians attacking and defending São Paulo bearing the brunt of the casualties.

Although the two sides were evenly matched in technological and strategic terms, the Europeans could count on a weapon far more powerful than firearms: disease. As in other parts of the sixteenth-century New World, epidemics had a devastating effect on the indigenous populations of the Brazilian coast. The first large-scale epidemic spread through the interior of the captaincy in 1554. "For these that we made Christians death came so quickly that it killed of ours three Headmen and many other male and female Indians," wrote a Jesuit contemporary despairingly.[77] Sometimes ravaging various captaincies at one time, the deadly epidemics became ever more frequent in the second half of the century. In 1559, for example, a Jesuit recounted the outbreak of a disease with massive numbers of victims along the coast and in the interior, from Rio de Janeiro to Espírito Santo.[78] Large-scale outbreaks of smallpox and measles erupted in São Vicente during the conflicts of the early 1560s, at once decimating and demoralizing the native population.[79]

In the meantime, the outcome of the broader conflict between the Portuguese and the Tupinambá was being decided along the coast, as the cumulative effect of diplomacy, war, and disease reduced the last Tamoios to allies, slaves, or corpses. The end of the war, which had produced such a negative outcome for indigenous peoples, illustrates some contradictions of indigenous warfare during this transitional period. The role of the Jesuits, above all of Nóbrega and Anchieta, was important, but not in the sense usually portrayed in the historiography. While the Jesuits did succeed in establishing an accord between certain warring groups, it did not result in peace. According to Anchieta's account, the Tupinambá were disposed to negotiate precisely because the configuration of alliances was shifting in the context of the war. Aware of the rebellion of some Tupinikin factions against their erstwhile Portuguese allies, the Tupinambá saw the opportunity to establish an alliance with the Portuguese in order to strike at their traditional rivals – the Tupinikin. Indeed, Anchieta confessed that the only reason the Tamoio agreed to negotiate was "the great desire that they have to make war on their Tupi enemies, who up to now had been our friends, and just now have risen up against us..."[80]

By 1567, when the Tamoio War ended, due to the aggressive military campaign led by Mem de Sá, the areas of Portuguese settlement in the captaincy of São Vicente had been pacified. With peace at hand, the prospect of economic development re-emerged and with it a struggle for Indian labor involving direct competition between the settlers and the Jesuits.[81] Up to a certain point, this problem revolved around the delicate ethical question of the nature and freedom of the Indians, a question that has been taken out of its proper historical context in conventional scholarship. What was at stake was the means by which newly contacted groups were to be integrated into the emergent Luso-Brazilian society and economy. Each side questioned the legitimacy of the other, as well as the methods their opponents used to bring Indians from the *sertão*, which ranged from peaceful persuasion and attraction to more violent forms of coerced relocation. Once this uprooting was accomplished, the contending colonial agents – Jesuits on the one side, settlers on the other – vied for the right to administer the labor of Indians recently dislodged from their homelands.

Although a simplified rendering of these conflicts allows a convenient distinction between two neat categories of well-defined interests, the actual situation involved greater complexity, which explains at least in part the contradictions that came to characterize Portuguese Indian policy in Brazil. Just as the settlers did not uniformly advocate slavery as the sole form of colonial integration, the Jesuits were not altogether opposed to Indian captivity. After all, everyone – except for the Indians, of course – agreed that outright domination offered the only way to guarantee the social control and economic exploitation of the natives once and for all. The thinking of Manuel da Nóbrega provides a telling example of Jesuit ambivalence. Among others of his order, Nóbrega defended Indian and African slavery as necessary for the development of the colony, suggesting at one point that captivity would represent an advance for the "heathenry." In discussing the most efficient way to execute the Jesuits' plans, Nóbrega insisted that he wanted to see the heathen "subjected to and placed under the yoke of obedience to the Christians, so that we may impress upon them everything we want, because [the Indian] is of a sort who, once subdued, we may well inscribe Christ's faith on their judgement and will, as was done in Peru and the Antilles."[82] Together with many of his contemporaries – priests and laypersons – Nóbrega upheld the basic notion that the Indians had to be dominated if Brazil was to prosper and that the only way to deal with particularly resistant groups was through the prosecution of "just wars" in which the Europeans' enemies would be reduced to slavery.

For Nóbrega, then, despite his defense of the freedom of most Indians, indigenous slavery would be permissible and even desirable in certain cases, not only for defense or punishment, but also because a supply of legitimate captives would attract Christian settlers to the New World. According to Nóbrega, the definitive prescription for development would require that "the heathen either be lorded over or driven off. . ."[83] Anchieta, for his part, expressed some frustration with the mixed results of his efforts among the Tupinikin of Piratininga, echoing the position of his mentor: "One cannot expect nor obtain anything in all this land with regard to the conversion of the heathens without many Christians coming here, who dedicating themselves and their lives to the will of God, will subject the Indians to the yoke of slavery and compel them to accept the banner of Christ."[84]

These considerations helped shape the first major legislative statement by the Crown on the Indian question, the law of March 20, 1570, which sought to regulate, but not outlaw, Indian slavery.[85] The new statute designated the legitimate means of acquiring Indian captives, restricting these to just wars duly authorized by the King or governor and the ransom of captives who would otherwise perish in anthropophagous rituals. All Indians captured through other means were declared free. The law had little effect on actual relations between colonists and Indians, as the gaping loophole of just war opened the way to abuses, but it did reflect the conciliatory tone adopted by an ambivalent Crown caught between Jesuit and settler interests. The posture in favor of Indian freedom certainly responded to the appeals of the Jesuits Luís da Grã and José de Anchieta, who sat on a commission organized by the Crown in 1566 to discuss the Indian question, from which the 1570 law emerged. At the same time, the just war clause emerged as an answer to the settlers' demands for slaves, while falling within the limits accepted by the Jesuits. This clause, well known on the Iberian Peninsula, had been first evoked in Brazil by Governor-General Mem de Sá in 1562, when he declared the entire Caeté people subject to enslavement as punishment for one group having killed and allegedly eaten Brazil's first bishop, who bore the appetizing name of Sardinha.[86]

Jesuit Counterpoint

Though the early Indian legislation of the sixteenth century treated the issues of warfare and captivity explicitly and in a detailed fashion, it was much less clear with respect to the distribution and regulation of labor. The destructive impact of war led the Portuguese to seek alternative ways of subordinating and transforming native peoples, including through missionary work. In creating a network of mission villages (*aldeamentos*), the Jesuits sought to restructure indigenous societies in order to provide a comprehensive solution to the problems of Indian domination and labor control. While the Jesuit project never fully met its goals, it became one of the pillars of Indian policy in colonial Brazil.[87]

The first mission village of the region, though not founded as such, was Piratininga, organized around Tibiriçá's village in 1554. However, it would seem that the population of the settlement never amounted to much, even by the standards of the time. In September 1556, Anchieta reported that only 36 Indians had been baptized, some of them *in extremis*. Over the same period, the priests only took on 130 Indians for catechism, "of every age and of both sexes."[88]

In the 1560s, with the founding of the town of São Paulo, three more mission villages were established: São Miguel, Nossa Senhora dos Pinheiros, and Itaquaquecetuba, all on the plateau near the new town, sheltering mainly Tupinikin and Guaianá. A fourth Jesuit mission village, Nossa Senhora da Conceição, became the home of a group of Indians identified as "Guarulhos," who were gathered there by the priests around 1580. The only mission village established on the coast of São Vicente in the sixteenth century was São João, which emerged alongside the town of Itanhaem in the 1560s and was founded and inhabited almost exclusively by Carijó.[89]

These new settlements soon replaced the independent villages, transferring control over indigenous land and labor into Portuguese hands. Though in principle designed to protect the declining population of Indians, in effect the mission villages hastened the disintegration of their communities. As the Jesuits subordinated new groups to their administration, the mission villages became improvised, unstable concentrations of Indians from diverse societies. Even so, in the early years at least, the Jesuits' correspondence shows a certain optimism regarding the potential for growth of the mission villages. In 1583, for example, Father Gouveia recorded that São Miguel and Pinheiros had a combined population of more than 500 souls, roughly matching the European population of the region, which he calculated at 120 households.[90] Two years later, another priest wrote enthusiastically of a large group of Maromini (Guarulhos) recently "reduced" and placed in a mission village alongside Guaianá, Carijó, and "Ibirabaquiyara" (probably southern Kayapó) Indians.[91] Finally, reports of baptisms, though numerically unspecific, also suggest a period of growth for the mission villages in the 1570s and 1580s.[92]

In the sixteenth century, the early but illusory promise of the Jesuit project impressed not only the missionaries, but also the Crown and even some settlers. According to an early seventeenth-century defender of the system, the mission villages were crucial to the defense of the sugar-producing zones of the northeast against external threats, such as those posed by the seaborne Dutch and English, as well as internal ones, namely those presented by the "Tapuias" of the interior and by runaway African slaves.[93] For the settlers, the existence of thriving, productive mission villages would provide a reserve of free labor for the colonial economy, thus reconciling the ideal of Indian freedom with the more general goal of developing the colony. Apparently pleased with such a prospect, Bishop Antonio Barreiro, addressing the pope in 1582, pointed out that while the Jesuits continued to defend the liberty of unjustly captured Indians, they at the same time generously served secular interests with their mission villages, "where they also assist the settlers in the planting of their cane and provisions and other things needed on their plantations."[94]

For their part, the settlers were probably willing to accept the mission-village system as an alternative to slavery so long as it provided cheap and abundant labor. In its ideal form, early Indian policy sought to develop a labor structure in which mission Indians would work for settlers through a system of contract labor. The mission village would provide the basic structures necessary for the reproduction of the labor force by maintaining certain aspects of precolonial social organization – including housing, subsistence agriculture, family bonds, and even political leadership, modified, of course, by the Jesuits' cultural project. Wages would be set well below the costs of reproduction of the labor force, which would be absorbed by these mission-village structures. Nevertheless, as we shall see, the mission villages were not able to fulfill the settlers' demands for labor.

Along with establishing a mechanism for access to indigenous labor, the mission-village project also addressed the question of Indian lands. Each village was apportioned a considerable amount of land, ostensibly intended to provide a base for Indian subsistence. At the same time, however, the land grants carried the less benevolent objective of restricting Indians to specific areas, thus giving European settlers access to lands previously occupied by native groups. The two major mission villages of the region, São Miguel and Pinheiros, received land grants in 1580, with the governor of the captaincy of São Vicente giving 6 leagues square (approximately 1,100 square kilometers) to each. While these grants were fairly large, they in no way reflected precolonial patterns of land use. The grant document itself points to radical alterations in the definition of property rights, as the former occupants of all of the land were now forced to petition for rights to a limited portion of it. In their petition, the Pinheiros Indians pointed out that the land they cultivated for the Jesuits was no longer viable and thus they were requesting title to land in Carapicuíba, some kilometers from the mission village, sandwiched between the properties of two prominent settlers, Domingos Luís Grou and Antonio Preto.[95] For their part, the Indians of São Miguel asked for lands more clearly associated with the indigenous past, as they sought title to lands near Ururaí, Piquerobi's old village. It is worth emphasizing, however, that the governor authorized these grants, *not* on the basis of the Indians' traditional rights to land, but rather because "most of them are Christians and have their churches and are always prepared to help and defend the land and to sustain it."[96]

Despite early expectations, the mission project turned out to be a miserable failure from almost every perspective. For the settlers, even during the sixteenth century, when the economy grew slowly and labor demands remained relatively modest, restricted access to Indian labor proved both inadequate and irritating. While visiting the mission villages of the south toward the end of the century, a Jesuit described the way in which labor was distributed: "[The Fathers] distribute the Indian servants [*índios de serviço*] and make themselves recipients of the daily wage... Whoever comes to request Indians for service asks the Padre, who calls the headman, who along with the Portuguese goes and gets them and then they agree on payment."[97] Clearly, the settlers wished to deal directly with the Indians, but to their great annoyance, the Jesuits always acted as intermediaries. In 1598, with tensions rising, the principal colonists protested to the Municipal Council of São Paulo against the "great oppression" they suffered at the hands of the Jesuits and the authorities, who impeded their direct negotiation with the mission-village Indians (their "friends and neighbors"), it being required that they first secure permission from the governor, who seldom visited the town. They proposed, in this instance, that the Council allow "the men to bring domesticated Indians into their service for a little while for small tasks" with the permission of any council member, thus circumventing the governor's authority.[98] This measure would not be sufficient, however, because even after having dispensed with the matter of the governor's authorization, the settlers would have to face the Jesuits in the mission villages before extracting the labor they sought so persistently.

By the early seventeenth century, it became clear that the experiment with free labor had failed. Enraged by the obstacles imposed by the Jesuits, a large group of colonists met before the Municipal Council in 1612, issuing a harsh indictment of the mission villages. The basic problem, they complained, lay in the fact that mission-village labor was extremely unreliable. Most Indians refused to work for the settlers, and even those who agreed generally did not comply with the terms that had been laid out, returning to the village as soon as they received their pay (half of which had to be handed over in advance) without carrying out their tasks to the satisfaction of the settlers. The colonists attributed this resistance to the absolute control exercised by the Jesuits: "Now a rumor is spreading among said heathen saying that they recognize no one but the padres as their superiors and said padres are saying that the villages are theirs and that they are lords in both the temporal and the spiritual..." Ever more indignant, the settlers argued that under existing conditions the Indians were useless and that they posed a threat to the colony, since their concentration and isolation could allow them "to rise up against the whites and townspeople as they have done in this captaincy and in other parts of this state." Finally, the settlers resolved that the mission villages should receive "neither slaves nor servants of whites unless there are in all [mission villages] lay captains who take special care and are sufficient to avoid [rebellion] and to put in order the things described above..."[99]

In spite of this final plea, the settlers recognized that even if the practical obstacles to their access to mission-village labor were removed, this source would not be enough to meet their growing need for workers. The mission villages failed to sustain and reproduce a reserve labor force. Already in the 1560s, the Jesuits feared for the survival of the mission villages, frequently struck by outbreaks of epidemic disease: "From time to time there are great dyings-off [*mortandades*] among them, as occurred a little while ago, when pieces of flesh fell from them, with great sufferings and a most foul stench," the priest Baltasar Fernandes observed somberly.[100] He was undoubtedly referring to the great smallpox epidemic that carried off much of the local population in 1653, striking residents of the new and unstable mission villages particularly harshly.

With their high mortality rates, the mission villages depended upon the constant introduction of new groups of previously uncontacted Indians to replenish their populations. As a result, the missions came to be characterized by their mixture of peoples and cultures, which, on the one hand, contributed to the Jesuit strategy of homogenization, but on the other tore apart particular indigenous societies. Indeed, in their attempts to make the mission villages the ideal medium for the manipulation and control of indigenous peoples, the Jesuits meticulously dismantled fundamental elements of the social organization and cultural orientation of diverse local groups, replacing them with radically different patterns. For example, the creation of permanent, fixed settlements with absolute territorial boundaries contrasted greatly with the conventional model in which villages were subject to periodic fragmentation and recomposition. The spatial organization of the missions, based on a European model and centered upon a church on a central square, also differed greatly from the organizational models of precolonial villages. The replacement of multi-family domestic units with nuclear households and the prohibition of polygamy had a significant impact, while the suppression of most native rites and the concomitant introduction of Christian rituals restructured the basic contours of Indian existence. Finally, and perhaps most significantly, the Jesuits attempted to inculcate a totally new conception of time and work into their Indian subordinates, in which the sexual division of labor and the regimentation of productive activities stood in marked contrast to precolonial patterns.[101]

In general, the Jesuits focused their efforts on three areas: the conversion of headmen, the indoctrination of the young, and the elimination of the shamans. But they faced resistance at every step, to a greater or lesser degree. Indeed, along with the devastating effects of epidemic disease, indigenous resistance was the main obstacle to the missionary project. The Jesuits, like other Europeans, counted naively on the blind acceptance of Christianity by their Brazilian flock: their accounts are filled with reports of mass baptisms, supposed miracles, and dramatic professions of faith by indigenous leaders. But their efforts did not always produce the desired effect, and even a headman's profession of faith did not guarantee the conversion of his followers. Nóbrega, for example, citing a case from Bahia, reported that a chief came "to be on bad terms with all his relatives for having accepted conversion and collaborated with the priests."[102]

During the early years, in part due to the resistance of older Indians, but also with the goal of subverting traditional forms of indigenous education, the Jesuits dedicated much of their energy to the education of boys.[103] However, the Jesuit fathers found it difficult to coordinate their efforts with the daily routines of their young catechumens. Referring to the mission village of São João, Nóbrega confessed that the boys only attended lessons in religion, reading, and music for three or four hours per day, after having performed other tasks, such as hunting and fishing. After lessons, the fathers would assemble the other inhabitants of the mission village for mass, which always included the singing of religious songs by the boys' choir. To bring the day's activities to their end, a final bell would ring out in the night, as the boys would be passing on their learning to the elder generation.[104] But even this intensive program, according to Anchieta, ended up having little effect. Initial successes often came undone at adolescence when, to the Jesuits' displeasure, many youths adopted their elders' customs.[105]

Throughout the sixteenth century, the missionaries' main line of attack was directed against the shamans and wandering prophets, who represented the last and most powerful line of defense of indigenous traditions. The offensive against the "sorcerers" was justified by the certainty that the charismatic presence and influence of the shamans threatened to subvert the priests' work. Anchieta observed at one point that the Jesuits in São Paulo found their strongest rival in a charismatic prophet "whom all follow and venerate as a great saint" and who intended to destroy the Catholic Church.[106] Within the mission villages, according to Nóbrega, the shamans spread the word that the holy water administered during baptisms was the cause of the illnesses that were laying waste to the native populations.[107]

The association between epidemic disease and Jesuit proselytizing went beyond the preaching of the shamans. According to one priest: "In the Village with the old women there is nothing that we can do to make them want to receive baptism, because they are very certain that death will strike them down with baptism."[108] There was some basis for this fear, considering that the fathers' baptismal ceremonies often gathered together Indians on the verge of death. Curiously, the priests themselves had their own suspicions regarding the efficacy of baptism. After witnessing innumerable examples of Indians who readopted their "heathen ways" after conversion, Father Afonso Brás, then working among the Tupinikin and Tememinó in Porto Seguro and Espírito Santo, affirmed: "I don't bother to baptize these heathen here so readily, unless they ask me many times, because I worry about their inconstancy and steadfastness, except when they are about to die."[109]

In this sense, it was not enough to discredit the shamans; the Jesuits would also have to take on the role of charismatic spiritual leader. Indeed, in their missionary activities, the Jesuits frequently adopted practices they believed would work well because they resembled precolonial practices. It was common, for example, for the Jesuits to preach at dawn, in the manner of the headmen and shamans. Likewise, Anchieta, in seeking to convert some Tupinambá villages along the coast, employed a rhetoric that was curiously similar to that of the charismatic shamans he so despised. "Speaking in a loud voice around their houses as is their custom," Anchieta proposed "that we want to stay among them and teach them the things of God, so that He may give them foodstuffs in abundance, health, and victory over their enemies and other similar things."[110] The priests also perceived that baptism, with its magical implications for the Indians, could serve to subvert certain rituals, especially cannibalism. Thus, when visiting a Tupinikin village in the interior of the captaincy in 1554, the Jesuits Nóbrega and Pedro Correia offered to baptize some captives as they were about to be sacrificed. The Tupinikin, however, did not allow the baptisms to occur, "saying that if they were killed after they were baptized, everyone who killed them and who ate of their flesh would die..."[111] In 1560, when Indians killed two captives in a village near the town of São Paulo, they refused to carry out the act of ritual cannibalism because Father Luís da Grã had baptized the victims earlier.[112]

In spite of the destructive impact that the missionary project had on indigenous societies, Indian groups were able to preserve at least some vestiges of their political organization and ethnic identity through the sixteenth-century transition to the mission-village regime. It would seem that the authority of the headman was preserved, providing the basis for some autonomy on the part of the different ethnic groups that made up the mission-village population. While the Portuguese found it necessary to maintain the leadership of the headmen in order to better control the broader subject population, this afforded the Indians a channel for protests and the airing of grievances. The chiefs, even while accepting their subordination to the Jesuits and lay authorities, could use the threat of violence to counterbalance unilateral impositions by the colonists. In 1607, for example, the headmen of the mission villages appeared before the Municipal Council of São Paulo to protest the appointment of one João Soares as captain of the Indians. After establishing that "they always have and always will obey the orders of captains and justices," the Indian leaders warned that Soares's presence in the mission villages would not be tolerated, "because the said João Soares had done them many injuries and does so each day, they do not want to obey him because they cannot suffer more than they have already suffered..." They complained further that Soares would send Indians to the coast, laden with goods, "without paying them for their labors." In addition to these abuses, Soares and his sons took mission-village women into their private homes. Finally, the Indians "could not have a single root of manioc nor livestock, all because of this João Soares..." Thus outraged with Soares, the Indians elected Antonio Obozio, "so that he as the eldest might speak for all," to issue an ultimatum to the Council: if measures were not taken immediately, the

Indians would rebel against the Europeans' authority and kill João Soares. Prudently, the members of the Council thought it best to notify Soares that if he did not stay away from the mission villages, he would suffer a hefty fine.[113]

In effect, the threat of unrest or outright rebellion became the ultimate measure of Indian resistance to Portuguese rule. In the long run, resistance furnished a powerful argument in favor of slavery as the most viable formula for Luso–Indian relations. On various occasions throughout the sixteenth century, the threat of resistance materialized in substantive violence, which, in turn, led to brutal repression and enslavement. As early as the 1550s, the Jesuits' fear of losing all that they had managed to build to the "inconstancy" of the Indians was strongly reinforced by events at Maniçoba, a village located some hundred kilometers from the chapel of São Paulo. In 1554, the Tupinikin there rebelled, threatening to kill the priest Gregório Serrão, who ended up being expelled from the village. It would appear that the Indians refused to tolerate the Jesuits' meddling in their warfare and sacrifice.[114]

This unsettled situation was exacerbated by inter-ethnic rivalries within the mission villages. In the 1590s, for example, factional violence erupted in São Miguel. More serious conflicts developed in the recently founded village of Barueri in 1611–1612, initially between Carijó and Tupinikin, and later between Carijó and Pé Largo (possibly Guaianá). Involving between 500 and 600 Indians, these conflicts caused great alarm among the white population, compelling the authorities to seek a solution to the conflict by relocating one faction to another mission village.[115] However, the most alarming occurrence was the revolt of 1590, in which the Indians of the Pinheiros mission village joined forces with warriors from independent villages in a general uprising against the Jesuits and the settlers. While loss of life and property was considerable, what most worried the colonists was the symbolic act of the destruction of the image of Our Lady of the Rosary, patron saint of the mission village, for it represented the rejection of Christianity and colonial authority.[116]

The principal justification for the mission-village project, controlling the Indians and preparing them for productive service, thus vanished. In attempting to manipulate elements of indigenous history and tradition, the Jesuits, with their mission-village project, ended by running up against the resistance of the Tupinikin, Carijó, Guaianá, and Guarulhos, among others. Instead of producing workers who would contribute to the development of the colony, the mission villages of São Paulo succeeded only in creating marginal communities of desolate Indians, weakened by diseases brought from abroad and barely able to provide for their own survival.

It was in this context that the settlers resolved to take the problem of Indian labor into their own hands.

Colonists on the Offensive

As it became increasingly clear that the mission-village project was insufficient as a means of providing a labor force, the colonists intensified other means of acquiring Indians for their service. Beginning in the 1580s, despite the restrictions imposed by Portuguese legislation, the settlers began to favor the direct appropriation of indigenous laborers through predatory expeditions into the wilderness. Actually, strict observance of the letter of the law was never among the favorite practices of the Paulistas. While the law of 1570 and subsequent legislation made allowance for slavery through the institution of just war, the captives that the Paulistas sought did not always match the provisions of the law.

Most of the groups that qualified as indomitable and subject to just war were so-called Tapuia, with the law of 1570 explicitly singling out the Aimoré, a denomination that included various Gê peoples who arduously resisted Portuguese expansion on the Bahian coast. From early on, though, the settlers showed a clear preference for Tupi and Guarani captives, for various reasons: greater demographic density, easier communication using the Tupian *lingua geral* spoken on much of the coast, and the greater likelihood of forming alliances; with the latter contacts established, the prospect of new captives vindicated their interest. The issue of labor also stood out in the somewhat stereotyped distinction between Tupi and Tapuia. Referring to the Guaianá of São Paulo, Gabriel Soares de Sousa remarked: "and whoever happens to have a Guaianá slave expects no service from him, because they are a people lazy by nature and do not know how to work."[117]

Until the mid-eighteenth century, colonists departing for the wilderness in search of captives employed this dichotomous distinction. Innumerable denunciations emerged throughout this long period, indicating that the settlers set out with the aim of subduing the most treacherous, barbarous, and indomitable peoples and bringing them into the bosom of the Church, but returned, more often than not, with Tupi captives, most of them women and children. Commenting on the activities of a troop of Paulistas who were recruited to combat the dreaded "Tapuias of Corso" in the late seventeenth century, the Governor-General explained to the Crown: "The Paulistas leave their land, and send out various bands throughout the wilderness, with no other intent but to capture heathen of the *lingua geral*, who are the ones who are already domesticated, and they do not bother with the Corso heathen, because these are no good for anything."[118]

A similar strategy, of taking Tupi and Guarani captives in the midst of just wars, had already manifested itself in the sixteenth century in the captaincy of São Vicente. The declaration of a just war against the Carijó in 1585 served as a precursor to what soon became general practice. At that time, the settlers of São Vicente, Santos, and São Paulo drafted a petition to the governor of the captaincy requesting authorization to organize a war party against the Carijó in the interior of the captaincy. The document made a point of detailing the real motive behind the enterprise: before recounting the hostilities perpetrated by the Carijó, the petition detailed the desperate need for slaves in the captaincy, particularly on the sugar-producing coast. Pointing out that 2,000 slaves had perished from disease in the previous six years, the settlers cautioned that without slaves they could not maintain commodity production, thus depriving the Crown of valuable tithes. Having established this basic need, the settlers sent a request to the governor

> that Your Mercy with the people of this captaincy make open war upon the Indians called Carijós, who have deserved such for many years for having killed in the last forty years more than 150 whites, both Portuguese and Spanish, they even killed fathers of the Company of Jesus who went to indoctrinate them and teach them our Holy Catholic Faith...[119]

Based on isolated incidents involving specific factions, this description of the Carijó as a barbarous and violent people contrasted sharply with the comments of settlers and missionaries alike, who considered the Guarani to be superior to other indigenous peoples. Furthermore, it did not justify indiscriminate war against all Carijó, as this generic denomination included groups that were allied with the Portuguese. In short, the settlers clearly sought to create a situation where they could legally and unrestrictedly fill their labor needs with the coveted Guarani.

A few weeks after the petition was submitted, Governor Jerônimo Leitão summoned representatives of the Municipal Councils of the three towns to a meeting at the Engenho São Jorge, in São Vicente, with the aim of delineating the conditions of a just war. Seeking to avoid any interference on the part of the Jesuits, the governor had called upon the vicar of São Vicente to represent the clergy, thus conferring greater legitimacy upon the resolution that the meeting produced. This resolution established that captives taken in battle would be divided between the three towns, with the municipal councils charged with distributing them among the settlers "for them to indoctrinate them and give them good treatment as *free heathen* and for them to help them in their service in what is licit..."[120] The treatment of the Indians as "free heathen" illustrates the contradictory nature of the whole process, for had the war really been just, following the strictures of the law of 1570, the settlers could have held the captives as legitimate slaves.

In effect, the strategy of legitimating the recruitment of Indian slaves through just war hardly disguised the settlers' aim of rapidly increasing their holdings of Guarani and non-Guarani captives.[121] The 1585 expedition, in this sense, reflected a general trend, on the upswing through the 1580s, as the settlers intensified their raids into the *sertão*, including private raids and expeditions sanctioned by representatives of the Crown. Jerônimo Leitão, for example, had already led an attack against the Tememinó in 1581, while other settlers organized forays of their own along the Tietê and Paraíba river valleys.

These actions provoked a new wave of unrest at the edges of Portuguese settlement, as Guaianá, Guarulhos, and Tupinikin groups received Europeans and their indigenous agents with increasing violence. In 1583, the Municipal Council of São Paulo warned settlers to avoid Guaianá villages because of the dangers involved. Four years later, the Council discussed the imminent danger of "there being here many Guaianá heathen and thus the greater part of the heathen of the *sertão* [who] speak badly [i.e., in non-Tupi languages] and are up in arms..."[122] More than ever before, indigenous resistance was explicitly tied to the question of slavery. In 1590, according to the Municipal Council, "all of the villages of the *sertão* of this captaincy joined together" to repel the European presence in the region. At that time, an allied force of Guaianá and Tupinikin destroyed an expedition of fifty men led by Domingos Luís Grou and Antonio Macedo, near where the town of Mogi das Cruzes would later be founded.[123] Following this victory, these allied indigenous groups launched new attacks on Portuguese farms along the Pinheiros River and, with the support of the residents of the Pinheiros mission village, staged a surprisingly broad-based rebellion against European control of the region. One year later, to the west of the town of São Paulo, at the locale called Parnaíba, Indians destroyed another slaving expedition on the Tietê River.[124]

The increasing hostility of the Indians was used to justify the organization of punitive forces that, in a wave of reprisals between 1590 and 1595, ended up destroying or enslaving the native population within a radius of at least 60 kilometers from the town. The principal victims, despite the energetic protests of the Jesuits, were the Tupinikin, who were singled out "because they were our neighbors and were friends with us and were our compadres and they interacted with us enjoying our barter goods and friendliness and this for many years..."[125] At the same time, the Guaianá and Guarulhos retreated to the Paraíba Valley or beyond the Cantareira Range, to become involved with the Paulistas again only in the 1640s.

Conclusion

With the close of the sixteenth century, the first cycle of Luso–indigenous relations came to an end. In the short span of two generations, the principal inhabitants of the São Paulo region had witnessed the destruction of their villages and the disintegration of their societies. The few who managed to survive these calamities found themselves subjected to the settlers or to the Jesuits. For the Portuguese, the significance of the conquest was twofold. While on the one hand, it had freed up lands for future settlement, on the other, in diminishing and destroying the local labor force, it imposed the need to introduce workers from other regions, which would mean the redefinition of the role and identity of the Indian in colonial society.

Over the course of the first century of Portuguese settlement in the captaincy of São Vicente, the character of Luso–indigenous relations underwent a profound transformation. During much of the sixteenth century, the dominant trend in these relations was defined by questions of alliance and exchange, and by the struggle for possession of the land. Though the appropriation of Indian labor was also an important consideration during this period, it too remained subordinate to the complex web of pre-existing inter-ethnic relations. Contact, however, in setting off a process of disintegration among indigenous societies, began to irreversibly shift the balance in favor of Portuguese domination. The disintegration of local structures was hastened by demographic decline resulting from disease and warfare, which then allowed the Portuguese to dominate significant sectors of the indigenous population. By the end of the century, vast stretches of land that had been Tupinikin and Guaianá territory lay securely in the hands of the conquerors.

The fact that the Portuguese were unable to integrate indigenous societies into the colonial sphere without destroying them resulted in the elaboration of historically new forms of labor, of which Indian and African slavery proved the most satisfactory from the colonial point of view. African slavery was ultimately favored for moral, legal, and commercial reasons, especially on the sugar-producing coast. In São Paulo, the settlers did not move toward large-scale African slavery in the seventeenth century, but they did create a labor system that was qualitatively, quantitatively, and institutionally different from the experiments of the first century. In order to expand the productive base of the colony, the Paulistas began to introduce larger numbers of Indians, from increasingly faraway lands. This mass of new captives, lacking any ancestral ties to the land where they now lived, would occupy the base of a colonial society defined by the social relations that drove the new system of production.

Notes

1. Gabriel Soares de Sousa, *Tratado descritivo do Brasil em 1587*, ed. Francisco Adolfo de Varnhagen, 4th edn. (São Paulo: Nacional, 1971 [1851]), 88.
2. See Curt Nimuendajú, *Mapa etno-histórico do Brasil e regiões adjacentes* (Rio de Janeiro: Instituto Brasileiro de Geografia e Estatística, 1981). Combining ethnological, linguistic, and historical data, Nimuendajú's study provides a very useful overview of native languages and societies across time and space.
3. Soares de Sousa, *Tratado*, 338. The early historian Pero de Magalhães Gândavo, in his *Tratado da terra do Brasil: história da província de Santa Cruz* (1576), ed. Rodolpho Garcia, 2nd edn. (Belo Horizonte: Itatiaia, 1980 [1924]), 141, also showed caution in referring to the Tapuia to avoid divulging "false informations due to the little news we yet have of the other heathen who live inland."
4. Fernão Cardim, *Tratados da terra e gente do Brasil*, ed. Baptista Caetano, Capistrano de Abreu, and Rodolpho Garcia, 3rd edn. (São Paulo: Nacional, 1978 [1925]), 123–127.
5. Soares de Sousa, *Tratado*, 299–300, provides a long digression on the subject, based on "information that has been taken from very old Indians," elucidating the indigenous perception of the historical succession of peoples in and around the shores of northeastern Brazil's Bay of All Saints.
6. Manuel da Nóbrega to Martin de Azpilcueta Navarro, Aug. 10, 1549, MB, 1:138.
7. Soares de Sousa, *Tratado*, 115.
8. Hans Staden, *Duas viagens ao Brasil*, trans. Guiomar de Carvalho Franco, 2nd edn. (Belo Horizonte: Itatiaia, 1974 [1942]), 153. For a more detailed discussion of the controversy surrounding the Guaianá of Piratininga, see John Monteiro, "Tupis, Tapuias e a história de São Paulo," *Novos Estudos CEBRAP* 34 (Nov. 1992): 125–135.
9. It should be pointed out that there were other Tupi groups in the captaincy during the sixteenth century. For a brief attempt at identifying these groups, see John Monteiro, "Vida e morte do índio," in Monteiro et al., *Índios no estado de São Paulo: resistência e transfiguração* (São Paulo: Comissão Pró-Índio de São Paulo, 1984), 21–44.
10. Staden, *Duas viagens*, 72.
11. Florestan Fernandes's apt summary of the difficulties involved in identifying the dynamics of relations between local communities is worth quoting here: "Little is known about the composition and functioning of the larger unit. The only evident point is that it included a certain number of smaller units, the villages (or local groups), spatially separate but united by kinship ties and the common interests they presupposed, in their relations with nature, in the preservation of tribal integrity, and in communication with the sacred." Fernandes, "Os Tupi e a reação tribal à conquista," in *A investigação etnológica no Brasil e outros ensaios* (Petrópolis: Vozes, 1975), 12–13. For a solid recent analysis of these "networks" among the Tupi of the coast, see Carlos Fausto, "Fragmentos de história e cultura Tupinambá," in Manuela Carneiro da Cunha (ed.), *História dos índios no Brasil* (São Paulo: Companhia das Letras, 1992), 381–396.
12. Despite the existence of other villages, only four are clearly identified in the mid-sixteenth century. Florestan Fernandes, in "Aspectos do povoamento de São Paulo no século XVI," in *Mudanças sociais no Brasil: aspectos do desenvolvimento da sociedade brasileira*, 3rd edn. (São Paulo: Difusão Européia do Livro, 1979 [1960]), 234, based on a letter by Anchieta, holds that there were twelve "not very large" villages. He might have misread

an ambiguous passage of the letter that may refer to twelve leagues, the supposed distance between São Vicente and the Paulista plateau. Nóbrega (MB, 2:284) refers to "many settlements [of Indians]" around Santo André in 1556.

13. The term *Piratininga* has provoked controversy in the historiography of São Paulo. In Jesuit accounts, Piratininga referred to the Tamanduateí River, as well as to the Tupinikin village located there. For an illuminating discussion of this and other matters relating to sixteenth-century São Paulo, see Mário Neme, *Notas de revisão da história de São Paulo: século XVI* (São Paulo: Anhambi, 1959).
14. Ulrich Schmidl, *Relato de la conquista del Río de la Plata y Paraguay, 1534–1554*, trans. Klaus Wagner (Madrid: Alianza Editorial, 1986), 105.
15. Diogo Jácome to the Colégio de Coimbra, June 1551, MB, 1:242.
16. José de Anchieta to Inácio Loyola, Sept. 1, 1554, MB, 2:114; Staden, *Duas viagens*, 87, where he refers to the Tupinambá village of Ubatuba.
17. For estimates of the size of villages in the sixteenth century, see Florestan Fernandes, *Organização social dos tupinambá*, 2nd edn. (São Paulo: Difusão Européia do Livro, 1963 [1949]), 62–63; and Pierre Clastres, *A sociedade contra o estado: pesquisas de antropologia política*, trans. Théo Santiago (Rio de Janeiro: Francisco Alves, 1978), 38, 56–69.
18. Luís da Grã to Inácio Loyola, Apr. 7, 1557, MB, 2:360–361. See also Anchieta to the Fathers and Brothers of Portugal, Apr. 1557, MB, 2:366. According to Anchieta, the Indians also moved as a way of resisting conversion.
19. For interesting analyses of the historical relationship between chieftainship and the fragmentation of local units among Tupi groups, see Dominique T. Gallois, *Migração, guerra e comércio: os Waiãpi na Guiana* (São Paulo: Faculdade de Filosofia, Letras e Ciências Humanas da Universidade de São Paulo, 1986), 60–62; and Waud H. Kracke, *Force and Persuasion: Leadership in an Amazonian Society* (University of Chicago Press, 1978), esp. 50–69.
20. Soares de Sousa, *Tratado*, 303.
21. See P. Clastres, *Sociedade contra o estado*, 30–31.
22. Staden, *Duas viagens*, 164.
23. Pedro Correia to Simão Rodrigues, June 20, 1551, MB, 1:231.
24. For a discussion of the relationship between different levels of political leadership, see P. Clastres, *Sociedade contra o estado*, 52–53. The close connection between chieftainship and war in another context is discussed in detail by David Price, "Nambiquara Leadership," *American Ethnologist* 8/4 (Nov. 1981): 686–708.
25. Anchieta to Loyola, Mar. 1555, MB, 2:205.
26. Cardim, *Tratados*, 105.
27. Nóbrega to Luís Gonçalves da Câmara, June 15, 1553, MB, 1:505.
28. Claude d'Abbeville, *História da missão dos padres capuchinhos na ilha do Maranhão e terras circumvizinhas*, trans. Sérgio Milliet, 2nd edn. (Belo Horizonte: Itatiaia, 1975 [1945]), 234.
29. On shamanism, see Hélène Clastres, *Terra sem mal: o profetismo tupi-guarani*, trans. Renato Janine Ribeiro (São Paulo: Brasiliense, 1978), esp. chap. 2; Alfred Métraux, *A religião dos Tupinambás e suas relações com a das demais tribos tupi-guaranis*, trans. Estêvão Pinto, 2nd edn. (São Paulo: Nacional, 1979 [1950]), chap. 7; and Pierre Clastres, *Arqueologia da violência: ensaios de antropologia política*, trans. Carlos Eugênio Marcondes de Moura (São Paulo: Brasiliense, 1982), 75–77.

30. Yves d'Évreux, *Viagem ao norte do Brasil, feita nos anos de 1613 e 1614*, quoted in H. Clastres, *Terra sem mal*, 35.
31. Nóbrega to Simão Rodrigues, Aug. 11, 1551, MB, 1:267–268.
32. Vicente Rodrigues to the Colégio de Coimbra, May 17, 1551, MB, 1:304. The association with food supply is linked to creation myths that emphasize knowledge of agriculture. Métraux, *A religião*, 148–149.
33. Nóbrega to the Colégio de Coimbra, Aug. 1549, MB, 1:150.
34. Ibid., MB, 1:150–151.
35. On these movements, see H. Clastres, *Terra sem mal*; Métraux, *A religião*, 175–194; P. Clastres, *Sociedade contra o estado*, 110–117; and Erland Nordenskiöld, "The Guarani Invasion of the Inca Empire in the Sixteenth Century: An Historical Indian Migration," *Geographical Review* 4/2 (Aug. 1917): 103–121.
36. Fausto, "Fragmentos de história e cultura tumpinambá."
37. Soares de Sousa, *Tratado*, 320.
38. Gandavo, *Tratado*, 54.
39. Anchieta to Diego Laynes, Jan. 8, 1565, in Anchieta, *Cartas: correspondência ativa e passiva*, ed. Hélio Abranches Viotti (São Paulo: Loyola, 1984), 216–217.
40. Jean de Léry, *Viagem à terra do Brasil*, trans. Sérgio Milliet, 2nd edn. (Belo Horizonte: Itatiaia, 1980 [1941]), 191.
41. Nóbrega to Martin de Azpilcueta Navarro, Aug. 10, 1549, MB, 1:137.
42. Staden, *Duas viagens*, 176.
43. Léry, *Viagem*, 184.
44. In a stimulating article on revenge among the Tupinambá, Manuela Carneiro da Cunha and Eduardo Viveiros de Castro present a new interpretation of Tupi warfare. Focusing on the meaning of revenge, the authors seek to show that warfare functioned as a kind of "memory technique" (*técnica de memória*), producing and sustaining the collective memory of Tupi groups, and linking the past to the future through actions in the present. Seen in this light, the primitive societies of conventional ethnology – stagnant, without a temporal dimension or history – acquire a new historical dimension. "Vingança e temporalidade: os Tupinambá," *Journal de la Société des Américanistes* 79 (1987): 191–208.
45. Ibid., 192–194. See also Carlos Fausto, "O ritual antropofágico," *Ciência Hoje* 86 (1992): 88–89.
46. Nóbrega to the Colégio de Coimbra, Aug. 1549, MB, 1:152.
47. Pedro Correia to Brás Lourenço, July 18, 1554, MB, 2:67.
48. See, for example, Anchieta to Loyola, Sept. 1, 1554, MB, 2:108.
49. Nóbrega to Luís Gonçalves da Câmara, June 15, 1553, MB, 1:498. Nóbrega's opinion of Ramalho softened soon thereafter, once he met Ramalho personally and affirmed that all of Ramalho's children had the same mother, who was known as Mbcy or Bartira. As for the accusation of bigamy, a shadow of doubt remained, as Ramalho could not say whether the wife he left in Portugal was still alive or not. Nóbrega to Câmara, Aug. 31, 1553, MB, 1:524. On Ramalho and other protagonists in the "accidental colonization" of Brazil by castaways, penal exiles, and fugitives, see the interesting analysis of Guillermo Giucci, "A colonização acidental," *Ciência Hoje* 86 (1992): 19–23.
50. Nóbrega to Luís Gonçalves da Câmara, Aug. 31, 1555, MB, 1:524.

51. Luís de Góis to the Crown, May 12, 1548, DI, 48:9–12. On the *engenho* of the Schetz family, see José Pedro Leite Cordeiro, *O engenho de São Jorge dos Erasmos* (São Paulo: Nacional, 1945), and Carl Laga, "O engenho dos Erasmos em São Vicente: resultado de pesquisas em arquivos belgas," *Estudos Históricos* 1 (1963): 113–143.
52. Pedro Correia to Simão Rodrigues, Mar. 10, 1553, MB, 1:445.
53. Leonardo Nunes to Nóbrega, June 29, 1552, MB, 1:339.
54. The debate over the meaning of barter is not new: as early as the 1940s, Alexander Marchant developed an interesting hypothesis regarding Amerindians' reaction to market stimuli. According to Marchant, the Portuguese found themselves having to provide goods of increasing value in order to obtain the same amounts of indigenous labor and produce: combs, scissors and fishhooks began to give way to sugar-cane brandy, larger tools, and firearms. Marchant, *From Barter to Slavery: The Economic Relations of Portuguese and Indians in the Settlement of Brazil, 1500–1580* (Baltimore: Johns Hopkins University Press, 1942). The Crown was concerned by this process, as in 1559 it prohibited the colonists from trading in anything but small tools and trinkets. *Alvará* of Aug. 3, 1559, DHA, 1:153–157. However, as Stuart Schwartz points out in his important article on Indian labor in Bahia, Marchant placed indigenous producers and consumers in an inappropriate theoretical context, assuming a Western, rational response to objective market conditions on the part of apparently irrational Brazilian Indians. Stuart B. Schwartz, "Indian Labor and New World Plantations: European Demands and Indian Responses in Northeastern Brazil," *American Historical Review* 83/1 (Feb. 1978): 43–79 (at 48–50).
55. See above, notes 52 and 53.
56. See, for example, the law of Feb. 24, 1587, which permitted the enslavement of Indians taken in just wars "or if they were purchased to prevent their being eaten by other Indians." The text of the law may be found in Georg Thomas, *Política indigenista dos portugueses no Brasil, 1500–1640* (São Paulo: Loyola, 1982), 222–224 (quotation at 223).
57. João de Azpilcueta Navarro to the Colégio de Coimbra, Aug. 1551, MB, 1:279.
58. Anchieta to Loyola, Sept. 1, 1554, MB, 2:110.
59. Schmidl, *Relato*, 106.
60. Nóbrega to Simão Rodrigues, Aug. 9, 1549, MB, 1:119. Anchieta would later elaborate on this subject in his "Informação dos casamentos dos indios do Brasil." See *RIHGB* 8 (1846): 254–262.
61. Pedro Correia to Simão Rodrigues, Mar. 10, 1553, MB, 1:438. On the category mamaluco/a (male/female), see below, Chapter 5.
62. Sexual relations between Portuguese men and Indian women have been the subject of some of the most picturesque accounts of colonial social life, which portray them as an outstanding factor in the making of Brazilian culture. It is worth recalling that inter-ethnic marriage became an important means of consolidating colonial control everywhere in the Portuguese empire, at least in the eyes of the Crown. In sixteenth-century Goa, the Portuguese Crown and local authorities promoted the marriages of soldiers, sailors, and artisans with women of the local elite, using cash payments or public offices as incentives. Charles R. Boxer, *Race Relations in the Portuguese Colonial Empire, 1415–1825* (Oxford University Press, 1963), chap. 2.

63. Anchieta to Loyola, Mar. 1555, MB, 2:206–207.
64. Léry, *Viagem*, 190–191. Nicholas Villegaignon – a military man, not a cleric – led the early French colony founded in 1555 on an island in Guanabara Bay.
65. For a careful study of the legislation, see Beatriz Perrone-Moisés, "Legislação indígena colonial: inventário e índice" (dissertação de mestrado, Universidade Estadual de Campinas, 1990). See also the same author's synthesis, "Índios livres e índios escravos: os princípios da legislação indigenista do período colonial (séculos XVI a XVIII)," in Cunha (ed.), *História dos índios no Brasil*, 115–132, along with the useful appendix listing the principal pieces of legislation.
66. *Regimento* of 1548, DHA, 1:45–62. The link between slavery and war is made explicit in Pedro Borges to João III, Feb. 7, 1550, MB, 1:175.
67. Nóbrega to Miguel de Torres, Sept. 2, 1557, MB, 2:416. The term "Campo" can be used as a common noun referring to the countryside or as a specific place name. See also note 70, below.
68. CMSP-Atas, 1:42, May 12, 1564. The settlement of the captaincy's southern coast, with the founding of the towns of Itanhaém and Cananéia, also obeyed this logic.
69. João Fernando de Almeida Prado, *São Vicente e as capitanias do sul, as origens, 1501–1531: história da formação da sociedade brasileira* (São Paulo: Nacional, 1961), 403ff. The existence of a slave-trading entrepôt in 1527 and its subsequent development into an established trading post (*feitoria*), a hypothesis raised by Ayres do Casal in the nineteenth century, is refuted by Neme, *Notas de revisão*, 23–32. On the presence of Carijó slaves at mid-century, see Leonardo Nunes to the Colégio de Coimbra, Nov. 1550, MB, 1:210; Staden, *Duas viagens*, also mentions the presence of Carijó captives among the Portuguese and the Tupinambá.
70. Most historians have maintained that the "campo" referred to the Campo de Piratininga. Neme, *Notas de revisão*, chaps. 11–14, shows that it referred instead to lands to the south and west. The official founding of Santo André was preceded by the raising of a small chapel at the suggestion of Father Leonardo Nunes, as the local Portuguese refused to resettle in the towns of the coast. Leonardo Nunes to the Colégio de Coimbra, Nov. 1550, MB, 1:208.
71. Francisco de Assis Carvalho Franco, *Dicionário de bandeirantes e sertanistas do Brasil* (São Paulo: Comissão do IV Centenário, 1954), entry on "Francisco Vidal."
72. Nóbrega to Luís Gonçalves da Câmara, June 15, 1553, MB, 1:504.
73. Nóbrega to João III, Oct. 1553, MB, 2:15.
74. See, for example, *Actas da Câmara de Sto. André da Borda do Campo* (São Paulo: Archivo Municipal, 1914–1915), 65.
75. Luís da Grã to Loyola, Apr. 1, 1557, MB, 2:360–361. Also, Anchieta to the fathers and brothers of Portugal, Apr. 1557, MB, 2:366. Anchieta believed that the reason for the dissolution of the villages was resistance to conversion.
76. Anchieta to Diego Laynes, Apr. 16, 1563, MB, 3:547–565; Antonio Barreto do Amaral, *Dicionário da história de São Paulo* (São Paulo: Governo do Estado, 1980), entries on "Jaguaranho" and "Piquerobi."
77. Pedro Correia to Brás Lourenço, July 18, 1554, MB, 2:70–71.
78. Antonio de Sá to the Colégio da Bahia, Feb. 1559, MB, 3:18–19.
79. The greatest outbreak was the smallpox epidemic that devastated the plateau in 1563–1564 (CMSP-Atas, 1:40, Apr. 29, 1564). This violent epidemic was related to

the outbreak that was spreading throughout the entire coast of the colony. Schwartz, "Indian Labor," 58, and Anchieta, *Cartas*, 257 (editorial note by Viotti).

80. Anchieta to Diego Laynes, Jan. 8, 1565, *Cartas*, 212–213.
81. On conflicts between settlers and Jesuits in colonial Brazil, see Dauril Alden, "Black Robes Versus White Settlers: The Struggle for Freedom of the Indians in Colonial Brazil," in Howard H. Peckham and Charles Gibson (eds.), *Attitudes of Colonial Powers Toward the American Indian* (Salt Lake City: University of Utah Press, 1969), 19–46; Stuart B. Schwartz, *Sovereignty and Society in Colonial Brazil: The High Court of Bahia and its Judges, 1609–1750* (Berkeley: University of California Press, 1973), chap. 6.
82. Nóbrega to João III, Sept. 14, 1551, MB, 1:291; and Nóbrega to ex-governor Tomé de Sousa, July 5, 1559, MB, 3:72.
83. Nóbrega to Miguel de Torres, May 1558, MB, 2:448.
84. Anchieta to Loyola, Mar. 1555, MB, 2:207. One must point out that, despite the passage of this letter cited above, Jesuit historians, notably Serafim Leite and Hélio A. Viotti, forcefully deny that Nóbrega or Anchieta tolerated the enslavement of Indians. See, for example, Viotti's emphatic note in Anchieta, *Cartas*, 108. It must be added that there was a simultaneous debate on African slavery, which produced no consensus. For a discussion of the position of the Jesuits on African slavery, see David G. Sweet, "Black Robes and 'Black Destiny': Jesuit Views of African Slavery in Seventeenth-Century Latin America," *Revista de História de América* 86 (July–Dec. 1978): 87–113.
85. The text of the law of 1570, together with a broad discussion of Portuguese policy, may be found in Thomas, *Política indigenista* (see appendix, 221–222, for the text).
86. On the legal limits placed on just war, see Beatriz Perrone-Moisés, "A guerra justa em Portugal no século XVI," *Revista da Sociedade Brasileira de Pesquisa Histórica* 5 (1989–1990): 5–10. It is worth observing that the 1566 Junta also counted on the presence of Mem de Sá and Bishop Leitão.
87. See Perrone-Moisés, "Índios livres e índios escravos."
88. Anchieta to Loyola, Sept. 1, 1554, MB, 2:106.
89. José Joaquim Machado de Oliveira, "Noticia raciocinada sobre as aldêas de indios da provincia de S. Paulo, desde o seu começo até à actualidade," *RIHGB* 8 (1846): 204–254.
90. Cristóvão de Gouveia, "Información de la provincia del Brasil," ARSI Brasilia 15, fols. 338–339.
91. Manuel Viegas to the provincial Acquaviva, Mar. 21, 1585, in Serafim Leite, *História da Companhia de Jesus no Brasil*, 10 vols. (Lisbon: Portugalia, 1938–1950), 9:385.
92. Anchieta, "Annua Brasiliae anno 1583," ARSI Brasilia 8, fol. 5v.
93. "Algumas advertências para a província do Brasil," BNVE-FG 1255/38 (3384).
94. Bishop Antonio Barreiro to the Pope, Mar. 26, 1582, ARSI Brasilia 15, fols. 330–330v.
95. The land that was no longer worthwhile, according to the petition, was an earlier donation to the Jesuits and not the grant the Indians requested in 1560. Sesmaria de Geraibatiba, May 26, 1560, MB, 3:197–201.
96. Sesmaria, Oct. 12, 1580, CMSP-Registro, 1:354–355. It is worth recalling that lands granted to mission villages were to have special characteristics, among which was that they were to be inalienable. A decree (*provisão*) of July 8, 1604 (CMSP-Registro, 1:357–359) codified matters relating to Indian land more specifically,

prohibiting settlers from residing on or cultivating lands belonging to mission villages. The position of the Jesuits, which upheld the Crown's prohibition, is laid out in detail in "Ordenações do visitador padre Manuel de Lima [1607]," BNVE-FG 1255/14, fol. 9v. For a broader discussion containing pertinent ethical and juridical commentary, see Manuela Carneiro da Cunha, "Terra indígena: história da doutrina e da legislação," in *Os direitos do índio: ensaios e documentos* (São Paulo: Brasiliense, 1987), 53–101.

97. Pedro Rodrigues to Acquaviva, Oct. 10, 1598, ARSI Brasilia 15, fol. 167v.
98. CMSP-Atas, 2:49, Dec. 13, 1598.
99. CMSP-Atas, 3:313–316, June 10, 1612. As implied by the distinction "this captaincy and in other parts of this state," the latter term referred to the whole of the Portuguese empire in South America, rather than to São Vicente or the present-day state of São Paulo alone.
100. Baltasar Fernandes to the Colégio de Coimbra, Dec. 5, 1567, MB, 4:426–427. For a general discussion of the impact of disease on indigenous demography and culture, see John Hemming, *Red Gold: The Conquest of the Brazilian Indians, 1500–1760* (Cambridge, MA: Harvard University Press, 1978), esp. 139–146.
101. On the impact and pedagogical strategies of the Jesuits in the sixteenth century, see Luis Felipe Baêta Neves, *O combate dos soldados de Cristo na Terra dos Papagaios: colonialismo e repressão cultural* (Rio de Janeiro: Forense-Universitária, 1978), and Roberto Gambini, *O espelho índio: os jesuítas e a destruição da alma indígena* (Rio de Janeiro: Espaço e Tempo, 1988).
102. Nóbrega to Simão Rodrigues, Apr. 10, 1549, MB, 1:112–113.
103. The education of youth in precolonial Tupi society receives exemplary treatment in Florestan Fernandes, "Notas sobre a educação na sociedade tupinambá," in *A investigação etnológica no Brasil*, 33–83.
104. Nóbrega to Miguel de Torres, July 5, 1559, MB, 3:51–52.
105. Anchieta to Diego Laynes, June 1, 1560, MB, 3:262.
106. Anchieta to the Colégio de Coimbra, Apr. 1557, MB, 2:366–367. See also Nóbrega to Miguel Torres, July 5, 1559, MB, 3:53–54.
107. Nóbrega to Azpilcueta Navarro, Aug. 10, 1549, MB, 1:143. See also Luís da Grã to Loyola, Dec. 27, 1554, MB, 2:134.
108. Antonio de Sá to the Colégio da Bahia, Feb. 1559, MB, 3:20.
109. Afonso Brás to the Colégio de Coimbra, Aug. 24, 1551, MB, 1:274.
110. Anchieta to Diego Laynes, Jan. 8, 1565, *Cartas*, 212. On the parallel situation of the Guarani of Paraguay, see Louis Necker, *Indiens guarani et chamanes franciscains: les premières réductions du Paraguay, 1580–1800* (Paris: Anthropos, 1979), esp. 88–91, and Maxime Haubert, *Índios e jesuítas no tempo das missões: séculos XVII–XVIII*, trans. Marina Appenzeller (São Paulo: Companhia das Letras, 1990), esp. chap. 5, in which he describes the struggle of "Messiah against Messiah."
111. Pedro Correia to Brás Lourenço, July 18, 1554, MB, 2:67.
112. Anchieta to Diego Laynes, June 1, 1560, MB, 3:259–262.
113. CMSP-Atas, 2:186, Jan. 20, 1607.
114. Anchieta to Loyola, Sept. 1, 1554, MB, 2:115, and Mar. 1555, MB, 2:194–195.
115. CMSP-Atas, 2:293–295, 312, Aug. 15, 1611, and Apr. 28, 1612, respectively.
116. CMSP-Registro, 1:22–23.

117. Soares de Sousa, *Tratado*, 115.
118. Governor Câmara Coutinho to the Crown, July 19, 1693, in BNRJ-DH, 34:85–86.
119. CMSP-Atas, 1:275–279, Sept. 1, 1585.
120. CMSP-Atas, 1:280, Sept. 1, 1585 (my emphasis).
121. It is worth noting that the Tupinambá were mentioned in the document not so much for the offenses they supposedly committed, as for the fact that they inhabited a region that the expedition would pass through.
122. CMSP-Atas, 1:211, 329, June 1, 1583, and Sept. 20, 1586, respectively.
123. CMSP-Atas, 1:403–404, July 7, 1590.
124. CMSP-Atas, 1:423–424, July 7, 1591. The second expedition was led by another man named Macedo and an Indian known as Maracujá. Carvalho Franco, *Dicionário de bandeirantes*, appears to confuse the two expeditions, citing them as if they were a single one.
125. CMSP-Atas, 1:404, July 7, 1590.

2

Backcountry Incursions and the Expansion of the Labor Force

Throughout the seventeenth century, colonists from São Paulo and neighboring towns attacked hundreds of indigenous villages in various regions, bringing thousands of Amerindians from different societies to their estates and farms in a state of "compulsory service." These expeditions into the interior provided a growing mass of indigenous manual labor on the Paulista plateau, which, in turn, enabled the production and transport of an agricultural surplus, linking – albeit modestly – the region to other parts of the Portuguese colony and even to the commercial circuits of the South Atlantic. Without these constant infusions of new captives, the fragile servile population would have soon disappeared, since, as with the institution of African slavery in the plantation zones, the reproduction of the labor force was absolutely dependent on a continuous supply of fresh captives. Unlike the slaveholding planters of the coast, however, the Paulistas turned away from the commercial circuit of the Atlantic as a source of labor. Instead, employing distinctive organizational techniques, they tackled the issue of labor supply on their own.

In attempting to secure a prominent place for their ancestors in the pantheon of national history, traditional Paulista historians – ironically enough – overlooked the local context in their interpretations of the evolution and meaning of so-called *bandeirantismo*. It became historical convention to divide this movement into stages characterized by distinct objectives: defending the fledgling settlement from the attacks of hostile indigenous groups, hunting for Tupi captives to sell as slaves on the coast, expanding outward from the earliest settlements, serving as Crown mercenaries against indomitable indigenous groups and fugitive African slaves, and prospecting for mineral wealth.[1] While the Paulistas' expeditions into the wilderness did vary in their pretexts and outcomes, the basic motivation behind them remained unchanged throughout the entire seventeenth century: the chronic need for Indian labor in local agricultural enterprises.

What did change over time were conditions of supply, which were determined by such variables as geographic bearings, distances travelled, outfitting costs, and the differing reactions of the indigenous peoples they encountered. Until the 1640s, Paulistas filled their needs with prodigious infusions of Guarani laborers, the scale of which closely accompanied the expansion of commercial agriculture on the plateau. Once large numbers of new Guarani captives were no longer to be had, the colonists faced a crisis that had profound repercussions on local structures, as it became difficult to maintain the labor pool at the level reached up to that point. To make matters worse, a smallpox epidemic in the mid-1660s exacerbated the shortage. In response, the settlers changed their slaving strategies, developing new kinds of expedition into the interior. Although these expeditions achieved some success, they unexpectedly altered the ethnic composition and sex ratio of the labor force. Ultimately, while slaving expeditions reflected the demand for labor on the plateau, their outcomes came to determine the economic options available to the settlers. This complex relationship between slaving and the local economy of São Paulo is this chapter's central concern.

The Riches of the Wilderness

Slaving expeditions to the interior and the Indian slave trade in São Paulo date back to the remote origins of the colony, but in the seventeenth century they began to assume new qualitative and quantitative dimensions. The experience of the sixteenth century had introduced diverse methods of acquiring Indian labor, ranging from *resgate* (barter), to *saltos* (raids), to the larger-scale punitive expeditions of the 1580s and 1590s. These models were perfected and expanded by the settlers to meet the demands of the new century. While the small-scale barter and raiding activities of the sixteenth century had been restricted to the Tietê River valley and nearby areas, expeditions now projected themselves over greater distances and became integrated with an emergent intra-colonial trade network. And while the punitive campaigns of the 1590s manifested defensive and territorial goals, the larger-scale expeditions became more explicitly tied to a program of colonial development.

The development project of Dom Francisco de Sousa provided powerful incentives for the intensification of Portuguese incursions into the backlands. As Governor-General of Brazil between 1591 and 1601, Dom Francisco doggedly focused on the search for mineral wealth, a fixation stimulated by the Tupinikin legend of Itaberaba-açu, a shining mountain range supposedly located at the headwaters of the São Francisco River. In the Portuguese imaginary, the legendary range was transmuted into a single peak of silver studded with emeralds, and its name was corrupted to Sabarabuçu. In 1596, Dom Francisco outfitted three expeditions, which departed simultaneously from Bahia, Espírito Santo, and São Paulo in search of the source of the

São Francisco. The Paulista expedition, led by João Pereira de Sousa Botafogo, had in its ranks at least twenty-five settlers, each with his own retinue of Indians. The explorers marched along the Paraíba Valley, crossed the Mantiqueira Range, and believed that they had reached their destination at a point some 70 or 80 leagues (approximately 400 kilometers) from São Paulo. One part of the group continued on to Salvador bearing samples of precious stones, and another went on to explore the region of the Paraupava (Araguaia-Tocantins), but the majority returned to São Paulo satisfied with the Tupinambá they had captured in the Paraíba Valley.

Encouraged by the results of the Sousa Botafogo expedition, Dom Francisco turned his attention to the south, where he assembled an entourage of practical miners from Germany, Holland, and Spain. Subsequent expeditions to the São Francisco River region yielded little in terms of mineral wealth, but during Dom Francisco's time in São Paulo gold and iron deposits were discovered not far from the town. After his mandate as governor of Brazil came to an end, Dom Francisco traveled to Portugal, where he lobbied the King to obtain the requisites that would allow him to follow through on an ambitious plan for the development of the southern captaincies of São Paulo, Rio de Janeiro, and Espírito Santo. By 1608, he was once again in São Paulo, armed with the titles of Governor of the South and Marquis of the Mines.[2]

Dom Francisco's plan was to create an economy made up of interlinked mining, agricultural, and industrial sectors, each of which would rely upon a solid base of Indian workers. His proposal was perhaps inspired by the model then in place in Spanish America, where the Indian masses, laboring in an integrated network of agricultural and mining enterprises, generated large fortunes for Spanish settlers while filling the royal coffers. However, in Brazil the plan soon failed. Unlike the Spanish in Andean South America, who found a seemingly inexhaustible source of silver ore at Potosí, in present-day Bolivia, the Portuguese under Dom Francisco made only the modest discoveries of the Jaraguá, Parnaíba, and Voturuna mines, which yielded disappointingly small amounts of gold. At the same time, in spite of the establishment of an ironworks in Santo Amaro around 1609 and the supposed founding of a town near where the city of Sorocaba would be founded years later, and where significant deposits of iron ore did in fact exist, the plan's industrial aspects failed as well.[3] Even so, the attempt by Dom Francisco and his associates to transform the backcountry of southern Brazil into a lively and dynamic hub of European enterprise affected the organization of the local economy of São Paulo. On the one hand, as we shall see, the growth of commercial agriculture was stimulated and, on the other, the enslavement of Indian laborers reached unprecedented proportions.

Between 1599, when he arrived in São Paulo for the first time, and 1611, when he died, Dom Francisco authorized several expeditions in search of mines and Indians, some of which he also outfitted. Only one of these journeys – led by André de Leão in 1601 and backed by Dom Francisco's inner circle – returned to the Sabarabuçu region, spending nine months in a futile search for silver that produced little beyond the fascinating account of the Dutch practical miner Willem Jost Ten Glimmer.[4] In view of the high cost and negligible success of this excursion, Dom Francisco and his coterie began to concentrate on the potential of the São Paulo region. Expeditions into the interior now sought the indiscriminate capture of Indians of the *sertões* that surrounded São Paulo. Indeed, early seventeenth-century expeditions produced identical returns: large numbers of captives and no mineral wealth. In 1602–1603, an expedition led by Nicolau Barreto, with about 100 settlers in its ranks, captured around 2,000 Tememinó while scouring the Paranapanema River valley.[5] Four years later, an expedition under the command of the *mamaluco* Belchior Dias Carneiro returned to São Paulo with hundreds of captives from the Sertão dos Bilreiros, despite the attacks of the southern Kayapó, who slaughtered several colonists. The band captained by Martim Rodrigues Tenorio de Aguilar met a similar fate at the hands of the Kayapó a couple of years later. But the slavers found greater success to the south and west, where there were dense populations of Tememinó and Guarani. Two expeditions of 1610, connected with the exploration of iron mines near Sorocaba, took many captives belonging to those two groups. Finally, in 1611, on the last journey sponsored by Dom Francisco, Pedro Vaz de Barros succeeded in enslaving 500 Guarani from the region of Guairá.[6]

Settlers who took part in these expeditions may have harbored vague hopes of striking it rich with the discovery of silver, but the vast majority enlisted in these ventures because they offered the opportunity to create or expand slaveholdings. The search for mineral wealth thus provided a veil of legitimacy for the explorers' real intentions. The importance of this artifice should not be underestimated, as once the Crown began to enact legal restrictions on Indian slavery, settlers sought any pretext that might safeguard their slaving activities. Afonso Sardinha, for example, setting out for the *sertão* in 1598 with "other young men and more than 100 Christian Indians," alleged that his only intention was to search for "gold and other metals."[7] The Municipal Council of São Paulo, always ready to defend the interests of prominent settlers, made use of another ploy at the time of the Nicolau Barreto expedition, requesting the governor's authorization for incursions to the *sertão* to recapture runaway Indians.[8]

Whatever the pretexts employed by the settlers to justify their incursions, their principal goal was clearly the acquisition of Carijó, or Guarani, who inhabited a vast territory to the south and southwest of São Paulo.

During the early decades of the seventeenth century, the Paulistas concentrated their activities in two regions, which came to be known as the Sertão dos Patos and the Sertão dos Carijós. The Sertão dos Patos, located in the interior of what is now the state of Santa Catarina, was inhabited almost exclusively by Guarani speakers, identified using such terms as Carijó, Araxá, and Patos, among others.

The Sertão dos Carijós included vast stretches of territory beyond the banks of the Paranapanema River, to the southwest of São Paulo, inhabited primarily by Guarani, though also by various non-Guarani groups. While the exact geographic location and dimensions of the Sertão dos Carijós are not clear, the term most likely referred to Guairá, an area circumscribed by the Piquiri, Paraná, Paranapanema, and Tibagi rivers. Because of its relatively easy access, at a forty to sixty day march from São Paulo, Guairá soon became the principal destination of the expeditions that set out from São Paulo.[9]

But this trek inevitably brought the Paulistas into contact with other indigenous groups occupying the lands between São Paulo and Guairá, particularly in the Paranapanema Valley. Two groups, the Tememinó and the Tupinaé, appear in the documentation of the era as the major victims of the expeditions that set out during the first decade of the seventeenth century. Little is known about relations between the Portuguese and these groups besides the fact that large numbers of Tememinó were introduced into São Paulo at two points: following the expedition of Nicolau Barreto of 1602–1604, and in 1607, when Manuel Barreto "peacefully" persuaded a large group, which he encountered on his return from Spanish Guairá, to move their village to his estate northwest of the town of São Paulo.[10]

Whereas wills and inventories from the early seventeenth century identified a wide variety of indigenous groups, beginning in the 1610s this diversity gave way to the predominance of Guarani captives in Paulista slaveholdings. This suggests that during the first decade of the new century the Paulistas occupied themselves mainly with preparing the way for the large-scale assaults on the Guarani that characterized the period 1610–1640. At that point, the most important aspect of the expeditions against the Tememinó lay precisely in building up the ranks of the Paulistas' Indian warriors, who would later play a key role in the Paulistas' raids against the Guarani of Guairá. It is possible that these Tememinó were the "Tupi" that appear in sixteenth-century chronicles as traditional enemies of the Guarani inhabiting the region between São Paulo and Paraguay. If so, they were also the Tupi frequently cited by Spanish Jesuits as the faithful auxiliaries of the Paulistas in their assaults on the missions. Manuel Preto, one of the principal leaders in the destruction of the Guairá missions, supposedly led a force of 999 archers, probably an inflated reference to warriors belonging to the the Tememinó group he had acquired in 1607.[11]

The mobilization of native warriors for the purpose of enslaving their traditional enemies, who would then serve the colonists, was nothing new in Portuguese–indigenous relations, but it took on entirely new proportions and characteristics in seventeenth-century São Paulo. Before they launched their large-scale, militarily organized assaults on the Guarani, the Portuguese acquired slaves primarily by dealing with Indian intermediaries. As in the sixteenth century, trade and alliance continued to play important roles in the strategies of settlers seeking to bring captives into the European sphere. Still novices in their knowledge of the *sertão* at that point, and with their paramilitary forces still in formation, the Paulistas depended upon these intermediaries, especially as they ventured further from São Paulo. In 1612, explaining why the Paulistas were so successful in the capture of Indians in Guairá, the governor of Buenos Aires informed the Spanish Crown that their success was due to the collaboration of certain Guarani chiefs, who "serve them as guides on these forays."[12]

All expeditions to the *sertão* were outfitted with copious supplies of trinkets and tools for bartering with Indians encountered along the way. Indeed, the Jesuits were not above trafficking in such articles. In providing an account of expenses incurred on a mission to the Patos region, the Jesuit Pedro Rodrigues noted that he spent 12 milréis on "barter goods of knives, fishhooks, glass beads, mirrors and other things of this sort, which I twice took to distribute in the villages of the southern captaincies, giving prizes to the male and female Indians who best knew Christian doctrine."[13] Among the scarce possessions of Francisco Ribeiro listed in an inventory hastily scribbled in the wilderness were "six scissors for barter" and "nine combs for barter."[14] A few years later, Manuel Pinto noted in his will that he once outfitted Fernão Gomes with "a red cap and some beads for barter in the Patos."[15] Each of these items was assessed at an exceedingly low value in Portuguese terms. It is impossible to assess, however, the returns such items brought the Portuguese or, from the opposite point of view, the destructive impact these objects had on the traditional practices of indigenous societies. For their part, the Portuguese harbored no illusions about the nature of barter: it was to serve short-term purposes and was often carried out with the cynical assumption that today's friends might become tomorrow's slaves. This position was especially clear when sugar-cane brandy was added to the array of barter goods. Describing trade with the villages of the south, a mill-owning planter from Rio de Janeiro is supposed to have said: "These people are very fond of sugar-cane brandy; consequently, we make them a present of it in order to please them all the more."[16]

The case of the southern Kayapó, or Bilreiros, a Gê-speaking group that occupied an extensive stretch of territory to the northwest of the town of São Paulo, offers a good example of the fate of an intermediary group. Early on, the Paulistas did view the Kayapó as potential captives; in fact, experience showed throughout the seventeenth and eighteenth centuries that the enslavement of Kayapó was very difficult. A Jesuit observer described the Kayapó as fearsome warriors, known for striking down their foes with unerring blows to the head. In their battles, he continued, they took many prisoners with the intention of eating them.[17] Though this last allegation is false, since the Kayapó did not practice cannibalism, the acquisition of captives may have been the key to the early, amicable relations between the Portuguese and this indigenous group. Several expeditions that set out for the Sertão dos Bilreiros in the early years of the seventeenth century brought back non-Kayapó captives, suggesting that these prisoners were acquired through trade with the Kayapó. Friendly relations, however, were short-lived. Two major expeditions were destroyed by the Kayapó between 1608 and 1612. From that point on, the Kayapó became the objects of Portuguese hostility. Threatened with enslavement or extermination, it was only by seeking refuge in remote *sertões* that the Kayapó were able to avoid new conflicts for more than a century thereafter.[18]

The principal intermediaries of the incipient trade in Indian slaves were to be found in the Patos region, where the so-called Port of Patos served as the main center in the organized traffic in Guarani captives.[19] According to the Jesuits who visited the region in the late sixteenth century, a few villages on the coast specialized in Portuguese–Guarani trade, while the main settlements of the region lay in the interior, 20 to 30 leagues away.[20] A few years later, trade having developed considerably, another priest outlined the methods of trade: "there are some villages of heathens friendly to the Portuguese to whom the latter carry barter goods of tools and clothing and in exchange they give up their own friends and relatives." At the Port of Patos, these captives were shackled and shipped to the captaincies of São Vicente or Rio de Janeiro.[21]

While the allegation that the Indians of the coast turned their own relatives and friends over to the Portuguese seems to be an exaggeration, there is no doubt at all that the Portuguese manipulated intercommunal and family relations in order to achieve their aims. By the same token, some Indian leaders strayed from custom and took advantage of their position as intermediaries, accumulating power and even wealth. Such was the case of a certain Tubarão, or Shark, who along with his three or four brothers, all supposedly shamans, became the main supplier of Guarani captives in the Patos region during the first decade of the seventeenth century. Once again, it falls to the Jesuits to describe, in rich detail, the system of supplying Indian slaves. Arriving in the Patos Lagoon in ships laden with tools, cloth, and other barter goods, Portuguese merchants would summon Tubarão and his brothers. These intermediaries, for their part, would furnish Araxá captives, taken by the Carijó in internecine conflicts, in exchange for the European goods. In addition to these war captives, Tubarão and his brothers would also bring "unattached people" – orphans and widows, for example – from the Carijó villages of the interior and trade them as well. Finally, other Indians would come on their own account to barter with the Portuguese, offering local products, such as the sturdy hammocks that were widely used in European settlements. According to the Jesuit account, these ingenuous peddlers would also be enslaved by the insatiable Portuguese.[22]

This maritime slave trade, probably quite small in scale before the 1630s, was also facilitated by royal officials acting in collusion with the settlers of São Vicente, Santos, and Rio de Janeiro. The Jesuits of southern Brazil, themselves interested in moving the Carijó of the Patos region to mission villages near Portuguese settlements, complained repeatedly that civil authorities were deeply involved in the unjust enslavement of the Guarani. According to one priest, the Crown officials who were supposed to assist the Jesuits in the establishment of mission villages acted duplicitously, collaborating with the priests in transporting Guarani to the coast, but then turning the Indians over to settlers to serve them as slaves. Referring to an expedition that took place around 1619, the same priest explained that the original objective was to bring together a large number of Araxá and Carijó Indians, already brought from the interior by both Jesuits and backwoodsmen, and to transfer them to mission villages in São Vicente, Rio de Janeiro, and Cabo Frio in a ship outfitted by Antonio Mendes de Vasconcelos, a Rio de Janeiro merchant. However, when the expedition arrived in São Vicente, the Jesuits' participation ended abruptly, as the Indians were turned over to private traders and sent on to the slave markets of Bahia, Pernambuco, and even Portugal.[23]

As the demand for slaves increased, violence became an increasingly important tool in the acquisition of captives. As in the case of the Kayapó, alliances and trade relations, even when strengthened by kinship ties between colonists and Indians, degenerated to the point where former allies were reduced to captivity. In the Patos region, barter between the Portuguese and the Guarani gave way to unprovoked attacks on the latter by the Europeans and their Indian henchmen. Pedro Rodrigues, a Jesuit missionary familiar with the region, related a specific case in which Portuguese traders arrived at the Port of Patos with the apparent intention of bartering with local headmen whom they had already engaged in "friendships and exchanges." Enticing the Indians to the port in order to trade, the Portuguese "in bad faith took an Indian headman with others who accompanied him, which would be about forty all told, and put them all in irons and took them by force to the ship and soon they arrived at the captaincy of São Vicente."[24]

Such acts of violence were not always preceded by the artifice of exchange. A rare criminal investigation, which inquired into the death of the Guarani chief Timacaúna, offers an exemplary account of straightforward enslavement. In this case, Timacaúna was in the process of moving his village to a site not far from São Paulo when he was suddenly attacked by "pombeiros negros" belonging to some Paulistas. Having murdered Timacaúna, these hostile Indians enslaved the remaining Guarani, who were brought to São Paulo and divided up among their masters.[25] The use of the term *pombeiro* in this context is noteworthy, it being a word of African origin referring to Africans or half-castes who were charged with providing slaves from the interior of that continent for the Portuguese merchants of the coast. The "black *pombeiros*" in this case were colonial Indian slaves who specialized in the enslavement of Indians from the *sertão*.[26] If this practice was indeed widespread, as it appears to have been, it would reflect a trend toward the internalization of the organizational aspects of slaving, as the Paulistas came to depend less on independent intermediaries and more on their own slaves. This represented a transformation in relations between whites and Indians, contributing significantly to the redefinition of captives as slaves.

This change in the organization of slave recruitment resulted in an immediate increase in the flow of Guarani captives to São Paulo. While it is difficult to assess the aggregate scale of the trade for this period accurately, somewhat more precise information on the composition and distribution of the captive population does exist for much of the seventeenth century. In 1615, for example, a detailed list was composed of Carijó recently brought from Guairá by an expedition authorized by Diogo de Quadros, Dom Francisco de Sousa's successor as superintendent of mines. In this case, rather than place them in mission villages, the authorities divided them among 78 settlers. Each settler assumed the responsibility of caring for the captives assigned to him, signing an agreement that recognized that the Indians were free (*forros*), though obligated to work "for the benefit of the mines." In reality, the list represented the distribution of the expedition's spoils, as the vast majority of the settlers in question were not involved in mining.[27]

At first sight, the most prominent feature of the list was the preponderance of women and children among the captives, representing almost 70 percent of the total. This apparent preference for Guarani women reflects, to a certain degree, the division of labor adopted in early settler agriculture, in which women and children performed the

Table 1 *Distribution of Indians in the Registry of 1615*

Size of the holding	(N)*	Men	Women	Children	Total
1 to 5	(29)	33	51	16	100
6 to 10	(29)	75	93	59	227
11 to 15	(13)	45	61	62	168
More than 15	(7)	41	40	52	133
Total	(78)	194	245	189	628

* (N): Number of owners within given range of holding size.
Source: CMSP-Registro, 7:115–157.

planting and harvesting functions, which reflected the sexual division of labor in many indigenous societies. In the colonial context, this division had the additional advantage, as far as the settlers were concerned, of making adult male captives available for other specialized functions, such as portage and participation in slaving expeditions. Nevertheless, the development of the slave system across the seventeenth century led to important changes in this division of labor, which made post-conquest labor increasingly different from its precolonial antecedents, while from the beginning the recruitment of captive women and children had represented a sharp break with precolonial patterns of captivity, in which the vast majority of captives were warriors taken in battle. In effect, this new colonial pattern of slaving appears to have reinforced the Portuguese strategy of imposing relations of domination upon the Indians: while the sexual division of labor on rural estates presented a certain measure of continuity with pre-conquest times, the discontinuity in how captives' roles were defined weighed more heavily in the composition of the Paulista slave population.[28]

By the late 1620s, when thousands of Guarani captives were driven to São Paulo, the local slave population had increased markedly. Due to the growth of the colonial economy of the plateau, the town of São Paulo became the main center of slaving activities; at the same time, the overland Guairá route generally came to be preferred over the maritime Patos connection. Nonetheless, the southern coast continued to be the target of increasingly large raids into the 1630s. Writing in 1637, a priest in Rio de Janeiro reported that in the previous ten years between 70,000 and 80,000 souls had been taken from the Patos region by the Paulistas, though few of them survived the journey to the Portuguese captaincies. Of the 7,000 enslaved in the Río de la Plata region, he further noted, only 1,000 had survived. Finally, to demonstrate the alarming proportions that the trade had begun to assume, the Jesuit claimed that in a single expedition 9,000 Indians were captured and delivered to Portuguese America in chains.[29]

The Portuguese of São Paulo and the Destruction of Guairá

Most of the large expeditions had as their destination the numerous Guarani villages of Guairá. By the late sixteenth century, the native inhabitants of this region found themselves caught up in the conflicting interests of Spaniards, Portuguese, and Jesuits. Both the Spanish settlers of Paraguay and the Portuguese of São Paulo competed for access to Indian labor in the vast, vaguely defined borderlands that separated the frontier outposts of the two Iberian empires. However, neither group appeared interested in the permanent settlement of the territory, seeking rather to take Guarani captives while avoiding conflict with other indigenous groups living in the borderlands, who were well known for their aggressiveness. In other words, instead of behaving like Iberian rivals, the Paraguayans and the Paulistas shared common interests, reinforced by the prospect of mutually beneficial commercial relations, with the Paulistas supplying European articles and even African slaves in exchange for Indian slaves and silver. During the period of the Iberian Union (1580–1640), despite royal prohibitions on trade between Portuguese and Spanish America, the members of the Municipal Council of São Paulo saw nothing wrong with opening a trail between São Paulo and Paraguay: "It seemed good to all due to the benefits expected of the opening of this trail and us having friendship and trade as we are all Christians and of a common King."[30]

If the Paraguayans and Paulistas had indeed succeeded in forging a harmonious relationship in the borderlands – at the expense of the Guarani, of course – their relations were unsettled by the Jesuit missionaries who arrived in the region beginning in 1609, when fathers Giuseppe Cataldino and Simon Maceta established the first reductions.[31] From the start, the Jesuits cultivated poor relations with both sets of settlers, neither of which looked kindly upon the arrival of a new contestant in the competition for Guarani labor. In Paraguay, the settlers counted on the support of the secular clergy and local Crown officials in their campaign against the Jesuit presence, fearing that the latter would severely limit the labor supply by taking Guarani captives out of circulation. That prospect threatened the precarious economic base of Spanish colonial society in the region, which depended upon Guarani labor in agriculture, particularly in the cultivation, harvesting, and transport of the tea-like leaves of the mate plant.[32]

For the Paulistas, who continued to take captives in Guairá without coming into direct conflict with the priests, the Jesuit presence was less threatening, at least during the early years. After all, Guairá extended through a vast territory and the unreduced population continued to outnumber that of the missions into the 1620s. Even on the eve of the Paulista invasion of 1628, the Jesuits only counted on fifteen reductions in Guairá, some of which were inhabited by non-Guarani catechumens. The picture had begun to change by then, however, as the cumulative effects of the slaving expeditions, missionization, and epidemic disease limited the numbers of Guarani available to slavers, who turned their gaze to the relatively larger proportion of the total population that was concentrated in the missions. Indeed, the reductions may have been seen by the Paulistas rather as amplifications, since the population density of the missions was much greater than the free villages of the Guarani, Guaianá, and Gualacho (Kaingang). Thus, the Paulistas attacked the missions not for moral or geopolitical reasons – as one strain of Paulista historiography would have it – but simply because considerable numbers of Guarani were to be found there. According to a Jesuit, at first the Paulistas respected the priests, but "with the growth of their greed" they began to attack the reductions. The problem, he continued, was that the Paulistas considered the region to be their exclusive preserve for the hunting of Indian captives. But the main reason for the attacks, the Jesuit concluded, was that the settlers simply wished to acquire "cheap" Indians.[33]

Historians have long claimed that the Paulistas attacked the reductions because these missions offered labor already transformed and disciplined by the Jesuits, thus better conditioned to the work rhythms demanded by Brazil's sugar plantations. This notion underestimates, on the one hand, the pre-contact importance of Guarani horticulture, while overestimating the efficacy of the Jesuits' cultural project on the other.[34] In fact, the Portuguese had been interested in the Guarani since the first half of the sixteenth century precisely because the Guarani were known for having practiced agriculture going back to precolonial times. Furthermore, even after the arrival of the Spanish Jesuits in Guairá, the Paulistas continued to raid independent villages as well as the missions. Finally, evidence from Jesuit documents written on the eve of the Paulista invasion clearly shows that the reductions of Guairá were not the prosperous, disciplined utopian communities that later came to characterize the Jesuit enterprise of Paraguay. In fact, the periodic raids by Paulistas and Spaniards were only one among many problems impeding the development of the mission system.

At the time of the largest Paulista raids on Guairá, which began in 1628, most of the missions were precarious and isolated communities that had been recently founded and were struggling to find a viable economic base that would ensure their survival. An account from 1625, referring to the material conditions of the Jesuit enterprise in the province of Paraguay, reported that the five reductions along the Paraná were in an impoverished state, entirely dependent upon a meager 400-peso stipend from Rome, since few subsistence plots had been planted. In Guairá, according to this report, the catechumens did not even produce enough to cover the barest expenses of the Church.[35] In 1628, with the Paulistas already camped on the banks of the Tibagi, Father Antonio Ruiz de Montoya, superior of the Guairá missions, wrote of other obstacles to the success of the missions in his annual missive. Outlining the situation of the province's eight reductions, Ruiz added disease, hunger, factional rivalries, and intertribal warfare to the slave raids by the Paulistas and Spaniards as their population's principal woes.[36] Of these, disease and intertribal warfare had certainly taken the greatest toll. Father Diego Salazar, charged with overseeing two of the largest missions, observed that most of the reductions "are filled with contagion"; in 1631, a violent epidemic raged between the Paraná and Paraguay rivers, which "peopled the heavens with new Christians."[37] Interethnic conflict was present in nearly all of the missions, and spelled real disaster on a few occasions, as in the case of Candelária, which soon after its founding was destroyed by "an army of infidels."[38]

The intensification of Paulista raids must thus be seen within this context of instability and uncertainty. The first of the large-scale enterprises, led by Antonio Raposo Tavares, set out from São Paulo in 1628, and though historians have taken this expedition to be a model for the organization of *bandeirante* slave raids, it was far from typical in its scale and structure. The size of Raposo Tavares's expeditionary force was disproportionately large when set against the scores of slaving missions that took place in the seventeenth century. Most accounts claim that 900 Paulistas (including Portuguese and *mamalucos*) and 2,000 Tupi warriors took part in the movement. However, the number of Paulistas was probably far lower, as only 119 can be identified from other sources, and because the ratio of two Indians for each Paulista seems exceedingly low when compared with other expeditions. At the same time, its disciplined military organization was atypical of the slaving expeditions that took place over the course of the century, which tended to be of a far more informal character. Testifying against the Paulistas in 1630, the Rio de Janeiro priest Pedro Homem Albernaz drew an interesting parallel between the Raposo Tavares expedition and the prevalent form of military organization in the colony: "and thus for these journeys they raise captains and militia officers with banners and drums," pointing out that this violated the law.[39] Indeed, the expedition had been organized in four companies, each with a standard and led by the principal leaders of the rural districts of São Paulo and Parnaíba. Raposo Tavares's company was further divided into advance and rear guards. While such tactical innovations were not incorporated into subsequent slaving expeditions, the great *bandeira* did represent a rupture with the past in that force and violence definitively replaced exchange and alliance as the predominant mode of labor recruitment in the *sertão*.

Though it is clear that the Raposo Tavares expedition left São Paulo with the explicit intent of capturing thousands of Guarani, its leaders did not state that they planned to raid the missions of Guairá. As in earlier collective expeditions, such as the punitive raid of 1585 and Nicolau Barreto's expedition of 1602, Raposo Tavares and his captains carefully developed pretexts for their warlike operation. According to the Jesuits Maceta and Mansilla, authors of a detailed denunciation of the Paulistas' activities, one of the principal participants, Francisco Paiva, went so far as to obtain a writ from the Holy Office of the Inquisition authorizing him to penetrate the *sertão* in pursuit of a heretic.[40] Dom Luiz Cespedes y Xería, the Spanish governor of Paraguay who joined one of the companies for part of the trek, was told that the Paulistas sought to recapture the many Tupi, Tememinó, Pé Largo, and Carijó slaves who had fled and sought refuge in Guairá. Backing up this justification, the company leaders André Fernandes and Pedro Vaz de Barros carried legal authorizations to recapture these fugitives.[41]

More substantive and palpable motives for the expedition emerged in a public meeting at the Municipal Council of São Paulo in late 1627. Leading citizens, among whom Raposo Tavares was especially vociferous, complained that the Spaniards of Villa Rica were encroaching on lands belonging to the Portuguese Crown, "taking all of the heathen of this Crown['s land] for their *repartimentos* and personal services."[42] It was a grave accusation to make amid the labor crisis facing the settlers in the 1620s. Less than three years earlier, the superintendent of the mission villages surrounding São Paulo, Manuel João Branco, had complained of their depopulation, as the colonists were transferring the inhabitants of the villages to their own properties.[43] Even the Governor-General of Brazil recognized the dearth of labor in São Paulo "due to the many deaths," which probably were the result of epidemic disease.[44]

The *bandeira* of 1628 began its activities cautiously, with Raposo Tavares setting up camp on the banks of the Tibagi, at the entrance to Guairá territory. From this base, the Paulistas began to raid independent Guarani villages and enslave their inhabitants, then turned their attention to the reductions. Their ends were achieved through naked violence. According to one Jesuit, the Paulistas' usual method was to surround a village and persuade its inhabitants, by force or by trickery, to accompany the settlers back to São Paulo. Villages that resisted met a terrible fate. In such cases, the Portuguese "enter, kill, burn, and destroy . . . and there have been cases in which they burned entire settlements merely to [instill] terror and awe in neighboring villages." The overland trip to São Paulo promised further horrors, "such as killing the sick, the aged, cripples and even children who delay their relatives or the others from continuing the journey with the haste and expediency that they [the Paulistas] expect and demand sometimes with such excess that they will cut off the arms of some and use them to whip the others."[45] Another priest accused the Paulistas of acting "with such cruelty that they do not seem to me to be Christians, killing the children and the old people who cannot keep up and giving them to their dogs to eat."[46]

By 1632, successive raids had destroyed many independent Guarani villages and virtually all of the Guairá reductions. Thousands of Guarani slaves were marched to São Paulo, a small number of which were traded to other captaincies. Precisely how many, though, remains a difficult question, given the wide variation of estimates in contemporary accounts, some swollen by the ulterior political motives of Jesuit witnesses. Total figures as high as 300,000 are cited by historians; this unlikely sum may derive from a faulty transcription by a scribe in the court of Philip IV.[47] Father Antonio Ruiz de Montoya stated that the Paulistas had destroyed eleven missions, each with a population of 3,000 to 5,000 souls, which would mean that anywhere from 33,000 to 55,000 Indians were enslaved, assuming that all inhabitants were captured.[48] Manuel Juan de Morales, a Spanish merchant resident in São Paulo, noted the destruction of fourteen reductions with an aggregate population of 40,000, of which 30,000 were enslaved.[49] Finally, Father Lourenço de Mendonça of Rio de Janeiro, citing a certificate passed by Spanish Jesuits, reported that 14 reductions with 1,000 or 2,000 families each fell victim to the Paulistas, who brought 60,000 Guarani captives to São Paulo.[50] We may add a fourth contemporary account, by the governor of Buenos Aires, based on information from Ruiz de Montoya, which asserts that the Paulistas took 60,000 Indians from the province of Paraguay between 1628 and 1630.[51]

These figures are probably not very far from the truth, especially considering that the Paulistas preyed on independent communities as well as the reductions in their attacks on the Indians of Guairá. As for the missions, there were fifteen in Guairá in 1628, thirteen of which were destroyed, while the remaining two were moved in 1631 to safer locations to the south, along the Uruguay River. The vast majority of the missions – twelve of them – had been established less than four years before the Paulista invasion. The only two reductions founded at a substantially earlier date, Loreto and San Ignacio, both set up in 1610, were the two that survived the onslaught. These two reductions were fully integrated into the Spanish economy of Guairá, which may explain their ability to hold off the invaders. But even they suffered significant misfortunes, including a major epidemic in 1618.[52] The other missions fell to the Paulistas rather rapidly, although the exact chronology of these events is unclear. According to a 1629 document, Raposo Tavares himself commanded the destruction of Jesús María, San Miguel, and at least one other reduction at the head of eighty-six other Paulistas.[53] It seems likely that the other missions were dismembered by other columns of the 1628 expedition, specifically those of André Fernandes and Manuel Preto.[54]

Once the Guarani population of Guairá was destroyed, the Paulistas turned their attention back to the Guarani further south. They began to attack the missions of Tape and Uruguay, located in what is today the southernmost Brazilian state of Rio Grande do Sul. The situation in Tape Province resembled that of Guairá, in that the missions had only recently been founded (1633–1634) at the time of the Paulista attacks (1635–1641). Of the six reductions founded by the Jesuits, three were destroyed by 1638, with Raposo Tavares and Fernão Dias Pais leading the most intense raids, in 1636 and 1637 respectively, while other groups found their leaders among the backwoodsmen who had acquired valuable experience in the Guairá campaigns. Nonetheless, this time the Paulistas faced major resistance on the part of the Indians. Raposo Tavares's expedition, reputed to have had an estimated 140 Paulistas and 1,500 armed Tupi in its ranks, struggled to overrun the Jesús María reduction, where 300 warriors put up stiff resistance. Shortly thereafter, fearing a general uprising as the inhabitants of San Cristóbal, Santa Ana, and San Joaquín grouped together in the Natividad mission, the raiders decided they had no choice but to retreat.[55]

A series of factors converged around 1640 to complicate the Paulista quest for Guarani captives. First, the Jesuits, who obviously counted on the support of powerful forces in the colonies and in Europe, began to fight back through legal channels, taking the problem of the missions to the Governor-General of Brazil, to Philip IV, and finally to the Pope, thereby securing the first successes in their counter-offensive against the Paulistas. After a fierce campaign in defense of the missions, the Spanish Jesuits convinced the Pope to hand down a strongly worded brief condemning the activities of the Paulista and Paraguayan slavers.[56] While publication of the brief provoked unrest in São Paulo, Santos, and Rio de Janeiro, it was not enough to discourage the Paulistas from continuing their assaults on Jesuit-run villages, for they returned to attack again in 1648 and 1676. In this context, the relocation and defensive organization of the missions was aimed at diminishing the threat posed by the Portuguese. As the Jesuits began to concentrate the reductions in less accessible locations, particularly along the Uruguay and Paraguay rivers, slaving expeditions had to face greater distances, harsher terrain, and the challenges of other indigenous groups – such as the Paiaguá and the Guaikurú – in their pursuit of Guarani labor. In addition, though the Spanish Crown prohibited the use of firearms by Indians, evidently as a precaution against native rebellion, the Jesuits began to arm and organize their wards to defend the missions against the attacks of Paulistas and enemy Indians. In some cases, the priests equipped the Indians with firearms, though it seems that most resistance depended upon traditional weaponry.[57]

The militarization of the Jesuit missions, more than any other factor, determined the end of large-scale raids on the Guarani. Unaccustomed to defeat, the Paulistas suffered major setbacks in Uruguay Province. In 1638, Guarani warriors killed nine backwoodsmen from São Paulo and took another seventeen prisoner at Caçapaguaçu, repelling the expedition led by Pedro Leite Pais (Fernão Dias's brother).[58] A more crushing defeat came in 1641, when the large *bandeira* of Jerônimo Pedroso de Moraes ran up against indigenous resistance at Mbororé. According to a Jesuit eyewitness, 300 Paulistas and 600 Tupi in 130 canoes attacked Jesuits and Indians in their camp on the banks of the Mbororé River, a tributary of the Uruguay. After a fierce riverine and land battle, the Paulistas were forced to retreat. Beaten on the field of battle, the expedition was subsequently annihilated by hunger and disease, an ironic twist that apparently delighted the Jesuit observer.[59] The following year, the Indians of Mbororé regaled a Jesuit visitor with a play recreating their heroic victory over the "Lusitanos," emphasizing the symbolic importance of the event.[60] Although a few, scattered expeditions returned to Guarani territory, for all practical purposes the Mbororé "disaster" marked the end of an era.

The Large-Scale *Bandeiras* and the Paulista Economy

The *bandeirante* surge of 1628–1641was intimately connected to the expansion of the local economy of São Paulo, and not, as most traditional Paulista historians have supposed, to the need for slave labor on the sugar plantations of the northeast. Without a doubt, some – perhaps many – of the Indian slaves taken by the Paulistas came to be sold in other captaincies, but such limited trade seems insufficient to explain the motives underlying the *bandeirante* enterprise, let alone its scale. Evidence indicates that the sale of captive Indians to the sugar planters of the coast was exaggerated by the Jesuits in order to build a stronger case against the Paulistas, since selling Indians who were not taken in just wars constituted a manifestly illegal act, even within the vague contours of Indian legislation. Using these arguments, one priest alleged that 11,000 to 13,000 souls had been sold at public market during a four-year period.[61] Even if that were so, it would still represent a small fraction of the total number of Indians taken captive.

In fact, the only categorical evidence linking the Raposo Tavares campaign with the inter-captaincy trade comes from a public investigation carried out in Salvador in 1629 in response to a complaint made by fathers Mansilla and Maceta.[62] According to the witnesses, a few Carijó captives had been shipped from Santos to be sold in Rio de Janeiro, Espírito Santo, and Bahia. One caravel carried forty-seven captives, most of whom were disembarked in Espírito Santo, while two small boys, aged eight or nine, were sent on to Salvador. A second vessel, chartered by Domingos Soares Guedes, a Portuguese merchant resident in Salvador, transported ten or eleven Carijó, leaving four captives in Rio de Janeiro. Finally, a third ship, belonging to the Benedictine order, carried twenty-five Indians, all of them from the missions raided by Raposo Tavares, to be delivered to the convent of São Bento in Salvador.

Despite the instances cited above, little in the evidence from other parts of Brazil would indicate that a growth in demand for Indian labor in the sugar-growing regions stimulated slaving in the south. Historiographical convention in Brazil once held that the large-scale campaigns against the reductions responded to the labor crisis in the sugar-growing northeast provoked by the Dutch invasions and the interruption of the African slave trade caused by the loss of Angola. However, this argument is chronologically inconsistent, as the Raposo Tavares expedition set out before the seizure of Pernambuco and well before the capture of Luanda.[63] That said, the sugar industry did depend on Indian labor for particular tasks and there is evidence that the supply of Indians dwindled in the early seventeenth century. In response to this situation, the Portuguese of Bahia organized slaving expeditions similar to those that set out from São Paulo, though without achieving the same measure of success. At the end of the sixteenth century, for example, a Jesuit wrote of a large expedition of 300 Portuguese and 600 Indians that, despite its size, brought back few captives.[64] In the same year as the invasion of Guairá, the Bahian Afonso Rodrigues Adorno led a large contingent of slave-hunters into the interior of Bahia, also with little success.[65] It would seem that during the seventeenth century a significant part of the Indian labor recruited for the sugar industry came from Maranhão. Indeed, Portuguese involvement in Maranhão was a response to the expanding sugar industry of the northeast, as the new colony was to supply foodstuffs and supplementary slave labor to the plantations, especially those of Pernambuco and the other captaincies of the north. This incipient connection is clear in Dutch documentation on Pernambuco, as the "Flemings" began to show an interest in the traffic in "Tapuia" slaves between Maranhão and Pernambuco.[66] It was perhaps in this way, ironically, that the Dutch invasion affected demand for Indian labor in the northeast.

Most likely, the Indians slaves who were "exported" from São Paulo represented a surplus in the economy of the plateau. Beyond the modest maritime traffic connecting the Patos region with markets to the north, it seems improbable that many captives were sent directly from the *sertão* or reductions to the sugar plantations. A baptismal register from a rural district of Rio de Janeiro in the 1640s reveals the existence of Indian captives who, instead of displaying Guarani origins, carried such tribal denominations as Guaianá, Guarulhos, and Nhambi (possibly a reference to

Table 2 *Proprietors and Indians, São Paulo Region, 1600–1729*

Decade	Proprietors	Indians	Average holding
1600–1609	12	154	12.8
1610–1619	49	863	17.6
1620–1629	38	852	22.4
1630–1639	99	2,804	28.3
1640–1649	111	4,060	36.6
1650–1659	142	5,375	37.9
1660–1669	148	3,752	25.3
1670–1679	138	3,686	26.7
1680–1689	159	3,623	22.8
1690–1699	71	1,058	14.9
1700–1709	63	948	15.0
1710–1719	100	927	9.3
1720–1729	40	435	9.9
1600–1729	1,174	28,537	24.3

Sources: Inventories of probated estates, São Paulo and Parnaíba. IT, vols. 1–44; AESP-INP, cxs. 1–40; AESP-IPO, various cxs.; AESP-IE, cxs. 1–6.

Anhembi, the indigenous term for the Tietê River).[67] These Indians were thus from the immediate region of São Paulo, which makes some sense when one considers the risks involved in the long-distance Indian slave trade. As we shall see, Indians recently brought from the *sertão* had very low values because of the reduced chances of their survival in their new environment. This, coupled with legal restrictions on Indian slavery, made the slave trade a poor business proposition, restricting it to the transfer of small groups or individuals whose values justified the cost of the voyage.[68]

Thus, almost all of the Indians captured in this period were integrated into the flourishing economy of the plateau. The Paulistas' own documentation indicates as much: one sees the increasing concentration of Indians listed in property inventories in the towns of São Paulo and Santana de Parnaíba (see Table 2). In this key moment in the development of commercial agriculture, as we shall see in Chapter 3, the large-scale expeditions proved effective as a way to constitute an aggregate stock of Indian labor. It is noteworthy that many if not most of the participants in the Guairá expeditions cut short their careers as backwoodsmen upon returning to the São Paulo region, turning to the more settled pursuit of wheat farming in the 1630s and 1640s. Raposo Tavares himself, despite several subsequent returns to the *sertão*, established a prosperous estate on the Tietê River at Quitaúna, between São Paulo and Parnaíba, which had a labor force of 117 Indians in 1632.[69] The other leaders of the Guairá raids also boasted large slaveholdings and became leading landowners on the plateau. Such was the case of the brothers André, Domingos, and Baltasar Fernandes, whose shares of the captives were the bases for the development of the towns of Parnaíba, Itu, and Sorocaba, respectively.

The Reorganization of Slaving

Beginning in the 1640s, large-scale expeditions gave way to new forms of organizing the pursuit of Indian slaves. In general, treks to the *sertão* became smaller, more frequent, and more geographically dispersed.[70] The most significant shift was in the geographical orientation of the expeditions, as the Paulistas sought a viable substitute for the Guarani captives that had impelled earlier operations. Initially, in spite of the distances involved, some expeditions set out for the very center of the continent, the Araguaia-Tocantins region, known as the Sertão do Paraupava. The Paulistas already knew of the region, since at least two expeditions had already traversed these backlands. The second of these two expeditions, in 1613, was the subject of a chronicle by a Jesuit who received a firsthand account from the backwoodsman Pedro Domingues. After a 120-day march, the Paulistas arrived at the island of Bananal, finding it inhabited by the non-Tupi Carajaúna and the Tupi-speaking Caatinga. They were favorably impressed by the region, which from then on was identified as an inexhaustible source of Indian labor.[71]

Although some captives from the Paraupava area appear in probate records, it would appear that few expeditions to the region were successful in satisfying the Paulistas' hunger for labor. The material and human costs of expeditions to such distant destinations meant that they generated little or no profit. Nonetheless, a few wealthier settlers were able to lead or commission slaving parties to that region, most notably the sons of Pedro Vaz de Barros. One, Sebastião Pais de Barros, traveled at least twice to the Tocantins, on his second expedition reaching Belém, at the mouth of the Amazon, where he died. Whatever the costs, he did manage to leave an inheritance of more than 370 Indians as part of his estate in Santana de Parnaíba. The variety of ethnic distinctions that appear in the inventory drawn up when his widow died suggests that a large part of his stock of slaves had been captured in central Brazil.[72]

The ambitious adventure that Antonio Raposo Tavares set out on in 1648 may also be seen in this light. Jaime Cortesão, among others, characterized the expedition as "the greatest *bandeira* of the greatest *bandeirante*," and insisted that it was driven by the geopolitical motives of exploring and expanding Portuguese claims in the interior of the continent. More likely, Raposo Tavares and his companions, most of them from Santana de Parnaíba, sought to recreate the successes of the Guairá raids by investigating the possibility of attacking the Itatim missions of the Paraguay River valley. In spite of being repelled by the Jesuits and their Indians, persecuted by the indomitable Paiaguá, and weakened by the maladies of the backlands, Raposo Tavares continued his voyage along the Madeira River to the Amazon, reaching Belém after three years spent wandering in the wilderness. Others of his party, unwilling to risk such a long journey, returned directly to São Paulo from Itatim with captives from the missions, which encouraged further expeditions in that direction. By the standards of the times, though, the "greatest *bandeira*" must have been viewed as a failure, as Raposo Tavares returned to São Paulo a shattered, impoverished man, and, according to some, so disfigured that his own relatives could not recognize him.[73]

Most settlers, who did not have the resources of Raposo Tavares or the Vaz de Barros family, restricted their pursuit of captives to regions closer to São Paulo. Several expeditions set out for the Paraíba Valley, a region neglected by the Indian slavers of the previous generation. This movement led to the founding of new towns in the region by Paulista pioneers in the 1640s and 1650s. At the same time, adventurers from the town of Parnaíba set out to the west and south, eventually founding the towns of Itu, Sorocaba, and Curitiba. To the northwest, residents of São Paulo founded the town of Jundiaí. The settlement of each of these towns reflected new directions in the search for Indian labor. The Paraíba Valley towns of Jacareí, Taubaté, and Guaratinguetá served as bases for incursions into the Mantiqueira Range and the vast area that would become Minas Gerais, where a predominantly Tupi population attracted the Paulistas. Jundiaí, in turn, lay on the so-called general trail of the *sertão*, the overland path that settlers took to the Indians and mines of Goiás, while the western towns of Itu and Sorocaba became starting points for expeditions to the westernmost reaches of the southern captaincies.[74]

The expansion of settlement, which was of course closely connected to the search for new sources of labor, reintroduced Guaianá and Guarulhos Indians to the Paulista labor force. Though these peoples had always been within reach of the slave-hunters, they were spared for a half-century because the Paulistas had tended to shun them in favor of the coveted Guarani. However, with the declining supply of Guarani, the enslavement of the Guaianá and Guarulhos emerged as a temporary solution to the crisis in labor recruitment. The expeditions of João Mendes Geraldo, Antonio Pedroso de Barros, and Fernão Dias Pais revisited what had been the Guairá region to capture the remaining Guaianá, returning in 1645, 1650, and 1661 with many captives. The expeditions of Jacques Félix and Jerônimo da Veiga enslaved many Guarulhos in the early 1640s, while more of the same ethnicity were taken in the mid-1660s along the Atibaia River.[75]

The largest post-1640 slaving enterprise, the *bandeira* of 1666, also was associated with a significant wave of settlement.[76] It would appear that the expedition penetrated the *sertão* of what would become Minas Gerais, perhaps to the headwaters of the São Francisco River, since scattered documents referring to the movement mention the capture of Amboapira (Tememinó) and Apuatiyara (Tobajara), groups that inhabited the region. Confirming this hypothesis, in 1682 one of the expedition's participants, Bartolomeu Bueno Cacunda, testified that he had established a subsistence plot along the Sapucaí River sixteen years earlier.[77] Further information emerges from the little-known will of Manuel Lopes, drawn up in 1666 on the Sertão dos Abeiguira. In this document, the dying man stated that he found himself "in this desert," listing twenty-four prominent backwoodsmen as witnesses.[78] The leader of the expedition was Jerônimo de Camargo, who shortly afterward established a prosperous estate in Atibaia, with 600 Indians and a chapel. Other participants, such as Francisco Cubas Preto, Baltasar da Veiga, Salvador de Oliveira, Antonio Bueno, and Bartolomeu Fernandes Faria likewise settled on good lands lying between the Juqueri and Atibaia rivers, each of them with holdings of more than one hundred Indians. These extensive slaveholdings, the last in São Paulo of any great significance until the sugar boom of the late eighteenth century, became the base for rural *bairros* in the area to the northwest of Jundiaí.[79]

The expeditions that sought Guaianá and Guarulhos captives resulted in a profound change in the ethnic composition of the slave population. Because of the massive infusion of captives during the first half of the century, the Guarani continued to make up the bulk of the Indian population, though they now shared the slave quarters with increasingly significant numbers of Guaianá and Guarulhos. Describing his vast holdings in his 1658 will, José Ortiz de Camargo left a forthright record of the resulting diversity: "I declare that I have in my service heathens of all nations."[80]

An important development related to this change in ethnic composition was a shift in the sex ratio of the slave population. Table 3 shows that women outnumbered men during the period of heaviest Guarani recruitment. But in the 1650s, precisely because of the increasing inflow of Guaianá captives, the number of men surpassed that of women for the first time. These general characteristics gain further meaning when the ethnic composition of the adult population is taken into account (Table 4). The sex ratio of the population identified as Guarani remained at around 80 men for every 100 women, while for the Guaianá there were around 112 men per 100 women.

The predominance of Guarani women and the disproportionate presence of men among Guaianá captives owed much to the conditions that the Paulistas encountered in the process of enslavement. Since the demographic

Table 3 *Males per 100 Females among Adult Indigenous Population, São Paulo and Santana de Parnaíba, 1600–1689*

Decades	São Paulo	Santana de Parnaíba
1600–1619	82.7	–
1620–1629	88.0	–
1630–1639	92.8	65.6
1640–1649	90.0	75.5
1650–1659	108.7	82.0
1660–1669	92.7	108.6
1670–1679	98.1	114.9
1680–1689	99.5	84.4

Sources: Inventories of probated estates, São Paulo and Parnaíba. IT, vols. 1–44; AESP-INP, cxs. 1–40; AESP-IPO, various cxs.; AESP-IE, cxs. 1–6.

Table 4 *Sex and Age Distribution of Indigenous Population by Ethnic Group*

Group	Men	Women	Children	M/100 W*
Carijó	194	242	205	80.2
Guaianá	66	59	26	111.9
Guarulhos	17	21	11	80.9
Total	277	322	242	86.0

* M/100 W: Rate of men per 100 women in the adult population.
Source: Inventories of probated estates, São Paulo and Parnaíba. IT, vols. 1–44; AESP-INP, cxs. 1–40; AESP-IPO, assorted cxs.; AESP-IE, cxs. 1–6.

density of the Guaianá, who were primarily hunters and foragers, was far lower than that of the Guarani, the Paulistas rarely captured many at one time. The absence of detailed descriptions of Guaianá villages suggests that the Paulistas preyed on hunting or war parties operating at a distance from the domestic sphere. In any case, whether due to their low population density or greater resistance to capture, the difficulties involved in Guaianá recruitment effectively raised the costs of supplying the European settlements with Indian labor. Indeed, several Paulistas recorded losses in the expeditions of the second half of the seventeenth century. Domingos de Góis, for example, testified that in the three expeditions undertaken by his son "he received more losses than profit due to the death of his Indians."[81]

That newly enslaved Indians were particularly susceptible to epidemic disease and less likely to submit to forced labor entailed further risks. Many soon succumbed to European and African diseases; among those who survived the initial immunological peril, some resisted the new work regime. For their part, the Paulistas, thoroughly accustomed to Guarani labor, faced significant obstacles in trying to communicate with non-Tupi speakers, let alone in attempting to transform them into productive workers. Captain Antonio Raposo Barreto of Taubaté, writing to a commercial correspondent in Rio de Janeiro in 1680, expressed the fear that he would lose the forty slaves (possibly Puri) that his son had brought him from the Mantiqueira Range since they were suffering from an outbreak of a flu-like illness. But Captain Barreto's greatest frustration was the difficulty of communicating with them, which left him unable to understand "what they are suffering, because there is not an interpreter who understands them."[82]

This new situation had serious implications when it came to social control on Paulista estates. The incidence of rebellion and flight increased markedly beginning in the 1650s, and this trend was closely related to shifts in the ethnic composition of the slave population, as Guaianá and Guarulhos captives made up most of the participants in all of the major revolts of this period. The vicissitudes of recruitment thus clearly influenced the formation of the Paulista variant of colonial slave society.

A Remedy for Poverty?

Facing the challenge of the uncertainties of the *sertão*, the Paulistas began to favor small expeditions – called *armações* (which may be translated literally as "armatures," but can also refer to nautical tackle and outfitting) – designed to fill specific labor needs. Unlike the great *bandeiras*, whose essential function was the reproduction of the aggregate labor force of the plateau, these new expeditions sought to reproduce the basic units of production more than anything else. Embarking on journeys to the interior, many young men wrote or dictated wills in which they expressed the need to penetrate the *sertão* in order "to seek a remedy for my impoverished state." Lucas Ortiz de Camargo, for example, declared that "he was presenting himself to go and Seek Remedy in the *sertão* which is the ordinary business of this land."[83]

Throughout the seventeenth century, the much sought-after "remedy" was holdings of captive Indians, which would help young male colonists establish their place in settler society, as well as offer a base for productive activities and some sort of income. Remarking on how driven young men were to risk their lives on these expeditions, a Governor-General of Brazil observed: "He whose great poverty does not permit him to have someone to serve him will subject himself to wander through the *sertão* for many years in search of someone to serve him, rather than serve someone else for a single day."[84] Indeed, in the economic context of seventeenth-century São Paulo, so dependent on Indian labor, opportunities for young settlers were restricted to winning a handsome dowry upon marriage, receiving a large inheritance, or participating in a profitable slaving expedition. With few exceptions, however, dowries included only a handful of "pieces of the heathen of the land," as Indian slaves were often called, while inheritances had to be shared equitably among all heirs. For most settlers seeking to establish their place in local society, slaving was the only option that offered any hope of establishing a reasonably large productive base.

In general, the young men who embarked in search of captives were outfitted by their fathers or fathers-in-law, who risked small outlays of capital and some Indians in the expeditions in the hope of expanding their own slaveholdings. The outfitter, called the *armador*, provided money, equipment, and Indians, and assumed all the resulting risk in exchange for one half of the captives eventually obtained on the journey. The *armação*, or expedition, was usually a family enterprise, for in the absence of institutional guarantees on such investments, it no doubt seemed safer to trust a kinsman. Nonetheless, the outfitter–backwoodsman relationship almost always took the shape of a contractual agreement. An example of this contractual relationship is provided by the will of Antonio Cordeiro of Jundiaí:

> I declare that I have an *armação* in the *sertão* with Antonio da Costa Colaço [and] that I gave him two blacks [Indians] and a chain of four and a half *braças* with ten collars and a canoe and one *arroba* of lead with powder and everything else needed so that we will divide in half between us whatever God gives for which I have a receipt in my power.[85]

As should be evident, the principal contribution of the outfitter was lead, gunpowder, chains, and, most importantly, Indians, essential elements for a slaving expedition. In effect, lead and powder were the greatest expenses, since it was necessary to procure these items in other markets. In 1647, for example, the merchant Antonio Castanho da Silva sent Diogo Rodrigues to Rio de Janeiro to buy ammunition for a journey into the *sertão*.[86] Toward the end of the century, to judge by the account book of Father Guilherme Pompeu de Almeida, the greatest part of the money spent on the outfitting of expeditions went to the purchase of arms and ammunition.[87] These cases demonstrate not only the need for venture capital, but also the violently aggressive strategies used by the slavers.

Agreements between fathers and sons, however, were more common than contractual arrangements, and generally reached verbally. Francisco Borges, for example, declared in his will that "I have outfitted my sons Gaspar Borges and Francisco Borges with all that is needed to go to the *sertão*, so that of the people they bring back from said *sertão* they will give me half and they will keep the other half for themselves."[88] It seems that sons expected financial and material assistance from their fathers for these journeys. Paternal help for the *armações* was so standard that its absence was noteworthy, as is shown by Domingos da Rocha's statement: "I have fourteen pieces of heathen of the land which I brought from the *sertão without help from my parents*."[89] It is worth pointing out that this was a prudent distinction to make while drawing up a will, for otherwise Indians could become the object of litigation after the death of their owner.

Typically, expeditions were composed of one or more experienced backwoodsmen, who guided a handful of young settlers on their first trek to the *sertão*. The composition of slaving parties thus shows that the conventional idea that all male residents of São Paulo were career *bandeirantes* has little basis in fact. To be sure, a few specialists, gifted interpreters knowledgeable of the ways of the wilderness, repeatedly penetrated the *sertão*. However, most male residents did not participate in more than one or two expeditions in their lifetimes. Fathers outfitting their sons often had them join up with a wilderness-bound expedition rather than organize one of their own. In 1681, for example, Luís Eanes Gil stated in his will that he had sent his son, Isidoro Rodrigues, to the *sertão* "with someone else's outfit." In fact, Isidoro had set off in 1679 with several young settlers led by captains Mateus Furtado and Antonio de Morais Madureira, both experienced backwoodsmen.[90] Other expeditions of known composition point to a basic structural similarity in their organization. The *armação* of Captain Fernão Bicudo de Brito and his uncle Antonio Bicudo Leme, mounted in the Paraíba Valley in 1673, had in its ranks seven young settlers of no relation to the Bicudo family.[91]

Expeditions to the *sertão* also received material support from sources other than fathers interested in launching their sons' careers by providing a few captives. Contractual agreements between unrelated parties were quite common, especially in the second half of the seventeenth century. The best surviving examples of such agreements come from the records of the Carmelite order, as at several junctures the friars contributed Indians, provisions, and even money to backwoodsmen who would bring them Indian slaves. A contract drafted in 1648, for example, read: "In view of the limited wealth of this convent, and that the remedy for this depends on the service of Indians, of which the convent is in great need, for which, it seems convenient to send some [Indian] youths to the *sertão* in support of a white man, paying him for all of the necessary costs and equipment." Likewise, in 1662 the Carmelites decided that "because of the lack of people on the estates, it seemed important to us that we send eight youths to the *sertão* in the company of Captain José Ortiz de Camargo, so that with the goodwill of Our Lady they can bring us some people, for without them not only the estates but the convent would be ruined." They resolved on that occasion to send four Indians from their Embiacica estate for that purpose. Finally, in 1665, the convent became the principal outfitter of the large-scale expedition led by Jerônimo de Camargo, Antonio Bueno, and

Salvador de Oliveira. These three captains signed an agreement to turn over fifty of the first one hundred captives taken, in return for the services of Brother João de Cristo, who would represent the interests of the convent while he accompanied the expedition. Captives taken beyond the first hundred would be shared in the same proportion "among the other soldiers of the *bandeira*."[92]

Another way of participating in slaving was for settlers to send Indians or weapons either in the care of an expedition's leader or with one of the other participants. Maria Bicudo, for example, sent thirteen Indians to the *sertão* with her son Salvador Bicudo de Mendonça in 1660, while also "wagering a few pieces [of heathen of the land] with Manuel Veloso" on the same expedition.[93] Such a practice, though, was risky. While it is true that the outfitter assumed all the risk for the venture capital he invested in an expedition, it was never altogether clear up to what point the backwoodsman could be held responsible for losses. Some outfitters sought legal protection in the drafting of the contract, stipulating that they would receive half of the captives brought to the settlement, so that the backwoodsmen would share in the losses that occurred on the return journey. This was a prudent strategy, since the captives were usually divided among the participants at the point of capture. If the outfitter or the expedition's leader died during the trek, from that point onward their captives traveled at the risk of their heirs. Confined to his hammock, dying and wary of the chance his heirs might be cheated, the backwoodsman Manuel Correia de Sá sought to guarantee the integrity of his portion of the slaves taken in the *sertão* by dictating in his will that his wife and son in São Paulo should receive either the captives or their monetary value.[94] To judge from the frequent litigation over possession of Indians brought from the *sertão*, even precautious backwoodsmen were left without sufficient guarantee.[95]

Along with young colonists and the experienced backwoodsmen who led the expeditions, a significant portion of the Indian population of the plateau participated in resupplying the stocks of captives. Lists of Indians in inventories often included the annotation "absent in the *sertão*" next to particular names. Mostly, though not exclusively, men, these Indians made up the rank and file of the expeditions, performing essential functions as guides, porters, cooks, and warriors. Settlers might be accompanied by anywhere from one to fifteen Indians, depending on how many they wanted to risk in the uncertainties of the *sertão* or how many captives they expected to obtain. Manuel Correia de Sá, for example, the owner of forty Indians, took ten along with him, including two women and a small boy, on the canoe flotilla led by his compadre João Anhaia de Almeida.[96]

It is difficult to establish a clear correlation between the size of an expedition and its return in captives. In 1675, the brothers Francisco and Domingos Cardoso, assisted by eleven Indians belonging to their father, spent several months in the *sertão* and, when they returned, delivered thirty Indians to the executor of their father's estate, their father having died in their absence. If one assumes that this expedition was carried out according to the typical agreement of the time, in which the total number of captives was split between expeditionaries and outfitters, this would indicate a return of sixty slaves.[97] For his part, another settler, Francisco Cubas Preto, evinced his uncertain expectations regarding a slaving expedition: "I declare that I thus also made an agreement with an Indian of the village of Marueri by the name of Marcos, whom I gave equipment, all supplies and two blacks of the heathen of the land to bring me all the people that he could acquire with this, for which I gave him a musket for him to have, whether he brings people or not, and nothing more for not one or another thing."[98]

In the search for captives in places never before explored by whites, the active participation of Indians in the expeditions was essential. For the settlers, exposed to fevers, wild animals, and unknown indigenous groups, their survival depended on the knowledge that these Indians had of the *sertão*.[99] On relatively short expeditions, slavers subsisted on game, fruit, and wild honey collected by the Indians. For longer expeditions, small camps or subsistence plots were established at strategic points in order to supply the backwoodsmen. Sometimes, advance parties of small numbers of Indians were sent ahead to plant crops with which to feed the principal body of the expedition and, on the return, the captives. A few of these camps eventually developed into towns, particularly on the routes to what later became Minas Gerais, Goiás, and Mato Grosso.

As expeditions cutting across the same territory became increasingly frequent, enterprising colonists set up subsistence plots along the way, tended by trusted Indian servants. In the 1670s, for example, there were the so-called Plantas do Urucujá, maintained by Ana Tobajara on a trail to the Minas Gerais area.[100] Another example is Batatais (literally, potato fields), situated north of São Paulo on the trail to Goiás, possibly at a junction with another trail headed east toward the region of the Sapucaí River. The Camp of Batatais was probably first established in the 1660s, when numerous expeditions began to cross that area; the first documentary evidence of its existence dates to 1663. According to the eighteenth-century chronicler Pedro Taques de Almeida Paes Leme, the wealthy Portuguese merchant Manuel Lobo Franco, related to the Bueno family by marriage and a frequent investor in slaving expeditions, received a land grant in 1678 in the incredible amount of 18 leagues near the Mogi River, "along the trail to Batatais, which was a shelter for heathen in 1678."[101] Batatais appears in the documentation again in 1683, in a fascinating lawsuit involving Manuel Lobo Franco's cousin, Francisco Bueno de Camargo. Camargo owned João, a *crioulo* Indian born in São Paulo who was charged with tending the subsistence plots at Batatais, who was also a carpenter and a "very great backwoodsman." According to Bueno de Camargo, João's responsibilities were "to plant and order to plant and to keep an account of all the supplies that [his owner] had ordered for the *sertão* convoy on the journey that he the Author was undertaking." However, before the "convoy" arrived, another slaver, Manuel Pinto Guedes, passed through Batatais and "took the said black to the *sertão* without permission or authorization of the Author, leaving his plots and plantings untended, which caused him great damages, in supplies as well as in the great loss of people that the Author had at his disposal due to the absence of said black and the supplies from Recolhida." Neither Pinto Guedes nor João ever returned, probably dying in what is today Goiás. In his lawsuit, Camargo sought to have Pinto Guedes's heirs compensate him for the value of the Indian he lost.[102]

If the establishment of subsistence plots on the way to the *sertão* represented an innovation in the organization of slaving expeditions, it also reflected an imminent crisis faced by the colonists. Projecting their incursions deeper and deeper into the vast continent's unknown wilderness, the settlers' hopes of encountering new sources of labor were increasingly frustrated. A simple equation held true: longer distances meant decreasing returns, for a number of different reasons. First, the time and outfitting costs involved tended to limit the size of expeditions, which limited the number of captives that could be taken. Second, these smaller bands were more vulnerable to the dangers of the backland, particularly those presented by previously uncontacted indigenous groups. Though they avoided the more lethal groups, such as the Paiaguá, Kayapó, and Guaikurú, slavers could not help but stumble upon warriors disinclined to cooperate with outsiders. Finally, greater distances increased the risk of mortality on the return voyage, for backwoodsmen as much as for captives. In sum, the acquisition of large numbers of new captives was quickly becoming an uneconomic proposition, even for the wealthiest settlers.

New Directions

While the reorganization of slaving presented itself as a partial solution to the crisis in the labor supply, the settlers also sought to maintain the influx of captives through other stratagems. By cooperating with the Crown's plans to intensify the search for precious metals and offering their military services in defense of the sugar-growing and cattle-raising riches of the northeast, the Paulistas opened up a new range of economic options. The continued expansion of the sugar industry and the rapid growth of cattle ranching created serious conflicts between settlers and Indians, first in the area around the Bay of All Saints and later throughout the entire northeastern interior. European expansion threatened the alteration or even the destruction of indigenous social formations and thus it engendered a series of indigenous responses, most of them violent. In turn, any act of violence on the part of the Indians was construed by the Portuguese as sufficient grounds to condemn all Indians to enslavement or extinction. Though several groups were spared for the moment because they collaborated with the settlers, by the end of the century much of the backlands of the northeast had been transformed from Indian territory into huge cattle ranches.[103]

At various points, governors, planters, and municipal councils called on São Paulo's backwoodsmen to wage "disinfestation" campaigns against indigenous peoples in revolt. Drawn by seductive promises of honorific titles, land, and money, Paulistas were mobilized to serve as mercenaries for determined periods. Well known for their warlike activities in the backlands, the Paulistas had previously been called upon to participate in the Luso–Dutch conflict of the late 1640s. But the column organized by Antonio Pereira de Azevedo at that time ended up following a different trajectory, accompanying Raposo Tavares to the Itatim missions in 1648.[104] The Portuguese of São Paulo showed somewhat greater enthusiasm when they were called upon to fight Indians in Bahia ten years later. In 1657, Governor-General Francisco Barreto decided to take decisive action against the so-called *Bárbaros* ("barbarians") who were terrorizing outlying settlements and sugar plantations in Bahia. Writing to the governor of São Vicente, Barreto observed: "I believe I understand that only the experience of the backwoodsmen of that captaincy will be able to overcome the difficulties that those of this one find in completely destroying those [indigenous] villages..." Sweetening his offer, the governor promised the Paulistas that "all whom they capture in this conquest they will take as their captives to that captaincy as described in the resolution that this Government made with the Bishop, Theologians, and Ministers who formed a council in which it was declared to be a just war, given the deaths, robberies, conflagrations and other hostilities," the Paulistas thus being able "to use them as slaves without the slightest scruple on their consciences."[105] In the following year, with the aim of pacifying the backlands of Bahia, Domingos Barbosa Calheiros embarked for Salvador, "on the current trade winds," with a band of 500 men, including Portuguese and Indians.[106]

Despite these measures, unrest persisted in the backlands of Bahia, such that in 1670 the Paulistas were once again summoned to fight "the very barbarous Indians who infest the vicinity of the Bay of All Saints."[107] Initially, Governor Alexandre de Sousa Freire invited Pedro Vaz de Barros – the feared "Vaz Guaçu," or "Great Vaz" – to lead an incursion, giving heed to "the good accounts that Dr. Sebastião Cardoso de Sampaio gave me of Your Worship's person, experience, and valor, and of the great knowledge that you have of Indians.[108] Notwithstanding, it fell to Estevão Ribeiro Baião Parente, Manuel Rodrigues de Arzão, Henrique da Cunha, and Pascoal Rodrigues – at the time the captains of the four mission villages of São Paulo – to sign a contract with the governor in which they agreed to carry out the conquest of the backlands on the condition that they would be authorized to legally enslave the prisoners of war, who would be transported to São Paulo at the royal treasury's expense.[109] One participant in the expedition, Feliciano Cardoso, indicated clearly in his will that his interest in fighting in Bahia derived from the desire to enslave Indians to add to his holdings in São Paulo.[110]

The result of the campaigns was somewhat different than what the Paulistas expected. Although thousands of captives were taken, very few reached the estates and smaller properties of the plateau, as many died of diseases contracted from the Europeans, which were aggravated by the conditions of the forced marches from the *sertão* to the settlement. Some indication of this immense waste of human life is found in a 1673 account by Governor-General Afonso Furtado de Castro do Rio de Mendonça. Lauding the Paulistas for their success against the *Bárbaros*, the governor noted that they "extinguished" the threat in one area by burning villages, killing many Indians, and taking 1,450 prisoners, 700 of whom died of a "quasi plague" in the *sertão*, many others dying after arriving in Salvador. A few months later, Mendonça reported the capture, by Estevão Ribeiro, of another 1,200 Maracá "souls" from three villages north of Salvador.[111] However, in spite of the governor's enthusiasm with the success of these forays into the *sertão*, his government lacked sufficient resources to ship the remaining captives to São Vicente, as too much had already been spent supplying the Paulistas in the martial phase of the conquest of the *sertão*. For their part, the Paulistas sought to make up for this violation of their contract by bringing the captives to market in Bahia: Estevão Ribeiro himself was accused of setting up a slave market across the Bay of All Saints from the colonial capital of Salvador. According to the written accusation, the Paulistas had spent most of their time and much public money in the capture of "friendly" Indians identified as Tupi, whom they then claimed were legitimate captives taken in a just war authorized by the royal government.[112]

In 1677, mercenaries from São Paulo were summoned to combat the Anayo of the São Francisco River valley and once again clear the way for cattle ranching. As in the previous invitation, the colonial government pledged to provide weapons and provisions, while temporarily revoking prohibitions on slaving. On this occasion, colonial authorities appealed to the principal settlers of São Paulo: Jerônimo Bueno, Fernão de Camargo, Baltasar da Costa Veiga, Bartolomeu Bueno, Antonio de Siqueira, and Father Mateus Nunes de Siqueira, who possessed more than 100 Indians apiece.[113] Though none of these men agreed to make the journey, a few bands of Paulistas did answer the call, eventually destroying the Anayo.

In the 1680s, when the situation in the cattle lands of the captaincies of the north became critical, the Governor-General recruited more Paulista troops. With the so-called *Bárbaros* of Rio Grande do Norte having slaughtered more than 100 people ("between whites and slaves"), while destroying more than 30,000 head of cattle and defeating the expeditions organized by local residents, royal authorities resolved to seek a solution in the vast experience of the settlers of São Paulo. Brother Resurreição, Bishop of Bahia and acting Governor-General of Brazil, remarked on the usefulness of the Paulistas in these circumstances:

> And if the Paulistas are so accustomed to penetrating the backlands to enslave Indians against the provisos of Your Majesty which prohibit it, I am certain that now that they may do so in the service of their King as your loyal vassals, and to such public benefit of those captaincies, they will do so with even greater willingness, not only to add to their fame, and [in] hope[s] of remuneration for which they work, but also for the value of the *Bárbaros* they take prisoner, who justly are captives according to the laws of the Lord my King.[114]

Several outfits were organized in São Paulo, including that of Domingos Jorge Velho – which would become famous for destroying the escaped-slave redoubt of Palmares – and the column led by Manuel Alvares de Morais Navarro. Though facing stiff opposition from the Janduim and other indigenous groups up in arms over the expansion of cattle ranching onto their lands, the Paulistas once again found the path to victory through alliances with select Indian groups, destroying most of the indigenous population of the captaincies of Rio Grande do Norte, Ceará, and Piauí over a thirty-year period ending in 1720.[115]

More than any other moment in Brazilian history, the northern campaigns demonstrate the wantonly destructive side of Indian policy in areas of unchecked economic growth. As in the conquest of the Bahian backlands, the Paulistas did not receive the return they had anticipated in Indian captives, and so they began to measure their success on a different scale. Attempting to make up for their dashed expectations with military victories, the Paulistas' slaving expeditions in these backlands soon assumed the sad character of pitiless massacres. Commenting on one of these episodes, Governor-General João de Lencastre wrote that a Paulista column "just now achieved a victory against the Indians, of whom they killed 136 and took 56 prisoner, not counting others who drowned in the River as they fled."[116] According to another crown official, the practical difficulties of battling the Tapuias compelled the Paulistas to opt for extermination rather than enslavement.[117] The Crown itself promoted a similar strategy, recommending that enemy peoples be driven into the state of Maranhão, where they would be annihilated by local indigenous groups.[118] In spite of all this, it must be acknowledged that these strategies achieved the goals of the government and met the needs of large-scale cattle ranchers.

The northern campaigns had important effects on the economy of the Paulista plateau, though not the ones participants had originally envisioned. On the one hand, in spite of the appearance in São Paulo of a few "pieces of heathen with straight hair" classified in estate inventories as legitimate slaves, the lengthy expeditions did not produce the flow of captives needed to supply the labor pool in the late seventeenth century. On the other, many of the Paulistas who participated in these campaigns did not return to São Paulo. Unable to bring back captives for their properties in the south, many soldiers ended up settling on newly conquered lands in the valleys of the São Francisco and the Açu, or even in the remote hinterland of Piauí. Many received land grants, which became the main form of compensation for mercenaries.[119] Paulista veterans and renegades were to be found throughout the interior of various captaincies, founding informal settlements and dedicating themselves to cattle raising.[120]

If some Paulistas collaborated with the policy of extermination promoted by colonial authorities and the large landholders of the northeast, others yoked slaving to the Crown project of searching for new sources of mineral wealth. Facing an increasingly severe fiscal and commercial crisis in the second half of the seventeenth century, Crown ministers pursued various mercantilist solutions, including more intensive prospecting in the hinterlands of its tropical colonies of Brazil, Angola, and Mozambique. In the São Paulo region, the renewed search for silver, gold, and emeralds was fundamentally tied to the pursuit of indigenous captives. Once again the convergence of local and international factors had important effects on the economy of the plateau.

As in the early seventeenth century, though, avowed intentions and outcomes were not always aligned, since the Paulistas continued to enslave  Indians under the cover of searching for mineral wealth. One settler, justifying the petition for lands he addressed to the Municipal Council of São Paulo, alleged that he had gone to the *sertão* "with the intention of making some discoveries for the aggrandizement of the royal crown, of which he found nothing but heathen of diverse nations."[121] For most Paulistas, Indians were the true riches to be extracted from the interior – "red gold" in the apt expression of Antonio Vieira. Interestingly, on various occasions the Crown itself acted to make the analogy less purely figurative by levying the royal fifth on captives, thereby applying a tax associated with the extraction of mineral riches.

The search for mineral wealth led to innumerable journeys to the *sertão*, some of them financed by the Crown, such as the expeditions of Jorge Soares de Macedo to the far south in 1679 and of Dom Rodrigo Castelo Branco to Sabarabuçu in 1681. Most, however, were privately funded because the Crown proved little disposed to make large outlays on searches that turned up more Indians than gold or precious stones, preferring to encourage such expeditions with promises of honorific titles.[122]

The most significant of these private expeditions was, without a doubt, that of Fernão Dias Pais, which set out from São Paulo in 1674 and remained in the backlands until its leader's death in 1681. Setting up camp near what was believed to be Sabarabuçu, Fernão Dias and his followers sought deposits of emeralds and silver in the very hills that would begin to yield copious amounts of gold as the century came to an end. Despite Fernão Dias believing he had discovered an emerald mine, the principal return of his protracted sojourn in the *sertão* was the flow of captives sent on to São Paulo, which explains why the mining areas were thoroughly depopulated by the time of the gold rush of the end of the century.[123] Like the adventurers who left São Paulo to fight the *Bárbaros*, not all of Fernão Dias Pais's companions returned to the plateau. Some of them became the first white settlers of what would become Minas Gerais, while others moved on to more distant regions, such as the Bahian portion of the São Francisco Valley. In short, as the century came to a close, the business of backcountry slaving – so fundamentally important to a once flourishing economy – was coming to a slow end of its own.

The process of recruiting indigenous labor thus came full circle over the course of the seventeenth century. The century had begun with the convergence of mining interests and the search for captives, and so it ended. Until the end of the century, when slaving was definitively supplanted by mining, the frequent expeditions to the wilderness both reflected and affected the needs and structure of the economy of the plateau. At the beginning, before the wholesale destruction of the Guarani, the colonists were restricted to small agricultural endeavors and to sending modest quantities of cured meats and quince paste to market on the coast, activities that required little labor. The rapid growth of the captive population due to the attacks on the Guarani missions and villages made possible larger, more labor-intensive agricultural enterprises. The crisis in the labor supply, which began in the 1640s and became more acute thereafter, compelled many colonists to take up other economic activities, such as cattle raising, in order to maximize the little labor available to them.

Ultimately, the principal function of the expeditions was the physical reproduction of the labor force and not, as historiographical convention would have it, to supply plantations along the coast, though some unfortunate victims were delivered to sugar planters. Thus, unlike other systems of slaving and labor supply – the African slave trade being the most noteworthy example – the Paulistas did not function as middlemen in the trade in captives, but were both suppliers and consumers of labor generated within an integrated system. While on the one hand, the Paulistas' peculiar pattern of appropriating indigenous labor was influenced by institutional constraints on Indian slavery; on the other, it was always the most economical means of fulfilling their needs. The viability of this scheme began to decline when distances, indigenous resistance, and outfitting costs increased. The result of this process was, inevitably, a steep decline in the returns on expeditions. Slave-hunting on the *sertão*, then, was not a business in the same sense that the African slave trade was. But even if the two colonial enterprises were organized quite differently, each played a fundamental role in the creation of a slave society.

Notes

1. For a well-executed summary of the traditional interpretation, see Myriam Ellis, "O bandeirantismo na expansão geográfica do Brasil," in Sérgio Buarque de Holanda (ed.), *História geral da civilização brasileira*, t. 1: *Época colonial* (São Paulo: Difusão Européia do Livro, 1960), vol. 1, 273–296
2. Carvalho Franco, *Dicionário de bandeirantes*, entry "Sousa, Francisco de." On these early, practical experiences, see Pedro Taques de Almeida Paes Leme, *Informações sobre as minas de São Paulo: a expulsão dos jesuítas do Colégio de São Paulo*, ed. Afonso d'Escragnolle Taunay (São Paulo: Melhoramentos, 1946); Myriam Ellis, "Pesquisas sobre a existência do ouro e da prata no planalto paulista nos séculos XVI e XVII," *Revista de História* 1 (1950): 51–71; Lucy de Abreu Maffei and Arlinda Rocha Nogueira, "O ouro na capitania de São Vicente nos séculos XVI e XVII," *Anais do Museu Paulista* 20 (1966): 7–136.
3. On Santo Amaro, see Sérgio Buarque de Holanda, "A fábrica de ferro de Santo Amaro," *Digesto Econômico*, Jan.–Feb. 1948, 78–81. The hypothesis, doubtful at best, of the founding of a town called São Felipe, is discussed in Aluísio de Almeida, "A fundação de Sorocaba," *Revista do Arquivo Municipal* 57 (May 1939): 197–202, and Neme, *Notas de revisão*, 341–350.
4. Carvalho Franco, *Dicionário de bandeirantes*, 393–396; Orville Derby, "As bandeiras paulistas de 1601 a 1604," *RIHGSP* 8 (1903): 399–423. Interestingly, this expedition was on the right track, since 70 leagues' further march would have put them in the area where emeralds and gold were found in the 1670s and 1690s; this distance falls far short of the headwaters of the São Francisco, though.
5. These Tememinó should not be confused with the Tememinó of Guanabara Bay, who were allies of the Portuguese in the sixteenth century. The name turns up in different places at various points in early Euro–indigenous encounters. It meant something like "grandson" or "descendant," offering an interesting point to the term Tamoio, which meant "grandfather" or "ancestor."
6. Carvalho Franco, *Dicionário de bandeirantes*, offers the best overview of the expeditions, while Afonso d'Escragnolle Taunay's chaotically organized *História geral das bandeiras paulistas*, 11 vols. (São Paulo: H. L. Canton, 1924–1950) remains useful as well. For

a summary listing of seventeenth-century expeditions and a note on sources, see John Monteiro, "São Paulo in the Seventeenth Century: Economy and Society" (Ph.D. dissertation, University of Chicago, 1985), 416–426.

7. CMSP-Atas, 2:46–47, Nov. 14, 1598.
8. CMSP-Atas, 2:112–115, Nov. 24, 1604.
9. Hélio Abranches Viotti, "A aldeia de Maniçoba e a fundação de Itu," *RIHGSP* 71 (1974): 389–401. On the trail to Paraguay in the sixteenth century, called Peabiru (among other names), see Neme, *Notas de revisão*, passim. This path may have followed a route used by Guarani migrants in precolonial times.
10. CMSP-Atas, 2:184–185, Jan. 7, 1607.
11. Pedro Taques de Almeida Paes Leme, *Nobiliarquia paulistana histórica e genealógica*, ed. Afonso d'Escragnolle Taunay, 5th edn., 3 vols. (Belo Horizonte: Itatiaia, 1980 [1926]), 1:79.
12. Governor Diego Negrón to the King, Jan. 8, 1612, AMP 1, pt. 2: 156–157. These intermediaries were sometimes referred to as *mus*. An interesting discussion may be found in Jaime Cortesão, *Raposo Tavares e a formação territorial do Brasil* (Rio de Janeiro: Imprensa Nacional, 1958), esp. chap. 3; see also Carlos Henrique Davidoff, *Bandeirantismo: verso e reverso* (São Paulo: Brasiliense, 1982).
13. Account of Dec. 9, 1594, ARSI Brasilia 3(2), fol. 358.
14. Inventory of Francisco Ribeiro, 1615, IT, 4:13.
15. Will of Manuel Pinto Suniga, 1627, IT, 7:336. The beads mentioned in the will, called *avelórios*, probably made of glass, were also used in the African slave trade. More details on the goods exchanged in southern Brazil are found in "Processo das despesas feitas por Martim de Sá, no Rio de Janeiro, 1628–1633," *Anais da Biblioteca Nacional do Rio de Janeiro* 59 (1937): 5–186.
16. "Descripção que faz o capitão Miguel Ayres Maldonado e o capitão Jozé de Castilho Pinto e seus companheiros dos trabalhos e fadigas das suas vidas, que tiveram nas conquistas da capitania do Rio de Janeiro e São Vicente, com a gentilidade e com os piratas n'esta costa" (1661), *Revista Trimensal do Instituto Historico e Geographico Brazileiro* 56, pt. 1 (1893): 352.
17. Jácome Monteiro, "Relação da província do Brasil, 1610," in Leite, *História*, 8:396.
18. Earlier accounts also showed a favorable view of the Kayapó, also known as "Ibirajaras." See, for example, José de Anchieta to Loyola, Sept. 1, 1554, MB, 2:117–118. For a well-reasoned assessment of the transformation of relations between the Portuguese and the Kayapó, see Mário Neme, "Dados para a história dos índios caiapó," *Anais do Museu Paulista* 23 (1969): 101–147.
19. The so-called Port of Patos, often confused with the Patos Lagoon of present-day Rio Grande do Sul, actually refers to the locale subsequently occupied by the town of Laguna (in the present-day Brazilian state of Santa Catarina). See "Informação do mestre de campo Diogo Pinto do Rego," Sept. 16, 1745, IT, 27:317, where Laguna is clearly identified as the Patos Lagoon of earlier colonial-era documents. Also, Hermann von Ihering, "Os indios patos e o nome da Lagoa dos Patos," *Revista do Museu Paulista* 7 (1907): 31–45.
20. Pedro Rodrigues to João Alvares, June 15, 1597, ARSI Brasilia 15, fol. 425.
21. Anonymous, "Relação certa do modo com que no Brasil se conquistam e cativam os indios," n.d. ARSI-FG, Missiones 721/I. The context suggests that this document was written by Father João de Almeida, S. J.

22. Jerônimo Rodrigues, "Relação sobre a missão dos Carijós, 1605–1607," in Serafim Leite (ed.), *Novas cartas jesuíticas* (São Paulo: Nacional, 1940), 196–246. Similar accusations were made some years later against the cacique Parapopi, probably in the same region. Letter of Francisco Ximenes, Feb. 4, 1635, in *Mss. de Angelis*, 3:100. The cultural and demographic effects of the trade in indigenous slaves has been the object of an interesting ethnohistorical literature; see, among others, Linda A. Newson, *The Cost of Conquest: Indian Decline in Honduras under Spanish Rule* (Boulder, CO: Westview Press, 1986); David R. Radell, "The Indian Slave Trade and Population of Nicaragua During the Sixteenth Century," in William M. Denevan (ed.), *The Native Population of the Americas in 1492*, (Madison: University of Wisconsin Press, 1976); Mary W. Helms, "Miskito Slaving and Culture Contact: Ethnicity and Opportunity in an Expanding Population," *Journal of Anthropological Research* 39/2 (1983): 179–197; Nádia Farage, *As muralhas dos sertões: os povos indígenas do Rio Branco e a colonização* (Rio de Janeiro: Paz e Terra, 1991); David G. Sweet, "A Rich Realm of Nature Destroyed: The Middle Amazon Valley, 1640–1750" (Ph.D. dissertation, University of Wisconsin, 1974). See also my article comparing São Paulo and Maranhão: "Escravidão indígena e despovoamento: São Paulo e Maranhão no século XVII," in Jill Dias (ed.), *Brasil nas vésperas do mundo moderno*, (Lisbon: Comissão dos Descobrimentos Portugueses, 1992), 137–167.
23. Simão Pinheiro, "Informação das ocupações dos padres e irmãos do Rio de Janeiro," c. 1619, ARSI Brasilia 3(1), fols. 199–201v. It is worth noting that similar accusations of corrupt authorities' connivance in the illegal trade in indigenous captives were made in colonial Maranhão. See Sweet, "A Rich Realm," and Monteiro, "Escravidão indígena e despovoamento."
24. Pedro Rodrigues to João Alvares, June 15, 1597, ARSI Brasilia 15, fol. 424v.
25. "Devassa tirada sobre a morte de um indio principal, Timacaúna, por uns pombeiros dos brancos," June 5, 1623, AHU-SP, doc. 3.
26. On *pombeiros* in the context of Portuguese colonialism, see Cortesão, *Raposo Tavares*, 194, and Edmundo Zenha, *Mamelucos* (São Paulo: Revista dos Tribunais, 1970), 52–53.
27. "Matrícula da gente carijó," 1615, CMSP-Registro, 7:115–157.
28. According to Sérgio Buarque de Holanda, this pattern emerged as early as the sixteenth century, following the *cuñajazgo* (female labor) structure of Spanish Paraguay. Holanda, "Expansão paulista em fins do século XVI e princípios do século XVII," *Boletim do Instituto de Administração* 29 (1948): 3–23 (at 14–15). The Portuguese Jesuit Francisco de Oliveira, assessing the character of the Paulistas in a public inquest, explained the sexual imbalance thus: "[The Paulistas] go about in concubinage with the heathen women, from whom they bring children to the settlement, and to be able to do this at greater ease, they kill the husbands." Sworn statement of Francisco de Oliveira, June 5, 1630, ARSI-FG, Collegia 203/1588/12, doc. 2.
29. Lourenço de Mendonça, "Súplica a Sua Magestade," 1637, IHGB, lata 219, doc. 17. This is a nineteenth-century copy of a document held probably in Spain. On the author of the "Súplica," a controversial figure in Rio de Janeiro in his time, see Cortesão, *Raposo Tavares*, 253. The immediate impact of this complaint in São Paulo may be judged by the proceedings of the Municipal Council meeting of Mar. 4, 1635 (CMSP-Atas, 4:245). The author probably was referring to the expedition of Luís Dias Leme, which indeed was uncharacteristically large. In 1635, with the authorization of the

governor of São Vicente, Dias Leme led around 200 Portuguese and their Indians to the Patos region. There, with the assistance of the cacique Aracambi, the Portuguese took many Carijó and Araxá captives. Dias Leme, Fernão Dias Pais's uncle, built seagoing vessels for regional trade in Santos. On the expedition, see the proceedings of May 12, 1635 (CMSP-Atas, 4:252–253); Carvalho Franco, *Dicionário de bandeirantes*, 212; Paes Leme, *Nobiliarquia paulistana*, chap. "Lemes," vol. 3; Luiz Gonzaga Jaeger, *As invasões bandeirantes no Rio Grande do Sul, 1635–1641* (Porto Alegre: Ginásio Estadual Anchieta, 1940); and Aurélio Porto, *História das missões orientais do Uruguai* (Rio de Janeiro: Imprensa Nacional, 1943).

30. CMSP-Atas, 2:138–139, 1603. Or, as Richard Morse put it: "It may well even be that except for its Jesuit missionary enclaves the Paulista-Paraguay region had a roughly homogenous society and culture in colonial times." Morse, introduction to Richard M. Morse (ed.), *The Bandeirantes: The Historical Role of the Brazilian Pathfinders* (New York: Knopf, 1965), 25. For an economic analysis of commercial relations during this period, see Alice P. Canabrava, *O comércio português no Rio da Prata: 1580–1640*, 2nd edn. (Belo Horizonte: Itatiaia, 1984 [1944]).

31. The Spanish term *reducciones* derived from the notion that non-Christian groups had to be "reduced" to live according to the civil and ecclesiastical codes of a Christian society – *ad ecclesiam et vitam civilem reducti*, as it were. Clovis Lugon, *A república comunista-cristã dos Guaranis, 1610–1678*, trans. Álvaro Cabral (Rio de Janeiro: Paz e Terra, 1968), 30.

32. For a general, though superficial background on the Guairá region, see Ramón Indalecio Cardozo, *El Guairá: historia de la antigua provincia, 1554–1676* (Asunción: El Arte, 1970). Interesting discussions of the Paraguayan economy during this era may be found in Elman R. Service, *Spanish–Guarani Relations in Early Colonial Paraguay* (Ann Arbor: University of Michigan Press, 1954); Regina A. Fonseca Gadelha, *As missões jesuíticas do Itatim: um estudo das estruturas sócio-econômicas do Paraguai, séculos XVI e XVII* (Rio de Janeiro: Paz e Terra, 1980); Juan Carlos Garavaglia, "Um modo de produção subsidiária: a organização econômica das comunidades guaranizadas durante os séculos XVII–XVIII na formação Alto-Peruano-Rio-Platense," in Philomena Gebran (ed.), *Conceito de modo de produção* (Rio de Janeiro: Paz e Terra, 1978), 247–275; Bartomeu Melià, *El Guaraní conquistado y reducido*, 2nd edn. (Asunción: Universidad Católica, 1988 [1986]); and John Monteiro, "Os Guarani e a história do Brasil meridional, séculos XVI–XVII," in Cunha (ed.), *História dos índios no Brasil*, 475–498. Ample evidence of the conflicts between Jesuits and Spanish royal and ecclesiastical authorities in Paraguay can be found in ARSI Paraquaria 11.

33. Anonymous, "Daños que han hecho los portugueses de la villa de San Pablo del Brasil a los indios de la provincia del Paraguay y su remedio," c. 1632, in Pablo Pastells, *Historia de la Compañía de Jesus en la provincia del Paraguay*, 8 vols. (Madrid: Victoriano Suárez, 1912–1949), 1:471–472.

34. A useful discussion of this theme can be found in Davidoff, *Bandeirantismo*, 55ff.

35. Catalogus Rerum, ARSI Paraquaria 4 (1), fols. 109–109v. This report may be biased, in the sense that it attempted to show the inadequacy of the stipend, and because other accounts of the era paint a more optimistic picture.

36. Antonio Ruiz de Montoya, "Carta anua," 1628, in *Mss. de Angelis*, 1:259–298.

37. Diego de Salazar, "Carta anua," 1626–1627, AMP 1, pt. 2 (1922): 213; Pierre-François-Xavier de Charlevoix, *Histoire du Paraguay* 3 vols. (Paris: Chez Didot, 1756), 2:309–310.

38. Charlevoix, *Histoire*, 2:221.
39. Sworn statement of Pedro Homem Albernaz, Apr. 18, 1630, ARSI-FG, Collegia 203/1588/12, doc. 2. It is noteworthy that several companies of troops were organized in São Paulo during these years in response to the Dutch invasion, but few ever saw action in the northeast, their members turning their attention to slaving instead. On the organization of four companies under the leadership of the backwoodsman Antonio Pedroso de Alvarenga, see CMSP-Registro, 2:6, Mar. 23, 1638. For a general study of the captaincy's military organization, see Nanci Leonzo, "As companhias de ordenanças na capitania de São Paulo, das origens ao governo do Morgado de Matheus," *Coleção Museu Paulista. Série de História* 6 (1977): 123–239.
40. Justo Mansilla and Simon Maceta, "Relación de los agravios," AMP 1, pt. 2 (1922): 247–270. This is the best account of the Raposo Tavares expedition. Davidoff, *Bandeirantismo*, provides a fine discussion of the role of violence in this and other expeditions.
41. D. Luis Cespedes y Xeria, "Testimonio de una relación de los sucesos ocurridos durante un viaje desde que salió del rio Paranapane [*sic*]," c. 1628, AMP 1, pt. 2 (1922): 211.
42. CMSP-Atas, 3:282, Oct. 2, 1627. This more aggressive posture on the part of the Municipal Council has bolstered Cortesão (in *Raposo Tavares*) and others in their belief that genuine geopolitical motives underlay the movement, but in reality it reflected more specifically the collective fear of losing the principal source of labor for São Paulo. The term "repartimento" refers to the Spanish American mode of forced indigenous labor known as *repartimiento*.
43. CMSP-Atas, 3:76, Jan. 13, 1624.
44. CMSP-Registro, 1:446–447, Oct. 27, 1624. In fact, the seventeenth century was punctuated by periodic outbreaks of disease, above all measles and smallpox. Significant epidemics were reported in 1611, 1624, 1654, 1666, 1676, 1695, and 1700. See Sérgio Buarque de Holanda, *Caminhos e fronteiras* (Rio de Janeiro: José Olympio, 1957), 105; Hemming, *Red Gold*, 139–146; Dauril Alden and Joseph C. Miller, "Out of Africa: The Slave Trade and the Transmission of Smallpox to Brazil, 1560–1831," *Journal of Interdisciplinary History* 18/2 (1987): 195–224.
45. Anonymous, "Relação certa," ARSI-FG, Missiones 721/I.
46. Nicolas Durán to Francisco Crespo, Sept. 24, 1627, AMP 2, pt. 1 (1925): 169–171.
47. Real cedula, Sept. 16, 1639, in Pastells, *Historia*, 2:32–34. For a discussion of these figures and their economic significance, see Roberto Simonsen, *História econômica do Brasil, 1500–1820*, 8th edn. (São Paulo: Nacional, 1978 [1937]), 245–246.
48. Antonio Ruiz de Montoya, "Primeira catechese dos indios selvagens feita pelos padres da Companhia de Jesus," *Annaes da Bibliotheca Nacional do Rio de Janeiro* 6 (1878–1879): 91–366 (at 235–236).
49. "Informe de Manuel Juan de Morales de las cosas de San Pablo y maldades de sus moradores," 1636, *Mss. de Angelis*, 1:182–193.
50. Mendonça, "Súplica," IHGB, lata 219, doc. 17, fol. 8.
51. Governor Avila to Crown, Dec. 10, 1637, in Pastells, *Historia*, 1:547.
52. Nicolás del Techo, *Historia provinciæ Paraquariæ Societatis Jesv* (Liège: Joan. Mathiae Hovii, 1673), 41.
53. "Relación de los portugueses que en compañía de Antonio Raposo Tavares deshicieron tres reducciones de indios carios," n.d., AMP 2, pt. 1 (1925): 245–246.

54. André Fernandes and Manuel Preto were held to be the scourge of the missions in subsequent Jesuit correspondence. The testimony of two Guarani headmen, taken in Buenos Aires nearly thirty years later, attributed much of the destruction of their people to Manuel Preto. "Declarações de indígenas, relativas a prisioneiros mulatos ou portuguêses de São Paulo, 28-IV-1657 [*sic*]" (Apr. 28–29, 1656, according to transcribed documents), in *Mss. de Angelis*, 4:326–333. On the life and times of Manuel Preto, see Victor de Azevedo, *Manuel Preto, "O Herói de Guairá"* (São Paulo: Governo do Estado, 1983). The map presented in Hemming, *Red Gold*, xx–xxi, provides the approximate locations of individual missions, as well as information on when they were founded and destroyed.
55. Letter of Diego de Boroa, Mar. 4, 1637, and account of Pedro Mola, Mar. 24, 1637, in *Mss. de Angelis*, 3:143–152.
56. The brief is summarized in Thomas, *Política indigenista*, 191.
57. For an excellent discussion of the militarization of the missions, see Arno Alvarez Kern, *Missões: uma utopia política* (Porto Alegre: Mercado Aberto, 1982), 149–207.
58. Report of the Cabildo Eclesiastico of Asunción, Apr. 18, 1639, in *Mss. de Angelis*, 3:269.
59. Claudio Ruyer, "Relación de la guerra y victoria alcanzada contra los portugueses del Brasil, año 1641 en 6 de abril," *RIHGSP* 10 (1905): 529–553. It would appear from the documents that the defenders of Mbororé were not Guarani but in fact Itatim, a group described by the Jesuits as Tememinó. See, for example, Diego Ferreira, "Carta anua," *Mss. de Angelis*, 2:29–49.
60. Lupercio Zurbano, "Carta anua," 1642 (Pastells, *Historia*, 2:342).
61. Francisco Ferreira, "La causa del Brasil estar en el triste estado en que está son las injusticias notables que en el se hacen contra los indios," n.d., ARSI-FG, Missiones 721/1.
62. "Información sobre los excessos que cometieron en las reducciones," Sept. 17, 1629, AMP 1, pt. 2 (1922): 239–246.
63. The best general treatment of these international events and their impact on local societies is Charles R. Boxer, *Salvador de Sá and the Struggle for Brazil and Angola, 1602–1686* (London: Athlone, 1952).
64. Inacio de Tolosa to General Acquaviva, Aug. 19, 1597, ARSI Brasilia 15, fols. 433–433v. On the use of Indian labor in the sugar economy, see Schwartz, "Indian Labor," esp. 72–78.
65. Carvalho Franco, *Dicionário de bandeirantes*, 9.
66. Adriaen van der Dussen, "Relatório sobre as capitanias conquistadas no Brasil," in José Antônio Gonsalves de Mello (ed.), *Fontes para a história do Brasil holandês,* vol. 1: *A economia açucareira* (Recife: Museu do Açúcar, 1981), 186. Before the Dutch invasion, a Jesuit wrote that the main activity of the settlers in Maranhão was enslaving Indians to supply Pernambuco. Ferreira, "La causa," ARSI-FG, Missiones 721/1.
67. "Assentos de batismos, casamentos e obitos feitos pelos padres jesuitas na igreja de São Francisco Xavier [Engenho Velho]," 1641–1759, ACMRJ, uncatalogued.
68. Transport costs were apparently quite high relative to the value of the slave. In 1701, for example, Father Guilherme Pompeu de Almeida registered in his account book that he had spent 11$000 to bring an African slave from Bahia; however, at the height of the trade in Indian slaves, in the 1630s, indigenous captives were sold in Rio de Janeiro for as little as 4$800. Even allowing for the fact that the trip from Bahia to São Paulo was

more costly than that from the principal slaving sites of the 1630s to Rio de Janeiro, as well as the time elapsed between these two accounts, it seems clear that the Indian slave trade could not have operated on the scale suggested by Simonsen, among others. On prices in Rio de Janeiro, see Ruiz de Montoya to Juan de Ornos, Jan. 25, 1638, *Mss. de Angelis*, 3:291–293. On the African slave, see José Pedro Leite Cordeiro (ed.), "Documentação sobre o capitão-mor Guilherme Pompeu de Almeida, morador que foi na vila de Parnaíba," *RIHGSP* 58 (1960): 510. It should be noted that Cordeiro wrongly attributes this document to the governor of São Vicente, but in truth it was the account book of his son and namesake, the priest Guilherme Pompeu de Almeida, one of southern Brazil's richest merchants during the period.

69. Inventory of Beatriz Bicudo, 1632, IT, 11:89–96.
70. For a summary listing of these expeditions, see Monteiro, "São Paulo in the Seventeenth Century," 419–425.
71. Antonio de Araújo, "Informação da entrada que se pode fazer da vila de São Paulo ao grande rio Pará," in Serafim Leite, *Páginas de história do Brasil* (São Paulo: Nacional, 1937), 103–110. A detailed and measured discussion of the expeditions to the Paraupava may be found in Manoel Rodrigues Ferreira, *As bandeiras do Paraupava* (São Paulo: Prefeitura Municipal, 1979).
72. Inventory of Catarina Tavares, Parnaíba, 1671, AESP-INP, cx. 12.
73. The best contemporary account is the letter of Antonio Vieira to the Provincial of Brazil, n.d. [1654], in Vieira, *Cartas*, 3 vols., ed. João Lúcio de Azevedo (Coimbra: Imprensa da Universidade, 1925–1928), 1:383–416. See also Jaime Cortesão, "A maior bandeira do maior bandeirante," *Revista de História* 22 (1961): 3–27; and Myriam Ellis, "A presença de Raposo Tavares na expansão paulista," *Revista do Instituto de Estudos Brasileiros* 9 (1970): 23–61.
74. The first expeditions to Minas Gerais are listed in Oiliam José, *Indígenas de Minas Gerais: aspectos sociais, políticos e etnológicos* (Belo Horizonte: Movimento-Perspectiva, 1965). Afonso Botelho de S. Paio e Sousa, "Notícia da conquista, e descobrimento dos sertões do Tibagi," *Anais da Biblioteca Nacional do Rio de Janeiro* 76 (1956): 1–290 (at 76), presents an interesting account of a 1644 expedition to Sabarabuçu, written by Luís de Góis Sanches, which shows the new geographic orientation of slaving activities and the reproduction of violent patterns in new areas. On the westward movement, see Sérgio Buarque de Holanda's posthumously published *O extremo oeste* (São Paulo: Brasiliense, 1986) and, with particular reference to Sorocaba, Luiz Castanho de Almeida, "Bandeirantes no ocidente," *RIHGSP* 40 (1941): 343–381. Antonio Pires de Campos, who was among the men who discovered the Cuiabá mines, left a description of the Indians who inhabited the area, enumerating several groups that are difficult to identify today: "Breve noticia que dá o capitão Antonio Pires de Campos do gentio barbaro que ha na derrota da viagem das Minas do Cuyabá e seu reconcavo," *RIHGB* 25 (1862): 437–449.
75. Paes Leme, *Nobiliarquia paulistana*, 3:223.
76. Despite its size, little is known about this expedition, which was considered by some to be a simple exaggeration on the part of Alfredo Ellis Júnior, who took as basis for its existence a passing mention in the documentation of the Municipal Council of São Paulo that states that "many Indians went to the wilderness in the company of some colonists." CMSP-Atas, 6a:496, July 3, 1666; Ellis, *O bandeirismo paulista e o recuo do*

meridiano, 2nd edn. (São Paulo: Nacional, 1934 [1923]), 258. However, the discovery of new documentation, brought to light here for the first time, indicates that Ellis was on the right track.

77. Catarina do Prado v. Bartolomeu Bueno Cacunda, 1682, AESP-AC, cx. 1, doc. 14.
78. Will and inventory of Manuel Lopes, 1666–1668, AESP-INP, cx. 9.
79. These men were among the larger contributors on the lists of the Donativo Real of 1679–1682 (see discussion in Chapter 6). "Livro do rol das pessoas para o pedido real do ano de 1679," AHMSP, CM-1-19. Further biographical information may be found in Carvalho Franco, *Dicionário de bandeirantes;* Paes Leme, *Nobiliarquia paulista*; and Luiz Gonzaga da Silva Leme, *Genealogia paulistana*, 9 vols. (São Paulo: Duprat, 1903–1905).
80. Will of José Ortiz de Camargo, 1658, AESP-INP, cx. 7. Despite having drawn up his will in 1658, shortly before a voyage to the *sertão*, Camargo would not die until 1663.
81. Domingos de Gois vs. Antonio da Cunha de Abreu, in inventory of João Furtado, 1653, AESP-INP, cx. 1.
82. Antonio Raposo Barreto to Pedro João Malio, n.d., in inventory of Antonio Raposo Barreto, Taubaté, 1684, Museu de Taubaté, Inventários e testamentos, cx. 1, doc. 10.
83. CMSP-Atas, 7:92, Feb. 1, 1681.
84. Letter of Antonio Pais de Sande, 1692, quoted in José Gonçalves Salvador, *Os cristãos novos e o comércio do Atlântico meridional, com enfoque nas capitanias do sul, 1530–1680* (São Paulo: Pioneira, 1978), 99.
85. Will of Antonio de Oliveira Cordeiro, Jundiaí, 1711, AESP-INP, cx. 24. To a certain degree, the relationship between the *armador* and the backwoodsman resembled the relationship between outfitters and ship captains in the Portuguese trade in slaves in the South Atlantic, though the respective destinations of the captives involved was a major difference. For an interesting discussion of the organizational aspects of the African slave trade during this period, see Joseph C. Miller, "Capitalism and Slaving: The Financial and Commercial Organization of the Angolan Slave Trade, according to the Accounts of Antonio Coelho Guerreiro (1684–1692)," *International Journal of African Historical Studies* 17/1 (1984): 1–56.
86. IT, 36:122–123.
87. Cordeiro (ed.), "Documentação sobre o capitão-mor," 528–529.
88. Will of Francisco Borges, 1649, IT, 39:89.
89. Will of Domingos da Rocha, 1683, AESP-INP, cx. 17 (my emphasis).
90. Inventory of Jerônimo de Lemos, 1679, AESP-IPO, 13.839; will of Luis Eanes Gil, 1681, IT, 21:143.
91. Inventory of Manuel Correia de Andrade, Taubaté, 1673, Museu de Taubaté, Inventários e testamentos, cx. 1, doc. 6.
92. Taunay, *História geral*, 4:271–274; Manuel Eufrásio de Azevedo Marques, *Apontamentos históricos, geográficos, biográficos, estatísticos e noticiosos da província do São Paulo*, 3rd edn., 2 vols. (Belo Horizonte: Itatiaia, 1980 [1879]), 2:341–343. Both date the last of these documents to 1685, though the context makes clear that it refers to the *bandeira* of 1666; Azevedo Marques was the last to transcribe the document from the original.
93. Will and inventory of Maria Bicudo, Parnaíba, 1660, IT, 16:72, 83–84.
94. Will of Manuel Correia de Sá, Parnaíba, 1677, AESP-INP, cx. 15.
95. See, for example, Domingos de Gois v. Antonio da Cunha de Abreu, in inventory of João Furtado, 1653, AESP-INP, cx. 1; João Rodrigues da Fonseca v. João Pires Rodrigues,

AESP-AC, cx. 6033-1; and "Termo de concerto" between Manuel Varoja and his mother-in-law, Mariana Rodrigues, AESP-Notas São Paulo, Jan. 27, 1685.

96. Will of Manuel Correia de Sá, Parnaíba, 1677, AESP-INP, cx. 15.
97. Inventories of Manuel Cardoso and Catarina Rodrigues, 1674 and 1675, AESP-INP, cx. 14.
98. Will of Francisco Cubas Preto, 1672, IT, 18:324.
99. Sérgio Buarque de Holanda, *Caminhos e fronteiras*, 13–148, offers a deep, stimulating discussion of this issue.
100. Catarina do Prado v. Bartolomeu Bueno Cacunda, 1682, AESP-AC, cx. 1, doc. 14; Sebastião Rodrigues v. heirs of Antonio Pedroso Leite, 1678, AESP-AC, cx. 6034–2.
101. Paes Leme, *Nobiliarquia paulistana*, 1:103.
102. Francisco Bueno de Camargo v. heirs of Manuel Pinto Guedes, 1683, AESP-AC, cx. 6033-1. See also Carvalho Franco, *Dicionário de bandeirantes*, 124, 433, for information on the 1663 expedition to Batatais.
103. Although Capistrano de Abreu identified the importance of the subject for the study of colonial history, there are few works of real value on the Indian wars of the late seventeenth century. A good, concise survey can be found in Stuart B. Schwartz's introduction to Schwartz (ed.), *A Governor and his Image in Baroque Brazil: The Funereal Eulogy of Afonso Furtado de Castro do Rio de Mendonça* (Minneapolis: University of Minnesota Press, 1979), while Ivan Alves Filho, *Memorial dos Palmares* (Rio de Janeiro: Xenon, 1988), presents new documents and interesting ideas, despite focusing more closely on episodes related to the destruction of the escaped-slave community at Palmares. As could not but be the case, the Paulista side of the story is told in Taunay, "A guerra dos barbaros," *Revista do Arquivo Municipal* 22 (April 1936): 7–331, while the Indian angle is approached by Hemming, *Red Gold*, chap. 16, and in a more synthetic form by Beatriz G. Dantas, José Augusto L. Sampaio, and Maria Rosário G. de Carvalho, "Os povos indígenas no nordeste brasileiro," in Cunha (ed.), *História dos índios do Brasil*, 431–456. An excellent study of the effects of the expansion of cattle raising on indigenous peoples may be found in Luiz R. B. Mott, "Os índios e a pecuária nas fazendas de gado do Piauí colonial," *Revista de Antropologia* 22 (1979): 61–78.
104. Paes Leme, *Nobiliarquia paulistana*, 1:235–236; Carvalho Franco, *Dicionário de bandeirantes*, 44–45; and Cortesão, *Raposo Tavares*, chap. "A bandeira em marcha."
105. Governor Barreto to the Capitão-Mór of São Vicente, Sept. 21, 1657, BNRJ-DH, 3:395–398.
106. CMSP-Atas, 6a:81–82, Mar. 17, 1658.
107. CMSP-Atas, 6:206, May 26, 1670.
108. Governor Sousa Freire to Pedro Vaz de Barros, Nov. 15, 1669, BNRJ-DH, 6:135.
109. Cartas Patentes to Antonio [*sic*] Ribeiro Baião (São Miguel), Manuel Rodrigues de Arzão (Barueri), Henrique da Cunha Machado (Conceição), and Pascoal Rodrigues da Costa (Pinheiros), Oct. 5, 1671, BNRJ, 1.2.9, docs. 140–143; and "Portaria para o provedor mor fretar embarcação para os prisioneiros que tomaram na conquista," Jan. 19, 1673, BNRJ, 7.1.30, doc. 815.
110. Will of Feliciano Cardoso, 1673, AESP-INP, cx. 7.
111. Governor Mendonça to Municipal Council of São Paulo, Feb. 11, 1673, and to Crown, July 10, 1673, BNRJ-DH, 6:239–241, 252.

112. "Papel feito a Sua Alteza contra Estevão Ribeirão Baião sobre as insolências que com outros de São Paulo fazia ao gentio para os cativar e vender," n.d., Ajuda, cód. 50-v-37, doc. 80.
113. Governor (actually, an interim junta) to various Paulistas, Feb. 20, 1677, BNRJ-DH, 11:71–74.
114. Frei Ressurreição to Crown, Nov. 30, 1688, BNRJ-DH, 11:142–245; and Governor Matias da Cunha to the Municipal Council of São Paulo, BNRJ-DH, 11:139.
115. Hemming, *Red Gold*, 351–376.
116. Governor Lencastre to Crown, July 10, 1699, Ajuda, cód. 49-X-32, fol. 487v.
117. Report of José Lopes de Ulhoa, Mar. 22, 1688, AHU, Rio Grande do Norte, cx. 1, doc. 18.
118. Crown to Governor Lencastre, Mar. 10, 1695, AMP 3 (1927): 307.
119. Toward the end of the century, Crown authorities began to offer land instead of slaving privileges to the mercenaries (Governor Lencastre to Municipal Council of São Paulo, Oct. 19, 1697, BNRJ-DH, 11:254). Royal grants of land for cattle ranching were usually very large. For example, Francisco Dias de Siqueira received one measuring 1 by 5 leagues at Canindeí, near the São Francisco River in the interior of Bahia (AESP-Notas São Paulo, 1686).
120. Governor Camara Coutinho to Crown, 1692, Ajuda, cód. 51-v-42.
121. Land Grant by Municipal Council of São Paulo to Pedro de la Guarda, June 25, 1684, in *Cartas de datas de terra*, 20 vols. (São Paulo: Departamento de Cultura, 1937–1940), 3:167–168.
122. While the Crown spent large sums on the northeastern campaigns, expeditions to the south received relatively few resources. For example, the outfitting costs of the Jorge Soares Macedo expedition came to 3 contos de réis, while nearly 29 contos were spent keeping the Paulistas on the field in Rio Grande do Norte. CMSP-Atas, 6:495, Dec. 31, 1678; and "Relação das despesas do terço paulista," Aug. 19, 1702, IEB, ms. 4–25.
123. It seems likely that this expedition discovered gold, which would explain the murder of D. Rodrigo Castelo Branco at the hands of Fernão Dias Pais's son-in-law, Manuel da Borba Gato. Borba Gato spent the twenty years following the crime hiding out in the Mantiqueira Range, where he became the leader of an Indian group, maintaining a safe distance between himself and royal justice. When the principal deposits of gold ore were discovered, the Crown – in need of Borba Gato's knowledge – pardoned him, and he soon became one of the wealthiest men in the new gold-mining region. The saga of Borba Gato is told in the Costa Matoso codex, Biblioteca Municipal de São Paulo. For details on the Dias Pais expedition, see Manuel Cardozo, "Dom Rodrigo de Castel-Blanco and the Brazilian El Dorado, 1673–1682," *The Americas* 1/2 (Oct. 1944): 131–159, and Eduardo Canabrava Barreiros, *Roteiro das esmeraldas: a bandeira de Fernão Dias Pais* (Rio de Janeiro: José Olympio, 1979), which focuses on its geographic aspects.

3
The Granary of Brazil

Late in the eighteenth century, writing to congratulate the governor of São Paulo on the opening of a new road connecting São Paulo and Santos, the chronicler Frei Gaspar da Madre de Deus evoked the captaincy's better days, "when, as Sicily was to Rome, it was called the granary of Brazil, since wheat, meats, and many other provisions were sent from here to all of the settlements of the State, when navigation from the Port of Santos to the Kingdoms of Portugal and Angola was frequent."[1] In another work, Frei Gaspar elaborated upon this nostalgic reflection, identifying the fundamental bases of the Paulista economy:

> The old Paulistas did not lack for servants because, as the captivity of Indians captured in just war and the administration of the same were permitted to them by our laws, and those of Spain, when we were subject to her, according to the circumstances prescribed in the same laws, so they had large numbers of Indians, as well as black slaves from the coast of Africa, with which everyone had many lands cultivated and lived in opulence.[2]

This vital connection between Indian slavery and colonial production – so evident to the chroniclers and genealogists of the eighteenth century – has been relegated to oblivion by modern historians. By uncovering the essential link between so-called *bandeirantismo* and the agrarian evolution of the plateau, demonstrating the interdependence of the process of slave-hunting and that of production, we may view the seventeenth-century history of São Paulo in a different light. The emergence of commercial agriculture on the plateau, particularly in wheat production, explains a good deal about the constitution of colonial society in the region, as the presence of large numbers of captive Indians enabled the articulation of the economy of the plateau with that of the coast, while at the same time resulting in an extremely unequal distribution of wealth in that society.

A Space for Development

The definitive conquest of the Indians of the plateau in the late sixteenth century opened the way for a new phase in the development of the colony. No longer restricted to the immediate environs of the town of São Paulo, the colonists began to occupy and exploit surrounding lands. At the same time, as we saw in the previous chapter, they sought to establish a permanent, bonded labor force of Guarani Indians brought forcibly from areas to the south and southwest.

As the seventeenth century began, these new patterns of settlement and labor recruitment were spurred by two external impulses. First, the rapid growth of the sugar economy after 1580, particularly in the captaincies of Pernambuco and Bahia, and, to a lesser extent, Rio de Janeiro, led to the emergence of new opportunities for cattle ranchers and producers of basic foodstuffs in other areas.[3] The growing plantation market, as well as the port towns from which sugar was shipped, with their growing slave and free populations, faced the threat of serious food shortages. In response, Paulista agriculturalists, along with those of southern Bahia, Espírito Santo, and, later, Maranhão, redirected their activities toward this incipient intra-colonial trade circuit. Second, and more immediately, Crown efforts to create an integrated agricultural and mining economy in the captaincies of the south beginning in the last decade of the sixteenth century had the dual effect of stimulating production for the market and intensifying the recruitment of Indian labor.

In short, the objectives that had lain behind the settlement of the plateau a half-century earlier only began to be realized at the beginning of the seventeenth century. While Indian slavery had developed slowly and unsteadily over the first century of the Portuguese presence in South America, now it could flourish in all its plenitude, since it was connected to a collective project of development involving colonists and the Crown. In a general sense, settlers and royal authorities recognized the intimate relationship between Indian labor and the production of a surplus, which, even when not oriented toward the commercial economy, at least could sustain a non-producing class of settlers, bureaucrats, and ecclesiastics.

By the final decades of the sixteenth century, settlers had already begun to look to the coastal market as a potential source of income. Initially focusing their efforts on raising cattle on the outskirts of the town of São Paulo, the settlers supplied the small market provided by the plantations and mills of São Vicente, the latter working once more following the end of the Tamoio War. It would seem, however, that much of the cattle that roamed the plateau belonged to coastal entrepreneurs, a matter that concerned members of the Municipal Council of São Paulo. In 1583, Council members complained that in spite of the abundance of livestock in the region, there was a shortage of meat, since all of the cattle was brought to market in Santos and São Vicente.[4] On several occasions, the Council also had to reprimand cattle-drivers whose herds damaged croplands on their way to the trail leading to the coast. In these years, the Council registered numerous cattle brands, while tithes were paid in hides and cured meats.[5]

In the 1580s, the settlers began to occupy the lands beyond the Tamanduateí and Anhangabaú rivers, which had marked the limits of European occupation up to that point. One motive for the expansion was the exhaustion of local resources: as much is suggested by the town council's ban on fishing using the *tingui* method, an indigenous technique that used a poisonous substance to kill fish, since it was leading to the extinction of the Tamanduateí's piscifauna.[6] In addition, the demarcation of mission-village lands in 1580 established an unmistakable legal distinction between the collective property of these reconstituted Indian communities and the private property of Portuguese settlers, opening the way for permanent white occupation. The process was slow, however. Until the end of the sixteenth century, colonists who dared settle too far from town still faced the threat of annihilation. But the major restriction on the expansion of settlement was the scarce supply of available labor, which in these years was limited to the precarious population of the three mission villages belonging to the town.

It is thus no surprise that the early settlement of new lands was limited to areas immediately abutting the town and its mission villages, at least until the early seventeenth century, when new methods of recruiting Indians and new forms of labor came to allow wider-ranging territorial expansion. Indeed, much of the land distributed between 1580 and 1600 belonged, at least in theory, to the Municipal Council of São Paulo. Although the *rocio* (commons) of the town was not clearly defined until 1598, the Council began distributing parcels concentrated in three areas beginning in 1583.[7] The first soon became the *bairro* (rural neighborhood) of Ipiranga, situated alongside the trail linking São Paulo to the coast; the second, which lay between the town's initial center of settlement and the Tietê River, came to be known as Guaré or Piratininga;[8] and the third was concentrated along both banks of the Pinheiros, or Jerubatuba, River, and was closely linked to the mission village of Pinheiros. Settlers of these lands received plots of public land ranging in size from 3,000 to 48,000 square meters.[9] The first settlers of Ipiranga, for example, each received homesteads of 12,100 square meters, which was enough for living quarters for family and slaves, as well as for planting subsistence crops.

From the outset, this first wave of territorial expansion was closely tied to the coastal economy. One of the founders of Ipiranga, Antonio de Proença, previously had settled in Santos, moving to the plateau in the early 1580s to raise cattle for the coastal market.[10] It was along the

Pinheiros River, though, that the strongest signs of a well-articulated commercial economy emerged. Inventories of its early settlers record the constant movement of salted meats and produce from establishments along the Pinheiros to the coast. At the same time, the regular appearance of coastal merchants in the debt and credit lists of these inventories indicates the creation of solid ties between the more prosperous producers of the São Paulo region and mercantile interests in Santos and Rio de Janeiro.[11]

While the growth of the coastal market offered new incentives to Paulista producers, a second impulse for the economic development of the region came from the Crown, in the person of Dom Francisco de Sousa. As we saw in the previous chapter, Dom Francisco and his entourage of practical miners from Europe sought to implant a model of integrated mining, agricultural, and manufacturing sectors. In spite of efforts at exploiting placer mines at Voturuna and Jaraguá and the first experiments with iron foundries, it was in the agricultural sphere that Dom Francisco's plan advanced furthest, if not exactly in the way he had projected. One of his explicit aims was the transformation of São Paulo into the "granary of Brazil," in which wheat-growing estates, organized on the model of the Spanish American hacienda, would provision cities and mines. Some of his entourage introduced technical elements necessary for wheat production and processing, installing the first flour mill in 1609. The first major wheat farmers founded some of the most important lineages in São Paulo, including the Taques, Pedroso de Barros, and Arzão families, all of them initially associated with Dom Francisco.

The expansion of the labor force, stimulated by Dom Francisco de Sousa in the first decade of the seventeenth century, was another decisive element in the development of Paulista agriculture. While defending the principle of Indian liberty, Dom Francisco sought to revive the old mission-village plan. Indians brought from the *sertão* were to be placed in mission villages belonging to the Crown, from which they would be drafted into temporary, remunerated service to settlers and the state. To this end, Dom Francisco sponsored the establishment of the mission village of Barueri, located to the west of the town of São Paulo, relatively close to the recently discovered mines of Jaraguá and Voturuna. Initially, it would seem, the Jesuits were charged with administering the sacraments to its largely Carijó and Guaianá residents, while control over the distribution of labor remained with the Crown. These stipulations were never defined clearly, though, and so Barueri became the object of permanent conflict between private, municipal, ecclesiastical, and royal interests.[12]

By the time of his sudden death in 1611, Dom Francisco and his followers had planted the seeds for the agricultural economy that would develop over the course of the seventeenth century. They had encouraged the growth of the labor force with the creation of the mission village of

Barueri, stimulated the occupation of lands beyond the Tietê and to the west of the town of São Paulo, and introduced a new staple crop that could be brought to market on the coast. But the new model soon revealed its limitations, as the expansion of agriculture made clear that local demands for labor could never be satisfied by the mission-village plan. As a result, and as the frontier of settlement extended further into the interior, the settlers came to appropriate for themselves the Indians they brought from the *sertão*, especially after Dom Francisco's death, instead of handing them over to the mission villages.

Even so, since the transformation of the labor force was a cumulative process, settlement in the early part of the century remained relatively close to the mission villages. Dom Francisco and his successors may have accelerated the distribution of land through official grants known as *sesmarias* (the term may refer to both grants by Crown officials and the lands so bestowed), but exploitation of these lands depended upon access to Indian labor, without which they were worthless in monetary terms. Land in itself had little intrinsic value in the seventeenth century, as demonstrated by inventories of probated estates during this period: in these it was rare for lands to be assigned any monetary value at all, while records of land sales show that prices were generally quite low.[13] Notwithstanding that fact, the existence of vast tracts of apparently unoccupied lands was a compelling attraction to settlers, one that resulted in generally dispersed settlement patterns. Still, the land question must be placed in the ideological and economic context of colonial Brazil, in which the occupation of successive agricultural frontiers – at least in areas where settlers aspired to more than mere subsistence – depended ultimately on the expansion of forced labor.

This situation was apparent to the settlers of late sixteenth-century São Paulo, and this led to an increase in the number of slaving expeditions sweeping through the vast wildernesses of Brazil. Thereafter – the year 1600 may serve as an approximate marker – territorial expansion assumed new characteristics, with modest grants of municipal lands giving way to immense *sesmarias* as the principal means of distributing rural landholdings. In general, a settler seeking definitive title to lands he already occupied as a squatter would petition the highest authority in the captaincy, who would most often authorize the grant in the terms of the petition. In theory, the grantee was to improve the lands granted him within a fixed period of time (usually five years) and to pay the ecclesiastical tithe on any fruits the land yielded. But these provisions were not strictly observed in Brazil. And, despite the condition that unimproved lands would revert to the Crown as idle public lands (*terras devolutas*), many grants remained uncultivated for generations.

Though the records of these grants for the São Paulo area are far from complete, a few conclusions can be drawn from the evidence that is available for the first half of the seventeenth century.[14] Between 1600 and 1644, at least 250 grants were made, covering the townships (*termos*) of São Paulo, Mogi das Cruzes, and Santana de Parnaíba (lands that at that point included the territories that would become the *termos* of the towns of Jundiaí, Itu, and Sorocaba, which would be founded between 1655 and 1661). Of these, a significant portion measured one half-league of frontage by one-half league of *sertão*, for a total area of about 750 hectares. However, it is difficult to assess the exact size of a fair portion of the grants as the petitions themselves are unclear. Usually, only the size of the property's frontage was mentioned, while its extension was described as "the *sertão* that is found there." Still other petitions resorted to unusual units of measure: for example, Pedro da Silva requested a "piece of countryside that is about one arrow's flight, a little more or a little less."[15]

The uneven frequency of grants, which often appeared in concentrated clusters, is another important characteristic of the way in which lands were distributed. This clustering owed as much to successive waves of settlement as to the infrequency of visits to the plateau by the captaincy's governors, who resided on the coast until the 1680s. One notes, for example, a cluster of grants in the Mogi das Cruzes area between 1609 and 1611, which were directly related to the founding of that town. Similarly, the great concentration of grants in 1638–1639, when Governor Antonio de Aguiar Barriga distributed large amounts of land between the Juqueri and Atibaia rivers, reveals a different strategy on the part of the settlers: much of this land was only effectively occupied in the 1660s. At the same time, significant stretches of land were given out near the mission village of Conceição dos Guarulhos, an area that was only settled by whites beginning in the 1650s. One may thus conclude that settlers also acquired *sesmarias* for future use.[16]

However, if the granting of *sesmarias* can elucidate the process of land alienation, it cannot satisfactorily explain patterns of settlement and territorial expansion, which were more closely linked to agricultural practices and the availability of native labor. Dispersive agricultural techniques, which followed indigenous models to some extent, led to the opening of successive areas of settlement. In the early seventeenth century, according to probate inventories, the only item of any significant value in the colonists' property holdings was the *roça* planted in corn or manioc.[17] The productive life of these plots rarely exceeded three years, when they would have to be abandoned in favor of virgin forest (*matos maninhos*) or plots that had been left fallow for several years and were now covered in secondary growth (*capoeiras*). Frequently, applicants for *sesmarias* would allege that their lands were no longer productive and that therefore it was necessary for them to expand onto an adjacent plot. Francisco de Alvarenga, among others, justified his need for new land by affirming that his current landholdings were "tired."[18] This process of abandonment and reconstitution of agricultural lands – closely resembling Indian practices – troubled royal authorities in São Paulo, who considered the constant mobility of the settlers to be excessive. In the middle of the seventeenth century, the crown judge Manuel Franco, for one, criticized the slash-and-burn technique because it compelled the settlers to constantly "move about like gypsies" (*se azingaram*), which presented obvious problems for a colonial bureaucracy organized to deal with permanently settled populations.[19]

The process of settlement also reflected different stages in the development of labor recruitment strategies. Once a well-defined system of forced native labor freed the settlers from their dependence on the mission villages, they were able to expand onto more distant lands. A new wave of settlement, which by the 1620s reached beyond the Serra da Cantareira, included the principal sites for wheat production and the largest concentrations of Indian slaves in the region. Petitions from the period are illustrative of the relationship between labor and landholding: Antonio Pedroso de Alvarenga, later one of the principal producers in the region, stated in 1638 that "he had some Indians and did not have any land on which to farm."[20] Sebastião Fernandes Camacho, like Pedroso de Alvarenga a future wheat farmer, as well as the "son and grandson of settlers and conquerors of the captaincy," outlined the relationship between labor and landholding in his own explicit terms: "he, the supplicant, is married with a wife and sons and daughters and has many heathen in his service, and he has no lands to farm and raise his livestock, from which must result much profit to the Royal Treasury."[21]

Finally, in addition to agricultural practices and the labor issue, demographic growth was a third major factor influencing the settlement patterns of Portuguese colonists, though the available demographic data is too sparse to support definitive conclusions. It is clear that the total population of the captaincy grew rapidly during the first half of the seventeenth century. While this growth was primarily due to the great influx of Guarani captives through 1640, the European population increased as the result of two waves of immigration, the first of new Portuguese elements at the beginning of the century, the second of Spanish-Paraguayan colonists between 1620 and 1640, with the latter becoming integrated into the Bueno, Camargo, and Fernandes families.[22] It is very likely that this general pattern of population growth was reversed in the later seventeenth century with the decline of slaving expeditions and out-migration by both the white and indigenous population.

In the first half of the century, however, population growth put a strain on existing resources, stimulating territorial expansion. In spite of the presence of seemingly infinite stretches of unoccupied territory, some documents indicate that there was a shortage of land available to settlers, particularly beginning in the 1640s. By that point, the flood of *sesmaria* grants distributed in the late 1630s had placed the best lands in the hands of a few settlers. Though much of this land remained unused, its owners defended their property rights energetically, including by taking legal action against squatters, neighbors, and other potential intruders. Joana do Prado, for example, sued the widow of Salvador de Oliveira in 1680, requesting damages amounting to 300 milréis because Oliveira had invaded her property, "forcibly felling virgin forests of good land [and] planting on them stands of cotton, wheat fields, plots of corn..." Prado justified this unusually high sum, "for their being the best lands there are in the district and close to the town." At that point, she owned 2,200 meters of frontage in the rural neighborhood of Juqueri, bounded on either side by the prosperous estates of Oliveira and the "matron" Inês Monteiro de Alvarenga.[23]

The establishment of new municipal jurisdictions on the plateau also illustrates the relationship between the appropriation of land and the demand for labor. The first new towns to be established in the region since the chartering of São Paulo dos Campos de Piratininga in 1560, Mogi das Cruzes and Santana de Parnaíba, founded in 1611 and 1625, respectively, emerged alongside reconstituted indigenous communities. The area of Mogi, to the east of the town of São Paulo along the Tietê River, was settled at the end of the sixteenth century after the annihilation of the indigenous people who had lived there. During the first decade of the new century, under the governorship of Dom Francisco de Sousa, several *sesmarias* were distributed and in 1611 a group of twenty colonists drew up a petition requesting that their settlement be raised to the status of a town.[24] At about the same time, the reconstituted Indian village of Nossa Senhora da Escada was established nearby, to the northeast of the site of Mogi, on the banks of the Paraíba River. Unlike other such villages, Escada was neither founded nor controlled by Jesuits. According to most accounts, it was Gaspar Vaz, the founding captain of the town of Mogi, who created the village; according to an ecclesiastical census from the 1680s, however, Escada had been established "by the Indians."[25]

The transformation of Santana de Parnaíba into an independent town, meanwhile, occurred more slowly. According to historiographical convention, the Portuguese Manuel Fernandes Ramos and his *mamaluca* wife, Suzana Dias, had founded the settlement in 1580, when they erected a rural chapel named for Santo Antônio. This seems unlikely, however, since the area was still considered "sertão" when a slaving expedition was wiped out there in 1591.[26] In any case, several colonists staked mining claims in the area and settled in the environs of the future town in the late sixteenth century and early seventeenth, by which time it was a flourishing rural *bairro* of São Paulo. It would seem that Suzana Dias, by then a widow, established the rural chapel of Santana around 1609 along with her sons and sons-in-law.[27]

The two or three decades' delay between the effective occupation of the area and its elevation to the status of town, it would appear, was due in large part to the resistance of the Municipal Council of São Paulo, wary of its potential loss of control over the mission village of Barueri, also established during this period. The settlement of Santana de Parnaíba lay only 39 kilometers from São Paulo and a mere 8 from Barueri. The settlers of São Paulo thus invoked royal legislation prohibiting the creation of new towns near established ones. The truth, however, was that the São Paulo settlers were on guard against losing the Indians of Barueri to the settlers of Parnaíba, accusing several of the latter of using force in recruiting mission-village residents. Antonio Furtado, for example, a son-in-law of Suzana Dias and pioneer wheat grower, at one point was ordered by the Municipal Council of São Paulo to return the Indians he had wrested from the mission village and pressed into service. A few years later, upon Furtado's death, his widow Benta Dias confessed that most of the Indians in their service belonged to the mission village and that "she could not place them in inventory in good conscience."[28] Even the principal colonist of Parnaíba, André Fernandes, son of Suzana Dias and co-founder of the original chapel, had an uncounted number of Indians from the mission village in his personal service, in addition to the more than one hundred captives who also worked on his estate in Parnaíba.[29]

The mixed slaveholdings of Furtado and Fernandes clearly illustrate the character of the transition that the economy of São Paulo was undergoing at that point. The emergence of new population centers, increasingly distant from the first towns, accompanied the development of slave-hunting as a way of meeting the need for labor. Indeed, the fragmentation of administrative units increased in pace at mid-century, together with the rapid reproduction of the basic social, economic, and institutional structures that the colonists implanted in new settlements and towns further inland.

Each new rural community followed an administrative trajectory that was to accompany the transformation of *sertão* into settled territory. The more populous *bairros* quickly became parish seats, while most of the parishes created in the seventeenth century became towns sooner or later. These transformations could take generations to occur, requiring prolonged periods of demographic growth to justify the fragmentation of older municipal units and the creation of new ones. In mid-seventeenth-century São Paulo, however, this process was accelerated in a number of cases, as new towns sprang up in the interior with astonishing rapidity.[30]

This second phase of town-founding, which began in the 1640s, also had much to do with access to Indian labor and patterns of its recruitment. Responding to the crisis in the supply of Guarani captives that emerged after 1640, the colonists of São Paulo, Santana de Parnaíba, and Mogi das Cruzes began to redirect their slaving expeditions to the Paraíba Valley, east of the so-called Paulista plateau, where the towns of Taubaté (1643), Guaratinguetá (1651), and Jacareí (1653) were established. Subsequent expansion on the plateau resulted in the founding of the towns of Jundiaí (1655), Itu (1656–1658), and Sorocaba (1661) to the northwest and west of São Paulo and Santana de Parnaíba. With their small-scale agricultural production based on Indian labor, these new towns provisioned expeditions passing through in search of new sources of Indian labor and served as staging grounds for further slaving parties mounted by local settlers.

The raising of a *bairro* or informal settlement to the status of a town was not always the result of a cumulative process of demographic or economic growth, since there were other reasons for the fragmentation of municipal units and the founding of new ones. In effect, the creation of a new town brought into being the administrative apparatus necessary for the organization of a new cycle of pioneer settlement. As in the case of the town of São Paulo, the founding of a new town often preceded the settlement of the outlying rural areas belonging to it. The importance of the town lay precisely in the basic institutions it provided, the most important of which were the Municipal Council, the notarial office, and the probate office. Together with religious and private institutions (which were also based in the town seat), each of these institutions played an important role in the creation, protection, and transmission of property rights, the latter including property in land and moveable assets as well as rights of control over and ownership of the Indian labor force.

Until royal justice became more firmly established in the region in the early part of the eighteenth century, an elected municipal body (the Municipal Council) wielded broad judicial and administrative powers within the township, though subject to periodic inspection by a visiting judge, a process that was called a *correição* (literally, "correction"). As an institution of government, the Council functioned on two levels. In the context of the Portuguese empire, it served as a royally sanctioned representative body that voiced collective settler interests before the colonial authorities of Rio de Janeiro, Salvador, and Lisbon. Within the local context, it was a political forum for divergent factions or class interests. Control of the Council could represent the consolidation of wealth and power for these factions or interests, which led to bitter disputes in local elections throughout this period.[31]

Indeed, as the administrative functions of the councils expanded in the seventeenth century, conflicts between local factions became more intense, stimulating the creation of new municipal units. From the beginning, the councils exercised a prominent role in almost every sphere of economic life, controlling the distribution of municipal lands and of the labor of the mission-village Indians. With the expulsion of the Jesuits in 1640, they likewise came to administer the lands held by the mission villages, which were often leased to private settlers. They also regulated trade by setting prices, farming out monopoly contracts, and levying taxes. Finally, the task of investigating and punishing offenses in civil and criminal law fell to the councils, which afforded local factions an institutional apparatus that could bolster their interests.

The notary's office, in turn, was particularly important in safeguarding property rights, since the formal registration of transactions, of delegations of power of attorney, and even of pardons for murder constituted the legal basis for any commercial or litigious action. Each town had at least one notary, who would carefully transcribe all business in a record book. São Paulo, the largest town, did not have a second notary's office until 1737, a development that would not occur in the other towns of the region until the nineteenth century.

Although little studied by historians, the probate office was another fundamentally important institution. As the authority responsible for the partition of the estates of deceased colonists, the probate judge (or, in his absence, a member of the Municipal Council acting as *juiz ordinário*, or "ordinary judge") had the arduous task of guaranteeing the strict observance of inheritance law.[32] In seventeenth-century São Paulo, the legal processing of inventories was especially significant because it was through this medium that the existing supply of Indian labor was redistributed. Along with this function, the probate judge had another, perhaps even more important one: to lend at interest the equivalent value of properties belonging to orphaned minors or dependent heirs, which was one of the colonists' principal sources of credit. Indeed, throughout colonial Brazil, though especially in small towns and remote regions where religious institutions were poor and wealthy merchants were few, many settlers resorted to the "orphans' fund" (*cofre dos órfãos*) for loans. In São Paulo, colonists paid a hefty 8 percent annual interest on probate loans, which was justified as "practice and custom of the land."

Along with the services performed by these essential municipal institutions – services that expanded as the town grew – in the years immediately following a town's founding, its Council had the central function of distributing property in land among settlers. As we have seen, the municipal lands of the town of São Paulo were divided up quickly in the late sixteenth century. Throughout the following century, most of the grants made by the Municipal Council were tiny urban allotments, at least until the Council began the distribution of Indian lands belonging to the mission villages. This means of access to land was one of the most obvious reasons for colonists to petition for the establishment of new towns, since each new municipality would have a given amount of public land belonging to the Municipal Council that could be divided up among the first settlers. At least that is what one may conclude from the petition that the settlers of Mogi das Cruzes presented to the governor of São Vicente in 1611. By that time, the settlers claimed, there was not enough land available in the township of São Paulo for their numerous offspring, which was why a new town needed to be founded.[33]

The mid-century founding of Jundiaí provides another example of the importance of municipal land grants in the development of a new community. The area along the Jundiaí River was first settled around 1640, by a group of colonists led by Rafael de Oliveira. A *bairro* soon grew around Oliveira's estate, bolstered by the in-migration of former residents of the neighboring settlement of Juqueri, each with their own holdings of Indian captives. In 1651, Oliveira and the widow Petronilha Antunes, both of them supposedly fugitives from justice at that point, established the rural chapel of Nossa Senhora do Desterro, which soon became the center for the *bairro*'s social and religious activities and the nucleus of the parish and town it would become. In 1655, the *bairro*'s settlers sent a petition to the proprietor of the captaincy requesting the creation of a municipality with the none-too-modest name of Vila Formosa da Nossa Senhora do Desterro de Jundiaí, a request that was granted later the same year.[34]

According to what one can gather from a municipal record book that has survived the ravages of time, the founding of the town of Jundiaí represented a response to the perceived need to distribute lands among the settlers.[35] The book lists eighty-five municipal land grants distributed between December 1656 and April 1657, alongside the minutes of the Municipal Council. Thus, it would seem that the central function of the Council in its earliest years was the distribution of the town's public lands. A second book, used to record municipal business in the following decade, shows that by the 1660s the distribution of lands was no longer a concern of the Municipal Council, which had decided that meetings should take place only once a month because of the lack of important business to be discussed.[36]

The Jundiaí land grants, in addition to defining the boundaries of deeded properties, indicate the reasons cited in petitions for lands. Most of the petitioners – nearly 60 percent – claimed to have been among the earliest settlers or to be somehow related to someone belonging to this select group. This fact reveals something of the spirit of town-founding, in that most colonists apparently felt that having been involved in the original settlement of the area meant they merited an award of land. It would seem that some settlers regarded such grants as a nearly exclusive privilege, since two of the earliest settlers, Francisco da Gaia and Manuel Preto Jorge, addressed petitions to the Municipal Council complaining of outsiders requesting lands "under the guise of coming to settle."[37] Notwithstanding, some municipal lands were settled by recently arrived colonists, since approximately 36 percent of grantees indicated no justification for their petitions beyond their alleged lack of property in land.

In sum, expanded access to land and Indian labor was a critical factor in the economic development of the São Paulo region in the seventeenth century. However, for agricultural production to become a source of income for settlers, its commercialization was required. In response to a growing market for provisions on the coast, the colonists of São Paulo embarked on an experiment with commercial agriculture yoked to a system of forced Indian labor, an experience that would prove significant in shaping the evolution of Paulista society.

Pathways of Paulista Agriculture

The golden age of wheat production in the São Paulo region spanned the years 1630–1680. It was during this period that the concentration of Indian captives reached its highest levels (see Table 2, in Chapter 2). The vital connection between an abundance of Indian labor and commercial agriculture was the cornerstone of a peripheral economy linked to the market of coastal Brazil, itself on the fringe of the Atlantic world. Around 1640, the Municipal Council of São Paulo described this relationship in a letter to the Pope, writing that with the labor of the Indians the colonists

> raise the grains, the meats, and produce for their everyday sustenance and with it feed much of the state of Brazil, because from this town and settlement every year are sent many thousand *alqueires* of wheat flour and great quantity of Meats and produce to feed said state, and even for the conquest of Angola, and all this would have been lacking were the Indians not in our service.[38]

In the early years of the seventeenth century, wheat was integrated into the regular output of Paulista agriculturalists as a lesser product. Even so, it was clearly distinguished from other crops because it was produced exclusively for the market. At no point in the seventeenth century was it produced to sustain the local population. Production for local consumption revolved around the cultivation of manioc, beans, and, above all, maize, the population thus forming part of what Sérgio Buarque de Holanda called the "maize civilization" of indigenous southern Brazil.[39] Wheat, on the other hand, was destined to feed the European population of the cities and towns of the coast and the Portuguese fleets, for which it was requisitioned by the colonial government on several occasions throughout the century. An incident that occurred on the estate of Valentim de Barros is revealing in this sense. After Barros's death, his Indians consumed much of the wheat on the estate, to the evident surprise and displeasure of his executor, who anticipated sending it to market on the coast.[40]

The records of the Municipal Council attest to the commercial orientation of wheat production, as in various meetings Council members complained of a lack of wheat for local consumption in spite of its abundance in the region.[41] This orientation is also evident in wills and inventories from the period. In the early years of the century, the products grown on subsistence plots (*roças*) generally were not evaluated in monetary terms, and served explicitly for the sustenance of the Indians on the property. In contrast, wheat fields (*searas*) and stocks of harvested grain always had their commercial value declared. Throughout the century, wheat-flour credits circulated as a form of payment, frequently making up part of dowries and even serving as a means to liquidate gambling debts.[42]

Specialized production of wheat became widespread in the 1620s, with wheat farms and flour mills soon assuming a pattern of geographical concentration. Three areas became centers for wheat farming: the rural neighborhoods of Santana de Parnaíba, to the west of São Paulo; the settlement of Cotia, to the south of Parnaíba; and the region called Juqueri, bathed by the river of the same name, to the north of São Paulo and Parnaíba. By the 1640s, almost every rural estate or farm probated in Parnaíba showed signs of wheat production, though in many cases these were quite modest. At about the same time, the first large-scale estates emerged, above all in the neighborhood of Juqueri, having grown out of the *sesmarias* granted there between 1617 and 1639. This growth in the scale of production was duly accompanied by the development of Indian slavery, as beginning in this period several estates emerged with holdings of over 100 Indians.

While it is clear that most of the wheat produced in São Paulo was destined for markets outside the region, the lack of precision that characterizes contemporary documentation makes it difficult to capture the mechanisms or scale of this intra-colonial trade. In the 1650s, for example, the Jesuit Antonio Pinto described the town of Santos as "a great port for carracks, much frequented by navigation, for the abundant foodstuffs that depart from there for all of Brazil."[43] While this description evokes the image of a bustling emporium, in reality seventeenth-century Santos was little more than a small town with a very irregular maritime traffic. Nevertheless, it did serve as the principal outlet for goods from São Paulo, linking Paulista producers and merchants to other captaincies and to the mother country.

Although there is evidence of commercial ties between Paulistas and merchants in Bahia, Pernambuco, and even Angola, the major market for the wheat of São Paulo seems to have been Rio de Janeiro, with its growing white population of planters, merchants, and bureaucrats.[44] Portugal, a grain importer since the late Middle Ages, was unable to supply the colonies with wheat, while the output of the Azores was destined first for the metropolis and later for the North Atlantic commercial circuit. The population of the Brazilian coast therefore depended upon the São Paulo region to supply its needs.[45] In the years 1630–1654, the Royal Treasury was a particularly eager buyer of wheat from São Paulo, as it fell to the Crown to supply the fleets and troops involved in the struggles against the Dutch in the northeast and in Angola. Throughout these years, colonial authorities sent several requests to the Municipal Council of São Paulo requesting provisions to feed Portuguese combatants.[46] Without a doubt, various Paulistas responded to this opportunity, among them João Martins de Sousa, whose inventory shows that he sent 70 *alqueires* of wheat flour to Pernambuco in 1652, entrusting them to the merchant João Rodrigues da Fonseca, also a resident of São Paulo.[47]

While it is clear that most of the wheat produced in São Paulo was destined for markets outside of the region, the volume of this intra-colonial trade remains unknown due to the spottiness of colonial-era sources. For two isolated moments in the seventeenth century, however, there exist sufficiently precise indicators to allow estimates of the total output of commercial agriculture in São Paulo. The first can be found in the sharply critical survey of the Paulista economy drawn up in 1636 by the Spanish merchant Manuel Juan de Morales, a resident of São Paulo. He wrote: "from sixteen years to the present all of this captaincy has had an abundance of wheat and not only in São Paulo." This abundance, according to Morales, was responsible for the growth of tithes in the captaincy, which evolved from a modest 70,000 *maravedis* (*c.* 82 milréis) in 1603 to 3,600 *cruzados* (1,440 milréis) in 1636. "And if in this land there were justice, which enforced the payment of tithes, they would amount to 4,500 cruzados [1,800 milréis] each year." In a given year, Morales calculated, the Paulistas produced as much as 120,000 *alqueires* of wheat, which would correspond to a tithe revenue in the order of 1,920 milréis, taking as the value per *alqueire* the average price at that time, which was 160 réis.[48]

More than anything else, these figures reflect the precariousness of relying on tithes as a source for statistical estimates of production. Tithe revenues never corresponded faithfully to the actual volume of production, as they were set by contract at three-year intervals. In addition, the evasion of tithe payments was widespread, which was due as much to the inefficiency of tithe collection as the failure of many rural producers to meet their obligations. It was in this context, in 1661, that a colonial administrator evaluated tithe returns in the southern captaincies: "These evasions have also been the cause of the lack of increase in tithes from the captaincy of São Vicente, which has many products and good ones, and a good output of them."[49]

A second indicator of the total output of the captaincy comes from the tithes gathered in 1666. Lourenço Castanho Taques, holder of the tithe-collecting contract for the town of São Paulo, led a protest by all of the captaincy's collectors, asking that the sums they were obligated to pay be reduced because an outbreak of smallpox in Santos had forced the Municipal Council of São Paulo to close the road to the coast, cutting off commerce. The value of tithe returns for that year was set at 5,200 milréis, while the loss caused by the interruption of trade was estimated at 2,800 milréis. For the purposes of calculation, keeping in mind that the main product sent down to Santos was wheat, we may take the latter figure as an approximate value of total wheat production. Annual output, then, would amount to 175,000 *alqueires*, nearly 50 percent more than in 1636.[50]

Such growth was not beyond the means of local producers, particularly if one considers the notable expansion of their productive base in the 1640s and 1650s, when the concentration of Indians on rural estates reached its peak. Few constraints on the production of wheat existed in seventeenth-century São Paulo, which explains the widespread cultivation of the crop, including by relatively poor farmers. While creating a unit of agrarian production required access to land and labor, these two factors of production remained abundant for much of the seventeenth century, though their distribution was highly unequal. Little capital was needed to outfit a farm, leaving aside the larger investments made by wealthy Paulistas who installed flour mills on their estates. The *foice de segar* (a sort of hand sickle) was the only specialized instrument used in wheat farming, and not only was it assigned little value when listed in estate inventories, it represented little technical advance on the tools wielded by indigenous peoples before the conquest.[51]

When compared with sugar-cane agriculture, with its constant demand for intensive labor, the planting and harvesting of wheat involved relatively little labor. Nonetheless, the scale of production could be increased in proportion to the expansion of the workforce, especially at two points in the agricultural cycle: in the dry months, during the clearing of areas to be planted, and later, during the harvest, as the entire crop had to be reaped and milled almost all at once. Thus, a small labor force would limit the amount of wheat that could be planted and harvested.[52] Even so, unlike in sugar-cane cultivation, it is difficult to establish a clear correlation between output and the size of a unit's labor force, especially since we have so little information on the size of areas planted in crops. Planted areas were measured in *alqueires*, but the size of that unit in the seventeenth century is unknown; in the early seventeenth century, the Jesuit Jácome Monteiro stated that each *alqueire* under cultivation yielded 100 *alqueires* of grain. But the ratio of a hundred to one does not match the evidence from inventories, in which small productive units might be listed as having as many as fifteen *alqueires* under cultivation, while large estates rarely produced more than 1,000 *alqueires* in a single year.[53]

Table 5 *Distribution of Indians in Wheat Production by Sex, Age, and Size of Holding, Santana de Parnaíba, 1628–1682*

Size of holding	(N)*	Men	Women	Children	Total
1 to 10	(12)	39	41	12	92
11 to 25	(22)	137	177	60	374
26 to 50	(24)	272	345	285	902
Over 51	(18)	688	772	514	1,974
Total	(76)	1,136	1,335	771	3,342

* (N) = Number of estates within given range of holding size.
Sources: Inventories of probated estates, Parnaíba. IT, vols. 7–44; AESP-INP, cxs. 1–40; AESP-IPO, various cxs.; AESP-IE, cxs. 1–6.

The organization of labor in wheat farming also differed from that adopted in sugar-cane cultivation, even when the latter relied upon Indian labor.[54] To a certain extent, the Paulistas adopted a division of labor characteristic of the indigenous societies they had attacked in their search for captives, though they would impose significant modifications of this scheme over the course of the century. The predominance of women in agricultural activities in São Paulo reflected the sexual division of labor in the production of basic foodstuffs among Tupi-Guarani peoples, which had the added advantage of making men available for other specialized functions, such as transporting goods to the coast and participating in slaving expeditions in the interior. For example, in the inventory of a wheat farm belonging to Pedro de Miranda, most of the male Indians on the list of "compulsory servants" were described as absent in the *sertão*, which suggests that the cultivation and harvest of the crop fell to the women who remained on the estate.[55] The significant presence of children in slaveholdings may have further contributed to this continuity in the division of labor, preserving, to a certain degree, the role played by youths in production in Guarani societies.[56]

An analysis of the inventories of wheat-producing properties in the township of Parnaíba offers a clearer picture of the composition of the Indian labor force (Table 5). It is worth emphasizing, however, that these figures provide only a partial view. To a certain extent, the demands of the organization of production favored continuity in the sexual division of labor. But, at the same time, vicissitudes in the supply of captive Indians, which changed radically after 1640, also profoundly influenced the makeup of the laboring population. In any case, a different tendency can be found on the largest, most specialized estates, where men in many cases outnumbered women (Table 6). This pattern suggests an attempt, on the part of some of the largest Paulista producers, to create plantation structures

Table 6 *Composition of Indigenous Population on Selected Wheat Farms, São Paulo Region, 1638–1682*

Owner	Year	Men	Women	Children	Total
Cornélio de Arzão	1638	34	36	28	98
Francisco Bueno	1638	36	37	8	81
Clemente Alvares	1641	43	42	38	123
João Barreto	1642	57	57	38	152
João de Oliveira	1653	18	22	10	50
Diogo C. de Melo	1654	60	42	n/a	102
Gaspar de G. Moreira	1658	64	38	25	127
Paulo P. de Abreu	1658	37	33	39	109
Domingos da Rocha	1661	49	28	15	92
João Pires Monteiro	1667	47	51	49	147
Francisco de Camargo	1672	25	19	14	58
Garcia R. Velho	1672	41	38	33	112
João R. Bejarano	1672	48	37	7	92
Pedro F. Arangonês	1682	41	47	27	115
Total	–	600	527	331	1,458

Sources: Inventories of Cornélio de Arzão (Embu), 1638, IT, 12; Francisco Bueno, 1638, IT, 14; Clemente Alvares, Parnaíba (Jaraguá), 1641, IT, 14; Dona Maria (Juqueri), 1642, IT, 28; João de Oliveira, Parnaíba (Pirapora?), 1653, AESP-INP, cx. 1; Diogo Coutinho de Melo, Parnaíba (Japi), 1654, IT, 15; Gaspar de Godoi Moreira (Carapicuíba), 1658, AESP-INP, cx. 3; Benta Dias, Parnaíba, 1658, AESP-INP, cx. 1; Domingos da Rocha do Canto, Parnaíba, 1661, AESP-IE, cx. 3, doc. 17; João Pires Monteiro (Juqueri), 1667, AESP-INP, cx. 9; Francisco de Camargo e Isabel Ribeiro (Tremembé), 1672, AESP-INP, cx. 10; Garcia Rodrigues Velho (Juqueri), 1672, AESP-IPO, 13.768; João Rodrigues Bejarano, Parnaíba, 1672, AESP-AC, cx. 1, doc. 12; Pedro Fernandes Aragonês (Juqueri), 1682, AESP-INP, cx. 12.

resembling those of the sugar-growing coast, in which men always outnumbered women among the enslaved population, with planters displaying a marked preference for young male slaves. This would have meant a significant rupture with the indigenous past and thus an important step in the making of a well-defined slave society.[57] At this point a few wheat producers, including Paulo Proença de Abreu, Domingos da Rocha do Canto, and Pedro Fernandes Aragonês, had already begun a transition to African slavery, shifting some of the resources accumulated in the exploitation of Indian labor into the purchase of "tapanhunos," or African slaves. In 1661, on the estate of Domingos da Rocha do Canto, for example, twenty-four African slaves worked alongside ninety-two Indians.[58]

Another feature that distinguished small producers from the owners of large estates was ownership of or easy access to flour mills. In São Paulo, flour mills variedly greatly in terms of size and value, but properties with mills were always worth a great deal more than those without. Even so, the most valuable farm with a mill in Parnaíba, belonging to Domingos Fernandes, was purchased by his brother-in-law Paulo Proença de Abreu, for only 350 milréis, about one-tenth the value of a mid-sized sugar mill in Rio de Janeiro at that time. However, one must bear in mind that the sale price did not include the estate's Indians, while the value of sugar mills usually included African slaves as well as fixed capital in equipment.[59]

In spite of the relatively low cost of milling equipment, there were few mills in the region. The establishment and operation of flour mills depended upon the authorization of the proprietor of the captaincy, who usually delegated the task to the municipal councils. In turn, the councils distributed land and water rights to qualified applicants, who in return would pay an annual fee, called *pensão*.[60] The exact qualifications are not specified in the surviving documentation, but apparently it was a guarded privilege, limited to a few persons. In 1628, Pedro Gonçalves Varejão suffered legal action for operating a mill without the authorization of the proprietor of the captaincy of São Vicente.[61]

Though in Europe at that time ownership of a mill did not confer much status, mill-ownership in seventeenth-century São Paulo correlated with the power and prestige of certain individuals, families, and religious institutions. The Fernandes family, made up of descendants of the first European inhabitants of the plateau, controlled the wheat business in Parnaíba, while the Pires, Bueno, and Camargo families dominated different rural settlements to the north of the town of São Paulo. The correlation between wheat production, holdings of captive Indians, and the concentration of wealth is clear in tax rolls from 1679 and 1682, which show the incommensurate share of total wealth held by these families. Among residents of the township of São Paulo in the highest decile of total wealth-holding, half belonged to the Bueno or Camargo families.[62]

This inequality was reflected in relations between mill-owners and wheat farmers. In the early seventeenth century, the mill-owner had the right to at least one-eighth of the wheat processed in his mill, though some charged as much as one-fifth. Profiteering led the Municipal Council to intervene in 1619 and to set the rate, called the *maquia*, at one of every seven *alqueires* that were milled.[63] In many cases, especially as the century wore on, producers chose to sell their grain to the mill-owners rather than be left in a state of dependence upon them, which spared individual producers the trouble, risk, and cost of placing the grain on the Santos or Rio de Janeiro market. Over the long term, this trend had the effect of concentrating even greater wealth and power in the hands of a few families.

Perhaps the greatest constraint on the commercial production of wheat was transportation, which further separated producers who held large holdings of captive Indians from less privileged ones. Internal transport, from farms to mills and from mills to towns, generally depended on Indian laborers, as porters and as the crews of freight-bearing canoes. Rural roads, most no more than trails, precariously connected farms, estates, settlements, and towns. Colonial documents distinguished between three types of road: royal, neighborhood, and private. Royal roads, which included trails between towns, such as the Caminho do Mar linking São Paulo and Santos, were maintained by the municipal councils. The maintenance of trails providing access to rural settlements fell to local residents, led by the captain of the neighborhood. Private trails were built on some of the larger estates at the initiative of their owners, such as Guilherme Pompeu de Almeida and Pedro Vaz de Barros, whose properties became rural neighborhoods after their deaths.[64] The region's rivers also played an important role in short- and medium-range transport, especially in the towns to the west of São Paulo along the Tietê River. Scattered references to the "ports" of Parnaíba and Barueri testify to the use of riverine transport. In Parnaíba, several inventories included specialized canoes used in wheat transport, some of which could carry up to 120 *alqueires* of flour.[65]

The route down the Serra do Mar from São Paulo to Santos, linking the plateau to the coast, also combined overland and riverine transport. The first and most difficult stretch, from São Paulo to Cubatão, was traveled on foot, while the rest of the journey to Santos was completed by canoe. Cubatão, at the base of the coastal escarpment, functioned as a toll site and, at least in the 1620s, as a location for warehousing grain.[66] In the second half of the century, the Jesuit College of São Paulo controlled the toll contract, establishing a large estate there to provision travelers. The contract, however, never provided the priests with much revenue, as the Municipal Council of São Paulo set the rates low, allowing them to charge little more than 1 percent of the value of each load.[67]

The trail from São Paulo to Cubatão was the most costly stretch of the route between São Paulo and Santos. The historiography on São Paulo has made much of the difficulties involved in scaling the coastal escarpment, but these accounts are almost entirely based on the observations of Portuguese newly arrived in Brazil, who were subjected to an uncomfortable ride in a hammock, borne by Indians or African slaves. Certainly, the trail to the coast remained a "rugged path," in the words of a seventeenth-century nobleman, at least until the end of the following century, but this hardly isolated the Paulista economy from the rest of the colony.[68] Indian porters overcame its obstacles with great frequency and speed, completing the trip from São Paulo to Cubatão in two to four days.

It was precisely in transport that the need for Indian captives was most acute, as their work as porters was the only means by which the produce of the plateau could be brought to market on the coast. During the seventeenth century, as long as Indian labor was abundant, the Caminho do Mar sustained a regular traffic in grains, cured meats, and even cattle. The steady flow of commerce was interrupted only twice, once during the smallpox epidemic of the mid-1660s, and on another occasion due to the fear instilled in merchants and Indian porters by a particularly ferocious jaguar. On both occasions, it should be noted, producers and merchants alike showed great concern over losses resulting from the interruption of traffic.[69]

Long-distance transport fell almost exclusively to Indian porters, and for this reason continued access to Indian labor proved especially critical to the survival of commercial agriculture. Indeed, transport was one of the basic occupations of captive male Indians in São Paulo, as suggested by one Paulista slaveholder in his will: "I have in my power two old blacks of the heathen of the land one already incapable of portering."[70] In the wheat trade, Indians carried their loads in baskets – each load (*carga*) was measured at 2 *alqueires* and weighed around 30 kilograms – strapped onto their backs in the Guarani fashion.[71] Porters were almost always men, which again indicates an attempt to modify the division of labor characteristic of indigenous societies, or at least of Guarani societies, in which women usually did the work of transport. Cargo parties, in their structure, resembled slaving expeditions: an experienced man leading a group of younger men or boys to the coast. For example, in a letter to a mill-owner in Parnaíba, a wheat merchant explained that he sent a *ladino* (acculturated Indian) to Cubatão with ten young men laden with flour.[72]

Human carriers, who required only rudimentary trails, offered a clear advantage over pack animals. From the settlers' point of view, as long as Indian labor was relatively abundant, porterage provided the most economical option, which explains its use through much of the century. It is the case that other solutions were sought at certain junctures, as in the very beginning of the seventeenth century, when Indian laborers were still relatively scarce. At that point, Governor Francisco de Sousa proposed to introduce 200 "pack sheep like those used to carry the silver of Potosí" (i.e., alpaca) and "to breed them and never want for them."[73] Likewise, toward the end of the century, when the influx of Indian captives began to decrease noticeably, some producers began to raise pack animals, as is shown by their increasingly frequent appearance in inventories beginning in the early 1670s.[74]

Indian porters were ultimately the cheapest form of transport, since they were swifter, could survive on less food, and could carry considerable amounts of goods at the lowest cost relative to the value of their loads. The Jesuit Antonio Ruiz de Montoya, in one of his many denunciations of the Paulistas, condemned the use of Indian porters, declaring that the colonists used the Indians "as if they were mere animals." Summing up the principal function of Indians in the Paulista economy, he observed: "Upon their shoulders are placed enormous loads, [the settlers] continually making them carry to other settlements the things that they deal in, tiring them with the burden of their property and their merchandise."[75] Antonio Vieira also observed that the Paulistas sought to maximize their gains through the relentless exploitation of their Indian porters: "In the *cáfilas* [caravans] from São Paulo to Santos they not only went burdened as men but overburdened like pack animals, almost all naked or covered by a rag and with an ear of corn for each day's ration."[76] As a Jesuit visitor noted in 1701, even the priests of the College of São Paulo availed themselves of this service, neglecting to pay the Indians for their "comings and goings with loads to Santos, and from Santos to São Paulo."[77]

Freight rates, insofar as they can be calculated in monetary terms, remained low in the first half of the century, when the supply of Indian captives was large, which indicates that the availability of surplus labor was critical in determining whether commercial agriculture was viable or not. After all, wheat was not the only product borne on the backs of Indian porters, who also carried products of much lesser value to the coast, showing just how low transport costs were. For example, Pedro Nunes sent a dozen Indian porters to the coast laden with beans in 1623.[78] And, in 1647, another Paulista sent twenty-eight loads of manioc to Santos, with a declared value of only 50 réis per load.[79]

Most Paulistas did not themselves possess the surplus labor necessary for transportation and thus had to rent Indians from the region's larger slave-owners or from the mission villages. Rental rates varied throughout the century, but the general tendency was toward higher fees by the end of the century, which corresponded to the increasing scarcity of labor. At the beginning of the seventeenth century, when the supply of Indian labor was still relatively low, freight rates were high. In 1613, for example, Domingos Luís paid 3 pesos (960 réis) for the rental of three Indians to carry goods to the coast, or 320 réis each.[80] By mid-century, the rate had dropped in half, to 160 réis, as when Gaspar Correia paid 3,200 réis to rent 20 Indians.[81] Shortly thereafter, the rate rose to 240 réis, where it remained until late in the century, when the labor shortage reached crisis proportions, exacerbated by the gold rush that began in the 1690s, provoking rate hikes that were considered scandalous. By 1700, the Jesuits were charging 1,280 milréis round trip, plus provisions for the Indian, while by 1730 the rate reached 1,600 each way.[82]

The relationship between transport costs and profit rates depended ultimately on the price fetched by wheat flour in Santos or Rio de Janeiro. Only the maintenance of a delicate balance between fluctuating transport costs and insecure, occasionally volatile market conditions on the coast allowed profitable trade to occur. In the 1630s, both Jesuits and private settlers were charging between 200 and 240 réis per porter for the trip from São Paulo to Cubatão. However, in 1633 the Municipal Council of Santos set the price of flour at 200 réis per *alqueire*, which, according to the councilmen of São Paulo, was a disincentive to trade. In response, the São Paulo Council demanded that its Santos counterpart raise the price of wheat flour to 320 réis per *alqueire*.[83]

In sum, Indian porters provided settlers with a generally efficient and economical mode of transport. At mid-century, even producers with relatively little Indian labor at their disposal could send their wheat flour to market in Santos. This situation began to change in the last decades of the century, when the wheat trade, due mainly to the crisis in the supply of Indian labor, began to decline dramatically. At the same time, the distances involved in the occupation and exploitation of new lands that were increasingly distant from the towns of São Paulo and Parnaíba restricted wheat production and transport in these areas to those producers who possessed large slaveholdings or who had sufficient resources to meet rising freight costs. Concurrently, the Santos market began to reveal its limitations. In 1672, for example, the accounts of one producer showed losses on an unspecified amount of "wheat flours [*sic*] that were in the Port of Santos, to be sent to Rio de Janeiro because they could not be sold in the Port of Santos."[84] Wheat sellers could thus find themselves in an increasingly precarious state of dependency on the irregular flow of intra-colonial trade.

While one consequence of these new conditions was an increase in the concentration of wealth in the region, a more serious, generalized effect was the abandonment of wheat growing by most agriculturalists. A survey of inventories from the period indicates that in the 1670s rural producers began to show a renewed interest in cattle raising, particularly in older areas, where one or two generations of farming had adversely affected soil productivity. This suggests a transfer of resources to activities that were less labor-intensive. Even so, the region's dependence on forced Indian labor persisted, despite most settlers having given up on commercial agriculture.

A noteworthy example of the transfer of resources – and of the decline of the seventeenth-century Paulista economy – is provided by the personal trajectory of Fernão Dias Pais. An experienced backwoodsman, beginning in the 1650s Fernão Dias dedicated himself to wheat farming on his vast estate near Santana de Parnaíba, populated by a large parcel of Indians he had brought from the *sertão*. According to the Municipal Council of Parnaíba, at one point he turned annual profits of 2,000 to 3,000 *cruzados* (800–1,200 milréis). However, perhaps due to the epidemics that ravaged the indigenous population of the plateau in the 1660s, Fernão Dias shifted practically all of his wealth to the search for emerald mines in the interior beginning in 1674. With the Indians he enslaved there, he was indeed able to establish a populous camp (*arraial*) in the area that later became Minas

Gerais. However, by the time of his death in 1681, his prosperity was only a memory. At that point he owed nearly 3,000 milréis to his cousins Fernão Pais de Barros and João Monteiro, and to Gonçalo Lopes, the wealthiest merchant in São Paulo at the time.[85] His case, among many others, shows how quickly the wheat trade was losing ground in the second half of the century, destined as it was to disappear along with the once numerous population of captive Indians.

The rapid rise and no less sudden decline of commercial wheat production in São Paulo is a little-known episode in the economic history of colonial Brazil, no doubt due to the apparently modest amounts of revenue it generated. Some estate-owners and merchants grew rich from the surpluses generated by Indian labor, but no great, lasting colonial fortunes were made in this way. In comparative terms, the aggregate wealth produced in the captaincy of São Vicente at the time of its greatest commercial output placed it a distant fourth among Brazilian captaincies, as indicated by the assessments of the Donativo Real tax for 1662, which established an obligation of 32,000 milréis for Bahia, 10,400 for Rio de Janeiro, 10,000 for Pernambuco, and only 1,600 for São Vicente.[86]

Nevertheless, a comparison of the aggregate wealth of the regional economy of São Vicente to that of major sugar-producing regions that were thoroughly integrated into the Atlantic economy reveals only one side of the story. Examined in its local and regional contexts, the experiment with commercial agriculture had a fundamental role in the creation of the structures that defined colonial São Paulo and the world that the Paulistas made.

Notes

1. Frei Gaspar da Madre de Deus to Governor Lorena, Mar. 6, 1792, BNL-Pombalina, cód. 643. Here, once again, the "State" referred to in the documentation encompassed Portugal's New World colonies as a unit, rather than the captaincy of São Vicente/São Paulo, embryo of the federal state of São Paulo.
2. Frei Gaspar da Madre de Deus, *Memórias para a história da capitania de São Vicente, hoje chamada São Paulo*, 2nd edn. (Belo Horizonte: Itatiaia, 1975 [1797]), 83.
3. On the growth and development of sugar-cane agriculture in colonial Brazil, see Stuart B. Schwartz's excellent study, *Sugar Plantations in the Formation of Brazilian Society: Bahia, 1550–1835* (Cambridge University Press, 1985), esp. parts I and II.
4. CMSP-Atas, 1:211–212, June 15, 1583.
5. CMSP-Atas, 1:99–100, 106–107, and passim, Sept. 30, 1576.
6. CMSP-Atas, 1:421–422, June 15, 1591. For a discussion of the *tingui* method, see Holanda, *Caminhos e fronteiras*, 81–82. A similar conflict emerged in Sorocaba in the early eighteenth century, when its Municipal Council launched an investigation into the contamination of local rivers by *tingui*. "Auto de inquirição," AESP-AC, cx. 26, no. 440.
7. The grants of these lands are published in *Cartas de datas de terra*, vol. 1, passim.

8. In 1603, the chapel of Nossa Senhora da Luz was transferred from Ipiranga to its current location, near the historic center of the city of São Paulo, then called Guaré. "Auto de tombo," Sept. 4, 1603, AMDDLS, Livro de tombo da paróquia da Sé, 1747. This document clearly equates Guaré to Piratininga, though historians have identified the latter with other locations. Wilson Maia Fina, for example, in his meticulous work *O chão de Piratininga* (São Paulo: Anhambí, 1965), places Piratininga to the north of the Tietê River, near what is now the Tremembé district of the city.
9. Municipal lands were usually measured in *braças*, which I have converted at 2.2 meters per *braça*. See Joel Serrão (ed.), *Dicionário de história portuguesa*, 5 vols., published in various edns., entry "Pesos e Medidas."
10. Paes Leme, in his *Nobiliarquia paulistana*, 1:113, indicates that Proença was married in Santos.
11. Solid examples from the first decade of the seventeenth century include the inventories of Fernão Dias (1605), Francisco Barreto (1607), and Isabel Fernandes (1607), in IT, vols. 1, 2, and 5. Barreto had been tithe collector for the captaincy, which means that his relocation to São Paulo may be seen as evidence of the shift in the productive focus of the colony from the coast to the plateau. The extent of Fernão Dias's influence in the areas along the Pinheiros River may be appraised from the beautiful maps made by Nicolau Alekhine in his exhaustive, but unpublished and practically unknown, work on public lands in the municipality of São Paulo, held by the regional archive of the SPHAN/Pró-Memória.
12. These conflicts are treated in greater detail in Chapter 4.
13. Property transfers were registered in the *Livros de notas*, the few surviving seventeenth-century examples of which are in terrible condition. The most complete series consulted for this study were those of Parnaíba (AESP-Notas Parnaíba) and Jundiaí (Cartório do Primeiro Ofício, Jundiaí).
14. For a more or less comprehensive list of the *sesmarias* granted in the first half of the century, see Monteiro, "São Paulo in the Seventeenth Century," 398–415. See also the incomplete listing by João Batista de Campos Aguirra, "Relação das sesmarias concedidas na comarca da capital entre os anos de 1559 a 1820," *RIHGSP* 25 (1927): 493–567.
15. CMSP-Registro, 1:364. With the passage of time, measurements assumed greater precision, and in the 1630s the Municipal Council found it necessary to name Pedro Rodrigues Guerreiro "surveyor of all the lands seeing that he is a man of the sea and understands the bearing of the needle since it is a post necessary for the common good of this people." CMSP-Atas, 4:306, July 19, 1636.
16. Discussion of this issue continues in Chapter 6.
17. IT, esp. vols. 1–7.
18. *Sesmaria* of Feb. 19, 1617, in Departamento do Arquivo do Estado de São Paulo, *Sesmarias*, 3 vols. in 5 (São Paulo: Archivo/Arquivo do Estado, 1921–1940), 1:225.
19. CMSP-Atas, 5:365–366, Mar. 16, 1649.
20. Quoted in *sesmaria* of Aug. 28, 1639, in Departamento do Arquivo do Estado de São Paulo, *Sesmarias*, 1:392.
21. *Sesmaria* of Oct. 10, 1641, in Departamento do Arquivo do Estado de São Paulo, *Sesmarias*, 1:471.
22. Paes Leme, *Nobiliarquia paulistana*, 1:269.

23. Joana do Prado v. Antonio Pais de Queiroz, Auto civil de 1680, AESP, cx. 357, no. 107.
24. "Petição dos moradores e povoadores para a formação da vila," Registro do foral da vila de Mogi das Cruzes, Arquivo da Prefeitura de Mogi das Cruzes. This volume contains copies of various documents that refer to the founding of Mogi das Cruzes that were transcribed in 1748 from originals that have since been lost. See also Isaac Grinberg, *Gaspar Vaz, fundador de Mogi das Cruzes* (São Paulo: by the author, 1980).
25. Ecclesiastical Census of the Bishopric of Rio de Janeiro, n.d., ACMRJ, uncatalogued. I am grateful to Wanderley dos Santos, formerly director of the Arquivo da Cúria Metropolitana de São Paulo, for providing me with a summary of this important document.
26. CMSP-Atas, 1:423–424, July 7, 1591.
27. The early history of the town is covered in Paulo Florêncio da Silveira Camargo's *História de Santana de Parnaíba* (São Paulo: Conselho Estadual de Cultura, 1971), which remains noteworthy despite its many errors. See also Alida Metcalf, *Family and Frontier in Colonial Brazil: Santana de Parnaíba, 1580–1822* (Berkeley: University of California Press, 1992), which – its subtitle notwithstanding – focuses on the eighteenth century.
28. CMSP-Atas, 2:486, Oct. 15, 1622; inventory of Antonio Furtado de Vasconcelos, Parnaíba, 1628, IT, 7:23.
29. Will and inventory of Antonia de Oliveira, Parnaíba, 1632, IT, 8:309–334.
30. In seeking to explain the rapid emergence of new towns in seventeenth-century São Vicente, historians have identified different motivating factors. Traditional Paulista historiography characterizes the founding of these new towns as "expeditions of colonization" (*bandeiras de colonização*) that followed logically upon the collective enterprises that focused on slave-hunting prior to 1640. See, for example, Myriam Ellis, "O bandeirantismo." Without completely breaking with this tradition, Sérgio Buarque de Holanda sought an explanation for seventeenth-century shifts in settlement in demographic factors in his magisterial, if misleadingly titled, essay, "Movimentos da população em São Paulo no século XVIII," *Revista do Instituto de Estudos Brasileiros* 1 (1966): 55–111. More recently, in *Household Economy and Urban Development: São Paulo, 1765 to 1836* (Boulder, CO: Westview Press, 1986), Elizabeth Kuznesof provides an interesting interpretation that associates the migration that lay behind the founding of new towns with the unstable character of settlement and the factional disputes that punctuated the colonial history of São Paulo, though she makes the mistake of identifying the founding of Parnaíba with the struggle between the Pires and Camargo families. See also the interesting approach in Metcalf, *Family and Frontier*, which highlights the importance of family strategies in the settlement of the region.
31. On the municipal councils, a topic still wanting for innovative studies, see the exploratory essays by Charles R. Boxer, *Portuguese Society in the Tropics: The Municipal Councils of Goa, Macau, Bahia, and Luanda, 1510–1800* (Madison: University of Wisconsin Press, 1965), 72–109; A. J. R. Russell-Wood, "Local Government in Portuguese America: A Study in Cultural Divergence," *Comparative Studies in Society and History* 16/2 (Mar. 1974): 187–231; and Edmundo Zenha, *O município no Brasil, 1552–1700* (São Paulo: Progresso, 1948).
32. On inheritance and the division of estates among eligible heirs (*partilha*) in colonial São Paulo, and Parnaíba in particular, see the excellent study by Alida Metcalf, "Fathers and Sons: The Politics of Inheritance in a Colonial Brazilian Township," *Hispanic American*

Historical Review 66/3 (Aug. 1986): 455–484; as well as A. J. R. Russell-Wood, "Women and Society in Colonial Brazil," *Journal of Latin American Studies* 9/1 (May 1977): 1–34.

33. "Petição dos moradores," 1611 (1748 transcription), Arquivo da Prefeitura de Mogi das Cruzes.
34. The circumstances surrounding the founding of Jundiaí have been the subject of much controversy among Paulista historians. In the nineteenth century, when the chronicler Azevedo Marques reprinted a section of the parish's *livro de tombo* that attributed the founding of the original chapel in 1651 to the fugitives Rafael de Oliveira and Petronilha Antunes, a typographical error inverted the date to 1615, an error that was reproduced in the official emblems adopted by the city Jundiaí in the twentieth century. As far as the crime that supposedly led the founders to flee from justice is concerned, scholars hold that it was a reference to the "crime" of hunting indigenous captives, a crime of which almost all Paulistas were guilty. It is worth emphasizing, however, that Jundiaí was a known refuge for various criminal fugitives, including Pedro Leme do Prado and Fernão "o Tigre" (the Tiger) Camargo, the killers of Pedro Taques, and maintained that reputation until the middle of the eighteenth century. It is possible that Pedro Leme do Prado – who was related to Rafael de Oliveira by marriage – participated in the founding of the chapel, as Paes Leme, *Nobiliarquia paulistana* (3:13) indicates that he was the founder of a chapel with the name Nossa Senhora da Estrela (perhaps a faulty transcription of Desterro) around 1645. In any case, the origins of the town were without a doubt linked to the factional conflicts that characterized São Paulo in the 1650s, which supports Kuznesof's general hypothesis (see note 30, above, this chapter). Azevedo Marques, *Apontamentos históricos*, entry "Jundiahy"; Mário Mazzuia, *Jundiaí e sua história* (Jundiaí: Prefeitura Municipal, 1979); and "Documentos sobre a fundação de Jundiaí," manuscript collection of the Instituto Histórico e Geográfico de São Paulo.
35. "Cartas de datas de terras," 1656–1657, Museu Histórico e Cultural de Jundiaí, uncatalogued.
36. "Atas da Câmara Municipal de Jundiaí," 1663–1669, Museu Histórico e Cultural de Jundiaí, uncatalogued.
37. "Cartas de datas de terras," Jundiaí, fols. 43v–44.
38. Municipal Council of São Paulo to the Pope, n.d., ARSI-FG, Missiones 721/I. In general, wheat cultivation has attracted little scholarly attention to this point. See, for example, Afonso d'Escragnolle Taunay, *Trigaes paulistanos dos seculos XVI e XVII* (São Paulo: Secretaria da Agricultura, Industria e Commercio, 1929); Sérgio Milliet, "Trigais de São Paulo," in his *Roteiro do café e outros ensaios*, 2nd edn. (São Paulo: Hucitec, 1982 [1939]), 147–151; and Holanda, *Caminhos e fronteiras*, 205–214. In a revised edition of a classic study first published in 1945, Holanda re-evaluated his earlier position on Paulista agriculture, but he maintained the conclusion that "wheat . . . did not reveal itself to be here [in São Paulo] the dynamic element that sugar would later become, and coffee much later." See *Monções*, 3rd edn. (São Paulo: Brasiliense, 1990 [1945]), 177.
39. Holanda, *Caminhos e fronteiras*, 215–225.
40. Inventory of Valentim de Barros, Parnaíba, 1651, IT, 15:226. Other sources suggest that the Indians, particularly the Guarani, refused to eat wheat bread, preferring corn.

In the missions of Guairá, for instance, the Jesuits attempted to introduce wheat to support the reduced population, but faced with the resistance of the Indians they began to produce the grain on a commercial basis, sending modest amounts to the European outposts of the Platine region. See Magnus Mörner, *The Political and Economic Activities of the Jesuits in the La Plata Region: The Hapsburg Era* (Stockholm: Institute of Ibero-American Studies, 1953). This assertion is echoed by Holanda, in the revised edition of *Monções*, 172.

41. See, for example, CMSP-Atas, 3:63, Dec. 2, 1623; 4:336–337, Feb. 22, 1637; and 6a:127, Apr. 12, 1659.
42. Among others, see the dowry that André Fernandes provided for his niece Suzana Dias, Jan. 27, 1641, AESP-Notas Parnaíba, 1641; the gambling debts appear in the inventory of Pascoal Neto, 1637, IT, 11:139.
43. Antonio Pinto, cited in Leite, *História*, 6:282. Carracks (*naus* in Portuguese) were large, three- or four-masted sailing ships, built to carry sizeable loads of merchandise while armed for war.
44. The inventory of Maria Bicudo (1660, IT, 16) shows credits for wheat sales in Bahia. While it is unlikely that wheat was ever shipped to Angola, Paulistas did send other local products, such as cured meats and cane brandy. For example, about one-third of the estate of Manuel de Oliveira was tied up in shipments of goods to Angola. Inventory of Isabel Borges, 1655, AESP-IE, cx. 3, doc. 7.
45. Provisioning the colony with wheat remained a problem through the entire period of Portuguese rule. In the eighteenth century, after the collapse of production in São Paulo, the Crown attempted to solve the problem with a colonization scheme involving Azorean couples, who were to cultivate wheat in southern Brazil and provision the rest of the colony. For details, see Charles R. Boxer, *The Golden Age of Brazil, 1695–1750: Growing Pains of a Colonial Society* (Berkeley: University of California Press, 1962), 246–254. On the production of wheat in Rio Grande do Sul during the eighteenth century, see the interesting study by Corcino Medeiros dos Santos, *Economia e sociedade do Rio Grande do Sul* (São Paulo: Nacional, 1984).
46. Examples of these requests may be found in Salvador, *Os cristãos novos e o comércio*, 88–89. See also Antonio de Couros Carneiro (Governor of Ilheus) to the Conselho Ultramarino, Apr. 11, 1647, AHU-Bahia, doc. 1266; Pedro Vilhasanti to the Crown, Nov. 14, 1638, AHU-Bahia, doc. 810; Municipal Council of Rio de Janeiro to Municipal Council of São Paulo, June 12, 1648, AHMSP, Avulsos, cx. 4; Provisão of General Salvador de Sá, CMSP-Registro, 2:70–71; Provisão of Municipal Council of São Vicente, Nov. 20, 1654, BNRJ-DH, 4:33–34; and vol. 3 of BNRJ-DH, passim.
47. Inventory of João Martins de Sousa, Parnaíba, AESP-INP, cx. 9, 1666.
48. "Informe de Manuel Juan de Morales de las cosas de San Pablo y maldades de sus moradores," 1636, in *Mss. de Angelis*, 1:182–193. The *alqueire* is a unit of dry measure equivalent to approximately 13.8 liters, as well as a unit of planted land, theoretically equivalent to the amount of grain a given plot could yield.
49. João de Gois e Araújo, "Informação sobre o rendimento dos dízimos do Brasil," Aug. 19, 1661, BNL, cx. 208, doc. 16.
50. CMSP-Atas, 6a:485–487, Apr. 23, 1666. According to Maria de Lourdes Viana Lyra, "Os dízimos reais na capitania de São Paulo: contribuição à história tributária do Brasil colonial, 1640–1750" (dissertação de mestrado, Universidade de São Paulo, 1971), in

1665 Lourenço Castanho Tacques bought the contract for the township of São Paulo for 2,400 milréis.

51. In the inventories, *foices de segar* were assigned values of between 20 and 120 réis, though the most common value was 40. The technical aspects of colonial Paulista agriculture are explained in detail in Holanda, *Caminhos e fronteiras*, 183–250, and *Monções*, 163–206.
52. Similar observations have been made in studies of wheat farming in colonial North America. See James Henretta, *The Evolution of American Society, 1700–1815* (Lexington MA: D. C. Heath, 1973), 15–18, for a summary.
53. Jácome Monteiro, "Relação da província do Brasil, 1610," in Leite, *História*, 8:396. A technique for estimating grain yields from estate inventories may be found in Mark Overton, "Estimating Crop Yields From Probate Inventories: An Example from East Anglia, 1585–1735," *Journal of Economic History* 39/2 (June 1979): 363–378. Unfortunately, the data from São Paulo are vastly inferior to those for early modern England.
54. Schwartz, *Sugar Plantations*, chaps. 2–3.
55. Inventory of Isabel de Proença, 1648, IT, 37:103–104. Another indication that this sexual division of labor was adopted by Paulista landowners comes from an eighteenth-century inventory, where on a medium-sized farm featuring African slave labor, the male slaves were listed as absent in the mines while female slaves were assigned to the *roça*. Inventory of Pascoal Leite Penteado, 1712, AESP-IPO, 14.020.
56. Egon Schaden, *Aspectos fundamentais da cultura guarani* (São Paulo: Universidade de São Paulo, 1974), 74.
57. Schwartz shows that the composition of Indian slaveholdings on late sixteenth-century sugar plantations in Bahia was similar to that of their African counterparts of the following century, both of which were marked by the predominance of young males. Schwartz, *Sugar Plantations*, chap. 3.
58. Inventory of Domingos da Rocha do Canto, Parnaíba, AESP-IE, cx. 3, doc. 17. A similar process occurred in colonial Venezuela, where wheat farmers switched from the *encomienda* system of forced Indian labor to African slavery in the seventeenth century. Robert J. Ferry, "Encomienda, African Slavery, and Agriculture in Seventeenth-Century Caracas," *Hispanic American Historical Review* 61/4 (Nov. 1981): 609–635. It should be noted, however, that the expansion of wheat production in São Paulo was accompanied by a rapid growth in the supply of indigenous labor stemming from peculiar strategies of labor recruitment, while in Venezuela the Indian population shrank as the economy grew, tightening the supply of indigenous labor and making African slavery more attractive.
59. "Escritura de venda de um sítio com moinho," Baltasar Fernandes to Paulo Proença de Abreu, 1658, AESP-Notas Parnaíba, cx. 6076–28. Sugar mills sold in Rio de Janeiro during the first half of the seventeenth century usually commanded between 2,000 and 10,000 *milréis*. Arquivo Nacional do Rio de Janeiro, Notas Rio de Janeiro, cx. 1–2. In the 1630s, Bahia's Engenho Sergipe do Conde, one of the colony's largest, was valued at 40,000 milréis, while several mills in Pernambuco commanded similar sums. See "Descrezão da fazenda que o Collegio de Santo Antão tem no Brazil e de seus rendimentos, pelo Padre Estevam Pereira, S. J. (1635)," AMP 4 (1931): 778; and Mello (ed.), *Fontes para a história*.

60. Examples of licenses to operate mills (to João Fernandes Saiavedra, Cornélio de Arzão, Manuel João Branco, and Amador Bueno da Ribeira) may be found in CMSP-Atas, 2:363, 374–378. The Carmelites of São Paulo, Parnaíba, and Mogi das Cruzes also received licenses to mill wheat in the seventeenth century.
61. "Sentença sobre um moinho," in Jaime Cortesão (ed.), *Pauliceae lusitana monumenta historica*, 2 vols. (Rio de Janeiro: Real Gabinete Português de Leitura, 1956–1961), 2:25–27, doc. 5.
62. On the distribution of wealth, see Chapter 6.
63. CMSP-Atas, 2:369, Dec. 26, 1615; 2:404–405, Feb. 9 and 23, 1619.
64. For a description of some of the trails within the township of Parnaíba, see "Auto de medição do rocio de Parnaíba," AESP-AC, cx. 14, doc. 212.
65. The inventory of Pascoal da Penha included two canoes, one with a capacity of 40 *cargas*, the other with a capacity of 60 (one *carga* equaled two *alqueires*), while Paulo Proença de Abreu was the declared owner of three canoes with capacities of 30, 40, and 50 *cargas* at the time of his wife's death. Inventory of Pascoal da Penha, Parnaíba, 1656, AESP-INP, cx. 3; Benta Dias, Parnaíba, 1658, AESP-INP, cx. 1.
66. Salvador, *Os cristãos novos e o comércio*, 95, affirms that Cornélio de Arzão (the Fleming who is credited with introducing wheat to the captaincy of São Vicente) received a *sesmaria* in Cubatão in the 1620s for the purpose of storing grain and other goods sent down from the plateau. Also in the 1620s, the inventory of Domingos de Abreu shows large amounts of cured meats "placed at Cubatão." IT, 6:345.
67. CMSP-Atas, 6a:361, Apr. 7, 1664.
68. Antonio Raposo Silveira to the Crown, Dec. 1656, AHU-SP, doc. 12. On the reconstruction of the road in the late eighteenth century, see Elizabeth Anne Kuznesof, "The Role of the Merchants in the Economic Development of São Paulo, 1765–1836," *Hispanic American Historical Review* 60/4 (Nov. 1980): 571–592.
69. CMSP-Atas, 6a:485–487, Apr. 23, 1666; CMSP-Atas, 6:13, Feb. 19, 1655. In addition to playing an important role in Indian beliefs, jaguars were a real threat to Indians and backwoodsmen alike, both in the wilderness and around settlements; indeed, one of the most feared Indian-hunters, Manuel Preto, escaped all of the arrows and curses that the Guarani and Jesuits aimed at him, only to end his career in a jaguar's claws. See the interesting discussion in Holanda, *Caminhos e fronteiras*, 108ff.
70. Will of Francisco Pinto Guedes, 1701, AESP-IPO, 13.998.
71. On the size of the *carga*, which may have varied slightly throughout the century, see IT, 37:107. In 1730, the governor of São Paulo noted that the Jesuits tended to underload their Indians at 2 *arrobas*, while charging excessive rates for their services as porters. Governor Pimentel to Conselho Ultramarino, May 1, 1730, AHU-SP, doc. 712.
72. Antonio Pompeu to Paulo Proença de Abreu, Feb. 20, 1639, in inventory of Antonio Furtado, Parnaíba, 1627, IT, 7:25. For images of Guarani baskets used in transport, see the photographs in Schaden, *Aspectos fundamentais*.
73. CMSP-Registro, 1:202; and Holanda, *Caminhos e fronteiras*, 150–151.
74. For example, inventories of João de Camargo Ortiz, 1672, AESP-INP, cx. 12; Domingos Leme, 1673, IT, 18; Felipa de Almeida, AESP-INP, cx. 15; and Ines Pedrosa, 1677, AESP-INP, cx. 22.
75. Antonio Ruiz de Montoya, "Primeira catequese dos indios selvagens," BNRJ-Anais, 6: 235–236.

76. "Voto do Padre Antonio Vieira sobre as dúvidas dos moradores da cidade [sic] de São Paulo," July 12, 1692, IEB, Coleção Lamengo, 42.3.
77. Luís Mamiani, "Memorial sobre o Colégio de São Paulo," ARSI-FG, Collegia 1588/203/12, doc. 6, fol. 1.
78. Inventory of Pedro Nunes, 1623, IT, 6:55–58.
79. Inventory of Isabel Fernandes, Parnaíba, 1647, IT, 35:107–108.
80. Inventory of Domingos Luis, 1613, IT, 3:87.
81. Inventory of Gaspar Correia, 1647, IT, 35:38.
82. CMSP-Atas, 7:545–546, Aug. 3, 1700; Governor Pimentel to Conselho Ultramarino, May 1, 1730, AHU-SP, doc. 712; also, AHU-SP, doc. 751.
83. CMSP-Atas, 4:153–154, Jan. 24, 1633. The councilmen's argument was flawed, as they neglected to consider that each Indian could carry two *alqueires* in a single *carga*, and that ordinarily they returned laden with merchandise, the freight cost of which was absorbed by Santos merchants.
84. Partilha amigável (out-of-probate-court settlement) of João Rodrigues Bejarano, 1672, AESP-AC, cx. 1.
85. "Atestado da Câmara Municipal de Parnaíba sobre Fernão Dias Pais," Dec. 20, 1681, in Azevedo Marques, *Apontamentos históricos*, 1:267–269. Paes Leme, *Nobiliarquia paulistana*, 3:64–65, describes Fernão Dias's prosperous estate.
86. Provisão of Apr. 28, 1662, BNRJ-DH, 5:346.

4
The Regime of Personal Service

"In Brazil," observed Frei Gaspar da Madre de Deus, "where to all was given freely more land than they needed and in such quantities as colonists requested, no one ever needed to work another's property, obligating themselves to the payment of annual rents." However, he continued, "in this State he who does not engage in trade or lacks slaves lives in the greatest indigence; and furthermore, for someone to be rich, it is not enough to possess many slaves, for these are of no use to their masters if the latter are not industrious themselves, and do not personally oversee the said slaves."[1]

Abundant lands and a concomitant need for slaves, with these optimally under the personal supervision of their master: this formula certainly had much do to with the making of colonial Brazilian society. However, it falls short of a satisfactory explanation of the evolution, dynamics, and economic viability of a slave society. After all, it is important to remember that the origin of slavery in Brazil – Indian and African – was found in the articulation of a colonial system that sought to create and expropriate agricultural and extractive surpluses to be transformed into commercial wealth. Nonetheless, Frei Gaspar's observations should not be taken lightly, because in addition to constituting a set of relations of production, slavery represented a pervasive way of looking at the world, one which often functioned independently of the dictates of the Atlantic economy. In every corner of Brazil, slavery became the measure of society.[2]

In discussing the Paulista version of colonial slavery, one faces the additional task of explaining why and how *Indian* slavery developed into the dominant form of production. Inevitably, this set of questions leads to at least implicit comparisons with African slavery in Brazil, which is better documented and has been more fully studied. In making these comparisons, historians have focused on the profound cultural differences between Amerindians and Africans while neglecting the basic commonality, which was, of course, slavery.[3] Seen from the latter perspective, the basic structural features of colonial society in São Paulo do not seem so distinct from those of the sugar-producing zones.

As we have seen in the preceding chapters, in seventeenth-century São Paulo, Indian slavery grew out of the same sources as African slavery on the coast and revolved around similar kinds of economic exploitation. However, because of existing legal and moral restrictions on Indian slavery, the Paulistas had to go to much greater lengths than their Bahian and Pernambucan counterparts in attempting to rationalize and justify their dominion over their captives. Employing increasingly elaborate arguments, the Paulistas came to demand under the law that which they already exercised in fact: absolute control over Indian labor and personhood. However, this was no easy task, for in addition to confronting the hardened opposition of the Jesuits, whom they eventually expelled from the captaincy, the Paulistas also had to carry out a series of diplomatic entreaties aimed at convincing the Crown to uphold and preserve a peculiar form of slavery.

The Creation of a Pro-Slavery Worldview

From the beginnings of Portuguese colonization, the development of Indian slavery as a minimally stable institution faced serious obstacles. The stubborn resistance of indigenous peoples, the unyielding opposition of the Jesuits, and the ambiguous position of the Crown on the Indian question: all stood in the way of the settlers' access to Indian labor. Step by step, the colonists of the São Paulo region confronted and overcame these obstacles, gradually shaping a well-articulated system of production based on Indian servitude. The first obstacle fell in the sixteenth century, with the decimation of the local Tupi population and the expulsion of the Guaianá and Guarulhos from areas of projected European settlement. The second would fall in the first half of the seventeenth century, when pro-slavery interests prevailed over those of the Jesuits, as a series of smaller conflicts culminated in the tumultuous expulsion of the priests in 1640. Only the third was never fully overcome by the Paulistas, as the Crown maintained its somewhat ambiguous position in the formulation and execution of Indian policy. Yet even in this sphere, through a well-crafted political and legal struggle, the Paulistas succeeded in outlining the institutional contours that would legitimize Indian slavery.

The elements of conflict between competing colonial interests, which had already surfaced in the sixteenth century, began to assume greater intensity as that century came to an end and the flow of new captives to the plateau increased. What was fundamentally at stake was the fate of Indians brought from the *sertão*. The Jesuit position was that these Indians should be incorporated into mission villages, after which their labor would be distributed to individual settlers on a contractual basis. On the other hand, the settlers – who, after all, had introduced the vast majority of Indians at their own expense – sought to appropriate for themselves the right of direct administration over these Indians, using the powers of the Municipal Council of São Paulo to attain this objective.

Initially, however, the Council wavered on the question of how newly arrived Indians should be administered. Thus, for example, in 1587, after an expedition led by Domingos Luís returned to the town with a large number of Tupinaé captives, the councilmen thought it best to send the Indians to a mission village, in spite of settler pleas to the contrary. Their decision, however, was not a verdict on the settlers' economic interest in captive labor. Rather, it responded to the question of how best to defend the colony, as the town was threatened by indigenous groups who were resistant to conquest and enslavement.[4] Only in the 1590s, when the Portuguese presence was more secure, would the Council adopt an explicitly pro-slavery position on the Indian question, which placed it in opposition to the mission-village project and, by extension, against the Jesuits themselves.

An important factor in aggravating conflicts over the Indian question in São Paulo was an increase in the meddling of the Crown and its local representatives. In 1592, the arrival of a new governor of the captaincy of São Vicente exacerbated existing conflict. The position taken by Governor Jorge Correia diverged completely from those of his predecessors, who, of course, had encouraged offensive war and Indian slavery, as was clear in the case of Governor Jerônimo Leitão in the 1580s. In fact, shortly after setting foot in Brazil, Jorge Correia ordered that the Indians be turned over to the Jesuits, which provoked an immediate, vehement response from the principal settlers of São Paulo, who called a public meeting before the Municipal Council. In this meeting, while initially excusing the governor "for being newly arrived from the kingdom and not having grasped the way of the land and its needs," the settlers did not shrink from demonstrating their displeasure. Though willing to accept that the Jesuits might continue to "indoctrinate and teach [the Indians] in the way that they always have," the settlers objected to the prospect of rigid and exclusive Jesuit control over the working population, "in view of it being very harmful to the community and not in the service of his majesty." According to the settlers, the Indians themselves "are not pleased that possession of them should be given to said priests nor any other person if they are not to live as they have been living until now." Though a few voices were raised in favor of the Jesuits, the main thrust of the meeting was a clear warning that any Jesuit interference in settler control of Indian labor would be met with serious opposition.[5]

The royal decree of July 26, 1596 attempted to resolve this conflict by defining the role of the Jesuits more clearly. According to this decree, it would fall to the priests to bring uncontacted groups from the interior to areas closer to Portuguese settlements, where they would perform the task of "domesticating" the Indians in segregated villages. The Indian, in turn, would "be master of his own property" and could serve the settlers for no more than two months at a time in exchange for a just salary for his labor. In addition, the position of the Judge of the Indians (*juíz dos índios*) was created, with jurisdiction in both civil and criminal law.[6] In sum, the decree of 1596 merely formalized the mission-village project, seeking to bolster a set of arrangements that was already clearly in decline, particularly in São Paulo.

In spite of the Crown's efforts to guarantee a Jesuit monopoly on access to Indian labor, the colonists were able to circumvent these measures through the Municipal Council. Indeed, the settlers proved adept at negotiating questions of jurisdiction inherent to the administrative structure of the colony. These jurisdictional questions emerged in conflicts between the Crown bureaucracy and proprietary privilege, on the one hand, and between royal authority and municipal autonomy, on the other. In this context, the Municipal Council of São Paulo little by little gained a stronger position in the struggle over Indian labor. In 1600, for example, the Council determined that the Judge of the Indians designated in the 1596 decree only had jurisdiction over Indians brought from the *sertão* by the Jesuits, as a selective reading of the decree could restrict its application to the Indians residing in the mission villages of São Miguel, Pinheiros, and Conceição dos Guarulhos, who were already a minority of the indigenous population of the region. At the same time, the Council reaffirmed the authority over Indians exercised by "ordinary judges" (*juízes ordinários*) chosen from among the councilmen and by the *bairro* captains they also named, reaffirming the privileges laid out in Martim Afonso de Sousa's charter of 1534.[7] Three weeks later, the Council allotted some Indians to João Fernandes, "because he was a poor man," an action that ran unmistakably counter to the royal disposition of 1596.[8]

As the settlers increasingly appropriated control over the incoming population of indigenous captives, they also sought institutional legitimation for the relations of domination that underlay their exploitation of Indian labor. Indeed, they hardened their view of the necessity of forced native labor after 1600 as they came to realize the scale of the challenges they would face in achieving even modest economic growth on the plateau, challenges that were far more daunting than the Jesuits' arguments in favor of Indian liberty. Lacking capital and access to credit, the settlers recognized that the large-scale importation of African slaves would be impossible. At the same time, they came up against the rugged Serra do Mar, which made transport difficult and costly, especially for the relatively low-value commodities that were to issue from the rural properties of the plateau. In short, for the Paulistas to participate in the larger colonial economy, they would need to produce and transport a marketable surplus so cheaply that its low sale price on the coast would still make the enterprise a profitable one. The solution, as we have seen, lay in the relentless exploitation of thousands of Indian field hands and porters brought from other regions.

No one at any point doubted that Indians would form the principal base of all colonial production in São Paulo. Nonetheless, the question of where formal authority over the Indian population lay was not so easily resolved, despite the settlers having triumphed over their adversaries in practical terms, establishing as a matter of fact that they could and would create, control, and sustain the labor force. On ideological and legal grounds, however, their position vis-à-vis Jesuits and the Crown was far less secure. As long as moral or legal objections to forced native labor existed, the reproduction of the relations of production upon which the settlers depended faced the continual threat of disruption from extra-economic forces. Therefore it was of supreme importance that the settlers constantly justify before the Crown the absolute need for and positive benefits of the personal service of the Indians, which they linked to the very survival of the colony.

Evidence of the Paulistas' distinctive viewpoint on the Indian question appears here and there in different types of seventeenth-century documentation, above all in wills. However, the most coherent, yet concise statement of the settlers' outlook appears in a report compiled in the 1690s by Bartolomeu Lopes de Carvalho, a Crown representative who visited the southern captaincies to gather information "especially about the Indians conquered and reduced to captivity by the residents of S. Paulo."[9] Drawing on what the colonists told him firsthand, Carvalho ended up providing a faithful rendition of how they regarded their society and economy, and even of how they perceived their past.

In his report, after recalling that the Paulistas had performed "many great services to God and Your Majesty, may whom God save, in the conquest of the Indians," Carvalho turned to explaining the historic rights that the Portuguese had to Indian lands in Brazil. He claimed that at the time of the Portuguese arrival in the New World the Indians were "the true lords and owners" of the land, but after contact, "with them peace and friendship were established by pact in which they gave us the right that we have today over their lands." This right, enhanced by the fact that the Europeans had a "rational politic" and a superior religion, was justified by the dissemination of the Catholic faith, seen as sufficient recompense for the appropriation of Indian land and labor, a belief manifested time and again in settlers' wills. This benevolent spirit was exemplified, according to the report, by the occupation of São Vicente, where the first settlers had lived in "calmness, friendship, and ease" with the "tame" Indians brought from the interior by the Jesuits.

For the settlers, it was the rupture of this friendly and tranquil situation by hostile Indians that elicited the practical need and moral justification for slavery. "Wild" Indians had begun to attack Portuguese settlements because of the hatred they harbored for the "tame" Indians allied to the Portuguese and "in the exercise of their savagery for being accustomed to continuous wars in order to capture people and butcher them for their sustenance." The whites, set upon from all sides and unable to peacefully convert these peoples to the Christian faith because of "their great savagery and brutality," found it necessary to subdue them by force of arms, as well as "to enslave some of these heathens whom they brought to [areas of] settlement and made use of in their farming, instructing them as Catholics for them to be baptized as they always did."

Enslavement was thus justified by the traditional practice of subjugating infidels who consciously rejected the Catholic faith, a point of key relevance in that it adhered to the principles of just war set down by Catholic kings and popes. Therefore, the "barbarous nations," equated to infidels because they were up in arms against Christians, had to be subdued by force. At the same time, even the "tame" Indians," those who "by their free will sought the bosom of the church," would have to labor on behalf of the settlers, not as legal slaves but "for their interests."

In Carvalho's account, the moral and historic justifications for the emergence of forced native labor serve only as a preamble to the presentation of the deeper reasons for Indian slavery. Invoking the Paulistas' services to the Crown, Carvalho indicated "that none of these things could have been accomplished without the service of these heathen as with them they crossed the backlands and with them they discovered minerals and made use of the labor with which they sustained all of Brazil with wheat and manioc flours, meats, beans, cottons and many other goods on which they paid Your Majesty's tribute." In short, the author argued that without Indian labor there would be no reason for São Paulo's existence as a colony. Presenting a valuable summary of the crux of the Indian question in São Paulo, he concluded:

> Sir, all that I say is that those Captaincies are in great need of these same heathen, whether free or captive, because without them neither will Your Majesty have mines nor any other fruit of those lands, for such is the character of that people, that he who has no heathen to serve him lives as a heathen, without a house but one of straw, without a bed but a hammock, without a trade or tool other than canoe, fishing lines, fish hooks and arrows, arms with which they live to sustain themselves while forgetting all else, with no appetite for honors for esteem nor increase of households for the conservation of his heirs.

Here the fundamental link between Indian labor and colonial production becomes clear, both in the mentality of the Paulistas and in the eyes of outside observers. Without the Indians to hoe their fields, to plant their crops, and to carry their produce, the Portuguese settlers of São Paulo would work barely enough to keep themselves and their families alive, such was their disdain for manual labor. Anticipating the position later taken by Frei Gaspar, Carvalho sought an explanation for this disdain in the structure of colonial society:

If Your Majesty ordered those lands to be peopled by the most robust and rustic folk to be found in your kingdom, within four days they would be reduced in the same way as the Paulistas, because it is certain that in those parts there has not yet been seen a servant who comes from Portugal with his master who does not soon aspire to be more than him, and for all of the reasons common to all of Brazil there should be many Guinea negroes or native heathen there, as without these people no fruit can be extracted from Brazil because everything there is sloth itself as is verified by D. Francisco Manuel in the book he wrote, Preguiça do Brasil ["Brazil's Sloth"].[10]

In sum, for Carvalho and for many of his contemporaries, the absolute necessity of forced labor lay in the convergence of settler attitudes toward work and the drive for wealth that animated Portuguese colonialism. The Paulistas could not be deprived of their Indians, he argued, not only because it would put an end to the contributions the captaincy made to the Portuguese empire, but also because it would reduce the colonists themselves to an uncivilized state in which they would be compelled to live in the manner of the Indians, a condition already observed among the poorest stratum of settlers. Thus, the question of Indian slavery went well beyond the moral debate over the legitimacy of captivity. In fact, slavery touched the very nerve center of Portuguese colonialism, where reasons of state and private interests combined to produce mutual benefits at the expense of Amerindian and African peoples.

The Custom and Practice of the Land

The Portuguese Crown, more interested in the development of the colony than the liberty of the Indians, ended up giving tacit consent to the widespread use of forced native labor in São Paulo. Indian slavery as a formal, legally constituted institution, however, existed only in a restricted sense. After all, the only legitimate captives were those taken in just wars, which experience proved to be an inadequate way of acquiring slaves. Nonetheless, isolated cases appear in the inventories of probated estates. In the late sixteenth and early seventeenth centuries, Tamoio, Tupinikin, Biobeba, Pé Largo, and Goiá slaves – taken as captives in the conflicts of the second half of the sixteenth century – figured among the holdings of some Paulistas.[11] Limited numbers of captives taken in the Bahian campaigns appear as slaves in estate inventories from the 1670s, while the early eighteenth-century inventory of an important landowner from Parnaíba listed one Ana of Pernambuco, evidently brought back from the Bárbaro War, "who even though parda [i.e., Indian] is a slave and as such was worth 300-some drams of gold."[12] Finally, in 1730, a Paulista mentioned a few Goiá and Kayapó slaves in his will, fruits of the just wars carried out against those peoples during the settlement of Goiás.[13] Yet these few cases seem insignificant when set against the far greater numbers of illegitimate Indian captives listed in seventeenth-century inventories. Legal slaves were so exceedingly rare that the executor of Antonio Pedroso de Barros's estate fell into obsessive redundancy when declaring the value of a "slave of the slave heathen of Bahia at one hundred *patacas* [32 milréis] for being a slave," as if to eliminate any doubts regarding the captive's status.[14]

The rarity of legitimate Indian slaves did not impede the development of the ideological apparatus of Indian slavery in São Paulo over the course of the seventeenth century. In fact, the introduction of thousands of Indians demanded the creation of an institutional structure that would regulate relations between masters and slaves. Despite the legal impediments to the forced labor of native peoples, the Paulistas were able to skirt these juridical obstacles and create institutional arrangements that permitted the reproduction of master-slave relations. By assuming the role of private administrators of the natives – who were considered to be incapable of administering themselves – the settlers produced an expedient allowing them to exercise complete control over the persons and property of the Indians without their appropriation being characterized as slavery in juridical terms.[15]

In São Paulo, the enslavement of the vast majority of the Indian population assumed a certain degree of legitimacy through the evolution of this parallel regime of personal service. For their part, the Paulistas did not spare words in attempting to justify their right to exploit the labor of the Indians that they themselves had "descended" from the wilderness. To cite one example, Domingos Jorge Velho, in the well-known letter he wrote to King Pedro II during his campaign against the escaped-slave redoubt of Palmares, declared:

> and if after [the subjugation of the Indians] we use their services in our fields; we do them no injustice; for it is as much to sustain them and their children as it is ourselves and our own; and this [is] far from enslaving them, rather we do them an invaluable service in teaching them how to till, plant, harvest and work for their livelihood, something that before the whites taught them, they did not know how to do.[16]

This position was not only adopted in correspondence with the Crown. Rather, it was also reaffirmed repeatedly in other kinds of documentation. For example, Diogo Pires excused Indian slavery thusly: "I declare that the heathens that I have from the land, I brought them by force yet it is to the good that they later became Christians."[17] Anna Tenoria, emphasizing the paternalistic aspect of private administration, declared: "I have some pieces of heathen of the land who number more or less fourteen or fifteen who are free and as such my heirs should consider them, giving them all good treatment as such [while] using their services as is right and teaching them good customs."[18] It is worth pointing out that in both these cases – drawn from wills – the dying masters asked that these "free" Indians be divided fairly among their heirs, a clause appearing in almost every seventeenth-century Paulista will.

The apparent contradiction between the explicit illegality of Indian slavery and the widespread practice of holding Indians as slaves derived only in part from the inefficacy of royal authority in a remote territory of the Portuguese empire. From a legal perspective, the question was far more complex. If, on the one hand, the Crown codified an idealized and vague legislation for the colony, on the other, colonial authorities – including the municipal councils – developed legal and administrative procedures that better reflected the practical needs of the settlers and the conflicts generated by local conditions. Oftentimes, such procedures contradicted the very letter of the law, as in the case of Indian slavery.[19] The settlers themselves recognized this paradox. In their joint will, composed in 1684, Antonio Domingues and Isabel Fernandes expressed the consensus view when they declared that the ten Indians in their possession "are free by the laws of the Kingdom and only by the *practice and custom of the land* are they compelled to serve."[20] Similarly, another slaveowner, Inês Pedroso, stated in her will that "the heathen that we have are free by the law of the Kingdom and as such I cannot compel them to servitude," while adding, "I have used their compulsory service like the other residents and thus I leave them."[21]

These two examples, among many other similar cases, show how the settlers perceived their right to maintain control over the Indians. This right was based ideologically on the justification that the settlers lent an inestimable service to God, the King, and the Indians themselves in bringing the latter from the wilderness to European settlement – or, in the language of later centuries, from barbarism to civilization – and was confirmed juridically in the appeal to "practice and custom." As the century wore on, this perception of the law hardened, becoming – so to speak – tradition.

Even so, the ambiguity of the Indians' situation never ceased to show through, above all in the drafting of seventeenth-century wills, which were considered by critics of the Paulistas to be evidence of their moral weakness.

For example, Manuel Juan de Morales, one of the few non-Jesuit defenders of Indian liberty in São Paulo, observed in a letter to the King of Spain and Portugal: "Here many wills are made, and at the hour of judgement they take to be truth that which the fathers of the Company teach, the dying one declaring that his Indians are free . . . and leaving them free on paper, they are captive by judicial authority, [and] divided among the relatives of the deceased, so that they can serve them in the way that at the hour of death had been judged unjust."[22] He may well have been referring to the will of Lourenço Siqueira, penned by a Jesuit:

> I declare that I have some pieces of heathen of Brazil who by the law of His Majesty are unbound and free, and I as such leave them and declare, and I ask them forgiveness for any force or injustice I have done them, and for not having paid for their service as I was obligated to, and I ask them, for the love of God and for that [love] I have for them, I want them to stay all together and to serve my wife, who will pay them for their service in the manner that is customary in the land, [but] will not be able to separate or sell any person among them, thus I say, and I ask of His Majesty's justices that in order to clear my conscience they do uphold this last wish and disposition.[23]

Notwithstanding the weight on some settlers' consciences, the legitimation of Indian slavery at the local level developed rapidly. In inventories from the first decade of the seventeenth century, "free" Indians appear regularly alongside legitimate captives in lists of "pieces," and were divided among heirs in the same way. This practice was submitted to judicial review on a few occasions during the long period in which Indian slavery was customary. In 1609, for example, after promulgation of the law declaring the unconditional liberty of all Indians, Hilária Luís submitted a petition to the governor asking if the Indians captured by her recently deceased husband could be divided among his heirs. The governor's response was curt and direct: Indians could not be listed on inventories because they were free by the laws of Portugal. The probate judge, however, was also asked to weigh in. He asserted, "it is practice and custom to divide free pieces among heirs for their sustenance and service and not for them to be sold." Unsatisfied with this response, the governor requested the opinions of the Judge of the Indians and of a Crown magistrate, both of them, it is worth noting, holders of captive Indians. The former reaffirmed that such was indeed the "practice and custom" of the land, while the latter added that without their inheritance the heirs "would become paupers begging for alms." In the end, the governor backed down, authorizing the inclusion of free Indians in the inventory.[24]

This case probably had little influence in a general legal sense, although it did demonstrate the willingness of colonial authorities to leave the guardianship of Indians to private settlers, even if this practice had all of the characteristics of slavery. Given the Crown's unwillingness or inability to clearly define the rights of native peoples, the settlers were able to claim that they should be responsible for the administration of the Indians. Thus, Maria do Prado, who owned large numbers of Indian slaves, stated in her will: "I declare that I do not possess any slave or captive but that I only possess as is customary practice ninety souls of heathen of the land whom I always treated as [my] children and in the same formality I leave them to my heirs."[25] Another example of this position may be found in the will of Lucrécia Leme:

> I declare that I own nine pieces of the heathen of the land, and one child, whom I always treated as free, which they are by their nature; for being incapable of governing themselves, I administered them with that Christian care, making use of their service in order to feed them, and in this same order shall my heirs govern them, not as inheritances, but as minors in need of governance, not neglecting their doctrine, and ordinary service until the King should decide otherwise.[26]

Minors in need of governance, children: it was in this sense that the settlers' paternalist discourse approximated the Indian policy of the Crown, despite so many other areas in which the two sides clashed. If the Indians required tutors, why could the role not be played by individual colonists? Confident that right was on their side, the settlers came to adopt the role as exclusively theirs, particularly once they defeated the Jesuits.

Settlers and Jesuits: The Decisive Battle

In a general sense, the settlers' pro-slavery outlook did not clash with either Crown or even Jesuit perspectives on the labor question in Brazil. But since it included a stubborn insistence on illegal Indian bondage, it placed the settlers on a collision course with the Jesuits. After all, the Jesuits derived a good measure of their power and prestige from their energetic defense of Indian liberty, which did not entail the actual freedom of the Indians, but rather opposition to illegal captivity.[27] The alternative they presented was the limited freedom of the missions, which had the effect of withdrawing Indians from circulation in the colonial labor market. The Jesuits thus had good reasons to criticize the Paulistas, who acquired most of their Indians through illegal means; at the same time, the settlers opposed the Jesuits, claiming that they were retarding the development of their economic activities.

The confrontation was sustained at two distinct levels. At the local level, colonists opposed the control that the priests maintained over the mission villages in the vicinity of São Paulo. In the intercolonial sphere, the Paulistas came to confront the energetic protests of Spanish Jesuits stemming from Paulista attacks on the missions in the provinces of Guairá and

Tape. These irreconcilable differences prompted shows of force on both sides. Faced with Jesuit demands on Crown government and the Vatican, which led to the enactment of new measures attacking Indian slavery, the settlers responded with violence, forcibly expelling the fathers from the captaincy of São Vicente.

It is important to note that the local dimension erupted into violence at two points before the fateful expulsion of 1640. In 1612, the colonists threatened to expel the Jesuits from the mission village of Barueri, alleging that the priests were making access to Indian contract labor exceedingly difficult. Twenty years later, irate neighbors of the same mission village, including Antonio Raposo Tavares, invaded Barueri and expelled the Jesuits. To a certain degree, this incident can be seen as a local expression of the intensified search for native labor; after all, if the Paulistas could destroy Jesuit missions in Guairá, why not reprise this activity closer to home? More specifically, though, this outbreak of violence emerged from competition between the more prosperous colonists of the settlements west of the town of São Paulo and the Jesuits, who were accumulating increasingly greater amounts of property and larger numbers of laborers. Meanwhile, the uncertain legal status of the mission village of Barueri added fuel to the fire.

Barueri lay in the midst of one of the principal wheat-growing areas in the region, near the *bairros* of Cotia, Quitaúna, and Carapicuíba, as well as the town of Santana de Parnaíba. By the 1630s, the Jesuits had established themselves as the principal landowners in the area, and controlled a disproportionate part of the Indian labor force. In addition to their preferential access to mission-village Indians, who numbered around 1,500 in Barueri alone, the College of São Paulo had inherited two enormous estates in the area along with their large populations of captive Indians. The first bequest, from 1615, was the donation by Afonso Sardinha and his wife Maria Gonçalves of their estate, Nossa Senhora da Graça, along with a sizeable number of Guarulhos Indians, "as well as of other nations." In the second, in 1624, Fernão Dias and Catarina Camargo bequeathed their estate, Nossa Senhora do Rosário, and around 600 Carijó that Dias had captured in the south. These properties, though they functioned as agricultural estates in the seventeenth century, would become the mission villages of Embu and Carapicuíba, respectively.[28]

The Jesuits thus represented much more than an obstacle to settler access to the labor of mission-village residents, which, in any case, had been a long-standing grievance of the Paulistas. From the settler point of view, the fact that the priests were developing a considerable stake in the Paulista economy as producers and landowners was even more troubling. The colonists also claimed that the Jesuits took undue advantage of their control over the mission villages, cultivating and even renting out land designated for the use of the villagers to the benefit of the College. Similar conflicts had already arisen in other captaincies, where colonists watched with apprehension as the Jesuits came to control some of the most productive lands and the most valuable urban properties, often acquired through royal donations.[29]

Faced with the advance of such a formidable adversary, the colonists turned to the only administrative body that could represent them, the Municipal Council. Following the incident of 1632 in Barueri, the settlers began to demand the removal of the Jesuits, making accusations that not only sought to demoralize the priests, but that also provided substantive evidence of the abuses and illegal activities of the Jesuits of São Paulo. In 1633, the colonist João da Cunha, a landowner in Cotia, protested that the Jesuits had stolen the Indians that he had received from his father-in-law as a dowry, taking them to Barueri. Apparently unsatisfied with the simple return of the Indians, Cunha requested that the Council "order [the Jesuits] out of the villages and to have nothing to do with the Indians outside of their church." During the weeks that followed, the Council heard complaints that the Jesuits were monopolizing the lands of Cotia and Carapicuíba, not allowing the settlers to cultivate the soil. Finally, the principal residents of these *bairros* went before the Council and issued an ultimatum: if the Council would not remove the Jesuits from Barueri, they and their Indians would expel the priests by force, which is what they did.[30]

It is worth remembering that the settlers were able to take such radical measures in this case in part because of the peculiar legal status of Barueri. Similar conditions existed in the areas surrounding the other three mission villages of São Paulo; indeed, another 3,000 or so Indians were under Jesuit control in São Miguel, Conceição dos Guarulhos, and Pinheiros. Yet these three mission villages had been founded by Jesuits in the sixteenth century, and most settlers recognized the rights of the Society of Jesus over them. Barueri, however, was established in the first decade of the seventeenth century by Dom Francisco de Sousa and became the object of a three-way legal struggle between Dom Francisco's heirs, the Jesuits, and the Municipal Council of São Paulo, each claiming rights to its administration. In the 1630s, the Jesuits exercised control over Barueri. However, as the colonists saw it, the Jesuits were there by order of the provincial of the Society, and not of the Crown, and thus it was their right to expel the priests and restore the administration of the village to the Municipal Council, which had supposedly received the privilege from Dom Francisco himself. In the end, following the settlers' attack on the mission village, the Council took control of Barueri, setting a precedent for its actions in 1640, when it appropriated the administration of the remaining villages, calling them "royal villages" (*aldeias reais*) and managing them in its capacity as the loyal and legitimate local representative of the Crown.[31]

With tensions already running high, the conflict entered its decisive stage when the Spanish Jesuits of Paraguay began legal proceedings against the Paulistas, seeking to put an end to the slave-hunting expeditions that were laying waste to the missions. Counting on the support of their Jesuit colleagues in Rio de Janeiro and Salvador, Fathers Simon Maceta, Justo Mansilla, and Francisco Díaz Taño first brought their case to the Governor-General of Brazil – who handed down a sharp but ineffectual ban on slaving expeditions – and then to the King of Spain and Portugal, and finally to the Pope. They conducted an impressive campaign against the Paulistas, portraying them – perhaps accurately – as a fearsome band of disorderly ruffians and outlaws. The Bishop of Río de la Plata also took the side of the Jesuits and, making use of some of the distortions characteristic of the larger campaign, wrote to the Pope in 1637, affirming: "In Brazil there is a city [*sic*] (subject to a prelate that is not a bishop) that is called São Paulo, and in it there have assembled a large number of men of different nations, Englishmen, Dutchmen, and Jews who, in league with those from the land, like rabid wolves cause great damage to Your Worship's new flock."[32] The Jesuits also used religious rhetoric in attempting to guarantee their exclusive access to the Indians of the interior, lamenting "that the *sertão* that they call Patos is open to every Moor, Jew, Black and White, tall and short, who wishes to go there to attack and conquer and capture the Indians to later sell them where and to whom they please." Were it not for the Jesuits, they argued, the Indians would be left "in the mouth of the devil and in the claws of the Whites."[33] The Crown, clearly distracted by the conflicts that were to culminate in the Restoration of 1640, in which royal authority over Portugal passed from the Spanish Habsburgs to Dom João IV of Braganza, did not respond very energetically to Jesuit appeals. The Vatican, however, was more decisive, pressuring the settlers with the publication of the Papal Brief of December 3, 1639, which essentially upheld the Bull of 1537 that had proclaimed the liberty of the Indians of the Americas. In mid-1640, the Jesuits began to divulge the contents of the Brief, provoking unrest in São Paulo, Santos, and Rio de Janeiro. Shortly thereafter, in June, representatives of the municipal councils of the captaincy of São Vicente met to discuss the matter. Under pressure from the principal residents of the town of São Paulo, they decided on the unconditional expulsion of the Jesuits, the confiscation of their properties, and the transfer of the power of administration of the mission villages to local authorities.[34]

After the expulsion, the settlers developed elaborate arguments to justify so brash an action. Writing to the recently coronated João IV, the Municipal Council of São Paulo explained that with the publication of the Papal Brief the Jesuits had attempted "to take away, deprive and usurp from said residents the immortal and ancient possession, which was theirs from the founding of this State to the present."[35] The defense of these dubious historical rights was bolstered by widely shared anti-Jesuit sentiment. In Santos, for example, a rumor circulated among the settlers that it was permissible to raid Jesuit mission villages and properties because the fathers of Pernambuco had allegedly persuaded their Indians to side with the Dutch. It was also rumored that the Brief was a Jesuit forgery and that one could now enslave Indians of any "nation."[36]

In addition to the Municipal Council, members of the religious orders that remained in São Paulo – notably the Franciscans – also assembled arguments to justify the expulsion of the Jesuits. Thus, in 1649, amid bitter litigation between the Franciscans and the Jesuits, Crown justices received a list of eight "causes" of the expulsion identified by settlers: (1) the Jesuits were becoming too rich and powerful; (2) the Jesuits forced the heirs of Afonso Sardinha, Gonçalo Pires, and Francisco de Proença to make enormous concessions (presumably of land and Indians); (3) they took lands from poor farmers through lawsuits; (4) they pressed a suit against Antonio Raposo Tavares and Paulo do Amaral (probably for their slave-hunting activities); (5) they won all of their legal actions because of their enormous wealth; (6) "They make greater use of the service of the Indians than the residents in their wheat fields, sugar mills, flour mills, and [the Indians] even carry them on their backs"; (7) "They take advantage of Indian lands and grants, trading and selling them, and putting their cattle on them"; (8) the Indians indoctrinated by them had proven rebellious and seditious in Cabo Frio, Espírito Santo, Rio de Janeiro, and Pernambuco.[37]

Despite the mutual hatreds and recriminations unleashed by the expulsion, the Jesuits were permitted to return to the captaincy thirteen years later. In an agreement hammered out by the principal settler factions and a Crown judge, the colonists made clear the conditions under which the priests would be allowed to return. First, the Jesuits would have to abandon any litigation challenging the original expulsion and give up asking for damages suffered in the incident. As far as the Indian question was concerned, the Jesuits were to desist from attempting to execute the Brief of 1639 or any other legal instrument aimed at defending Indian liberty. Moreover, the Jesuits were to refuse to harbor Indians who fled their masters. Finally, in a conciliatory tone, the colonists agreed to assist in the reconstruction of the College, which was completed in 1671.[38]

The expulsion, together with the conditions that were set for the return of the Jesuits, decisively removed the Jesuit obstacle to unfettered settler access to the Indians. The Jesuits, for their part, continued to be important landowners, once their properties in Embu and Carapicuíba were restored, to which were later added the donations of the Santana estate and the extensive Araçariguama property, which lay in the townships of São Paulo and Santana de Parnaíba, respectively. However, despite this undeniable economic power, the Jesuits had lost control over the mission villages, and their voice of opposition to Indian slavery had been muted. According to one father, writing at the end of the century, the situation was such that the Jesuits could never touch on the subject of Indian slavery in their sermons or in any other public statements. Nonetheless, he observed with some pride that they made use of "industrious dissemblance" in private conversations, ever trying to make the settlers see the errors of their ways. However, "the residents of that town were so firm[ly convinced] that the Indians were slaves that even if the Eternal Father came down from heaven with Christ crucified in his hands to preach to them that the Indians were free, they would not believe it."[39]

Slaves or Wards?

In the second half of the seventeenth century, the struggle over the legal status of the Indian captives of São Paulo reached another stage. In spite of their convictions, the colonists still faced the legal paradox that was the administration system. The regime of personal service differed little from slavery, which did not escape the attention of the Crown or of Jesuits working outside the region. According to a historical account from the early nineteenth century, it was little more than a matter of terminology: "The Paulistas, although they did not call the domesticated Indians *captives*, or slaves, but only *administrados* [wards], nonetheless used them as such, giving them in dowries and to their creditors in payment of debts."[40] In fact, practically every seventeenth-century dowry for which there is a record includes at least one "black of the land." Moreover, "pieces of heathen of the land" figured as collateral in loans and mortgages, and were sold on various occasions to satisfy debts or for other purposes. In 1664, for example, the executor of Antonio de Quadros's estate sold a young Indian girl for 18 milréis so that the proceeds could be lent out at interest, "as is the practice and custom."[41]

Two routine practices reveal with particular clarity the real status of Indians under this ambiguous regime. First was the sale of Indians, which despite falling beyond the legal bounds of personal administration, was frequent in the seventeenth century. However, when sales appear in the documentation they are almost always accompanied by some kind of justification. Thus, João Leite felt compelled to sell Paula because of "her threats and the distress she caused him."[42] In other cases, the sale of Indians provoked serious legal conflicts, which always brought to light the fundamental contradiction of a regime of thinly disguised slavery. In 1666, for example, João Pires Rodrigues accused João Rodrigues da Fonseca of the illegal sale of a captive, a transaction that was registered at the office of the notary. In Fonseca's defense, his counsel developed the argument that the contractual sale of property outweighed any consideration of Indian liberty.[43] Later in the century, when a widow attempted to sell Indians that had been left to heirs who had not yet attained their majority, the executor retroactively barred the sale, alleging that "pieces were sold that should not have been sold, [for the] reason that no honorable and property-owning man has died in this land and had his pieces sold for such a low price as it appears [*como consta*] those that were left to the aforesaid your charges [*seus curados*, i.e., minor heirs] have been sold. . ."[44]

The second practice that betrayed the essential identity of slavery and the regime of personal service was manumission. The two principal means by which captives might escape the shackles of personal service were by obtaining a letter of freedom that would then be registered by the notary's office or through a provision in their master's will. As we will see in greater detail in the final chapter, the uncertain status of captives presented a theoretical and practical problem in colonial jurisprudence, particularly once some Indians began to claim freedom for themselves under colonial legislation.[45]

The controversy over Indian freedom began to heat up again in the last quarter of the seventeenth century. Pressures came initially from Rio de Janeiro, in the 1670s, when the newly created bishopric attempted to impose an ecclesiastical tax of 160 réis for each "heathen brought back" from the wilderness. Soon thereafter, the governor of Rio de Janeiro proclaimed the unconditional liberty of all Indians. These developments immediately affected the Paulistas, who were nominally subordinate to the civil and ecclesiastical authority of Rio de Janeiro and who therefore felt threatened by the new measures. Their greatest fear was that their Indians might flee the captaincy of São Vicente en masse in order to live in freedom in Rio de Janeiro. Insecure once again, the Paulistas sought to reaffirm their control over the labor force, first through the now-traditional demonstration before the Municipal Council and then in negotiations.[46]

Yet again, the conflict centered on the settlers' right to administer Indians brought from the *sertão*, which had been the principal driver of the Indian question in São Vicente since the sixteenth century. However, the colonists proved somewhat more conciliatory than in 1640, though there appears to have been at least an attempt at expelling the Jesuits once again in early 1685. Tempers having cooled, they began a long process of negotiation with royal authorities. Mediated by the Jesuit Provincial, Alexandre de Gusmão, these negotiations sought a solution that would satisfy all parties, except for the Indians, of course. As was to be expected, two diametrically opposed positions emerged: the settlers, reaffirming the absolute need for forced native labor, sought to reassert their right over the

Indians they had brought from the wilderness "with the pretext of bringing them into the bosom of the Church," while the Jesuits proposed to revive the mission-village project and its "repartition" of contracted Indian labor.[47]

The settlers could never accept the Jesuits' proposals, however, because along with raising questions regarding the social control of the laboring population, they threatened the entire material basis of Paulista society. In 1692, the settlers drew up a list of sixteen "doubts" that would have to be resolved if a satisfactory agreement was to be reached.[48] Their concerns centered on four basic issues, all of them, in one form or another, having to do with the definition of Indians as property. These four issues were runaways, remuneration, inheritance, and alienation. First, the settlers wanted to make sure that the Indians under their administration could not flee to freedom, a question raised by the prospect of mass flights to Rio de Janeiro. Their second concern was more controversial, since the proposed freedom of the Indians was intimately associated with the question of the wages they were to be paid. According to the settlers, food, clothing, medical care, and spiritual indoctrination was just and sufficient compensation for the labor the Indians provided. The third problem, inheritance, struck at the core of the system. On the one hand, inheritance provided the principal mechanism for the transfer of the administration of Indians. On the other, it clearly defined the Indians as partible property. Both the mechanism and the definition were stubbornly defended by the settlers. Fourth, on the issue of alienation, the colonists sought legal ways to transfer administration from one colonist to another by means of sale, proposing a set of hypothetical situations in which such a sale would be permissible. Finally – and here the issue of property was also at stake – the settlers questioned whether creditors could demand the services of Indians who were put up as collateral for debts.[49]

The doubts expressed by the colonists summarized the position of the Paulistas in favor of Indian slavery. Antonio Vieira, when asked to comment on the matter, set down perhaps his last great diatribe against the institution.[50] In his striking rhetorical style, he asked himself the question of what the Indians of São Paulo were, then answered:

> They are thus the said Indians, those, who living free as natural masters of their lands, were torn from them with great violence and tyranny, and brought in irons with the cruelties that the world knows, dying naturally and violently on trails of many leagues until reaching the lands of São Paulo, where the residents used their services and use their services as slaves. This is injustice, this is misery, this is the present state, this is what the Indians of São Paulo are.

According to Vieira, the Indians could not be slaves, because they had not been taken in just wars. Furthermore, in a set of salvos aimed at the principal arguments of the Paulistas, Vieira reaffirmed the explicit illegality of administration by pointing to some of its most basic characteristics: runaways were restored to their masters through the use of force; administration was transmitted through inventories and dowries; and, finally, what was listed as the value of Indians' service bore no relation to any wage rate, but rather was equivalent to slave prices.[51]

This last point was crucial to the controversy over the formulation of Indian policy. Vieira rejected the settlers' proposal that providing food, shelter, clothing, and conversion constituted acceptable "payment" for Indian labor; on the contrary, administrators should pay a just wage. In their "doubts," the Paulistas justified not paying salaries with the allegation that the Indians were lazy. To this Vieira retorted: "But very practical and trustworthy people of that land affirm that the Paulistas usually use the services of said Indians from morning to night, as is done with the Blacks of Brazil." In short, the Indians of São Paulo suffered the most complete expropriation of their liberty, "such that nothing of him or of his remains that is not for all his life subject to the administrators; and not only as long as these live, but even after their deaths."

In spite of the charges of such a formidable opponent, the Paulistas got the better end of the agreement that was reached in 1694. Infuriated, Vieira criticized the Jesuits who participated in negotiations and signed the accord, claiming that they had no experience with Indians and did not even speak the *lingua geral*. He referred specifically to the "foreign" priests Jacob Roland and Jorge Benci, the latter "an Italian who never set eyes on an Indian and only listened to the Paulistas." For his part, Roland was the author of "Apologia pro paulistis," which according to Vieira was so hypocritical that the general of the Company of Jesus ordered it incinerated.[52] In fact, the Apologia upheld many of the Paulistas' most basic propositions, particularly with regard to the Christian mission that they executed in bringing Indians from the wilderness to civilization. What upset Vieira most, however, was the manipulation of his own ideas and statements, twisted to support the colonists' side: "The fables make believe that the wolves made peace with the sheepdogs, and now the sacred apologia wants the same wolves to be the pastors of the sheep."[53]

Indeed, even the Jesuits were unable to resolve the fundamental contradiction that characterized Indian labor in São Paulo. That is what is suggested by a report on the economic activities of the College of São Paulo by the *padre visitador*, or Jesuit inspector, Luís Mamiani.[54] In his report, Mamiani showed how the Jesuits themselves, though they professed loftier principles, in fact treated their Indians little differently than did the colonists they so criticized. Written at the end of the seventeenth century, Mamiani's perceptive comments captured several of the fundamental issues that needed rethinking in the face of ongoing controversy. The income of the College, Mamiani began, came from the output of agricultural laborers and artisans, "the greater part of it earned with the sweat and toil of the Indians of our administration." On its estates, no distinction was made in the division of labor among the 300 or so Indians administered by the Jesuits and the few dozen African slaves who worked alongside them. The priests distributed tasks to slaves and Indians alike on working days: males were sent to the fields, workshops, and corrals, while women were charged with weaving. Both slaves and Indians sustained themselves with the subsistence plots they cultivated on Saturdays and holidays. Finally, African slaves and Indian wards received equal "remuneration" in lengths of cotton cloth. The only difference detected by Father Mamiani was that the Indians, unlike the Africans, were *supposed* to be free and, as such, should have been compensated for their labor.

This last question – of just compensation for the labor of free persons – was central to the controversy. While he recognized that a certain degree of unremunerated labor was legal, Mamiani argued that it was immoral. Legitimate or not, the conditions under which the personal service of Indians was permitted were very specific: "some hold as licit the forced personal service of the Indians, either in their capacity as administrators or parish priests, since the Indians are obligated to pay either some tribute or the pension of their parish priest, and if they do not have the means to pay this, they can be forced to pay in personal service." Mamiani emphasized, however, that "the service can never be greater than the obligation."[55]

According to Mamiani, the abuse of compulsory labor on the Jesuit estates was the basic flaw in the regime of personal service. It was a strictly economic question, as Mamiani calculated the savings generated by "personal service" and revealed that around 80 percent of the income of the College derived from Indian labor. Even if the College were to pay an exceptionally low daily wage while continuing to make use of compulsory Indian labor at an appropriate level, its expenses would more than double. In short, the College would be unable to pay for Indian labor and still support its resident priests and other ecclesiastical activities.

Obviously, these contradictions were never resolved, and the outcome of the process of negotiation between settlers, Jesuits, and Crown was the royal decree of 1696. In spite of the law of five years earlier and its proclamation of Indian liberty, the new decree recognized the settlers' rights to the administration of Indians, thus legitimating a form of forced labor that was slavery in all but name.[56] Indeed, the distinction between the two kinds of labor was a mere formality, as a nineteenth-century governor of the province of Amazonas, Francisco José Furtado, would assert more than 160 years later: "The history of the Indians is the opprobrium of our civilization. Despite so many laws proclaiming their freedom and proscribing their slavery, the latter endures almost in fact!"[57]

Notes

1. Gaspar da Madre de Deus, *Memórias*, 82–83.
2. The role of the slave trade and of African slavery in the making of Portugal's New World colony inspired lively historiographical debate in Brazil, epitomized by two seminal works: Fernando A. Novais, *Estrutura e dinâmica do antigo sistema colonial*, 5th edn. (São Paulo: Brasiliense, 1986 [1974]), and Jacob Gorender, *O escravismo colonial*, 4th edn. (São Paulo: Ática, 1985 [1978]). New perspectives on the subject have been provided by the work of Luiz Felipe de Alencastro; see, for example, his important essay, "O aprendizado da colonização," *Economia e Sociedade* 1 (Aug. 1992): 135–162.
3. A notable exception is Gorender, *O escravismo colonial*, 468–486, in which the author incorporates Indian slavery into his general argument in favor of the idea of a colonial slave mode of production, albeit while considering it to be an "incomplete" institution (in comparison with African slavery).
4. CMSP-Atas, 1:333–334, Nov. 18, 1587.
5. CMSP-Atas, 1:446–447, Sept. 20, 1592.
6. *Alvará* of July 26, 1596, in Leite, *História*, 2:623–624, and Thomas, *Política indigenista*, 225–226.
7. CMSP-Atas, 2:70–71, Jan. 16, 1600.
8. CMSP-Atas, 2:75–76, Feb. 6, 1600.
9. Bartolomeu Lopes de Carvalho, "Manifesto a Sua Magestade," n.d., Ajuda, cód. 51-IX-33, fols. 370–373v.
10. The author Dom Francisco Manuel de Melo was well known in seventeenth-century Iberian intellectual circles. In citing him, Carvalho likely refers to the text *Descrição do Brasil*, which is among the works of Melo that have been lost. The subtitle of this work – *Paraíso dos mulatos, purgatório dos brancos e inferno dos negros* ("a paradise for mulatos, a purgatory for whites, and a hell for blacks") – became a popular saying in the second half of the century, though it was only recorded in 1711, by André João Antonil, in his *Cultura e opulência do Brasil*, facs. edn. (Recife: Universidade Federal de Pernambuco, 1969 [1711]). On Dom Francisco's life and work, see Edgar Prestage's excellent book, *D. Francisco Manuel de Mello, esboço biographico* (Coimbra: Imprensa da Universidade, 1914).
11. See IT, esp. vols. 1–3.
12. Inventories of Manuel de Lemos, 1673, AESP-INP, cx. 13; Feliciano Cardoso, 1674, AESP-INP, cx. 7; Antonio Pedroso de Barros, Parnaíba, 1677, AESP-INP, cx. 14; João de Almeida Naves, Parnaíba, 1715, AESP-IPO, 14.758.
13. Inventory of João Leite da Silva Ortiz, 1730, IT, 25:383–441.
14. Inventory of Antonio Pedroso de Barros, Parnaíba, 1677, AESP-INP, cx. 14.
15. For discussions of the legality and legitimacy of Indian slavery in colonial Brazil, see José Vicente César, "Situação legal do índio durante o período colonial, 1500–1822," *América Indígena* 45/2 (1985): 391–426; Manuela Carneiro da Cunha, "Sobre a escravidão voluntária," in her *Antropologia do Brasil: mito, história, etnicidade* (São Paulo: Brasiliense, 1986), 145–158; Elizabeth Madureira Siqueira, "O segmento indígena: uma tentativa de recuperação histórica," *Leopoldianum* 33 (1985): 129–141; and Perrone-Moisés, "Índios livres e índios escravos."
16. Domingos Jorge Velho to the Crown, July 15, 1694, quoted in Ernesto Ennes, *As guerras nos Palmares: subsídios para a sua história* (São Paulo: Nacional, 1938), 77.

Domingos Jorge Velho's letter is printed in full, in an approximation of its original orthography, as an appendix to Ennes' book. See ibid., 204–207.

17. Will of Diogo Pires, Parnaíba, 1642, IT, 28:264.
18. Will of Anna Tenoria, 1658, IT, 12:449.
19. It is worth pointing out that Indian slavery was not the only juridical issue over which seventeenth-century royal officialdom and settler-dominated institutions differed. The interest rate in São Paulo was generally kept at a robust 8 percent per annum, higher than the 6.75 percent permissible under Catholic usury codes. When pressed on the matter in the early seventeenth century, the Municipal Council of São Paulo defended the local rate as "practice and custom of the land."
20. Joint will of Antonio Domingues and Isabel Fernandes, Parnaíba, 1684, AESP-INP, cx. 18 (my emphasis).
21. Will of Inês Pedroso, 1663, AESP-INP, cx. 11.
22. "Informe de Manuel Juan de Morales de las cosas de San Pablo y maldades de sus moradores," 1636, in *Mss. de Angelis*, 1:189–190.
23. Will of Lourenço de Siqueira, 1633, IT, 13:9.
24. Petition of Hilária Luís, Nov. 3, 1609, in the inventory of Belchior Dias Carneiro, 1607, IT, 2:163–165. For a fascinating discussion of the coexistence of positive law and customary law in reference to slave manumission, see Cunha, "Sobre os silêncios da lei," in her *Antropologia do Brasil*, 123–144.
25. Will of Maria do Prado, 1663, AESP-INP, cx. 7.
26. Will of Lucrécia Leme, Itu, 1706, IT, 25:215.
27. Leite, *História*, vol. 2, chap. 4.
28. Copies of these donations may be found in DI, 44:360–370.
29. For a similar conflict in Rio de Janeiro, see letter of Pedro Rodrigues, Sept. 16, 1600, ARSI Brasilia, 3(1), fol. 193.
30. CMSP-Atas, 4:160, 171–173, Mar. 12, June 18, and Aug. 20, 1633. See also CMSP-Atas, 4:121–122, May 22, 1632, and Francisco Ferreira, "La causa del Brasil estar en el triste estado en que está son las injusticias notables que se hacen contra los indios," n.d., ARSI-FG, Missiones 721/I.
31. CMSP-Atas, 4:172–175, Aug. 20 and 21, 1633. In 1657, witnesses testifying in a royal inquest affirmed that Barueri indeed was founded by Dom Francisco and that the Jesuits had no legitimate claim to the administration of the village. "Inquirição de testemunhas," Aug. 28, 1657, Biblioteca Pública de Evora, cód. CXVI/2–13, doc. 17. Many historians, following the dubious account of Simão de Vasconcelos, S. J., written at the time of the controversy, have asserted that it had been founded by Anchieta or João de Almeida as a mission village. Vasconcelos, *Vida do p. Joam d'Almeida da Companhia de Iesu na provincia do Brazil* (Lisbon: Officina Craesbeeckiana, 1658); Duarte Leopoldo e Silva, *Notas de história ecclesiástica*, vol. 3: *Baruery-Parnahyba* (São Paulo: Augusto Siqueira, 1916), 25ff.; Camargo, *História de Parnaíba*, 87.
32. Bishop of Río de la Plata to the Pope, Sept. 30, 1637, in *Mss. de Angelis*, 3:281–282. From its founding in 1560 until 1711, São Paulo was a town (*vila*) rather than a city (*cidade*), a formal distinction that had jurisdictional significance.
33. Anon., "Resposta a uns capítulos," ARSI-FG, Collegia 202/3, doc. 2, fol. 11; anon., "Razões por onde não convém nem é lícito largarmos as aldeias dos índios no Brasil," ARSI Brasilia, 8, fols. 512–512v. José Gonçalves Salvador has taken these and other

accusations quite literally in trying to show the strong presence of Jews and new Christians in the southern captaincies. See his *Os cristãos novos*.

34. The standard account of the expulsion, supposedly written by Pedro de Moraes Madureira in the late seventeenth century, is "Expulsão dos jesuitas e causas que tiveram para ella os paulistas desde o anno de 1611 até o de 1640, em que os lançaram fóra de toda a capitania de São Paulo e S. Vicente," *RIHGSP* 3 (1898): 57–123. This document, the basic source for the interpretation of Pedro Taques de Almeida Paes Leme, includes the interesting suggestion of a link between the expulsion of the Jesuits and the restoration of the Portuguese Crown. Settlers of both principal factions supported the ouster of the priests, though the Pires were less enthusiastic about it and more willing to discuss their readmission. Curiously, one of the accusations the settlers levied against the Jesuits was that they supported the Sebastianist movement in Portugal and were spreading this atavistic political movement among the Indians of the backlands of Brazil. It is not entirely implausible, then, that some connection existed between the expulsion of the Jesuits, the restoration of the Portuguese Crown, and the acclamation of Amador Bueno, despite the efforts of Taunay and Aureliano Leite to invalidate this interpretation. In any case, it is clear that the basic motive underlying the colonists' actions was the Indian question. For a good discussion of the larger context of the expulsion, see Boxer, *Salvador de Sá*, chap. 4. It is worth recalling that the São Paulo conflict was hardly an isolated case, as similar conflicts emerged in Salvador and Rio de Janeiro, while in Maranhão the colonists expelled the padres on two occasions, in 1661 and 1684 (Monteiro, "Escravidão indígena e despovoamento"). Interesting, too, is that the Spanish settlers of Paraguay also expelled the Jesuits on various occasions (Melià, "Las siete expulsiones," in his *El Guaraní conquistado*, 220–234).
35. Remonstrance of the Municipal Council of São Paulo to the Crown, n.d., in *RIHGSP* 3 (1898): 98–104.
36. Anon., "Relação do que se sucedeu nesta vila de Santos sobre a publicação das bulas," ARSI Brasilia 8, fol. 558v. See also, "Representação da Câmara Municipal," Apr. 15, 1648, AHU-SP, doc. 14.
37. "Causas que os moradores de São Paulo apontam da expulsão dos padres da Companhia de Jesus," 1649, BNRJ II, 35.21.53, doc. 2.
38. CMSP-Atas, 6:24–26, May 12, 1653.
39. *Visita* of Padre Antonio Rodrigues, Jan. 25, 1700, ARSI Brasilia 10, fol. 2v.
40. Manuel Ayres de Casal, *Corografia brazilica, ou, relação historico-geografica do reino do Brazil, composta e dedicada a Sua Magestade fidelissima por hum presbitero secular do gram priorado do Crato*, 2 vols. (Rio de Janeiro: Impressão Regia, 1817), 1:223. He also remarked: "The Paulistas of today pass for good folk; but their ancestors certainly were not" (1:222).
41. Inventory of Antonio de Quadros, 1664, AESP-IE, cx. 4. This practice was contested in an early eighteenth-century lawsuit: José de Sousa Araújo v. Catarina da Cunha, 1721, AESP-AC, cx. 9, doc. 136. For an analysis of the debt issue, see Muriel Nazzari, "Transition Toward Slavery: Changing Legal Practice Regarding Indians in Seventeenth-Century São Paulo," *The Americas* 49/2 (Oct. 1992): 131–155.
42. Will of Isabel Rodrigues, 1661, AESP-INP, cx. 6.

43. João Pires Rodrigues v. João Rodrigues da Fonseca, 1666, AESP-AC, cx. 1.
44. Inventory of Miguel Leite de Carvalho, IT, 22:88–89.
45. The question of the juridical status of Indians and slaves came up with some frequency in colonial Brazil. See, for instance, "Carta dos desembargadores da relação da Bahia ao Conselho Ultramarino," May 10, 1673, AHU-Bahia, doc. 2531. In São Paulo, Indians were usually equated to African slaves in civil and criminal proceedings. See AESP-AC, various cases, as well as CMSP-Atas, 6a:253, Nov. 26, 1661, where masters are held responsible for infractions of municipal ordinances committed by their Indians. See also "Dúvidas que se oferecem pelos moradores da vila de São Paulo à Sua Magestade, e ao senhor governador de estado, sobre o modo de guardar o ajustamento da administração na matéria pertencente ao uso do gentio da terra, cuja resolução se espera," n.d., in Leite, *História*, 6:328–330.
46. CMSP-Atas, 6:447–448, June 22, 1677.
47. CMSP-Atas, 7:275–276, Mar. 8, 1685; see also CMSP-Atas, 7:309–310, Sept. 18, 1686. The Jesuit proposal was similar to the arrangement that was being worked out in Maranhão at the time. On Maranhão, see Dauril Alden, "Indian versus Black Slavery in the State of Maranhão during the Seventeenth and Eighteenth Centuries," *Bibliotheca Americana* 1/3 (1983): 91–142; José Oscar Beozzo, *Leis e regimentos das missões: política indigenista no Brasil* (São Paulo: Loyola, 1983); and Monteiro, "Escravidão indígena e despovoamento."
48. "Dúvidas que se oferecem pelos moradores. . .," in Leite, *História*, 6:328–330.
49. For a different approach to this issue, see Nazzari, "Transition Toward Slavery."
50. "Voto do reverendo padre Antonio Vieira sobre as dúvidas dos moradores da cidade [*sic*] de São Paulo acerca da administração dos indios," July 12, 1692, IEB, Coleção Lamego, 42.3 (nineteenth-century manuscript transcription).
51. In the second half of the seventeenth century, inventories came to indicate the appraised value (*alvidração*) of the services of "heathen of the land," principally to facilitate the division of estates among heirs, but also to pay off debts. This frequently resulted in the illegal sale of "pieces" under the pretext of exchanging their "service" for its appraised value.
52. However, the Apologia was not burned, for it still exists in the Biblioteca Nacionale Centrale Vittorio Emanuele in Rome. Jacob Roland, "Apologia pro paulistis," n.d., BNVE-FG, 1249/3 (2278). See also Leite, *História*, 6:344.
53. Vieira to Manuel Luis, July 21, 1695, in Vieira, *Cartas*, 3:666–669.
54. Luís Mamiani, "Memorial sobre o governo temporal do Colégio de São Paulo," 1701, ARSI-FG, Collegia 1588/203/12. A similar discussion emerged among the Jesuits of the Río de la Plata region at around the same time. It is analyzed in Nicholas P. Cushner, *Jesuit Ranches and the Agrarian Development of Colonial Argentina, 1650–1767* (Albany: State University of New York Press, 1983), 110–114.
55. When the Jesuit estates were expropriated in 1759, the new administrators of these properties sought to maintain certain labor practices that reveal the continued influence of this concept of mutual obligations. The Indians "were obliged to provide three days of the week in service to the estate, and in return the padres gave them quarters [*senzalas*, literally, "slave quarters"] in which to live and lands on which to plant foodstuffs." See "Relações dos bens aprehendidos e confiscados aos jesuitas da capitania de São Paulo," DI, 44:353–354.

56. Royal decrees of Jan. 26 and Feb. 19, 1696. For a general discussion of this legislation, see Agostinho Marques Perdigão Malheiro, *A escravidão no Brasil: ensaio histórico-jurídico-social*, 2 vols., 3rd edn. (Petrópolis: Vozes, 1976 [1866–1867]), 1:147–249; and Perrone-Moisés, "Legislação indígena colonial."
57. Report of the President of the Province of Amazonas, Francisco José Furtado, 1858, cited in Francisco Adolfo de Varnhagen, *Os indios bravos e o sr. Lisboa* (Lima: Imprensa Liberal, 1867), 45.

5
Masters and Indians

In the early seventeenth century, the colonists of São Paulo began to impose a greater distance – geographic and social – between the Indians they captured and the societies from which these slaves originated. Indeed, as we saw in the previous chapter, the introduction of thousands of captives provoked the elaboration of an ideological and institutional structure that could organize relations between settlers and Indians. However, the agency and experience of indigenous captives within colonial society also contributed in significant ways to the historical construction of Indian slavery. In this regard, it is important to remember that the active participation of native peoples shaped the structures of domination that characterized seventeenth-century Paulista society, and that Indians, in turn, confronted colonial subordination and captivity in multiple, sometimes contradictory ways, their actions constituting a dimension of their history that has gone largely unexplored.

To be sure, the shock of conquest, aggravated by repeated outbreaks of epidemic disease, debilitated and disarticulated indigenous societies. However, the many Indians who survived this initial impact, and who were then subjected to one of several modalities of colonial domination, hardly disappeared. Rather, they underwent a transformation through which members of once vigorous societies came to form the most miserable and exploited ranks of colonial society. From hinterland to settlement, from Indian to slave – this was the process endured by the majority. Yet, we should not think of it as a straightforward process, since it involved the development of complex relations between masters and Indians, relations that were shaped by the ties that bound them together, and by the Indians' own actions and experiences.

From Survival to Slavery

"It is well known," declared a colonist involved in a suit over Indian slaves, "that one piece from the settlement is worth more than four newly brought from the wilderness."[1] It was a simple, direct statement that expressed the difference between Indians recently introduced from the hinterland and those born in captivity or considered acculturated, a difference that manifested itself, throughout the seventeenth century, in the prices paid for captives.[2] To some extent, the higher prices commanded by Indians born into slavery, who were called *crioulos* ("creoles"), reflected the colonists' expectation of those Indians' greater longevity and, especially, productivity. But the larger significance of this differentiated scale lay in the implicit process of transformation of native peoples into chattel slaves.[3] The very term *índio* – redefined over the course of the century – serves as evidence of this process: in documentation from the period the term refers only to the inhabitants of mission villages, the vast majority of the indigenous population receiving the suggestive denomination of *negros da terra* (literally, "blacks of the land," hence "native blacks").

As slaveowners attempted to transform new captives into productive laborers, they encountered a series of obstacles that stood in the way of the formation of a well-defined slave class. Expeditions to the wilderness yielded a wide variety of ethnic types, and every Indian introduced from the interior faced a period of adaptation to the new regime of forced labor. Masters proved sensitive to distinctions within the captive population, and different types of slaves were valued accordingly. Maria Pacheco, for example, in seeking compensation for an Indian who had been murdered on the estate of Bento de Alvarenga, demanded that the victim be replaced with "a black of the same nation as the deceased."[4] In another case, Cornélio Rodrigues de Arzão allowed four fugitive slaves to remain on the estate of Antonio Lopes Benavides so long as Benavides agreed to give him "four equal pieces" in exchange.[5] Maria da Cunha of Mogi das Cruzes remarked in her will that her slave Domingas, a *bastarda* (as the illegitimate daughter of an Indian woman and Portuguese settler would be called), could be traded, but only "for another of her quality."[6] Not all Paulistas were so easily satisfied with equal trades, though. When João Barreto achieved a favorable judgment over Pedro Porrate de Penedo and was to receive twenty-two Indians in satisfaction of a debt, he requested that the Indians be auctioned, preferring money over flesh, "inasmuch as pieces are not permanent goods but mortals and may dwindle away and cause losses to heirs."[7]

Though slave price information is scarce for the seventeenth century, the available figures show variations that reflected the diversity of the population in terms of ethnic background and occupational specialization. The clearest distinction was drawn between Indians recently introduced from the hinterland and those born in captivity (the *crioulos*) or considered fully adapted to the regime (*ladinos*). Throughout this period, it would seem that the value of a *crioulo* or *ladino* slave remained four or five times higher than that of an unseasoned captive; in the second half of the seventeenth century, the price of a seasoned Indian ranged between 20 and 25 milréis, while Indians recently arrived from the backlands were sold for 4 or 5 milréis each.[8] In one specific case, Antonio Rodrigues Velho arranged with his brother-in-law to exchange 20 Indians from the backlands for 12 from the colonial settlement. Believing himself to have struck an excellent bargain, Antonio was subsequently disappointed to learn that his brother-in-law was only willing to deliver five adults and one young boy as payment for the 20 captives from the backlands, an exchange that probably more accurately reflected their relative value.[9]

At the other end of the price spectrum, Indians with well-defined specializations were valued accordingly. For example, "a native black carpenter named Tomás," was listed separately from 61 other Indians in the inventory of Antonio Correia da Silva and his value was assessed at 50 milréis, nearly equivalent to the price of an African slave. In another inventory, an Indian weaver was included on a list of African and mulato slaves and assigned a monetary value.[10] At the same time, *crioulos* and *mestiços* (metis, in the first generation, nearly always the offspring of European fathers and Indian mothers) usually commanded high prices, in some cases as high or higher than the average price of an African slave. In 1653, for example, a *bastarda* belonging to Simão de Araujo was appraised at 80 milréis, about twice the value of an African captive.[11] Similarly high values were assigned to the offspring of Indian-African unions, who were quite often listed in estate inventories as slaves, even when their mothers' status as Indians should have led to their being registered separately, as personal servants.[12]

The preference for locally born over recently captured Indians, and for *mestiços* over either, undoubtedly had a great deal to do with the vicissitudes of slave-hunting, which profoundly shaped the formation of São Paulo's slave society. While in the early seventeenth century colonists believed that the wilderness offered an inexhaustible supply of Indians, they soon discovered that it was an unreliable source for the physical reproduction of their labor force. After all, mortality rates were bound to be high in a regime characterized by wasteful exploitation, in which Indian captives were considered expendable so long as replacing them remained cheap and easy.

Though the records offer only a fleeting glimpse at patterns of mortality within the regime of personal service, the question of longevity certainly played a vital role in determining the continued viability of Indian slavery. It would seem that the survival rate for captives immediately following their capture remained very low. The long marches that captives were forced to make from their communities of origin to São Paulo, during which food supplies were always scarce, was one of the main reasons so many died. Those who survived the tribulations of the long journey faced further ordeals, especially in their first few years in São Paulo: illness, hunger, and abusive treatment decimated this population. Documentary evidence, though spotty, indicates that the attrition rate for the captive Indian population remained high, which meant that slaveholdings tended to diminish when not replenished with new captives.[13]

Periodic calamities aggravated this negative demographic balance. The Indian population, especially the recently captured segment of it, proved extremely susceptible to Old World disease, which, in turn, made it necessary to continually reconstitute the workforce through new slaving expeditions. For example, the smallpox epidemic that afflicted the captaincy in 1665–1666 precipitated a sharp decline in the local population, which served as justification for the large-scale expedition of 1666. Other epidemics were recorded in 1624, 1630, and 1635, each related to a recent influx of large contingents of Guarani captives, just as the intensified introduction of African slaves in the 1690s led to new outbreaks.[14] Though it is not clear how many Indians perished, each of these outbreaks provoked the intensification of raiding, as the colonists desperately tried to reconstitute their holdings.[15]

On other occasions, disease struck isolated estates with devastating results. Domingos Leite de Carvalho, master of many Indian slaves, observed in his will: "I do not declare the heathen of the land as they are sick and go on dying."[16] In the late 1680s, the wealthy couple Pedro Vaz de Barros and Maria Leite de Mesquita boasted of having more than 500 Indians among their holdings west of the town of São Paulo, but a measles epidemic decimated the ranks, leaving only 47 at the time of Vaz de Barros's death in 1697.[17]

Hunger was another factor contributing to high mortality rates among captives. The irregular influx of new captives, which caused the colonial population to grow in spurts, placed significant pressure on the food supply, since the vast majority of slaves were destined for activities linked to commercial production and transport, rather than the cultivation of subsistence crops for local consumption. In 1652, the Municipal Council discussed on multiple occasions the great hunger that the Indians suffered, in spite of the regular transport of large quantities of meat and wheat to the coast.[18]

The colonists were well aware of the high attrition rate for Indians in captivity, which is why they clung so dearly to the right to "descend" Indians from the wilderness. Indeed, the death of Indian servants came often enough to be a constant concern for the colonists. Martim Rodrigues Tenorio, for example, recorded slave obituaries in his account book: "Silvestre passed away on March 29, 1601, on a Thursday at around noon. Apollonia died on May 22."[19] Manuel Temudo and Gaspar de Oliveira, who died nearly forty years apart, each took care to set aside small sums in their wills so that masses could be delivered for the "heathen of my service who died in my household."[20] In 1660, when he petitioned to establish the rural chapel of Conceição de Taiassupeva on his property in Mogi das Cruzes, Baltasar de Godoi Moreira requested authorization to establish a cemetery for the *serviços* (literally, "services," thus servants) and other poor people of the neighborhood, since it was too costly and difficult to bring them all the way to town for a Christian burial.[21]

This concern for Indians at the hour of their deaths reflected a more general attempt to impose some cohesiveness on the fragile structures that made up the local slave system. As raiding expeditions became more difficult, dangerous, and costly, the colonists attempted to forge structures that would foster the preservation of the system. Somewhat like the Jesuits, they had the creation of an ideal Indian in mind: docile, disciplined, and Christian. The result – an increasingly disappointing one over time – was the development of fragile structures that could not offset the trend of demographic decline.

Paths to Integration

If the transformation of indigenous captives into Indian slaves required adjustments on the part of masters, it also involved a process of adaptation on the part of enslaved peoples. This process unfolded over the course of the seventeenth century, contributing to the development of the precarious structures that were to hold together the regime of personal service. One of the central elements in this process was religion, which served as a means of putting a definitive distance between Indian servants and the social organization and culture from which they had been torn. Thus, to the slave-owners, at least, the ideal of conversion went well beyond its use as the principal justification for Indian slavery.

It is not entirely clear to what point the Paulistas inculcated Christianity in their slaves. Clearly, though, the masters' religion reaffirmed existing relations of domination and served as an instrument to enforce authority. One example of this comes from a judicial inquest in which an Indian informant, ironically named Inocêncio, was cautioned by the interpreter who took his oath "that he speak the truth and not lie because he had sworn on the evangelical saints and the Devil would take him should he not speak the truth."[22]

For such warnings to have any significance required introducing Indians to the world of Catholicism through baptism and the assignment of Christian names. Parish registers reveal that many masters were content with baptizing Indians in collective rites shortly after bringing them from the interior. Other masters, however, evidently made a conscious effort to indoctrinate their slaves before baptizing them, as indicated by the interval between the arrival of some Indians and their baptisms. Many estate inventories included unbaptized Indians who were listed either without names or with their native appellations transcribed into often indecipherable Portuguese. For example, Maria Moreira's inventory included "Jacó and his wife with two children who being Tapuios [i.e., Tapuias] and unbaptized do not have names," while Catarina Tavares's inventory contained names so garbled by the imaginative scribe who penned them as to be incomprehensible to the modern researcher, though they may refer to personal names or the names of local Indian groups from around the Tocantins River in the Amazonian north.[23] Those Indians who did not yet have Christian names apparently went through some religious instruction before baptism. Thus, when the infant Albana was christened, the vicar noted that Albana's mother, "now pagan, is to be called Luzia when she is baptized," which occurred more than a year later.[24]

In addition to bestowing Christian names on Indians, the baptism ritual also introduced them to the practice of *compadrio*, or ritual coparentage, an important element of the Luso-Christian world of colonial Brazil. Analysis of seventeenth-century parish registers reveals patterns in relationships between masters and Indians that afford a better understanding of the structure of slave society on the Paulista plateau. The richest evidence comes from the parish of Sorocaba, where several collective baptisms of recently enslaved Indians took place in the 1680s. An analysis of these records reveals two interesting features of the baptism of new slaves. First, almost all of the Indians christened were children, registered as *filhos de pagãos* ("children of pagans"), which suggests that newly enslaved adults were not immediately subjected to baptism. Second, Indians who had already converted to Christianity, generally ones belonging to the same estate as those being baptized, served as godparents in most cases. For example, of the fifty-three captives belonging to André de Zúñega who were baptized on the same day in 1685, forty-six had Indian godparents. The following day, when thirty-one Indians belonging to Diogo Domingues de Faria were baptized in a single ceremony, all had Indian godparents.[25] Based on these figures, we may assume that seasoned Indian slaves, as godparents, served as intermediaries in the process of transforming more recent arrivals into Christian slaves, at least in a symbolic sense.

Beyond this relationship between *ladinos* and new captives, there is some evidence that suggests greater complexity in the ritual kinship of *compadrio*. For example, Martinho Garcia personally oversaw the baptism of thirty-six Indians he had enslaved on the Zúñega expedition, assuming the role of godfather to all the adults and to seven children who received Christian names. His brother Miguel Garcia served as godfather to eleven children, while the remaining eleven, all girls, became the godchildren of the African slave Simão and the Indian Laura, both of whom belonged to the neighboring estate of Diogo Domingues de Faria.[26]

Table 7 *Ethnicity of Parents and Godparents of Children Baptized in Sorocaba, 1684–1692**

	Godparents					
Parents	Wh/Wh	I/I	Wh/I	I/Wh	AS/I	I/AS
I + I	127	238	44	6	13	2
U + I	35	17	8	1	–	–
Wh + I	15	–	–	–	–	–
Wh + Wh	184	–	–	–	–	–
TOTAL	361	255	52	7	13	2

* I = Indian, U = undeclared father, Wh = white, AS = African slave. Men precede women in the order of couples and godparents.

Source: Batizados de Sorocaba, servos, 1684–1694 (inserted in Batizados Livro 1), Arquivo da Cúria Diocesana de Sorocaba.

Such proximity between masters and captive children was rare, though. In the Sorocaba registers, masters appear as godfathers of their own slaves in a mere 25 instances out of nearly 700 baptisms. Significantly, masters appeared as godfathers to their own Indians only in cases where no father was declared, in adult baptisms, or where they themselves were the father of the child to be christened – a pattern also observed in the parish registers of Santo Amaro, Itu, and Conceição dos Guarulhos during this period. Masters, in other words, might choose to be godfathers to their slaves, but not in cases where it would mean becoming a coparent with a male slave. They thereby avoided creating bonds of equality or solidarity with their slaves, while allowing the godfather–godchild relationship to reinforce the paternalistic ethos of slave mastery.

Figures on infant baptisms registered in the parishes of Sorocaba and Santo Amaro beginning in the late seventeenth century illustrate other interesting features of *compadrio* in São Paulo during that era (see Tables 7 and 8). The results differ slightly in the two cases, the differences reflecting the contrasting demographic structures of the two parishes. Sorocaba had a much greater concentration of Indians in its overall population, as 62 percent of registered baptisms were of children born to Indian parents, compared to only 24 percent for Santo Amaro. At the same time, there was a substantially higher percentage of children whose fathers were unidentified in Santo Amaro (22 percent) than in Sorocaba (9 percent). This difference becomes especially clear when expressed in terms of the Indian population: among the children born to Indian mothers in Santo Amaro, 49 percent did not have fathers who recognized their paternity, while in Sorocaba this figure stood at only 12 percent. These figures reflect the different stages of development of the two parishes. Santo Amaro included communities that had existed for three generations, while Sorocaba was an

Table 8 *Ethnicity of Parents and Godparents of Children Baptized in Santo Amaro, 1686–1710**

Parents	Godparents					
	Wh/Wh	I/I	Wh/I	I/Wh	AS/I	I/AS
I + I	138	70	18	7	1	1
U + I	169	31	20	5	–	1
Wh + I	10	–	–	–	–	–
AS + AS	4	3	4	–	–	–
U + AS	7	2	2	–	–	1
I + AS	2	–	1	–	1	–
AS + I	1	–	–	–	–	–
Wh + Wh	508	–	–	–	–	–
Total	839	106	45	12	2	3

* I = Indian, U = undeclared father, Wh = white, AS = African slave. Men precede women in the order of couples and godparents.

Source: Batizados de Santo Amaro, Livro 1 (1686–1725), Arquivo da Cúria Metropolitana de São Paulo, 04-02-23.

area of relatively recent settlement. Moreover, the Indian population of Sorocaba received large infusions of new captives during this period.

Differences between the two parishes also appear in the composition of godparents. In Sorocaba, 55 percent of the children born to Indian parents where the father was declared had two Indians as godparents, while 30 percent had a pair of white godparents and 11 percent had mixed godparents, usually a white godfather and an Indian godmother. These percentages were practically reversed in Santo Amaro, where only 30 percent of the children baptized had two Indians as godparents, while a full 59 percent had two white godparents.[27] This apparent preference for white godparents in Santo Amaro was even more acute in the case of illegitimate children whose fathers were not declared in the register. About 75 percent of the children born to unmarried Indian mothers had two white godparents, while only 14 percent had two Indian godparents. In every case in which a colonist assumed paternity of a child born to an unmarried Indian woman, the godparents were both white. The results from Sorocaba show a smaller concentration of white godparents, but a preference for them nonetheless: 57 percent of children born to unmarried Indian mothers had two white godparents, 28 percent had a pair of Indian godparents, and 15 percent had mixed godparents.[28]

The hierarchical patterns suggested in the baptismal registers may reflect differentiated strategies of socialization. However, they reveal little about the significance of ritual coparentage to the Indians themselves. Any conclusions derived from these figures, therefore, must be regarded with some suspicion. Oftentimes, the choice of godparents was no choice at all, as candidates were selected by masters. In other cases, godparents assumed the role only because they were present at the time of the ceremony, which is suggested by the repeated appearance of certain godparents on the same date. On other occasions, when likely candidates were lacking, the responsibility of serving as godmother fell to Indian women belonging to the officiating priest or even to the mother of the christened child herself. Even when the choice was apparently made more or less freely, it sometimes followed a logic of its own. That was the case of the twins Amaro and Sebastião, sons of an unmarried Indian woman and an unidentified father, the former (Amaro) receiving two whites as godparents and the latter (Sebastião) two Indians.[29]

Even if ritual coparentage did not have the same meaning for converted Indians as it did for the colonists, it nevertheless represented a significant step in the integration of Indians into Paulista society. On the one hand, in cases in which godparents and parents alike were Indians, it produced bonds of solidarity defined by the shared experience of slavery. On the other hand, particularly in cases where colonists served as godparents to the children of unmarried Indian women, ties of ritual kinship reinforced the master–slave relationship.

Much as the acceptance of ritual coparents at the baptismal ceremony may have represented little more than pro forma compliance with general ecclesiastical practice, the adoption of a Christian name was not necessarily a sign of acculturation. Frequently, names were chosen – or assigned – according to the Christian calendar, which appears to have served mainly to help masters identify their slaves. For example, during the compilation of the inventory of Maria Tenoria's estate, three Indian children entered the list unnamed, "as they are on the roça and no one remembers their names."[30] Other Indians, particularly ones brought from the *sertão*, appear in the documentation as having two names, one Christian and the other pagan.

The question of language, though little studied, offers further traces of the complex social processes that characterized seventeenth-century São Paulo. Historians have long held that Tupi was widely spoken in São Paulo until at least the middle of the eighteenth century, when it gave way to Portuguese and, in rural areas, the *caipira* dialect.[31] The Bishop of Pernambuco's commentary regarding Domingos Jorge Velho has been frequently cited in support of this view: "This man is one of the worst savages I have ever encountered: when he met with me he brought an interpreter with him, for he does not even know how to speak, nor does he differ from the most barbarous Tapuia, except in saying that he is a Christian."[32] In truth, however, not only could Domingos Jorge Velho speak Portuguese, but he could also write it, an uncommon attribute for any "Tapuia." Though hardly a fluent writer, he did manage to pen a letter to the Crown, and his quite readable signature appears with some frequency in the notary books of Santana de Parnaíba.[33] As it happens, the Bishop of Pernambuco, like other new arrivals from Portugal, apparently was quick to classify creole Portuguese, with its smattering of Indian and African elements, as an Indian language. As to the more general question of how conversant most Paulistas were in Tupi, it is worth pointing out that command of the Tupian *lingua geral* or any other indigenous language was regarded as a special skill even in São Paulo, where only the greatest backwoodsmen were fluent speakers of indigenous languages. In the 1690s, when a Paulista mercenary petitioned the Bishop of Rio de Janeiro for permission to spread the gospel among a recently contacted Tupi group in one of the northeastern captaincies, ecclesiastical authorities collected sworn statements by leading citizens of São Paulo attesting to his expertise in the *lingua geral*.[34]

It seems likely that an ancestral form of the *caipira* dialect, which remained heavily laced with words of Tupi-Guarani origin into the twentieth century, developed during the seventeenth century alongside the regime of personal service.[35] The slave population, primarily Guarani though increasingly heterogeneous beginning in the second half of the century, was basically bilingual, though many Indians found it difficult to express themselves in Portuguese. When called to the witness stand in judicial proceedings, first-generation Indian captives often used interpreters, while Indians born into slavery usually testified in Portuguese. In short, the language division followed the bipolar structure of colonial society. At the base, slaves from different ethnic and linguistic groups communicated in increasingly corrupted forms of Guarani, which amounted to the Paulista version of the *lingua geral*. At the top, the Luso-Brazilian community distinguished itself from the great mass of captives through their use of the colonial tongue, even as they inevitably came into daily contact with bastardized Guarani.

This dual pattern was also reflected in the terminology employed to describe Indians and Africans in São Paulo.[36] Over the course of the seventeenth century, Indian slavery produced a rich and varied terminology, which is evidence not only of the ethnic, racial, and occupational diversity of the local population, but also of the complex historical process involved in its formation.[37] In general, due to the legal restrictions on Indian enslavement, the colonists avoided the use of terms such as "slave" or "captive," though both appear in private correspondence as well as in public documentation. Until the late seventeenth century, the term used to refer to Indians most often was *negro*, though it gradually gave way to other terms with the increasing presence of Africans in the captive population. By the end of the seventeenth century, colonists called their Indians *gentio do cabelo corredio* ("straight-haired heathen"), *administrados* ("administered ones," in deference to the 1696 agreement), *servos* ("servants"), *pardos* ("dark-skinned ones"), and, finally, *carijós.* This last term encapsulates a great deal of the indigenous experience in the region, particularly the process of transformation that the captive population underwent.[38]

Beginning in the mid-sixteenth century, the ethnonym *carijó* served as a general term for the Guarani, the main object of Paulista slave-hunters as well as of the Jesuit and Franciscan missionaries of Spanish and Portuguese America. Until 1640 Paulista society was profoundly marked by the constant influx of Guarani captives, originating particularly from the Sertão dos Patos and Guairá. From that date onward, however, the supply of Guarani captives abruptly declined due to Indian and Jesuit resistance. As a solution to this crisis in the labor supply, the Paulistas redirected their slaving expeditions, introducing captives of the most varied origins into São Paulo.

The adoption of the term *carijó* to refer to an ethnically diverse captive population, long after the massive inflow of Guarani had ceased, is thus curious. Yet it makes perfect sense in the context of colonial São Paulo. First of all, the extraordinarily high number of Guarani captives introduced before 1640 – reaching, perhaps, 50,000 individuals – left indelible marks on the social composition of the captaincy. More important, however, was the fact that the ethnic diversity of the subaltern stratum of colonial society in the post-1640 period destabilized the system of private administration. Abrupt changes in the age structure, sexual makeup, and ethnic base of the captive population had profound repercussions in the organization of production and the sphere of social control. As we shall see, the 1650s saw the outbreak of a series of violent revolts, which called into question the viability of Indian slavery. In this context, the resignification of the term *carijó* almost certainly reflected a strategic attempt on the part of colonists to render a varied population more uniform by imposing Guarani captivity as a model.

In any case, it is clear that by the early eighteenth century the term had ceased to indicate Guarani origins and was used to refer to any subjugated Indian. For example, in the manumission letter that freed Maria Carijó in Sorocaba in 1722, Maria appears as a "Carijó of the Vargis nation."[39] Thus, *carijó* came to acquire a generic meaning associated directly with Indian slavery. Another example comes from the 1726 will of Pedro Dias, of Parnaíba, which states "that I possess some straight-haired Carijó which I leave free and unbound [*forros e livres*] by any kind of slavery and they may go wherever they like."[40] Similarly, in the will of Margarida da Silva, the Indian servant Catarina was freed, while her husband and children "shall remain in the status of the other Carijó" (*correrão o foro dos mais carijós*).[41] In short, placing the entire captive population into a single, standardized ethnic category represented much more than the express policy of the slave-owning stratum or a simple semantic exercise: it was, rather, part of a larger historical process involving the transformation of Indians into slaves.

One may note a similar process of change over time involving the terminology that referred to persons of mixed origins. Two terms, often taken to be synonyms, actually expressed a critical distinction in the seventeenth century: *mamaluco* and *bastardo*.[42] Both terms referred to the progeny of an Indian mother and a white father. The fathers of *mamalucos*, however, publicly recognized their paternity, while the fathers of *bastardos* did not. As a result, *mamalucos* usually were considered free and Portuguese, while *bastardos* remained tied to the Indian segment of society, having inherited their mothers' status as servants. By the eighteenth century, the term *mamaluco* fell into disuse, while *bastardo* came to refer generically to anyone of Indian ancestry, as in the 1765 census, which referred to the neighborhood of Pari as being inhabited "mainly by *bastardos*."[43]

While shifts in terminology are indicative of the disintegration – or, in the case of the term *carijó*, reconstitution – of Indian identity, marriage practices and the composition of slave families followed the same general trend. Some masters displayed concern with the maintenance of families on their estates, perhaps with the natural reproduction of their slaveholdings in mind. Estevão Furquim, for example, stressed in his will that the Indian families passed on to his heirs were not to be split up under any circumstances.[44] In another case, an heir had to make do with a different Indian than the one left to him in his father's will, because the latter was married and therefore "they cannot be separated."[45] Francisco Cabral de Távora of Jundiaí stated in his will: "I declare that the pieces that we possess of heathen of the land are not to be sold and that they remain in the allotments as they are so that my wife and my son Francisco may administer them and give them good treatment as I gave them."[46]

In general, however, family stability was more the exception than the rule on seventeenth-century estates. Few Indian couples catalogued on inventory lists had Church-sanctioned marriages, a trend confirmed by the almost complete absence of the latter in parish registers. On numerous occasions, ecclesiastical authorities pointed to informal marital arrangements among Indians in São Paulo as evidence of priestly neglect or the lack of qualified clergy. In 1700, during his ecclesiastical inspection of the interior of the captaincy, the Jesuit Antonio Rodrigues performed ninety-seven marriages under the Law of Grace and "revalidated" ninety others.[47] In certain cases, informal marital arrangements facilitated the splitting up of families when estates were divided. For example, in the inventory of Antonio Ribeiro Roxo, the Indians Pedro and Branca appear as a married couple in the initial listing of goods, but in the partition they were classified as "single" and were assigned to different

Table 9 *Married Indians as Percentage of Adult Population, São Paulo and Santana de Parnaíba, 1600–1689*

Decades	%M*	%F**
1600–1619	40.2	33.3
1620–1629	49.6	43.6
1630–1639	45.3	40.6
1640–1649	49.7	42.9
1650–1659	30.8	29.7
1660–1669	33.9	33.1
1670–1679	29.2	30.6
1680–1689	30.5	29.8

* %M: Percent of adult male population listed as married.
** %F: Percent of adult female population listed as married.
Sources: Inventories of probated estates, São Paulo and Parnaíba. IT, vols. 1–44; AESP-INP, cxs. 1–40; AESP-IPO, various cxs.; AESP-IE, cxs. 1–6.

heirs.[48] Other inventories indicate the persistence of indigenous practice, as in the case of Cristóvão, a Guarani who was listed "with two wives one Hilária the other Luzia," an arrangement that clashed with the Christian concept of monogamy.[49]

Over the course of the seventeenth century, the proportion of married couples in the Indian population declined slightly. Table 9 demonstrates this downward trend, showing the most precipitous drop in the 1650s. These figures confirm the hypothesis that the slave population underwent a trying phase of readjustment in these years, during which new patterns of slave-hunting resulted in a general shift in the ethnic composition and sexual balance of the servant population. A similar pattern emerges on the largest estates, which tended to have the most pronounced family structures. Before 1640, more than 50 percent of adult males and 40 percent of adult females on estates with 100 or more slaves had marriage partners. These rates declined slightly thereafter, though they remained higher than the average shown.[50]

The instability of the Indian family in seventeenth-century São Paulo is also shown in the age structure of the slave population. The number of children listed as dependents in inventories of "pieces" fluctuated with shifting patterns of slave-hunting and slave marriage.[51] As we have emphasized, in the Paulistas' attacks on Guarani villages and the missions of Guairá, women and children predominated among the resulting captives, which explains the higher percentage of children in the population early in the century. In the 1640s and 1650s, when the Paulistas mainly captured adult males on their raids among the Guaianá and Guarulhos, this percentage fell. The relative stability of such figures beginning in the 1660s was due – in part, at least – to higher birth rates among the slave population. However, it is important to note that there was an increase in the number of children born to unmarried women during these years, which undoubtedly contributed to the destabilization of family structures in the Indian population. This trend is clearly visible in the parish register of Santo Amaro, which shows that more than half of all the Indian children baptized between 1686 and 1727 were born to unmarried Indian mothers and "unknown" fathers.[52]

Rates of mixed marriage – between Indians of different ethnic groups, between mission-village residents and personal servants, and between African and Indian slaves – also appear to have increased toward the end of the century. The royal decree of 1696, which laid down regulations for private administration, expressly prohibited marriage between personal servants and the Indians of the mission villages, as well as between personal servants and African slaves. Throughout the seventeenth century, colonial authorities were greatly concerned that mission-village Indians were being transferred into personal service through marriage. Colonists were generally conscious of the distinction, however, and despite occasional abuses, they tended to exclude free Indians and mission villagers from the partitioning of estate inventories, even when they were married to Indian slaves. In 1632, Antonia de Oliveira, whose husband André Fernandes commanded a large labor force of slaves and mission-village Indians, wrote in her will that the many Indians from the mission village of Barueri who served her and her husband were not to be listed in the inventory because of their status.[53] A half-century later, Maria Diniz referred to "a young man by the name of Custódio, who is free and unbound [*forro e livre*], and no one may force him into any servitude save of his free will should he want to be in the company of his wife."[54]

Marriage between Indians and African slaves appears to have been infrequent in the seventeenth century. If seventeenth-century masters promoted such marriages in order to increase their slaveholdings, they were surely disappointed, as these marriages proved remarkably unfruitful, with a negligible number of children of these mixed unions appearing in the baptismal records of Santo Amaro, Sorocaba, and Itu. In the eighteenth century, however, this situation began to change due to a dramatic increase in São Paulo's population of African origin and heightened competition over available labor. The earliest evidence of forced marriages emerges in this context. When questioned by the authorities about his participation in a series of crimes, the slave tailor Pedro Mulato Papudo claimed that he had been kidnapped by Bartolomeu Fernandes de Faria and forced to marry Teresa, an Indian servant. The records of the same case also indicate that

Faria had forced Isabel, a free *bastarda*, to marry the slave Luciano, described as a mulato.[55]

The Pursuit of Autonomy

The different ways in which Indian labor was appropriated and Indians were integrated into Paulista slave society reflected the basic changes faced by the indigenous population of the region. In the sixteenth and early seventeenth centuries, when the regime of personal service was still in formation, the colonists relied upon precolonial forms of organization in order to extract labor from the Indians. Thus, at the inception of colonialism, the terms of exchange and of alliances mitigated the exploitation of native labor. As the seventeenth century proceeded, however, and slave relations were firmly established, this situation was reversed, and the indigenous population was forced to adjust to a new reality. While unable to reproduce pre-conquest organizational forms, the Indians of São Paulo pursued a somewhat separate existence within colonial society. This pursuit, though it yielded results that were as often as not ambiguous, came to be expressed in the everyday struggle for survival as well as in multiple forms of resistance.

The spatial organization of towns and rural estates illustrates the process by which Indians were transformed into slaves. Throughout the seventeenth century, Indian living quarters figured prominently in urban and rural landscapes, and in both settings were associated explicitly with the sphere of work. In the towns, Indians' quarters invariably were located in the rear of properties, usually alongside the kitchen, separated from the main house by a garden. In the countryside, the dwellings of Indian workers were located near the subsistence plots where corn, manioc, and other staples were grown.

To a certain extent, the evolution of Indian dwelling-places during the seventeenth century reflected the general transformation of Luso–indigenous relations in São Paulo. At the beginning of the century, Indians on rural estates lived in large, straw-covered huts or lodges, called *tijupares*, probably similar to those found in precolonial Guarani societies. Over time, however, these constructions began to assume some of the broad characteristics associated with the Paulista variety of colonial architecture. Collective housing gave way to single family units in such a way as to mirror the rural and urban living arrangements of the dominant class, while building materials gradually approached the European norm as new constructions were increasingly roofed with ceramic shingles instead of straw.[56] Finally, in the early eighteenth century, when the African presence began to be firmly established in the region, Indian housing came to be referred to by the Kimbundo-derived term *senzala*.[57]

Meanwhile, colonial forms of labor organization, by imposing radical changes in the traditional division of labor in indigenous societies, also contributed to the transformation of the native population. In the countryside, Indians maintained subsistence plots to feed themselves, which may have afforded some continuity between precolonial and colonial forms of organizing production. But the exigencies of the colonial economy altered the division of labor such that subsistence agriculture no longer followed traditional patterns. While most Indian women continued to work in agriculture – since the Paulistas used so many men in transport and backwoods raiding – some colonists seemed to prefer them as domestic servants. For example, in the inventory of Antonia de Chaves, eleven of fifteen female Indians were listed as house servants.[58] In the inventory of José Preto of Mogi das Cruzes, who owned 106 Indians, 22 female Indians were listed under the heading *negros de casa de serviço*, or "house-servant blacks."[59]

This division left some agricultural chores to men, whose increasing presence in agricultural activities served to further distance Indian slaves from their indigenous past, in which the planting and harvesting of crops was carried out almost entirely by women. At the same time, the use of European tools exacerbated the rupture with tradition. The will of Jerônimo de Brito, the owner of a large number of Indian slaves, provides suggestive evidence of this trajectory. Granting freedom to all of his Indians, he left each man a scythe, a hoe, and an axe "for them to make their plots to feed themselves."[60] Pedro Morais Dantas left his Indians to his son, the Jesuit Antonio Ribeiro, who was finishing his studies in Portugal. Dantas's will explained: "while the aforementioned my son Antonio Ribeiro is absent [the Indians] will be on their plots that at present they are planting for their food and sustenance."[61] In some cases, Indians established independent production units of their own, according to several land-sale documents that refer to Indian farmers as neighbors.[62]

Other roles assigned to Indians in the colonial economy also distanced them from indigenous traditions. In the seventeenth century, almost all artisanal activities were executed by Indian craftsmen and apprentices. Many slaveowners, particularly town-dwelling ones, lived off the earnings of their artisan slaves. Others concentrated larger numbers of Indian craftsmen on their estates. Such was the case of José Ortiz de Camargo, who counted five cobblers, two blacksmiths, and two carpenters among his slaves. Captain Guilherme Pompeu de Almeida, who commanded hundreds of Indian and African slaves on his massive estate of Voturana, dominated the crafts market of the town of Parnaíba with his many master artisans, a tradition maintained by his son and namesake.[63] Likewise, according to Pedro Taques de Almeida's description, Lourenço Castanho Taques, the younger, had "numerous slaves, who were destined to labor in workshops, in which worked masters and craftsmen of various trades, his slaves, from which he received the profits from the salaries they earned."[64]

The modest market provided by local towns created opportunities for Indian artisans, producers, and vendors, some of whom worked on their own rather than for masters. By the 1650s, Indian vendors began to compete seriously with Portuguese peddlers in the town of São Paulo, especially in the trade in local products, such as flour and hides. Wills and inventories frequently attest to this activity, as many colonists listed outstanding debts to Indians for goods and services the latter had provided. Manuel Alves Pimentel, for example, owed an Indian named Pedro more than 1 milréis for a certain amount of sweets. Before he passed away, Antonio Vieira Tavares settled a debt with "a black blacksmith by the name of Salomão for having made a scythe."[65]

On several occasions over the course of the seventeenth century, colonial authorities inveighed against this Indian-run informal economy. The Municipal Council of São Paulo established stiff fines as punishment for colonists who bought specific kinds of goods from Indians. In 1647, the Council registered a complaint of "thefts and other disorders and excesses" resulting from trade with the "blacks of the land [in] compulsory service," then instructed settlers that they should only trade with Indians who had permission from their masters to sell local goods. In 1660, the Council suddenly became stricter, prohibiting all trade with the Indians, "under penalty of being charged with theft." Shortly thereafter, however, the councilmen relented, making an allowance for trade with the "blacks of the land" in transactions of 200 réis or less, which excluded almost everything except small amounts of locally grown produce.[66]

Despite its repeated insistence, the Municipal Council was unable to suppress the independent, informal commercial activities of the Indians. It nevertheless demonstrated this persistent, if futile concern for two important reasons. First, the development of a black market in hides and meat violated the monopoly privileges bestowed upon local Portuguese merchants, whose purchase of municipal contracts gave them exclusive rights to the sale of fresh meat. Second, much of the meat and hides sold in town by Indians was the product of plunder, which presented serious problems in terms of social control and public order.

By the 1660s, the situation was practically out of hand, with complaints of Indian plunder regularly being brought to colonial authorities. For example, in her will Grácia de Abreu referred to a suit brought against her by Salvador Bicudo because her "people" had stolen two loads of wheat flour that belonged to him and slaughtered some of his pigs.[67] It seems likely that both of these items, with significant commercial value in the context of the local economy, found their way to the marketplace. In a similar, if more violent case, Francisco Cubas pressed a lawsuit against the heirs of José Ortiz de Camargo, claiming that Camargo's Indians had repeatedly raided his estate, slaughtering cattle and plundering the fields. At one point they attacked Cubas's son, who was minding the estate, "with offensive and defensive weapons ... saying kill, kill João Cubas," who escaped "miraculously," hiding from the raiders, though the Indian Agostinho died "with the many arrow wounds they gave him and they split his head and ransacked and robbed the house and property."[68]

To a certain extent, this wave of "criminal" activity reflected the patterns of adjustment to slave society experienced by Indians. Cattle rustling, the pilfering of crops, and monetary theft were very common in São Paulo in the seventeenth century. However, slave crime was far more than a simple reaction to the disorientation inherent in the transformation of Indians into slaves, though in some cases hunger and despair contributed to such acts. In many ways, the crimes perpetrated by Indians resembled those attributed to African and Afro-American slaves in other contexts.[69] Their values in manifest conflict with the values of the dominant society that held them as slaves, Indians were unlikely to consider the appropriation of a pig or a calf from a neighboring estate to be stealing, especially if their own well-being depended upon it. At the same time, masters tacitly accepted such activities, assuming responsibility – including legal responsibility – for property stolen or destroyed by their Indians.[70]

It is useful at this point to distinguish between the independent native hunter, who, living on the margins of colonial society, attacked cattle either as game or as a reaction to the threat that cattle posed to his society, and the Indian slave who slaughtered cattle in order to sell meat and hides on the internal colonial market. Though both were described as criminals by colonial society, the hunter would suffer reprisals and even extermination, while the slave rarely was punished. In this sense, while crimes perpetrated by Indian slaves appeared to threaten the stability of the slave regime, more than anything they reflected a determined level of integration – what others have called "resistant adaptation" – in which the Indian slave forged spaces of survival within his new social reality.[71]

The Inevitable Conflict

Municipal authorities confronted the unruly behavior of Indians with increasingly repressive legislation, which tended to exacerbate the inherent conflict between settlers and their captives. The power exercised by local councils rarely reached beyond their respective municipal seats, but that was precisely where unrest erupted most frequently. As early as 1623, the Municipal Council of São Paulo dedicated a session to discussing "the heathen that in this town have many dances both day and night and whereas at said dances occur many mortal sins and insolent acts against the service of God and the common good in committing flights and uprisings and other things that are too indecent to declare."[72] In 1685, the Council posted an order prohibiting the sale of sugar-cane brandy (*aguardente*) to Indians during Holy Week "to avoid some damages and offenses that they commit on those days."[73] Finally, near the end of the period of Indian slavery, the councilmen drafted an edict that prescribed corporal punishment for "carijó and black youths" who disrupted religious processions with roguish behavior.[74]

More serious measures were taken in response to cattle rustling and physical assaults committed by armed Indians. These measures included the construction of a gallows in the 1620s. Though there is no evidence that it was ever used, its symbolism was not lost on its potential victims, as a defiant group of Indians set fire to it in the 1640s.[75] Similar precautions were taken in the towns of the interior, beset by disorder throughout the colonial period. The municipal councils of Parnaíba and Sorocaba repeatedly prohibited the carrying of knives, sharpened sticks, and muskets by Indians within the urban perimeter, while authorities in Guaratinguetá built a jail specifically for "the heathens who bring so much confusion to this town."[76] The records of the Municipal Council of Sorocaba, though fragmentary, refer to repeated melees, generally involving the Indians of the Benedictine convent. In 1672, for example, the wedding of Pedro Leme da Silva, one of the principal colonists of Sorocaba, was disrupted by a street brawl between the convent's Indians and the "blacks" of Captain Jacinto Moreira Cabral.[77] Three years later, the heirs of Baltasar Fernandes, who had founded Sorocaba twenty years earlier, complained that the Indians of the convent were causing great damage to the crops and livestock left them by the town father.[78]

If slaveowners could rely to a certain extent on the municipal councils for the control of the Indian population in urban areas, they were on their own when it came to social control on their rural estates. The regimentation of the Indian population was hardly achieved by peaceful means alone. Like other slave systems, the Paulista version included a fair amount of coercion and violence exercised by the master class in its efforts to impose discipline on its subordinates. The paternalist mentality had its violent side, which paralleled the disciplinarian approach that authoritarian Portuguese fathers adopted in child-rearing. Pedro Taques mentions a Paulista, Francisco de Almeida Lara, "well known for the ardor of his temper in punishing his slaves and instructing his children, because of the rigor of which he was known by the nickname *Caga-fogo*" (literally, "shit-fire").[79] Another, Fernão Pais de Barros of Sorocaba, so brutalized his Indian and African slaves that complaints reached royal authorities in Lisbon.[80] Antonio Bororo, under the administration of João Lopes Fernandes, sued for his freedom, alleging that his master held him in "torturous captivity as the blows and marked instances of violence never ceased."[81] In a similar case, Grimaneza and other Indians who belonged to Manuel Moreira claimed that their late master had stipulated in his will that they were to serve his heirs as free persons, but that these treated them as slaves, administering frequent beatings to remind them of their social position.[82] It would seem that the second of the three P's of the popular colonial-era saying – *pão, pau, e pano*, or bread, rod, and cloth – figured prominently in the Paulista slaveholders' lexicon.

Many of the repressive measures taken by the municipal councils and by individual colonists reflected a genuine concern with the possibility of revolt. Colonists certainly had genuine reason to fear, particularly in the 1650s – it was in this decade that a series of bloody revolts broke out – when the concentration of the Indian population rose to alarming levels and proportions as high as eight Indians to each white were reached in many rural areas.[83] This situation was aggravated by the fact that the ethnic composition of the Indian population was undergoing important changes, with the introduction of many Guarulhos and Guaianá captives. It was thus a period of readjustment, since the colonists faced greater difficulties in subjugating non-Tupi peoples, not only because of the language barrier and the new captives' unfamiliarity with the colonial labor regime, but also because these peoples proved more prone to revolt. Another aggravating circumstance was the apparent crisis in the food supply, which must have weighed most heavily on the Indian population. In addition to the complaints registered by the Municipal Council of São Paulo during these years, one may gauge the degree of dearth by the excessive value attributed to corn plantings in an inventory from 1653. The appraisers of the estate left by João de Oliveira estimated that his three *alqueires* sown in corn were worth 15 milréis, an extremely high quantity when compared with the negligible value attributed to corn in other inventories from throughout the century. One may also compare it to the five *alqueires* that were listed in the inventory of Manuel Alves Pimentel in 1666 with a value of 5 milréis.[84]

The 1650s were likewise marked by the conflict between the Pires and Camargo factions, a rift in the dominant class that created a climate of social instability. Both sides mobilized large numbers of Indians, who fought pitched battles in the town of São Paulo. During his inspection of 1653, a crown magistrate observed: "there is the great scandal that the Indians roam this town with clubs, bows and arrows from which results brawls and disasters."[85] A final source of tension emerged as rumors circulated that the Governor of the South, Salvador de Sá, intended to declare the Indians free as part of his plans for the development of mining. The colonists feared that such news would incite the Indians to a mass uprising.[86]

The most dire forecasts began to be confirmed in 1652, when the first great revolt by Indian slaves broke out on the estate of Antonio Pedroso de Barros, in the *bairro* of Juqueri. Pedroso de Barros, a major wheat producer, owned between 500 and 600 Indians, some of them Carijó, others Guaianá, most of whom would have been recently brought from the wilderness. It is difficult to assess the causes of the rebellion, but all available evidence indicates that the Indians struck at the very system of personal service itself. Not only did they murder Pedroso de Barros and other whites found on the estate, they also destroyed crops and livestock. It fell to Pedro Vaz de Barros, the victim's brother, to describe the devastation: "So great was the number of heathen that on that occasion flocked to the murder of their master and still others that they did not leave a living thing that they did not destroy, kill and eat since they are perverse by nature as is notorious in all of this captaincy."[87] The authorities had a difficult time putting down the revolt, which they accomplished only after a large number of rebels had fled.

The process of assessing and dividing Pedroso de Barros's assets reveals some interesting details about the structure of the slave population on a large estate and is suggestive of some of the conditions that prompted the uprising. At first, colonial authorities were unable to approach the estate, fearing that the Indians would "rise up and flee for being an indomitable people and not having names in our common Portuguese for not being baptized." This was a reference to the Guaianá, as "only the Carijó are called by their names." Even so, the Carijó were so numerous that they were organized in "lots" headed by Indian leaders, who ended up working out a peaceful solution to the impasse. Only in 1670 was an inventory of slaves composed, listing 318 captives who were partitioned among the heirs of Antonio Pedroso de Barros. In the eighteen-year interval between the revolt and the inventory, however, many Indians had sought refuge on other estates in the region, while a large group of Guaianá had escaped to the wilderness and established a community on the Atibaia River. Though unusually large, this rebellion set the tone for subsequent unrest.[88]

Another, smaller-scale revolt occurred in the same year near the mission village of Conceição dos Guarulhos. In this case, some Guarulhos Indians rose up, killing João Sutil de Oliveira and his wife, Maria Ribeira, who had established a rural property with fifty-nine Indian laborers shortly before. The causes of this rebellion remain obscure as well, though the inventory that was made of the couple's estate offers some clues. The rebellion broke out at a time when settlers were beginning to usurp lands belonging to Conceição dos Guarulhos and to transform its residents into forced laborers, which must have heightened friction between the two sides, and it may be seen as a response to this situation. However, not all of the Indians on the Sutil de Oliveira estate were from the mission village. It appears that many

Indians who took part in the uprising had been brought from the *sertão* recently. As much is suggested by the listing of Indians in the inventory, where the names of several couples are curiously similar: Ascenso and his wife Ascensa, Ambrósio and Ambrósia, Simão and Simoa, Luís and Luísa, a pattern suggestive of recent, pro forma baptisms. Two women who fled the scene had odd names – Sefaroza and Perina – that suggest they had not been baptized at all. Yet another clue comes from the statement of Sutil de Oliveira's father-in-law, who declared: "the Guarulhos murderers abducted some youths who have not been heard from since and [it would seem] that the others are dead." It is possible, then, that the rebels included Guarulhos from outside the property, perhaps from the mission village or, more likely, from the group that had been raided recently, who were attempting to rescue relatives who had been enslaved. Speculation aside, is it worth noting that most of the Indians remained on the estate after the crime, as only two men and nine women ran away.[89]

Another wave of unrest broke out in 1660, when various revolts claimed the lives of several slaveholders. In Mogi das Cruzes, the Guaianá of Bartolomeu Nunes do Passo rebelled, killing their master and destroying his property. When the probate judge arrived to make an inventory of the property of the deceased, the distraught widow, Maria Diniz de Mendonça, stated that it would scarcely be worthwhile, "as there is little wealth left over from the destruction that the heathen made of their goods on the occasion of the murder they committed." She added that "what else [the couple] owned said blacks have taken with them to find refuge in the bush." Of the twenty-eight Indian slaves that the couple had possessed, only nine remained on the property at the time of the inventory. The other "pieces" fled after the murder, "of which all named belong to her and her children and that if one or another should reappear one day the law will be informed to do what is fitting and good." It is worth noting that unlike in the other cases, most of the Indians involved in the rebellion were not new captives. Indeed, some of the culprits listed by the widow had been part of the inheritance she received nine years earlier from her first husband.[90]

At around the same time, other revolts broke out in the *bairro* of Juqueri. In this area characterized by large wheat-producing properties and the greatest concentration of Indian slaves in the region, there were uprisings on the estates of Manuel de Morais, Ascenso de Morais Dantas, Fernão Bicudo Tavares, and Francisco Coelho da Cruz. The latter two were killed, though detailed information exists only in the case of Coelho da Cruz. As in the revolt in Conceição dos Guarulhos, Francisco Coelho da Cruz and his wife Maria Leme were newly established settlers. But contrary to the pattern, their holdings of Indian slaves were relatively small and unusual in composition. Among their ten slaves, there were five of each sex, four of them couples and the remaining two single. There were no children. All of them, except for the single man, took part in the killings and then fled the estate.[91]

The outbreak of five rebellions in a single year shook the foundations of Indian slavery, leaving the colonists in a state of panic. As is common in such situations, their first response was to imagine a conspiracy theory, attributing the rebellions to agitation stirred up by Salvador de Sá. Furthermore, there were rumors that they should expect the worst at the end of the year, "due to the great risk there is of the heathen rising up when it becomes public that the said General [Salvador de Sá] will free them, an idea that has them agitated, and part of them has risen up in the Bairro of Juqueri." According to the colonists, it was this inspiration that moved the Indians to kill Francisco Coelho da Cruz, Bartolomeu Nunes do Passo, and Fernão Bicudo Tavares.[92]

However, as hard as the settlers searched for an external trigger for the Indians' unrest, it became increasingly clear that the problem had its roots on the plateau. The concentration of captives in the overall population was a constant threat, particularly in the middle decades of the seventeenth century, when the Indians were at an indisputable numerical advantage. For the first time since the conflicts of the sixteenth century, the absolute domination exercised by the settlers was confronted head on by the Indians. In this new conjuncture characterized by social instability, some settlers apparently came to believe that only masters who could discipline their slaveholdings were capable of possessing large numbers of Indians. In 1662, for example, Leonor de Siqueira, whose husband Luís Pedroso de Barros had disappeared on an ambitious expedition destined for the Andes Mountains, hurriedly sold sixty slaves belonging to her Juqueri estate for 20 milréis apiece, "because they were mutinous and because of the risk involved." The purchaser was Fernão Pais de Barros, her brother-in-law and the owner of a vast property near São Roque. Pais de Barros certainly had the means to control the hundreds of Indians under his administration, having learned the painful lesson provided by the death of his elder brother, Antonio Pedroso de Barros.[93]

The Ambiguous Meaning of Flight

While cases of collective revolt were relatively rare, flight and truancy occurred frequently throughout the entire period of Indian slavery's existence. According to many historians, running away constituted a well-characterized form of resistance to the slave system; paradoxically, however, it also indicated an advanced degree of integration. This assertion stands at odds with the long-standing view in the historiography of colonial Brazil, which contended that Indians were much more likely to flee from slavery than their African counterparts, since they were native to Brazil and because their "backward" culture stood in the way of their adaptation to the rigors of forced labor. But an analysis of flight among Indians in São Paulo reveals, on the contrary, that a marked similarity existed between São Paulo and other slave societies.

The incidence of flight, like that of rebellion, increased after 1640, and probably for many of the same reasons.[94] The sharp rise in the proportion of fugitive slaves reported in the inventories may be attributed in part to the influx of Guaianá and Guarulhos captives. It also coincided with the period of greatest concentration of Indians in the general population. Predictably, with the decline of the Indian population, the runaway rate also fell.

Different aspects of the slave regime motivated individual fugitives. Bad treatment, the desire to be reunited with family members who lived on other estates, or simply the desire for freedom were all compelling reasons for abandoning a particular household. For example, the Carijó Tetecola declared that she had fled because she did not want to serve the heirs of her late mistress.[95] In a similar case, Manuel Ruivo, a *bastardo* of the administration of Bartolomeu Fernandes de Faria, explained how he ended up in Faria's service in his statement during a judicial inquest. He said that after the death of his master, Miguel da Costa, on whose estate he was born, he rejected the administration of Costa's heir Tomás Correia and fled to the estate of Bartolomeu Fernandes.[96] Cristóvão Diniz recalled in his will that several years before he had owned a Kayapó slave who ran away to a Jesuit estate, where he married and raised many children.[97]

As this last case suggests, most Indians identified as runaways were actually to be found on other properties in the region. It is difficult to distinguish between coercion and protection, however, as it is clear that some Indians sought refuge on other estates, while others were obviously held against their will and forced to serve other masters. In either case, the recuperation of runaways became a sticky legal issue, as the uncertain status of Indian slaves and the relative immunity of rural estates to colonial justice came into play. This may be illustrated by a suit pressed by Catarina do Prado in 1682, which reveals the ambiguity of fugitive status, while illustrating the roles played by Indians in conflicts over the ownership of particular slaves. In her suit, Catarina stated that four "blacks of the land" belonging to Bartolomeu Bueno Cacunda had invaded her estate and kidnapped Úrsula, an Indian in her service. Úrsula, she argued, belonged to her because her husband, Estévão Ribeiro de Alvarenga, had brought her from the wilderness sixteen years earlier. Unconvinced by this claim, the judge decided to question Úrsula. Through an interpreter, Úrsula, known as Bahehu "in her land," told her side of the story. In response to the question "Whose are you?" the scribe recorded her as having answered:

Only to Captain Bartolomeu Bueno Cacunda, for having brought her from her land to his fields at Sapucaí, where he left her . . . and when from the said fields she tried to make her living or at her leisure she was found by the said deceased Estévão Ribeiro de Alvarenga and he took her to [this] settlement to his house with all her children who were in her company.

The judge then asked, "Why did you remain so long without returning to the house of the aforementioned your master?"

She answered because they had imprisoned her in irons and [once] not having done so and finding herself unbound she came to seek the house of her owner without any person having induced or counseled her to do this but that she did all of the above of her own accord.

The defendant, Bartolomeu Bueno, was absolved, and the "fugitive" Úrsula remained with her original master. It is an interesting case, not only for what it reveals about the issue of flight, but also because it demonstrates the process of distancing the Indian slave from her indigenous past.[98]

While flight by individual slaves occurred frequently, cases of mass flight involving the wholesale rejection of slave society were rare in seventeenth-century São Paulo. Slaves who fled to the bush were invariably from local groups, mainly Guaianá and Guarulhos, and had been brought to the Portuguese settlements only recently. In general, fleeing to the wilderness made little sense for Indian captives brought from distant homelands who had witnessed the destruction of their societies by the Paulistas.[99] Except in rare cases in which entire groups succeeded in fleeing at once, as in the aftermath of the rebellion on Antonio Pedroso de Barros's estate in 1652, it was practically impossible to recreate the world that had been lost.

That said, numerous reports of individuals running away to the *sertão* appear in the documentation. Usually, though, these reports refer to cases in which the fugitive – an ambiguous term in this context – had joined or been forced to join a slaving expedition. In his will, drawn up in 1676, Pedro Vaz de Barros noted: "I declare that I have many fugitive pieces particularly with the people of Captain Fernão Dias Pais," who was in Minas Gerais.[100] Another master, distraught over the loss of two Indians he had rented to Captain Braz Moreira Cabral to serve as translators on a slaving expedition, lamented that they remained in the Vacaria region of Mato Grosso as Cabral's henchmen, only to be used "against their master."[101]

Most fugitive slaves, however, remained within the regional slave society. References to fugitives often included the location where they took refuge, as the masters of these fugitive Indians knew precisely where the runaways were to be found. For example, Antonia Chaves recorded in her will that the Indian Isabel "went about as a fugitive" and that "they say it is certain that she is in the household of Antonio Ribeiro de Morais, resident in the town of São Paulo."[102] Another settler, Manuel Rodrigues de Góis, declared "that I have a young man of the Carijó heathen whom I bought with my money by the name of Tomás who is fugitive in the household of Salvador de Miranda from which I order my heirs to collect him."[103] In a similar case, the widow of Estevão Furquim pressed a suit to recover a runaway who had been working for seven or eight years on the estate of Inês Rodrigues in distant Taubaté, "in plain sight of all the world." To consolidate her acquisition, Inês Rodrigues had married the fugitive to one of her own servants, a strategy that became more and more common as Indian labor became increasingly scarce.[104]

These cases indicate that many masters sheltered fugitives as a means of expanding their labor force at the expense of less powerful slaveowners. Ana Machado de Lima, who had ten Indians in her service, noted revealingly in her will that six of them belonged to other masters, "as my husband well knows."[105] João Missel Gigante, an important slaveowner in Parnaíba, included among his last wishes that the Indians found on his estate who belonged to other colonists should be returned to their rightful owners.[106] Similarly, Pedro Vidal declared that "on my estate there are three female blacks and an old black man, fugitives of the Goianá, heathen, and it is not known who they belong to [and] should their owners appear I order that they be turned over to them."[107]

The owners of Indian slaves were therefore able to turn a potential form of resistance to the system of forced labor to their own benefit, as in the context of the local economy Indian flight basically resulted in the redistribution of labor. For the Indians, this situation allowed for a certain measure of mobility, restricted as it was. It may well have been that the circulation of captives served to lessen the tensions inherent to the master–slave relationship. In the final analysis, however, this situation reinforced that relationship, even as it favored the wealthier and more powerful colonists, who were better able to resist attempts by other slaveowners to recover their fugitive or stolen property by force of arms or through the unreliable mechanisms of the colonial legal system.

Despite the unreliability of the latter, colonists proved increasingly litigious toward the end of the century, as Indian labor became increasingly scarce and the relative value of slaves rose. Authorities took an explicit stance on the issue as early as 1649, when a royal magistrate established fines and punishments for colonists who harbored fugitives. Interestingly, the fines clearly corresponded to the value of slaves as laborers. As time went on, however, legal ordinances became progressively tougher. In 1675, during his inspection of the captaincy, Crown Judge Castelo Branco established that owners of fugitive slaves were to receive compensation of 20 milréis in addition to the value of the Indian in question, to be paid by the colonist who was using that Indian's labor. The Indian would remain in the hands of the latter, who by sheltering a fugitive would effectively have bought a slave. As an alternative, the injured party could collect his slave along with an indemnity that corresponded to the going rate for renting a slave. In 1687 this amount was set according to location: the daily rate for an Indian fugitive who was put to work in the same *bairro* was 80 réis; around the town center, 200 réis; within the township, but at a considerable distance from the master's home, 640 réis; in a neighboring township, 1 milréis; and in the *sertão*, the considerable sum of 4 milréis.[108] While this measure may have discouraged the use of fugitive Indians on slaving expeditions and in the transport of goods to the coast, it placed no real onus on settlers who put fugitives to work locally, as the penalty remained below the going rate for renting an Indian. What seems most important to note, however, is that colonial authorities connived to manage – without formally regulating – the use and abuse of Indian slaves, which would be pointed out by Vieira in his polemic with the colonists five years later.

Some settlers appealed to these measures in attempting to recover personal losses provoked by the absenteeism or sequestration of their Indians. However, such an approach usually meant a costly, drawn-out suit that had to be brought before the probate judge (in cases involving inheritances), or the ordinary judge of the Municipal Council, or even a Crown magistrate on a periodic judicial inspection. Onofre Jorge, for example, spent nine years trying to recover an Indian he knew was being held by João Barreto, leaving the task to his heirs when he died.[109] João Vaz Madeira of Mogi das Cruzes was one of the few colonists who succeeded in recovering a runaway Indian, but tellingly, he did so outside of the judicial system, spending 6 milréis on the services of the man who recaptured the fugitive. This sum represented about 20 percent of the value of the captive.[110] In lawsuits, most colonists had to settle for simple restitution of the fugitive or, at most, payment of the Indian's approximate value. Such was the case of Captain Antonio João de Moura, who sued the estate of João Pires Monteiro, demanding restitution for the value of seven Indians at the rate of 20 milréis each, plus an amount equivalent to their rental for 750 days. While Moura won the case, he received only the 20 milréis per Indian.[111]

In the last analysis, as we will see in greater detail in the final chapter, the increase in litigation over fugitive Indians reflected the crisis that the regime of personal service was undergoing. All of the resulting tensions came together in the case of the outlaw Bartolomeu Fernandes de Faria, who in the early eighteenth century still held more than two hundred Indian and African slaves. In 1718, when Faria was arrested and charged with a double homicide, authorities confiscated 98 Indians from his estates in

Jacareí and Iguape. The list they compiled of these captives revealed that nearly all of them belonged to other estates. Most belonged to the rural chapel left by Brígida Sobrinha in 1694 in a will that was also in the power of Bartolomeu Fernandes. In addition, the list included four free *bastardas* – daughters of Indians, born into compulsory service, but since freed – who had been "seized by the old man to serve him," as well as a free *bastarda* who was forced to marry a mulato slave belonging to the old man.[112]

Few settlers went as far as Captain Bartolomeu Fernandes in their attempts to ensure the availability of Indian labor in the midst of a supply crisis, but it was becoming increasingly clear to all that other strategies for acquiring – and maintaining – labor were necessary.

From Indian to Slave: Final Comments

The trial of Captain Bartolomeu Fernandes de Faria also provides illuminating evidence of the process of transformation from Indian to slave. While the term *carijó* captured much of this historical experience, the imposition of this model by masters can be illustrated by the case of Joana de Siqueira, a free *bastarda* of twenty-eight years of age who was forced into slavery. At some point in the mid-1710s, henchmen of Bartolomeu Fernandes ambushed Joana along with two traveling companions. The latter were brutally murdered, while Joana was taken to the estate of Bartolomeu Fernandes, where she came face-to-face with her new master:

> who said to her, the witness, you come here that I want to take you to serve me and he ordered her to raise her skirt and placed a stick between her legs and ordered her whipped by his son João Fernandes and by Antonio Fernandes . . . which they did until a quantity of blood ran from her, the said Bartolomeu Fernandes saying that he did that so that from then on she would recognize him as her master . . . and after the said Bartolomeu Fernandes took her to his roça and dressed her in a *tipóia* and was using her until now as his captive.[113]

The case of Joana de Siqueira demonstrates how violence and submission figured as two crucial elements of the structure of domination that characterized Paulista society in the seventeenth century. Joana's humiliation played an important role in the affirmation of social relations of domination, which must have provoked strong resentment on her part, particularly since she had previously lived as a free person. Lashed like a slave, forced to wear a *tipóia*, the typical dress of Guarani women, thus was Joana reduced to slavery and identified as belonging to the enslaved community.[114]

But violence represented only one facet of the complex relationship between masters and slaves. Without it, to be sure, control over the Indian population would have been practically impossible. However, while the colonists may have been interested primarily in the fruits of Indian labor, every master recognized the need to create additional mechanisms to soften the inherently conflictual relationship between oppressors and oppressed. These mechanisms ultimately were couched in the paternalistic discourse with which the colonists sought to justify their domination over the Indians. More than simple rhetoric, though, this posture was also manifested in practice, in the sense that masters took care to establish extra-economic bonds with their slaves, with the aim of imposing some stability on the fragile structures of the slave system.[115] The protective attitude they adopted toward their presumed social inferiors, far from being incompatible with economic exploitation, reinforced the unequal relations that drove the system of production.

Notes

1. "Protesto de Domingos de Góis," in inventory of João Furtado, 1653, AESP-INP, cx. 1.
2. Because Indian slavery was technically illegal, there exist few records of sales of Indian slaves with which to chart changes in prices over time. Beginning in the 1670s, however, *alvidrações*, or appraisals of the values of *serviços* (literally "services," but in practice meaning "servants"), appearing in inventory lists of Indian wards permit the creation of price charts. For a preliminary attempt, see Monteiro, "São Paulo in the Seventeenth Century," 255 (table 11).
3. For an interesting discussion of the concept of "creolization," see Charles W. Joyner, *Down by the Riverside: A South Carolina Slave Community* (Urbana: University of Illinois Press, 1984), esp. the intro. and pp. 246–247.
4. Petition of Maria Pacheco, June 11, 1670, in inventory of João Pires Monteiro, 1667, AESP-INP, cx. 9.
5. Register of trade of Indians between Cornélio Rodrigues de Arzão and Antonio Lopes Benavides, Jan. 17, 1681, AESP-Notas Parnaíba, 1680.
6. Will of Maria da Cunha, Mogi das Cruzes, 1681, AESP-Mogi.
7. João Barreto v. Pedro Porrate Penedo, 1686, AESP-AC, cx. 3434-1.
8. See note 2, above.
9. Inventory of Antonio Rodrigues Velho, 1616, AESP-IE, cx. 1, doc. 3.
10. Inventory of Antonio Correia da Silva, Parnaíba, 1672, AESP-INP, cx. 12; inventory of Juliana Antunes, Mogi das Cruzes, 1682, AESP-INP, cx. 12.
11. Inventory of Simão de Araujo, Mogi das Cruzes, 1653, AESP-Mogi.
12. According to Pedro Taques de Almeida Paes Leme, young *mulatos* – the mixed offspring of Indian women and African men – frequently served as *pajens*, or page boys, in the seventeenth century.
13. For a more detailed discussion of Indian mortality, see John Monteiro, "Os escravos índios de São Paulo no século XVII: alguns aspectos demográficos," *Revista da Sociedade Brasileira de Pesquisa Histórica* 5 (1989–1990): 11–18.
14. No systematic study of colonial-era epidemics exists. Information on the outbreaks listed here was compiled from local documentation, especially the *Actas da Câmara de São Paulo*. See, among others, CMSP-Atas, 4:73, Dec. 14, 1630, as well as Camargo, *História de Parnaíba*, 101–103. See also the discussion in Chapter 2, above.

15. I explore this dynamic in Monteiro, "Escravidão indígena e despovoamento."
16. Will of Domingos Leite de Carvalho, 1692, AESP-INP, cx. 21.
17. Manuel da Fonseca, *Vida do veneravel padre Belchior de Pontes, da Companhia de Jesus da provincia do Brasil,* facs. edn. (São Paulo: Melhoramentos, 1932 [1752]), 128–129; inventory of Pedro Vaz de Barros, 1697, IT, 24:13–67.
18. For example, see CMSP-Atas, 5:535, Nov. 9, 1652.
19. Account book of Martim Rodrigues Tenorio [de Aguilar], IT, 2:75.
20. Will of Manuel Temudo, 1660, AESP-INP, cx. 5; will of Gaspar de Oliveira, 1696, AESP-IPO, 15.620.
21. "Treslado da concessão da ordem com que se eregiu a capela da Senhora da Conceição," 1660, in "Livro de tombo" of Mogi das Cruzes, 1747, Arquivo da Cúria Diocesana de Mogi das Cruzes.
22. "Protesto de Domingos de Góis," in inventory of João Furtado, 1653, AESP-INP, cx. 1.
23. Inventory of Maria Moreira, Taubaté, 1675, Museu de Taubaté, Inventários e testamentos, cx. 1; inventory of Catarina Tavares, Parnaíba, 1671, AESP-INP, cx. 12. Catarina Tavares was the wife of the backwoodsman Sebastião Pais de Barros, who led a large-scale expedition through the region of the Tocantins River that reached the city of Belém, at the mouth of the Amazon River.
24. Batisados, Santo Amaro, Mar. 25, 1699 and July 18, 1700, AMDDLS, 04-02-23.
25. Batisados, Sorocaba, Jan. 21, 1685, Jan. 31, 1685, and Feb. 1, 1685, ACDS, livro 1.
26. Batisados, Sorocaba, Feb. 20, 1685, ACDS, livro 1.
27. In this context, the term "white" refers to the free population, as distinct from the class of Indian servants. This population included, of course, a wide variety of ethnic types.
28. While the clear preference for white godparents is not surprising, the figures for the São Paulo region offer a strong contrast with the results found by Schwartz for the parish surrounding the Sergipe do Conde plantation. In Bahia, only 9 Indians appeared as godfathers and 21 as godmothers in 234 baptisms. It should be pointed out, however, that the level of detail found in the baptismal registers of Sergipe do Conde is inferior to that found in the Paulista registers, with the lack of specific indications of the ethnic origin of the parents and godparents in almost half of all cases. See Schwartz, *Sugar Plantations*, 61 (table 6).
29. Batisados, Sorocaba, Oct. 8, 1690, ACDS, livro 1.
30. Inventory of Maria Tenoria, 1620, IT, 44:33.
31. The "*caipira* dialect" refers to the form of Portuguese spoken by the native-born rural poor of São Paulo and parts of adjacent captaincies/provinces/states that were settled by Paulistas between the late eighteenth century and the early twentieth. Studies of the historical evolution of the *caipira* dialect are few, focusing mainly on folkloric aspects rather than on ethnolinguistics. Historians have clung to the notion that everyone in colonial São Paulo spoke Tupi. A curious exception, Joaquim Ribeiro, *Folclore dos bandeirantes* (Rio de Janeiro: José Olympio, 1946), contends that the Paulistas spoke a local dialect of Portuguese. For a good general introduction to the subject of caipira culture, see Carlos Rodrigues Brandão, *Os caipiras de São Paulo* (São Paulo: Brasiliense, 1983).
32. Letter of Frei Francisco de Lima, Bishop of Pernambuco, quoted in "Consulta da Juncta das Missões de 29 de outubro de 1697 sobre as cartas do Bispo e Gov.^{or} de Pernambuco. . .," in Ennes, *As guerras nos Palmares*, 353.
33. Domingos Jorge Velho to the Crown, July 15, 1694, in Ennes, *As guerras nos Palmares*, 204–207; AESP-Notas Parnaíba, 1691.

34. Auto de genere of Salvador Sutil, 1696, AMDDLS, 1-2-32. Guarani, like Tupi, belongs to the Tupian language family.
35. Examples of the Guarani etymology of various words from the *caipira* dialect may be found in Amadeu Amaral, *O dialeto caipira: gramática, vocabulário*, 4th edn. (São Paulo: Hucitec, 1982 [1920]).
36. A similar pattern was identified by Schwartz in his study of Indian labor in Bahia, where the Portuguese coined a series of terms that reflected European biases while attaching precise definitions to different social and occupational categories. Schwartz, "Indian Labor," 61–62.
37. On these terms, see John Monteiro, "A escravidão indígena e o problema da identidade étnica em São Paulo colonial," *Ciências Sociais Hoje* (1990): 237–252.
38. The diffusion of the term *carijó* has led to some ethnographic confusion, especially when it appears as an ethnonym in the regions of present-day Minas Gerais, Goiás, and Mato Grosso. In fact, the presence of so-called Carijó in those regions was related to Portuguese expansion in the first quarter of the eighteenth century. Colonists who traveled there were accompanied by numerous Indian slaves, whom they called *carijó* to distinguish them from African slaves, who were present in ever-greater numbers. In an interesting chapter in Luso–indigenous relations, a large group of Carijó captives fled from settlers in Goiás, then established autonomous communities along the Tocantins River and resisted the subsequent advance of European colonization. These groups came to be known as Canoeiro or Avá-Canoeiro (the latter term suggesting possible – if also debatable – Guarani origins). For a very interesting ethnohistorical account, see André Amaral de Toral, "Os índios negros ou os Carijó de Goiás: a história dos Avá-Canoeiro," *Revista de Antropologia* 27–28 (1984–1985): 287–325.
39. "Carta de liberdade a Maria Carijó," Sept. 30, 1722, AESP-Notas Sorocaba.
40. Will of Pedro Dias Pais, Parnaíba, 1726, AESP-INP, cx. 28.
41. Will of Margarida da Silva, 1726, AESP-INP, cx. 28.
42. There has been a long-standing debate on the origins of the term *mamaluco*, with some (including the Spanish Jesuits of the seventeenth century) suggesting that it derived from the Egyptian term *mamluk* (*mameluco* in Portuguese), which referred to the warrior-slaves of the fifteenth and sixteenth centuries. However, the word invariably appears as *mamaluco* in the Paulista documentation, which led Sérgio Buarque de Holanda to favor this spelling. A seventeenth-century glossary of Brazilian Tupi identifies the term with Tupi origins. "Vocabulario da lingua brasilica," Biblioteca Municipal de São Paulo, ms. a4. See also the linguistic analysis of Plínio Ayrosa, "Mameluco é termo árabe ou tupi?" *Revista do Arquivo Municipal* 1 (June 1934): 21–24.
43. Other late seventeenth-century terms point to the increased heterogeneity of the population of São Paulo. The terms *caboclo* and *curiboca* appeared for the first time in the 1680s, both of them referring to offspring of either white and Indian unions or African and Indian unions. The terms *cabra* and *pardo* had varied meanings, but increasingly referred to individuals of at least partial African ancestry. See Monteiro, "São Paulo in the Seventeenth Century," 283–284, 286.
44. Will of Estevão Furquim, IT, 16:201.
45. IT, 14:208.
46. Will of Francisco Cabral de Távora, Jundiaí, 1692, AESP-INP, cx. 21.

47. Antonio Rodrigues, "Carta da missão que no ano de 99 fizeram dois religiosos da Companhia de Jesus na vila de São Paulo e mais vilas adjacentes," Jan. 25, 1700, ARSI Brasilia 10, fol. 3v. Marriage patterns among poor whites followed this pattern well into the nineteenth century.
48. Inventory of Antonio Ribeiro Roxo, 1653, AESP-INP, cx. 1.
49. Inventory of Garcia Rodrigues, 1632, IT, 8:405.
50. Monteiro, "São Paulo in the Seventeenth Century," 427–429.
51. On this subject, see Monteiro, "Os escravos índios de São Paulo."
52. Batisados, Santo Amaro, livro 1 (1686–1725), AMDDLS, 04-02-23; Table 7, above.
53. Will of Antonia de Oliveira, Parnaíba, IT, 8:311–312.
54. Will of Maria Diniz, 1682, AESP-INP, cx. 16. At one point in its half-hearted efforts to maintain the mission-village system, the Municipal Council of São Paulo tried to discourage colonists from promoting marriages between their Indians and mission-village residents. CMSP-Atas, 6a:356, Mar. 1, 1664. Crown justice took a more serious approach, as one magistrate ordered that in the case of forced marriages, the master would lose *both* parties to the mission village. CMSP-Atas, 6:384–389, Nov. 10, 1675.
55. Testimony of Pedro Mulato Papudo, Oct. 10, 1718, Justice v. Bartolomeu Fernandes de Faria, AESP-AC, cx. 6, doc. 98. Notwithstanding its filing in AESP-AC, this document is actually a *Devassa*, or criminal investigation, and not an *Auto Civil*.
56. On Indian quarters, see, for example, inventory of Isabel da Cunha, 1616, IT, 4:319; inventory of Maria Pais, 1616, IT, 4:454; inventory of Matias de Oliveira, 1628, IT, 6:276; inventory of Paulo da Silva, 1633, IT, 32:73; "Cartas de datas de terras," Jundiaí, 1657, Museu Histórico e Cultural de Jundiaí; inventory of Antonio Correia da Silva, Parnaíba, 1672, AESP-INP, cx. 12; record of land sale by Francisco Proença to Antonio Dias Diniz, Oct. 26, 1682, AESP-Notas Parnaíba, 1680.
57. For example, the criminal José Grande Carijó casually mentioned his place in the "*sanzala*" in his testimony before a Crown magistrate. Justice v. Bartolomeu Fernandes de Faria, AESP-AC, cx. 6. The inventory of Bento Amaral da Silva, which dates from 1719, lists "various houses of straw and senzalas," evidently to house his 42 African slaves and 21 Indian servants. AESP-IPO, 14.308.
58. Inventory of Antonia de Chaves, 1640, IT, 14:lxii–lxiii.
59. Inventory of José Preto, 1653, AESP-Mogi, cx. 1.
60. Will of Jerônimo de Brito, 1644, AESP-IE, cx. 2, doc. 4.
61. Will of Pedro Morais Dantas, 1644, IT, 14:289.
62. For example, record of sale by Gaspar de Brito to Simão Jorge Velho, May 8, 1690, and by Paulo Proença to [illegible], Oct. 18, 1700, AESP-Notas Parnaíba.
63. Inventory of José Ortiz de Camargo, 1663, AESP-INP, cx. 7; donation by Guilherme Pompeu de Almeida, Feb. 11, 1687, in "Livro de tombo" of Santana de Parnaíba, fol. 31, Arquivo da Cúria Diocesana de Jundiaí, cód. 505.
64. Paes Leme, *Nobiliarquia paulistana*, 1:130.
65. Inventory of Manuel Alves Pimentel, 1626, IT, 31:168; will of Antonio Vieira Tavares, Itu, 1710, AESP-INP, cx. 26.
66. CMSP-Atas: 5:261, Feb. 2, 1647; 5:295, Mar. 2, 1647; 6a:216, Dec. 18, 1660; 6a:382, Aug. 8, 1664. Maria Odila Leite da Silva Dias, in *Quotidiano e poder em São Paulo no século XIX* (São Paulo: Brasiliense, 1984), also notes the constant presence

of the Municipal Council in the informal world of petty commerce in nineteenth-century São Paulo.

67. Will of Grácia de Abreu, Parnaíba, 1660, AESP-INP, cx. 5.
68. Francisco Cubas v. heirs of José Ortiz de Camargo, 1664, AESP-AC, cx. 6033-1.
69. For a solid analysis of slave crime in the province of São Paulo, including its relationship to market activities, see Maria Helena P. T. Machado, *Crime e escravidão: trabalho, luta e resistência nas lavouras paulistas, 1830–1888* (São Paulo: Brasiliense, 1987), esp. 100ff. See also the discussion in Eugene D. Genovese, *Roll, Jordan, Roll: The World the Slaves Made* (New York: Pantheon, 1974), 599–613. An excellent, pioneering article comparing indigenous and African resistance in the English Caribbean is Michael Craton, "From Caribs to Black Caribs: The Amerindian Roots of Servile Resistance in the Caribbean," in Gary Y. Okihiro (ed.), *In Resistance: Studies in African, Caribbean, and Afro-American History* (Amherst: University of Massachusetts Press, 1986), 96–116.
70. For example, in Padre Domingos Gomes Albernás v. Frei João Batista Pinto, 1691, a suit over a theft of money by one of Pinto's Indians, the litigant remarked that if one of his Indians were involved in such a case, he would pay damages immediately, "without contention in justice." AESP-AC, cx. 1, doc. 22.
71. On the concept, see Steve J. Stern (ed.), *Resistance, Rebellion, and Consciousness in the Andean Peasant World, 18th to 20th Centuries* (Madison: University of Wisconsin Press, 1987), 9–13.
72. CMSP-Atas, 3:56, Oct. 21, 1623.
73. CMSP-Atas, 7:280, Apr. 17, 1685.
74. CMSP-Atas, 8:275, Feb. 19, 1712.
75. CMSP-Atas, 3:79–80, Jan. 27, 1624; Afonso d'Escragnolle Taunay, *Piratininga: aspectos sociaes de S. Paulo seiscentista* (São Paulo: H. L. Canton, 1923), 28–29.
76. Câmara Municipal de Parnaíba, Atas, livro 1, fols. 19v–20, Feb. 17, 1680, AESP, cx. 6049-1; Câmara Municipal de Sorocaba, Vereanças, June 5, 1669, AESP, cx. 472-1; Municipal Council of Guaratinguetá to Municipal Council of São Paulo, n.d., AHMSP, Correspondência Avulsa, cx. 4.
77. "Protesto do Padre Presidente Frei Anselmo da Anunciação," 1672, Câmara Municipal de Sorocaba, Livros de Vereança, AESP, cx. 472-1.
78. "Requerimento do capitão do povo," June 24, 1675, Câmara Municipal de Sorocaba, Livros de Vereança, AESP, cx. 472-1.
79. Paes Leme, *Nobiliarquia paulistana*, 1:200.
80. Padre Manuel da Cruz ao Conselho Ultramarino, Aug. 24, 1739, AHU-SP, Aditamentos, cx. 252.
81. Antonio Bororo v. João Lopes Fernandes, 1733, in Departamento do Arquivo do Estado de São Paulo, *Boletim do Departamento do Arquivo do Estado* 7 (1947): 53–54.
82. Grimaneza, Filhos e Companheiros v. Maria Pedrosa and Domingas Moreira, 1717, AESP-AC, cx. 5, doc. 80.
83. This calculation is based on an estimate of forty Indians per slaveowner, the average for the decade (see Table 2, above), divided by five (the average figure for the size of a slaveowning family).
84. Inventory of João de Oliveira, 1653, AESP-INP, cx. 1; inventory of Manuel Alves de Aguirra, 1666, AESP-INP, cx. 9.

85. "Autos de correição, capitulo 18," June 7, 1653, CMSP-Atas, 6:37; and CMSP-Atas, 6a:101–102, Dec. 24, 1658.
86. CMSP-Atas, 6a:211–212, Nov. 8, 1660.
87. Inventory of Antonio Pedroso de Barros, 1652, IT, 20:55–56.
88. Inventory of Antonio Pedroso de Barros, 1652, IT, vol. 20, passim.
89. Inventory of João Sutil de Oliveira and Maria Ribeira, 1652, IT, 42:129–171 (quote on 147).
90. Inventory of Bartolomeu Nunes do Passo, Mogi das Cruzes, 1660, AESP-Mogi; inventory of Antonio Pedroso de Lima (first husband of Maria Diniz de Mendonça), 1651, IT, 41:257–290.
91. Inventory of Francisco Coelho da Cruz, Parnaíba, 1660, AESP-INP, cx. 5.
92. CMSP-Atas, 6a:209–212, Nov. 2 and 8, 1660. On the conspiracy thesis, see Municipal Council of Rio de Janeiro to Antonio Mariz, n.d., in *RIHGB* 3 (1841): 22–23.
93. Inventory of Luiz Pedrozo (Luis Pedroso de Barros), Parnaíba, 1662, IT, 43:289–290.
94. According to the inventories of probated estates in São Paulo, there was notable increase in slave flight in the 1660s, when the rate of male fugitives per 1,000 slaves reached 59. In the decades that followed, this rate fell to 39 per 1,000, still a high rate. The figures for Parnaíba, and for female slaves in both townships, show a similar pattern. See Monteiro, "São Paulo in the Seventeenth Century," 316.
95. Petition of Diogo Mendes, Oct. 29, 1619, in inventory of Isabel Fernandes, 1619, IT, 30:214–215.
96. Testimony of Manuel Ruivo Bastardo, Sept. 12, 1718, in Justice v. Bartolomeu Fernandes de Faria, AESP-AC, cx. 6.
97. Will of Cristóvão Diniz, Parnaíba (Itu), 1650, IT, 41:135.
98. Catarina do Prado v. Bartolomeu Bueno Cacunda, 1682, AESP-AC, cx. 1.
99. See, for example, inventory of Francisco Borges, 1649, IT, 39:97–98; will of Domingos Dias Felix, Taubaté, 1660, Museu de Taubaté, Inventários e testamentos, cx. 1; inventory of Maria da Cunha, 1670, IT, 17:488.
100. Will of Pedro Vaz de Barros, Parnaíba (São Roque), 1674, AESP-INP, cx. 22.
101. Salvador Moreira v. Braz Moreira Cabral, July 2, 1690, in inventory of Salvador Moreira, Parnaíba, 1697, IT, 24:97–100.
102. Inventory of Antonia de Chaves, Parnaíba, 1640, IT, 14:lxii.
103. Will of Manuel Rodrigues de Góis, 1662, AESP-INP, cx. 6.
104. Inventory of Estevão Furquim, 1660, IT, 16:278–279.
105. Will of Ana Machado de Lima, 1684, AESP-INP, cx. 17.
106. Will of João Missel Gigante, Parnaíba, 1645, IT, 32:122.
107. Will of Pedro Vidal, 1658, AESP-INP, cx. 4.
108. "Capítulo de correição," Mar. 16, 1649, CMSP-Atas, 5:367; "Correição, capítulo 9," June 7, 1653, CMSP-Atas, 6:34; "Capítulos de correição," Nov. 10, 1675, CMSP-Atas, 6:389; and "Capitulo de correição," Dec. 30, 1687, CMSP-Atas, 7:342–343.
109. Will of Onofre Jorge, 1688, AESP-IPO, 14.645.
110. Petition of João Vaz Madeira, n.d., in inventory of Antonio Pereira Magalhães, Mogi das Cruzes, 1679, AESP-Mogi.
111. Antonio João de Moura v. Heirs of João Pires Monteiro, Oct. 7, 1671, in inventory of João Pires Monteiro, 1667, AESP-INP, cx. 9.

112. "Auto de sequestro," June 18, 1718, in Justice v. Bartolomeu Fernandes de Faria, AESP-AC, cx. 6. The corresponding passage of *Negros da terra* refers to "a white girl who had been a foundling" among Fernandes's illicit holdings, but no such figure appears in a discussion of this situation in Monteiro's subsequently published "Sal, justiça social e autoridade régia: São Paulo no início do século XVIII," *Tempo* 8 (Aug. 1999): 23–40 which later appeared, with "some small modifications and corrections," as chap. 4 of the thesis he presented for the title of livre-docente at the University of Campinas in 2001. See Monteiro, "Tupis, tapuias e historiadores: estudos de história indígena e do indigenismo" (tese de livre-docência, Unicamp, 2001), 79–96 (quote on 79n). The editors and translators of this book have updated their text accordingly.
113. Justice v. Bartolomeu Fernandes de Faria, AESP-AC, cx. 6.
114. On the *tipóia*, originally associated with Guarani societies and perhaps spread to other groups by the Jesuits, see Alfred Métraux, "The Guarani," in Julian H. Steward (ed.), *Handbook of South American Indians*, 7 vols. (Washington, DC: Smithsonian Institution, 1946–1950), 3:82–83.
115. On the issue of paternalism, see, for example, Genovese, *Roll, Jordan, Roll*, esp. chap. 1. For nineteenth-century Brazil, see the interesting discussion in Robert W. Slenes, "The Demography and Economics of Brazilian Slavery, 1850–1888" (Ph.D. dissertation, Stanford University, 1976).

6

The Roots of Rural Poverty

Between 1679 and 1682, the residents of the town of São Paulo and its outlying rural districts were duly enrolled in a book kept by the Municipal Council that registered the contribution each head of household was to make to the Donativo Real (Royal Contribution).[1] The Donativo, a tax levied by municipal councils throughout the Portuguese empire, had existed since the early 1660s, but, at least in the captaincy of São Vicente, the criteria for its collection were laid out only in 1679, during the judicial inspection of the royal magistrate João da Rocha Pita.[2] The compiling of the Donativo created a valuable – indeed, indispensable – document for the study of Paulista society in the seventeenth century, one that has not yet provoked significant interest among historians.

The registry book contains lists of residents and the values of their annual contributions. The specific criteria employed to appraise the value of individual contributions are unclear, but Pita's general instructions were that all residents, rich and poor, should contribute "according to their means."[3] There are two reasons why it seems likely that holdings of Indians served as the principal basis for establishing the amounts to be paid. First, there is a strong correlation between the size of the contribution of property holders who died within a decade of the assessment and the number of Indians found in their estate inventories. Second, a similar tax roll composed for Itu in 1728 clearly used the number of African slaves and Indian servants to determine the amount that each taxpayer was to contribute.[4] Therefore, the Donativo lists should reflect not only general differences in wealth, but also the relative size of individual slaveholdings, the possession of captive labor having been the principal means of wealth-holding in the region.

Beginning with an analysis of the tax rolls of 1679–1682, this chapter seeks to examine the internal structure of the rural neighborhoods that surrounded the town of São Paulo in the seventeenth century. The rolls afford a partial glimpse at the distribution of wealth and of family relationships that defined each rural district, a view that may be enhanced by examining other documents from the period, particularly inventories and wills. The lists, in sum, provide statistical evidence that illustrates how processes of territorial expansion and rural development – though relatively modest in scale – determined, in large part, the basic contours of Paulista society.

The conclusions that emerge from this more comprehensive view refute certain ideas that have been fundamental to Paulista historiography. On the one hand, the tax rolls of 1679–1682 show that Paulista society in the "century of the *bandeirantes*," far from being egalitarian, was marked by profound inequalities in the distribution of wealth. On the other, these same lists show that the spread of rural poverty, which is often attributed to geographic isolation and the less intensive variety of agriculture supposedly practiced in São Paulo, resulted from a process in which Indian slavery and commercial agriculture played key roles.

Rural São Paulo, 1679: The Distribution of Wealth

The formation of Paulista society in the colonial period was closely tied to the process of transforming uncultivated wilderness into fairly stable population centers, a process accompanied by the evolution of large-scale Indian slavery. Over much of the seventeenth century, new groups of colonists extended the limits of European settlement and organized new communities on a broad base of Indian labor. Territorial expansion depended upon the availability of abundant land and labor.

In the second half of the seventeenth century, access to economically viable lands, as well as Indian captives, became much more difficult. During the first half of the century, the acquisition of virgin land through *sesmarias* and municipal grants had been relatively easy. At the same time, the collective organization of large-scale slaving expeditions, made viable by the proximity of numerous Guarani villages, had afforded an abundant supply of labor for an entire generation. This picture began to change in the 1640s. Between 1638 and 1641, almost all of the best lands between the town of São Paulo and the Atibaia River were distributed, along with vast tracts along the Tietê River to the west of Santana de Parnaíba. In these same years, the Jesuits and the Guarani began to repel slaving expeditions, severely limiting the recruitment of Indian labor and forcing the colonists to reorganize their expeditions along more modest lines. Finally, the region's wealth, based on the production and transport of a few commercial goods – wheat foremost among them – became increasingly concentrated in the hands of a few privileged and powerful families who, by the 1650s, were struggling among themselves for absolute control over the reins of power.

If, on the one hand, the organization of agricultural production led to a sharp division between slaveowners and Indian slaves, exploiters and exploited, on the other, it also determined that there would be profound differences in wealth within the free population. In brief, while the formation of new communities and the expansion of production offered the prospect of wealth, the principal result of these processes was, paradoxically, the spread of rural poverty.[5]

Much of the wealth, power, and prestige of the leading families of rural São Paulo was rooted in the rural *bairros* that had emerged with the expansion of colonial production. In administrative terms, the *bairro* was little more than an appendage of the town, designed to provide an organizational structure capable of meeting some of the collective needs of its residents. Thus, each *bairro* had an internal structure of its own, particularly during the colonial period, when the pull of the urban market was weak and the dominance of city over countryside lay in the future.[6]

As constellations of rural properties more or less linked to one another, the *bairros* were composed of units of production that varied greatly in size. Although the term *fazenda* (estate) appears here and there in the documentation, even some of the largest units were called *sítios* (literally, "site" or "place"), which presents a problem for the historian, as the latter term would come to refer exclusively to smallholdings.[7] Most seventeenth-century *bairros* originated with and grew around large commercial properties owned by the wealthiest and most prestigious residents. These leading residents reserved for themselves the position of local militia captain (*capitão do bairro*), a source of authority that ultimately mirrored the economic relations that predominated in the formation of the neighborhoods.

In many cases, the largest landowners raised chapels on their estates, which served as centers for the *bairro*'s religious and recreational activities. The founding of a chapel was an important event, as it reinforced the social prestige and economic power of its founder. Having raised a rural chapel, its founder would also assume the expenses associated with local religious services, which were the only way the Church reached much of the rural population under Portuguese colonialism. In seventeenth-century São Paulo, with few exceptions, the founding of a chapel was associated with the presence of large numbers of Indians. The spatial organization of the chapel itself mirrored the basic division in colonial society: the central and lateral areas were reserved for the free, while an ample area around the entryway was ceded to slaves and Indians who wanted "to glimpse the saints."[8] As a result of the subsequent economic and demographic development of their *bairros*, several of these early chapels came to have resident priests and, in some cases, became parish seats.

Each township had several *bairros*, though it remains difficult to recover the precise names and locations of all of them from the surviving documentation. Many had indigenous names, some of which have been

Table 10 *Distribution of the Donativo Real by Bairro and among Contributors (in réis), Rural São Paulo, 1679*

Bairro	Contributors	Total assessed	Average contribution
Antonio Bueno	72	62,640	870
Atibaia	100	101,640	1,016
Barueri	56	46,440	829
Caaguaçu	118	40,080	340
Caucaia	116	56,820	490
Cotia	53	33,220	627
Forte	32	22,960	718
Juqueri	35	28,340	810
Santo Amaro	146	40,970	281
São Miguel	46	25,540	555
Tremembé	55	30,280	551
Total	829	489,210	590

Source: "Livro do rol das pessoas para o pedido real," AHMSP, CM-1-19.

maintained down to the present. Others, particularly newer ones, carried the names of their founders. For example, on a list of taxpayers in Itu for 1728, three of the nine rural *bairros* bore the name of their richest resident.[9] Similarly, in 1679, one of the recently formed *bairros* in the township of São Paulo was called "*Bairro* of Antonio Bueno."

Table 10 summarizes the distribution of the Donativo Real of 1679 among the rural zones of São Paulo.[10] The number of contributors is a rough measure of the number of productive units in each *bairro*. In turn, the average assessment demonstrates the relative wealth of the various *bairros*. The wealthiest *bairros* – Atibaia, Antonio Bueno, Barueri, and Juqueri – all included areas of recent settlement and were the principal centers for commercial agriculture at that time. In contrast, the *bairros* of Santo Amaro, Caucaia, and Caaguaçu, more densely settled and closer to the town of São Paulo, were inhabited by small farmers and marginal stockmen.[11]

This picture is suggestive of a process of expansion and decline, in which older districts already felt the presence of widespread poverty while the newer, more dynamic *bairros* offered greater opportunities for the accumulation of wealth. In the seventeenth century, as territorial expansion was critical to the creation and maintenance of large fortunes, the wealthiest settlers constantly shifted resources to newer, more productive areas.

But that tells only part of the story. Soil exhaustion and demographic growth contributed to the spread of rural poverty and provoked territorial expansion at the same time. However, the roots of rural poverty lay not only

Table 11 *Distribution of Tax Contribution and Contributors by Amounts Assessed, Rural São Paulo, 1679*

		Value of contribution (in réis)				
Bairro		Under 400	400–639	640–999	1,000–1,999	Over 2,000
Antonio Bueno	%N*	37.5	15.3	16.7	19.4	11.1
	%R**	9.9	8.1	15.0	26.3	40.7
Atibaia	%N	58.0	10.0	8.0	11.0	13.0
	%R	12.5	5.2	6.1	15.6	60.6
Barueri	%N	55.4	12.5	12.5	8.9	10.7
	%R	9.6	7.6	11.2	13.5	58.1
Caaguaçu	%N	76.3	9.3	5.9	6.8	1.7
	%R	41.5	13.2	12.8	22.4	10.0
Caucaia	%N	67.2	6.9	6.9	13.8	5.2
	%R	23.7	6.9	11.2	33.5	24.7
Cotia	%N	52.8	15.1	17.0	9.4	5.6
	%R	18.2	11.8	21.1	18.3	30.6
Forte	%N	53.1	9.4	12.5	15.6	9.4
	%R	17.9	6.2	12.7	32.0	31.2
Juqueri	%N	62.8	8.6	8.6	11.4	8.6
	%R	11.3	5.8	7.0	15.2	60.7
Santo Amaro	%N	82.9	5.5	8.2	2.0	1.4
	%R	48.9	9.3	21.8	9.0	11.0
São Miguel	%N	56.5	15.2	17.4	2.2	8.7
	%R	15.9	14.6	23.5	3.9	42.1
Tremembé	%N	63.6	9.1	10.9	9.1	7.3
	%R	24.1	7.1	16.4	20.3	32.1

* %N = Percentage of total residents of *bairro*.
** %R = Percentage of total contribution of *bairro*.
Source: "Livro do rol das pessoas para o pedido real," AHMSP, CM-1-19.

in the decline of once prosperous *bairros*, but also in the structure of frontier expansion itself. On the Donativo rolls, even the wealthiest, most recently settled *bairros* included large concentrations of contributors at the lowest levels of wealth (Table 11 displays the distribution of taxpayers according to the size of their contributions). These figures suggest that a built-in structure of inequality accompanied frontier expansion, and that inequality probably tended to decrease in older zones as wealthier colonists moved on to new lands.

This assertion can be confirmed by two statistical measures of wealth concentration, the Gini coefficient of inequality, or Gini index, and the size share of the top 10 percent, sometimes referred to as the SSTT.[12] Table 12 presents these measures based on the Donativo lists. All the districts had relatively high concentrations of wealth in the hands of the richest

Table 12 *Indices of Wealth Distribution, Rural São Paulo, 1679*

Bairro	Gini*	DPMR (%)**
Antonio Bueno	.48	38
Atibaia	.61	54
Barueri	.64	49
Caaguaçu	.41	37
Caucaia	.50	40
Cotia	.49	39
Forte	.47	31
Juqueri	.65	35
Santo Amaro	.16	37
São Miguel	.53	46
Tremembé	.52	37

* Gini: Gini coefficient of inequality, in which 1.00 = perfect inequality and 0.00 = perfect equality.

** DPMR: share of total wealth controlled by top decile of *bairro* residents.

Source: "Livro do rol das pessoas para o pedido real," AHMSP, CM-1-19.

10 percent, with the wealthier *bairros*, especially Juqueri, Atibaia, and Barueri, showing more intense concentrations. The Gini index is more revealing, showing great levels of inequality, again particularly in the wealthier districts. The only major exception, Santo Amaro, with the low value of .16, is not surprising in that it was the oldest *bairro*, with few Indians and little wealth spread among its residents.

These figures may be compared with values calculated for eighteenth-century São Paulo by Alice Canabrava.[13] Using the 1765 and 1767 censuses, Canabrava worked out Gini values ranging from .60 to .75 for rural São Paulo, but found much greater concentrations of destitute colonists than those appearing in the rolls of 1679–1682. This suggests that the commercial opportunities offered by the development of the mining economy of the eighteenth century benefited only a limited segment of the population, and, predictably, served to increase inequality.

The Donativo Real tax rolls offer some notion of the distribution of wealth in rural São Paulo in the seventeenth century. Other relevant figures, taken from inventories and wills, also show concentrations in the holding of Indian slaves that seem to reflect the distribution of wealth in the *bairros*.[14] Indeed, statistical analysis of slaveholding over time shows that Indians were distributed very unevenly throughout the century.[15]

Once again, this indicates that the process of expansion incorporated strong elements of inequality from the start, which favored a few wealthier colonists to the detriment of an ever-increasing number of impoverished smallholders.

The Concentration and Consolidation of Wealth

In order to clarify these processes further, it is necessary to examine the trajectories of a few *bairros* and provide specific examples of these general patterns of wealth concentration and family consolidation. From their founding onward, the *bairros* shared certain characteristics, though their individual fortunes were not the same. The wealthier *bairros* grew out of *sesmarias* granted during the first half of the century and developed around prosperous wheat-producing estates. The original estates were subdivided among favored heirs, often through the careful application of a dowry rich in land and Indians. Each of these *bairros* was still thoroughly dominated by one family in 1679.

The rise, consolidation, and decline of the Pires family provides a noteworthy example of a more general trajectory taken by the leading kin groups of seventeenth-century São Paulo. During the first half of the century, the brothers Salvador and João Pires de Medeiros emerged as the premier wheat producers in São Paulo, settling the area that would later be known as Juqueri. As settlement advanced, Juqueri came to refer to the area north of the Cantareira Range but south of the Juqueri River.[16] In the 1620s, Salvador Pires and his wife Inês Monteiro de Alvarenga established an estate with hundreds of Guarani captives in the region. There they constructed the chapel of Nossa Senhora do Desterro, to accommodate the devotional needs of the *bairro*.

The wealth of this estate, measured in land and Indians, was transferred to the succeeding generation in the manner most characteristic of the reproduction of rural wealth in colonial Brazil. The ten children of Salvador Pires and Inês Monteiro by no means received equal shares in the partition of the property, despite essentially egalitarian inheritance laws.[17] The oldest son, Alberto Pires, married into the Camargo family in an ill-fated attempt at alliance between the two families, though he probably remained in the *bairro*. Of the five daughters, three were married with handsome dowries, thus establishing the foundations for large properties with ample holdings of Indian slaves. Two of the other sons were favored with lands and Indians, themselves leaving holdings of more than 150 captives at the times of their deaths in the 1660s. The youngest, João Pires Monteiro, became the captain of the *bairro* in the 1660s, following in his father's footsteps.[18]

In 1679, reminders of the imposing presence of Salvador Pires and Inês Monteiro continued to dominate the structure of the *bairro*. The two richest residents – a daughter of Salvador Pires and her son – accounted for nearly 54 percent of the Donativo contribution. Isabel Pires de Medeiros (listed as Isabel Gonçalves), widow of Domingos Jorge Velho (not to be confused with the leader of the campaign against Palmares), paid a substantial contribution of 6,720 réis, while her son, Captain Salvador Jorge Velho, contributed 8,500. Salvador Jorge Velho became even wealthier a few years later, when he inherited 560 Indians from his mother-in-law, who was also his godmother.[19]

The imprecise denomination Juqueri was also applied to the *bairro* of Antonio Bueno, which developed similarly to the Juqueri of Salvador Pires. The origins of the *bairro* date back to a 1627 concession of a *sesmaria* to Amador Bueno da Ribeiro, who had petitioned for 2 leagues (10,800 meters) of land to accommodate his large family.[20] The grant began on the banks of the Juqueri River and extended to the Atibaia River, including a village belonging to an Indian named Maracaña. It seems unlikely that Amador Bueno da Ribeira occupied the *sesmaria* himself, as he probably remained on his large wheat-growing estate in Mandaqui, closer to the town of São Paulo, where thanks to the labor of hundreds of Guarani captives brought from Guairá by his sons in the expeditions of 1628–1632, "he had every year abundant harvests of wheat, corn, beans and cotton."[21] The fact that the *bairro* was named for Amador Bueno's second son, Antonio, also suggests that the original owner never occupied his lands. Most likely, as he stated in his petition for the *sesmaria*, the land was acquired for future use, specifically by his sons and sons-in-law. Indeed, of Amador Bueno's nine children, seven established productive estates in the *bairro*. The first large-scale occupation of the area took place only in the 1650s, and benefited from an influx of Indians captured by the slaving expeditions then sweeping the region. The *bairro* was consolidated after the great expedition of 1666, which counted among its members Amador Bueno (*o moço*, or "the younger," son of the original grantee), Antonio Bueno, Baltasar da Costa Veiga (Amador moço's son-in-law), and Mateus de Siqueira, all masters of large numbers of Indian slaves and prominent residents of the *bairro* in 1679.[22]

The case of the *bairro* of Antonio Bueno illustrates better than any other the importance of the dowry in strategies for the reproduction of rural wealth. Dowries, in seventeenth-century São Paulo, served to consolidate or maintain the hegemony of a particular family or a larger family-based group. For example, Francisco Arruda de Sá saw three of his sons marry three Quadros sisters and, in a case of four brides for four brothers, Luzia Leme and Francisco de Alvarenga gave their daughters to the Bicudo de

Britos, thereby establishing uncontested control over one of the rural *bairros* of Santana de Parnaíba.[23]

Seventeenth-century dowries in São Paulo ordinarily included trousseaux, Indians, and landed property (usually in the form of virgin lands), to which were sometimes added capital, cattle, and credits for shipments of wheat to market. André Fernandes, for example, outfitted his niece Suzana Dias with 40 "servants [*serviços*] of the heathen of land," 800 *alqueires* of wheat "placed at Santos," and a section of virgin land measuring about 3 square kilometers.[24] Assets like these were essential to the creation of new units of production, given the limited possibilities offered in the economic context of rural society. As already observed, the most common strategy for young men seeking a livelihood was to combine a favorable marriage with the business of the *sertão* – that is, the acquisition of Indian labor through slaving expeditions – thereby obtaining the material basis for a new household.

The connections between the richest residents of the *bairro* of Antonio Bueno indicate that the dowry was the preferred mode by which to transmit wealth. The wealthiest, Baltasar da Costa Veiga, was the son-in-law of Amador Bueno, the younger, while the second- and third-richest, Captain Antonio Ribeiro de Morais and Captain Domingos da Silva Guimarães, were sons-in-law of Amador Bueno da Ribeira. Their contributions to the Donativo were assessed at 5,700, 4,100, and 3,500 réis, respectively. This ranked them far ahead of the sons of Amador Bueno da Ribeira, who also lived in the *bairro*. Captain Diogo Bueno, the youngest son, was to contribute 1,200, Captain Antonio Bueno, 1,000, and Amador Bueno, the eldest, 800. The *bairro*'s rural chapel also followed the female line, as the chapel of Belém, founded by Antonio Bueno on the Canduguá estate, to the north-northwest of the town of São Paulo, was administered by his son-in-law, Gervásio Mota de Vitória.[25]

Similar family relationships also intertwined the leading residents of the *bairro* of Atibaia, the newest and richest area of settlement in São Paulo when the Donativo lists were drawn up. Several *sesmarias* had been distributed in the area in 1639–1641, but it would seem that there was no direct connection between the holders of the original grants and the principal residents of 1679, as was the case in the *bairro* of Antonio Bueno. Only the *sesmarias* of Paulo Pereira de Avelar, whose sons figured among the most prominent residents of the *bairro*, and of Fernão de Camargo, whose family dominated the area, were exploited by the original grantees. Permanent settlement of the area did not begin until the 1660s, and the establishment of the *bairro* as such resulted from the *bandeira* of 1666. Before that date, the banks of the Atibaia River provided one of the last refuges of the Guarulhos Indians, who in 1665 were contacted by Father Mateus Nunes de Siqueira, who established a mission village there at his own expense. Within a year, settlers from neighboring *bairros* became interested in this new potential source of Indian labor and began to approach the banks of the Atibaia. At the same time, the Municipal Council of São Paulo attempted to drive Father Siqueira from the mission village and transfer its Indians to Conceição dos Guarulhos, a mission village located significantly closer to the municipal seat.[26]

Nothing more is known about the former mission village, but by 1669 several *sítios* dotted the area. In that year, the Municipal Council accused one Frei Gabriel, a Capuchin, of setting up a utopian community on the Atibaia, which was attracting Indians from the mission village of Conceição as well as from nearby estates. The Council expelled Frei Gabriel and supposedly returned the Indians to Conceição, though most likely this was a ruse and most of the Indians ended up in the hands of local slaveowners.[27]

It was around this time that Jerônimo de Camargo established his wheat-growing estate, for he had returned from the *sertão* in 1666 at the head of some 500 newly captured Indians.[28] He soon founded the chapel of São João, which by the 1680s had its own curate. According to the Donativo assessment, Camargo was the wealthiest man in São Paulo at that time, his contribution assessed at 12,000 réis. Three of his brothers and most of their sons-in-law also resided in the *bairro*, all appearing among the top 15 percent of contributors. Even so, their domination did not appear as complete as that achieved by other kinship groups in different *bairros*, since several families unrelated to the Camargos, most notably the Cardoso de Almeidas and the Pereira de Avelars, held significant shares of the local wealth. This may be due to distinct *bairros* being listed under the heading Atibaia. At least in the case of the Cardoso de Almeidas, their sphere of dominance was in the area that later became Bom Jesus dos Perdões, at some distance from the original settlement controlled by the Camargos. The list also includes the *bairro* that later became the parish of Juqueri, as it features the names of Pedro Fernandes Aragonês and Antonio de Sousa Dormundo, the founder of the chapel of Nossa Senhora do Desterro, which served as the nucleus of the original settlement.[29]

In any case, despite the geographic imprecision of the lists, it is clear that the Camargos and Buenos had become the dominant families in São Paulo in the second half of the seventeenth century. Nearly half (48 percent) of the wealthiest tenth of all taxpayers belonged to these two families. Members of the two families controlled several of the basic institutions of the town of São Paulo. The brotherhood of the Misericórdia, for example, was virtually dominated by the Camargos, who were also its principal benefactors.[30] By the 1690s, a Bueno was in control of the probate office, a key institution in the provision of credit. While they had to share leadership of the Municipal Council with the Pires, as stipulated by a formal agreement worked out in 1655, their interests were better served by that body.[31]

Perhaps most important of all, it was the Camargos who controlled the vast majority of the Indian population in the township of São Paulo, which, in the final analysis, guaranteed their wealth, power, and prestige.

The rise of the Camargos to their hegemonic position was one of the most significant events in seventeenth-century São Paulo. Their struggle with the Pires brought together a series of conflicts and pressure points that afflicted the plateau in the mid-1600s, including the explusion of the Jesuits, the question of Indian labor, and the problem of maintaining social control over a vast population of captives.[32] Moreover, commercial wheat production and the growth of large holdings of captive Indians had concentrated a disproportionate amount of wealth in the hands of very few families, most notably the Pires and Camargos, who struggled against one another for much of the seventeenth century.

One of the major sources of the struggle between the two families lay in the formation of the *bairro* of Tremembé, where the dominant interests came head to head in the 1640s. The relative decline of the Pires and the rise of the Camargo family is illustrated by the trajectory of this *bairro*. Once a major center for wheat production, by 1679 it was a site for small-scale cattle raising, with most of its settlers living in the shadow of the Jesuit estate at Santana. The major figures associated with the development of Tremembé were João Pires, whose distribution of dowries laid a firm base for the permanent settlement of the *bairro*, and Amador Bueno da Ribeira, whose wheat farm and mill at Mandaqui was one of the most important agricultural units in São Paulo in the first half of the seventeenth century. At the time of the Donativo Real, however, the heirs of João Pires no longer figured very prominently in Tremembé, where the Camargos now controlled much of the wealth. The Camargos had established marital alliances with Amador Bueno and were represented in the *bairro* by Captain Marcellino de Camargo. Some years earlier, Marcellino's brother Francisco had married a sister of Amador Bueno and established a valuable wheat-growing property, becoming one of the wealthiest mill-owners in the captaincy. When he died in 1672, he left no direct heirs, and so ownership of the estate passed to Marcellino, who kept it until his own death in 1684.[33]

Competition between the families peaked in the 1650s, when the two factions and their Indian followers fought pitched battles in the town of São Paulo. Faced with a state of near anarchy, aggravated by the problem of the general unrest of the Indian population, in 1655 the Governor-General approved an agreement that proposed that control over the Municipal Council alternate between the two families. While the principal result of the conflict between the two families was victory for the Camargos and conciliation for the Pires, it meant further alienation from power for most colonists, once and for all excluding those not aligned with the two principal factions from access to municipal institutions.

This exclusion, in turn, resulted in the migration of several families and the consequent founding of new towns deeper in the interior. The councils of São Paulo and Parnaíba reacted immediately to this new situation, as it threatened their control over the rural population. The situation also concerned colonial authorities because the new communities, particularly Itu and Jundiaí, were raised to the status of towns under circumstances that were irregular or otherwise suspect.[34] Most colonists, however, remained in the *bairros* of São Paulo, resigned to a reality of political exclusion, reduced access to economic resources, and, ultimately, rural poverty.

The Spread of Rural Poverty

One of the first consequences of increasingly restricted access to economic resources was a renewed cycle of predation on the region's mission villages, which already occupied a marginal position in the colonial economy. Some of the poorer *bairros* owed their existence to the occupation of Indian lands, a process that intensified after 1640. With the expulsion of the Jesuits, the mission villages of Pinheiros, Barueri, Conceição dos Guarulhos, and São Miguel were entirely exposed to land- and labor-hungry settlers, who promptly launched all-out efforts to transform the remaining mission villagers into personal servants and, at the same time, to carve up the 6 square leagues of land belonging to each community. Several colonists had already occupied Indian lands before that time, often acquiring them with the cooperation of officials charged with protecting Indian property. For example, when his late wife's inventory was drawn up, Gonçalo Ferreira declared to the probate judge that he "owned two hundred and fifty *braças* of frontage in the lands of the Indians where his estate is located . . . on which land they are by authority of the legal representatives of said Indians."[35] Other settlers on Indian lands had received authorization from the proprietor of the captaincy by claiming that deposits of mineral wealth were to be found on them, a condition under which the alienation of the inalienable was permitted. Finally, the Municipal Council of São Paulo, in its capacity as administrator of the mission villages after the first expulsion of the Jesuits, itself began to authorize the wholesale spoliation of Indian lands beginning in 1660.[36]

Colonists occupying Indian lands often justified their claims by alleging they were idle public lands, never effectively occupied by the Indians. One petitioner, in his request for an island in the Tietê River belonging to the Indians of Conceição, remarked that former Governor Diogo Luís de Oliveira had ordered that "the lands of the Indians be divided among the residents, without harming the Indians."[37] Under Portuguese law, unoccupied *sesmarias* did revert to the Crown after a certain period, but Indian lands were usually exempt from this clause. Though this juridical issue was not addressed in São Paulo until the early eighteenth century, there is reason to doubt the colonists' claims that Indian lands were unoccupied or idle. In fact, whenever possible the Indians of the mission villages maintained *roças* for their own subsistence, even supplying occasional surplus quantities of maize and manioc for the markets of the towns. In 1623, for example, the Municipal Council of São Paulo ordered cattle owners to remove their livestock from Indian lands because of the damage being done to the "seedbeds" (*sementeiras*) of the Indians.[38] A few years after the expulsion of the Jesuits, a magistrate suggested that the Indians were not planting their lands because the colonists did not let them, preferring to subject them to personal service. The Indians who were able to escape the settlers' clutches, he added, "withdrew and hid themselves in the woods because said residents took their lands and do not allow them to cultivate them."[39] Two years later, the Indians of the mission village of São Miguel complained that certain colonists "were planting on the lands of the Indians and pushing them off of them causing great harm with their livestock such as cattle and saddle animals and damaging their fields and crops for which reason all the heathen were dispersed and away from the village."[40]

The question of Indian land, therefore, remained inextricably linked to the struggle for labor. When the influx of Guarani captives was at its peak, during the era of great slaving expeditions that began in 1628 and ended definitively in 1641, the mission villages were a supplementary reserve of labor for the colonial economy. Beginning in the 1640s, however, with the deepening crisis in the supply of captives, the mission-village residents once again came to be the immediate objects of labor-seeking colonists. Indeed, with the expulsion of the Jesuits in 1640, the settlers counted on the authority of the Municipal Council to take possession of the Indians of the mission villages. In 1664, a royal official observed that the villages "are today much damaged and nearly extinct, for the officials [of the Municipal Council] ordinarily appoint their kinsmen as captains there that both take from them the Indian men and women as they see fit for the service of their homes and estates."[41] Not long thereafter, another authority observed of the villages: "Now they are found to be much despoiled, by the excess with which the various colonists take from them the Indians for their service, [and for] journeys to the wilderness, treating them as their slaves, and occasioning not only much harm to the service of Your Majesty, but the ruin of the villages themselves."[42] A few years later, the Indians of Pinheiros presented a petition requesting that the posts of lay captain and administrator be eliminated because both were only "a means for them to use their services."[43]

Under these conditions, the population of the mission villages declined rapidly after 1640. In a report presented to the Overseas Council, Salvador Correia de Sá expressed this decline in numerical terms, reporting that in 1640 there had been 2,800 *casais* (literally "couples," but referring to households) in the mission villages, a figure that had shrunk to 290 in 1679, the date of the report. Barueri, the largest mission village, had declined from 1,000 *casais* to 120; São Miguel, from 700 to 90; Conceição, from 800 to 70; and in Pinheiros only 20 *casais* remained of the 300 that had once inhabited the mission village.[44] Local sources indicate even lower figures. For example, in the same year as Salvador de Sá's report, representatives of the Municipal Council of São Paulo counted 58 Indians in São Miguel, while only 17 were found in Barueri the following year. As far as Conceição is concerned, twenty years earlier the councilmen charged with inspecting the mission village were surprised to find only the white "captain," Estevão Ribeiro, and the "Indian headman," Diogo Martins Guarulho. In each case, the missing Indians were reportedly dispersed throughout the rural estates of the region.[45]

Lands belonging to the mission villages of Conceição and São Miguel made up parts of at least three *bairros* listed in the Donativo rolls of 1679. The *bairro* of Caucaia, which later became the parish of Guarulhos, incorporated much of the lands of Conceição while also extending through the area along the Jaguari River, including the spot where Matias Lopes de Medeiros founded the chapel of Nazaré in 1676. The first colonial settlement in the region bordered on Indian lands, most likely encroaching upon them on various occasions. The origins of Caucaia as a properly constituted *bairro* probably can be traced back to the activities of Miguel de Almeida Miranda and his nephew Jerônimo da Veiga, each of whom established prosperous wheat-producing properties in the region around 1650, Miguel de Almeida having received *sesmarias* in the region in 1625 and 1639.[46] As in other *bairros*, most of the wealthiest residents listed in the Donativo rolls traced their lineage directly to these founders. Three sons-in-law of Miguel de Almeida lived in the *bairro*, while two others figured among the most prominent residents of Votorantim, occupying lands along the Juqueri-Mirim River. Of the three in Caucaia, Henrique da Cunha Gago was captain of the *bairro*, and in 1660 represented one of the three *parcialidades* (factions) called upon by authorities in an effort to resolve factional disputes.[47] Cunha Gago's son-in-law – Antonio Soares Ferreira, also the bearer of a quasi-military title – in turn emerged as the richest resident of the *bairro*.

A second wave of settlement concentrated expressly on Indian territory, beginning with the *sesmaria* of Geraldo Correia Soares, which covered the area that would later be called Minas de Geraldo Correia or Minas Velhas. Claiming that gold deposits existed along the Baquirivu River, on lands belonging to the mission village of Conceição, Correia opened the way for settlement. In the 1660s, the Municipal Council began attending to colonists' petitions for Indian lands in the area, transferring numerous plots to private settlers. Officially, these grants were lease agreements, though no quitrents were collected until 1679, during the judicial inspection of the Crown magistrate Rocha Pita. Like the municipal commons distributed by the Council, these plots were treated as settlers' private property. The expropriation of previously indigenous spaces was completed with the seizure of control over the mission village of Conceição, as Geraldo Correia Soares himself was named its "white captain" with the connivance of the Indian captain.[48]

The *bairro* of São Miguel also grew out of the expropriation of the lands and labor of a pre-existing mission village. The original *sesmaria* of Ururaí, granted in 1580, included lands on both sides of the Tietê River to the east of the town of São Paulo, though the colonists' *bairro* appears to have been on the north bank. The mission village was on the south bank, but the lands surrounding it apparently were considered part of the *bairro* of Caaguaçu. What appears on the Donativo rolls as the *bairro* of São Miguel consisted mainly of the small properties surrounding the chapel of Bonsucesso, on the estate of Francisco Cubas. Cubas, son-in-law of the great backwoodsman Manuel Preto, had inherited considerable holdings of Indian slaves from his father-in-law, to which he added many more through the slaving activities of his son, Francisco Cubas Preto, a skilled backwoodsman in his own right who participated in the expedition of 1666 and was the owner of nearly 200 Indians at the time of his death in 1673.[49] Thus, Francisco Cubas provides yet another example of the relationship between the founding of chapels – and, consequently, of rural *bairros* – and the arrival of large groups of captive Indians, a pattern also seen in the cases of Manuel Preto, Fernão Dias Pais, Afonso Sardinha, Jerônimo de Camargo, Fernão Pais de Barros, and Pedro Vaz de Barros, among others.[50]

Though several relatives of Francisco Cubas were among the leading residents of the *bairro* in 1679 – Cubas Preto's widow, for example, was the wealthiest, with a contribution of 4,000 réis – São Miguel departs from some of the patterns of wealth distribution and transmission observed in other *bairros*. Unlike the heads of other kinship groups, whose holdings were splintered by successive dowries, Cubas sought to keep his estate and his family intact. Toward the end of his life, Cubas transferred much of his wealth and Indians to the chapel of Bonsucesso. In his will, he instituted his four spinster daughters as administrators of the chapel, which of course gave them free access to its lands and Indian labor. This access, however, was conditional, as any daughter who married would lose the right of administration and would therefore have to move from the chapel. For some unknown reason, then,

Francisco Cubas declined to transmit his wealth through a well-chosen son-in-law, a procedure that was one of the cornerstones of the reproduction of rural society.[51] Within a generation of Cubas's death, the wealth and prestige of his family withered, and by the mid-eighteenth century the chapel itself was in a lamentable state.[52]

Even in the seventeenth century, however, the few wealthy wheat producers and stockmen of São Miguel shared their *bairro* with an ever-increasing number of poor farmers eking out a meager existence on the small plots of Indian lands distributed by the Municipal Council. In 1678, the Council surveyed the limits of the mission village of São Miguel and, as in Conceição, began to distribute parcels among petitioners. Unlike in its dealings with the settlers of Caucaia who occupied lands deeded to the mission village of Conceição, in São Miguel the Council began to charge an annual money rent, which varied from the trifling 100 réis to the still modest 640 réis. In addition, the Council sought to have settlers pay some rents in advance, with some tenants paying up to eleven years at one time.[53]

While at first glance this might be interpreted as having been a revenue-raising scheme intended to increase the Council's receipts in the short run, it was actually a way of limiting access even to these lands, often suitable only for small-scale cattle raising. It also placed poorer colonists in a dependent position as far as the Municipal Council was concerned. With the payment of rent, the occupant's chances of permanently alienating the property were slim and the security of their tenure remained uncertain. This problem emerged in an increasingly acute form in the eighteenth century, when wealthy proprietors, including the religious orders that came to administer the mission villages beginning in 1698, began to expel poor tenants and squatters. Such was the case of Antonio Ribeiro Maciel, who submitted a petition requesting possession of lands near the mission village of São Miguel that he had occupied for twenty-three years, "paying rent for them to said village." Together with other poor farmers of the area, Maciel had faced attempted evictions "by force of armed persons" acting on behalf of the Jesuits of the College of São Paulo, who alleged that their order had legal title to the lands. Even after hearing the corroborating testimonies of several neighbors, the authorities could not guarantee possession, as the lands in question were Indian lands.[54]

According to the lists of the Donativo Real of 1679–1782, a large proportion of the rural population of the São Paulo region lived in poverty, their material conditions barely a cut above the dwindling mass of Indian slaves. To a certain degree, the pattern of wealth distribution in the *bairros* of Santo Amaro and Caaguaçu presaged what was to be the general condition of rural São Paulo by the mid-eighteenth century. Excluded from access to large numbers of Indian laborers with which to cultivate virgin lands, inheriting run-down establishments and exhausted soils from the first Portuguese occupants, most free Paulistas, along with an ever-decreasing number of Indian subalterns whom they brought at great sacrifice from distant *sertões*, cultivated primitive subsistence plots to feed family, relatives, and Indian servants, only occasionally producing a tiny surplus that was sold in the limited markets of nearby towns. In short, the expansion of settlement and development of agriculture in São Paulo in the seventeenth century created the prospect of commercial wealth even as it set the measure for rural poverty.

Notes

1. "Livro do rol das pessoas para o pedido real do ano de 1679," AHMSP, CM-1-19.
2. On the early years of the Donativo, see CMSP-Atas, 6a:393, Nov. 1, 1664; also, Governor Francisco Barreto to Municipal Council of Guaratinguetá, Jan. 20, 1663, BNRJ-DH, 5:186.
3. "Auto de correição," Sept. 8, 1679, AESP, Atas da Câmara Municipal de Parnaíba, cx. 6063-1. In principle, the Donativo was a fiscal onus designed to pay for the dowry of Catherine of Braganza, who was married to Charles II of England in 1662, together with the indemnity Portugal owed the Netherlands under the 1661 treaty that brought a formal end to the Luso–Dutch War.
4. "Relação das quantias oferecidas pelos moradores do bairro de Araritaguaba," Nov. 24, 1728, AHU-SP, doc. 653. The title of this document is incomplete, as along with Araritaguaba (later renamed Porto Feliz) it lists residents of the town of Itu and its outlying settlements.
5. The spread of rural poverty in colonial and imperial Brazil has been the subject of an interesting array of works. See, for example, Laura de Mello e Souza, *Desclassificados do ouro: a pobreza mineira no século XVIII* (Rio de Janeiro: Graal, 1982), a noteworthy study of the process of marginalization of the majority of the free population in the development and decline of the mining centers of Minas Gerais in the eighteenth century; Luiza Rios Ricci Volpato, *A conquista da terra no universo da pobreza: formação da fronteira oeste do Brasil, 1719–1819* (São Paulo: Hucitec, 1987), which discusses the origins of colonial Mato Grosso in an innovative fashion while upholding some of the conventional approaches of Paulista historiography; and Dirceu Lindoso, *A utopia armada: rebeliões de pobres nas matas do Tombo Real, 1832–1850* (Rio de Janeiro: Paz e Terra, 1984), which contains revealing information on the poorer strata in the northeastern interior during the first half of the nineteenth century, emphasizing their relationship with the export economy in the context of the War of the Cabanos, a conflict that had as its apparent cause inter-elite conflict but that generated a mass rebellion by Indians, slaves, and the rural poor more generally along the border of the provinces of Pernambuco and Alagoas. On urban poverty, see the important work by Maria Odila Leite da Silva Dias, *Quotidiano e poder*.
6. The rural *bairros* of the São Paulo region have been the subject of numerous sociological studies, but a more detailed treatment of their historical dimension is lacking. See, among other works, Antonio Candido de Mello e Souza, *Os parceiros do Rio Bonito*, 5th edn. (São Paulo: Duas Cidades, 1979 [1964]), and Maria Isaura Pereira de Queiroz, *Bairros rurais paulistas: dinâmica das relações bairro rural-cidade* (São Paulo: Duas Cidades, 1973).

7. It is worth noting that Sérgio Buarque de Holanda debated this issue in a posthumously published essay in which he coined the binomial "Grande propriedade, pequena lavoura" ("Large property, small agriculture"). In addressing this apparent paradox, he countered the positions held by Alfredo Ellis Júnior and other historians, who asserted that smallholding was one of the pillars of the unique character of the old Paulistas. Holanda, *Monções*, 181–184.
8. On the founding and function of chapels in colonial Brazil, see Eduardo Hoornaert (ed.), *História da Igreja no Brasil: ensaio de interpertação a partir do povo*, 2 vols. (Petrópolis: Vozes, 1977–1980), 1:292–294. These private initiatives provide an interesting contrast to the collective projects that would later result in the founding of chapels in communities of the rural poor.
9. "Relação das quantias oferecidas pelos moradores do bairro de Araritaguaba," AHU-SP, doc. 653.
10. On the boundaries between townships, see "Auto de medição," Parnaíba, 1681, AESP, cx. 6066-18; "Demarcação do distrito de Mogi das Cruzes," Oct. 23, 1665, Arquivo da Prefeitura de Mogi das Cruzes, Registro do Foral.
11. Two of the last three *bairros* already boasted sufficiently dense populations in the 1680s to justify their being raised to the status of parishes, in spite of their proximity to São Paulo. The parishes of Santo Amaro and Guarulhos (Caucaia) were created in 1684 and 1686, respectively. Caaguaçu, its population much more dispersed, eventually became the poor parish of Penha in the eighteenth century.
12. The Gini index figures presented here were calculated according to the formula outlined in Charles M. Dollar and Richard Jensen, *Historian's Guide to Statistics: Quantitative Analysis and Historical Research* (New York: Holt, Rinehart and Winston, 1971), 121–124.
13. Alice P. Canabrava, "Uma economia de decadência: os níveis de riqueza na capitania de São Paulo, 1765–1767," *Revista Brasileira de Economia* 26/4 (Oct.–Dec. 1972): 95–123 (at 112).
14. A useful discussion of the use of inventories for analyzing the distribution of wealth may be found in Gloria L. Main, "Inequality in Early America: The Evidence from Probate Records of Massachusetts and Maryland," *Journal of Interdisciplinary History* 7/4 (1977): 559–581.
15. See the tables presented in John Monteiro, "Distribuição da riqueza e as origens da pobreza rural em São Paulo no século XVII," *Estudos Econômicos* 19/1 (1989): 109–130. The distribution of Indian slaves in São Paulo may be compared to the distribution of African slaves in other parts of colonial Brazil. See, in particular, Stuart B. Schwartz, "Patterns of Slaveholding in the Americas: New Evidence from Brazil," *American Historical Review* 87/1 (Feb. 1982): 55–86, and Francisco Vidal Luna, *Minas Gerais, escravos e senhores: análise da estrutura populacional e econômica de alguns centros mineratórios, 1718–1804* (São Paulo: Instituto de Pesquisas Econômicas, 1981), esp. 123–136.
16. This route through the Cantareira Range is discussed in Fina, *O chão de Piratininga*.
17. On this subject, with reference to Santa de Parnaíba in the eighteenth century, see Metcalf, "Fathers and Sons."

18. The genealogical information presented here comes from a variety of sources, including wills, inventories, and parish registers, as well as the following indispensable works: Paes Leme, *Nobiliarquia paulistana*, and Silva Leme, *Genealogia paulistana*.
19. Paes Leme, *Nobiliarquia paulistana*, 3:79.
20. "Traslado da sesmaria concedida a Amador Bueno (16 de agosto de 1627)," June 11, 1756, in Mazzuia, *Jundiaí e sua história*, 88–91.
21. Paes Leme, *Nobiliarquia paulistana*, 1:75–76.
22. On the expedition of 1666, see the discussion in Chapter 2, above.
23. Silva Leme, *Genealogia paulistana*, vol. 4; inventory of Luzia Leme, Parnaíba, 1653, AESP-INP, cx. 1.
24. "Escritura de dote," Jan. 27, 1641, AESP-Notas Parnaíba, 1641, cx. 6074-26. For interesting discussions of the dowry in colonial São Paulo, see Metcalf, "Fathers and Sons," and Muriel Nazzari, "Dotes paulistas: composição e transformações, 1600–1870," *Revista Brasileira de História* 17 (1988–1989): 87–100, as well as the latter author's broader study, *Disappearance of the Dowry: Women, Families, and Social Change in São Paulo, Brazil, 1600–1900* (Stanford University Press, 1991).
25. Inventory of Maria Bueno, 1673, IT, 18:387–398.
26. CMSP-Atas, 6a: 428–429 and 508–509, July 3, 1665 and Nov. 29, 1666.
27. CMSP-Atas, 6:161–162 and 165, May 13 and 25, 1669.
28. Pedro Taques de Almeida Paes Leme, *Historia da capitania de S. Vicente* (São Paulo: Melhoramentos, n.d.), 149, where the author asserts that Camargo possessed more than 500 warriors at that time. On the land grant and the chapel, see Waldomiro Franco da Silveira, *História de Atibaia* (São Paulo: by the author, 1950), 114, 119.
29. On the chapel of Nossa Senhora do Desterro do Juqueri, see "Livro de Tombo" of the Parish of Sé, 1747, AMDDLS.
30. For a list of the benefactors of the brotherhood, see Laima Mesgravis, *A Santa Casa de Misericórdia de São Paulo, 1599?–1884: contribuição ao estudo da assistência social no Brasil* (São Paulo: Conselho Estadual de Cultura, 1976), 48–55.
31. CMSP-Registro, 3:547–550.
32. On the social conflicts of the 1650s, see Monteiro, "São Paulo in the Seventeenth Century," 367–373. The standard work on feuds in colonial Brazil, though based on a very weak theoretical framework, remains Luiz de Aguiar da Costa Pinto, *Lutas de famílias no Brasil: introdução ao seu estudo*, 2nd edn. (São Paulo: Nacional, 1980 [1949]), 37–94 of which refer to the Pires and Camargos. See also Afonso d'Escragnolle Taunay, *História seiscentista da villa de S. Paulo: escripta á vista de avultada documentação inedita dos archivos brasileiros e extrangeiros*, 4 vols. (São Paulo: H. L. Canton, 1926–1929), where the author compares the two families to the Capulets and Montagues, "of Shakespearian memory" (vol. 2, quote on 55); and Francisco de Assis Carvalho Franco, *Os Camargos de São Paulo: noticia sobre os representantes dessa linhagem, na capitania vicentina, nos seculos XVI e XVII* (São Paulo: Editora S. P. S., 1937).
33. Inventories of Francisco de Camargo, 1672, AESP-INP, cx. 10, and Marcellino de Camargo, 1684, IT, 21:481–501.
34. BNRJ-DH, 3:271; Atas da Câmara, Parnaíba (June 23, 1679), AESP, cx. 6063-1.
35. Inventory of Isabel Fernandes, 1641, IT, 28:160. These lands belonged to the mission village of Barueri. On the spoliation of Barueri's lands, see the interesting anonymous

account from the eighteenth century, "Historia de Barueri," BNRJ, Coleção Morgado de Mateus, 30.24.19.

36. These grants of Indian land are registered in *Cartas de datas de terra*, vols. 2 and 3, and in CMSP-Registro, 3. The distribution of these lands was later sanctioned by the Crown magistrate João da Rocha Pita (CMSP, 7:27, auto de correição of May 8, 1679), but its legality would be challenged in the early eighteenth century.
37. Petition of Henrique da Cunha Gago, Jan. 15, 1661, CMSP-Registro, 3:12–13.
38. CMSP-Atas, 3:56, Oct. 21, 1623.
39. CMSP-Atas, 5:367, Mar. 16, 1649.
40. CMSP-Atas, 5:468–469, May 6, 1651.
41. Agostinho Barbalho Bezerra to Conselho Ultramarino, Aug. 18, 1664, AHU-SP, doc. 23.
42. Carta patente to Antonio [*sic*] Ribeiro Baião, Oct. 5, 1671, BNRJ, 1.2.9, no. 140.
43. CMSP-Atas, 7:217, July 3, 1683.
44. Boxer, *Salvador de Sá*, 126–127.
45. CMSP-Atas, 7:67–68, Sept. 7, 1680; CMSP-Registro, 3:467, provisão of Jan. 21, 1679; and 2:581–582, July 27, 1660.
46. Inventories of Jerônimo da Veiga, 1660, AESP-INP, cx. 5; Maria da Cunha, 1670, IT, 17:461–501; and Maria do Prado, 1670, AESP-INP, cx. 7.
47. CMSP-Registro, 3:547–550, Jan. 25, 1660.
48. CMSP-Atas, 6a:337, Oct. 6, 1663.
49. Inventory of Francisco Cubas Preto, 1673, IT, 18:309–350.
50. For a reasonably complete listing of rural chapels in seventeenth-century São Paulo, see Monteiro, "São Paulo in the Seventeenth Century," 431–435.
51. Will of Francisco Cubas (partial copy), "Livro de Tombo" of the parish of Conceição, 1747, Arquivo da Cúria Diocesana de Guarulhos. One of Cubas's daughters, Maria Antunes, married and petitioned to have her father's will legally annulled. Her three spinster sisters, however, won a favorable decision upholding the stipulation in question, preventing Maria Antunes and her husband from making use of the Indians and other property belonging to the chapel. AMDDLS, processo-crime de 1695.
52. For further details on the chapel of Bonsucesso, the subject of extended litigation, see Chapter 7.
53. *Cartas de datas de terra*, vol. 3, passim.
54. Petition of Antonio Ribeiro Maciel, 1723, AESP-AC, cx. 12, doc. 170.

7
The Final Years of Indian Slavery

Through the first half of the seventeenth century, the economic activities of the settlers of the São Paulo region rested on the firm base provided by ample numbers of Indian slaves, captured on the Paulistas' frequent expeditions to the wilderness. A constant influx of captives, which reached its peak at mid-century, supplied the estates and smaller farms of the plateau region, while at the same time providing surplus labor employed mainly in the transport of local products bound for the coastal market. This central relationship between abundant labor and commercial agriculture defined the contours of Paulista society in the seventeenth century and, at the same time, integrated São Paulo into the larger colonial economy.

Beginning in the second half of the century, the acquisition of Indian labor through slave-hunting became increasingly difficult, as expeditions came up against little-known stretches of wilderness, greater distances, and increasing Indian resistance. The resulting decline in the profitability of expeditions provoked a serious crisis in the Paulista economy. Most rural producers, now with limited access to Indian captives, ceased to produce for the market, while the few who had managed to maintain control of considerable numbers of laborers began to shift their resources toward other activities. Some introduced African slaves on their estates in a deliberate effort to make up for the decline in the population of Indian captives. Others began to raise pack animals to replace Indian porters. There were still others, such as Fernão Dias Pais, who sunk their hopes and their resources in the search for mineral wealth.

Nevertheless, in spite of obvious signs presaging the decline of Indian slavery, it remained deeply rooted in São Paulo when gold was discovered in the 1690s in what were then the northern reaches of the captaincy. In this period, some slaveowners continued to have holdings of more than a hundred slaves at their disposal. On the institutional plane, the viability of Indian slavery appeared to get a second wind with the agreement between colonists, Jesuits, and the Crown that was reached in 1696, which assured the colonists of their rights to the personal service of the Indians.

Even so, the gold rush deepened the crisis of Indian slavery in several ways. Many Paulistas, especially those with smaller slaveholdings, departed for the mines, taking their slaves with them, the cumulative result of which was a considerable exodus of local laborers, which became the subject of correspondence between Crown officials as well as of meetings of the municipal councils of the region. Indeed, one can observe in local documentation, especially estate inventories, a precipitous decline in the overall concentration of Indian labor in the region.

The problem of labor supply was made more acute by the fact that the economic opportunities presented by the mining boom led the Paulistas to practically suspend the slave-hunting activity that had been fundamental to the reproduction of Indian slavery.[1] Some captives from the areas surrounding the mines were brought to São Paulo in the early eighteenth century, but they were few in number, since much of the Amerindian population of the region had been displaced by the impact of slaving expeditions in the region beginning in the 1660s.[2] The few indigenous groups remaining in the immediate environs of the mines soon disappeared, decimated by epidemic disease or forced to flee in the face of white settlement.[3]

By the early eighteenth century, the process of domination that had characterized Luso–indigenous relations since the late sixteenth century had left deep and lasting impressions on Paulista society. The master–Indian relationship defined the framework of a larger structure of domination, thus laying the bases of a distinct slave society. Meanwhile, the unequal distribution of captives, which only worsened with the crisis in slave-hunting, established stark distinctions between a small minority of wealthy colonists and the vast majority, which found itself ever more deeply submerged in a state of rural poverty.

Paths to Freedom: Manumission

As the gulf between the rural poor and a handful of wealthy land- and slaveowners widened, the proximity between poor whites and Indian slaves became increasingly evident. In a certain sense, the social distance between Indians and whites in São Paulo had always been relatively narrow, as even the greatest slaveowners and those who considered themselves to be the nobility of the land could not hide a tinge of Indian ancestry in their genealogies.[4] The fact that São Paulo was a heavily mixed society, in which illicit unions and illegitimate births occurred on a large scale, meant that masters and Indians were enmeshed in furtive social relations that were cloaked by patterns of domination. Moreover, with the development of slavery, ethnic proximity gave way to distinctions based on social position and the relations of production. The importance of these distinctions to the slaveholding class is clear in the attitude of Amador Bueno da Veiga, the master of more than one hundred Indians and a few dozen African slaves, who became disgusted with his half-sister, a *mamaluca* born to an Indian woman, when she agreed to wed one of his Indian slaves.[5]

As the case of Amador Bueno's half-sister demonstrates, slavery itself produced situations that revealed the uncomfortable proximity between white masters and Indian slaves, the distinction between them diluted by the existence of a wide stratum of persons of uncertain condition. The will of Antonio Nunes reveals a fascinating detail in this respect: "I declare that I have a young man among the heathen of the land of my administration who is my uncle, the brother of my mother, married to an Indian of the mission village and for the good services he has rendered to me . . . I leave him free and unbound."[6] Another slaveowner observed in her will that one of the Indians in her holdings was not to appear in the inventory lists, since her son Antonio Varejão "ransomed the mulato Polinário with his own money for being his brother."[7] In an equally bizarre case, also involving siblings, one Domingas Mamaluca sued for her freedom, claiming that she had been sold by her brother, who had inherited her from their father. The defendant, who had purchased her from her brother, saw nothing out of the ordinary in these circumstances, because "it has been the custom and practice of these captaincies ever since they were first settled to buy and sell people of one's administration."[8] A more dramatic case emerged in Sorocaba: on April 17, 1722, Antonio Moreira exchanged a young woman "of the heathen of the land" for Maria, property of Captain Gabriel Antunes Maciel. According to the bill of sale, Maria was none other than Antonio Moreira's mother. Several months later, on September 30, Moreira issued a writ manumitting Maria.[9]

If the incorporation of former slaves into free society became more commonplace in the late seventeenth century, its broader effects were to hasten the decline of Indian slavery and swell the ranks of the rural and urban poor.[10] The parish records of Santo Amaro, for example, display a very high incidence of illegitimate births to Indian and *bastarda* mothers in which the father was not identified during the years 1686–1725.[11] In cases in which paternity was acknowledged, the children were always considered to be free, in spite of the legal disposition of *partus sequibus ventrum* (that is, that the child's status follows from the mother's). Some of the more prominent fathers of such children cleared up any doubts by granting freedom to these children's mothers, sometimes giving them land and slaves. For example, Pedro Vaz de Barros, the founder of the great estate of Carambeí and the chapel of São Roque, sired fourteen bastards with six different slaves, all of whom were freed and showered with landed property and Indians upon his death.[12]

Beginning in the final years of the seventeenth century, newly freed Indians contributed to the growth of a population of uncertain status, between slavery and freedom.[13] Manumission was practiced throughout the period of Indian slavery, but, with the decline of commercial agriculture and the resulting impoverishment of many settlers, masters seem to have become more willing to concede freedom to their Indians. In this sense, it is important to distinguish between wills that declared the freedom of Indian servants as a general principle and those that went further and actually set Indian servants free. It was most often the case that masters, on their deathbeds, would admit to doubts about the legitimacy of Indian captivity, in a sort of paternalistic last gasp, while also guaranteeing that their "free" Indians would be divided up among their heirs. The crucial difference came in cases in which wills included an additional stipulation freeing the Indians of any service obligations following the death of their master, which occurred much less frequently.

Freedom so conceded in a last will and testament, sometimes reiterated in a letter of manumission filed with a notary, was considered irreversible, despite occasional lawsuits pursued by recalcitrant heirs. Inês Pedroso, for example, upon freeing Generosa and Custódia "for [their] good works," emphasized that the two "would remain free and unbound by any obligation of servitude whatsoever not to son nor to daughter and they may go to the mission village or to wherever they see fit."[14] In another case, Madalena, an Indian woman set free in similar circumstances by her mistress, Luzia Leme, had to resort to the law in order to guarantee the freedom granted her, as an heir to Luzia Leme continued to hold her in captivity. In his sentence, the judge issued a fine of 20,000 réis, the approximate value of the Indian woman, against the person "who impeded her."[15] Unwilling to place his faith in the law alone, another master took a different approach to protecting a woman he freed, prohibiting her exploitation by his heirs under threat of their coming "under my curse."[16]

In São Paulo, conditional manumission was the most common means of passage from slavery to freedom. Masters often stipulated that Indians would have to serve their heirs, manumission only taking effect upon the death of the latter. From the point of view of the master, this act had the dual advantage of alleviating their conscience as they were facing death while guaranteeing some labor or income to their heirs. For Indian slaves, this kind of conditional freedom was practically meaningless, except in cases in which the heir in question was an aged spouse. For most, however, resigned to serve the offspring of their "benevolent" master, freedom remained a distant prospect, except in very rare cases in which heirs actually executed their parents' wishes and issued definitive letters of manumission. For example, Captain Guilherme Pompeu de Almeida filed a letter of manumission with the notary of Parnaíba, conceding freedom to the couple

João and Isabel, both of them *bastardos*, together with their children, thus carrying out the letter of his mother's will, which had given the family its freedom on the condition that its members serve her heirs.[17]

Other conditional manumissions stipulated specific tasks or terms of service. For example, the letter of manumission granted to the Indian slave Paulo, an artisan or skilled worker of some sort, outlined a complicated arrangement. According to its terms, Paulo would be allowed to spend one week each month with his wife, a slave living on another property, in exchange for teaching eight young Indian slaves the secrets of his craft. After six years, he was to be freed unconditionally.[18]

Such conditions could cause some confusion, as in the case of the *bastardas* Mônica and Felipa. Margarida Gonçalves, owner of the pair, found it necessary and just to revoke the manumission that had been conceded to them, as the two girls went straightaway to the town of São Paulo, thinking that they were already free instead of awaiting her demise, as laid out in their letter of manumission. Gonçalves justified this action by observing that the two "were ungrateful and were her slaves, as they are daughters of her black woman."[19] José Mamaluco, son of a white man and a Tememinó woman, met a similar fate. His master, Father Antonio Rodrigues Velho of Jundiaí, had issued a letter of manumission in his name in 1672, but revoked it nine years later "for ingratitude."[20]

Unconditional manumissions were much rarer. In one case, the "black of the land" Maria secured her immediate freedom upon depositing 32,000 réis, her market value, in the hands of the heirs of Luzia Leme.[21] In a similar case, Sebastiana de Oliveira granted freedom to an Indian woman named Páscoa upon receiving 200,000 réis, "which she gave me out of gratitude for my leaving her free and unbound."[22]

In general, masters sought to keep freed slaves on their properties, even in cases of unconditional manumission. Oftentimes, certain members of a family would be manumitted, while their spouses or children would remain in the condition of "compulsory services." For example, Gaspar Favacho granted freedom to several Indians in his will, but all of them would have had to remain on the estate in order to keep their families intact.[23] Throughout the period of Indian slavery, it was common to find freed slaves as part of the labor force on Paulista estates, either to be with their families or because they were subject to coercion.

In any case, the choice between leaving or staying on the lands of the former master depended, in the final analysis, on the opportunities for survival in the economic and social context of colonial São Paulo. Thus, perhaps because of a lack of alternatives, the ten former slaves of Maria de Lima Barbosa opted to remain on her son's property after she died.[24] But some slaveowners showed some concern with the fate of their former slaves, giving them tools, land, and even money to help them in their new lives.

Ângela de Siqueira, for example, gave 20,000 réis to a *bastarda* "who assists in my house . . . for good services."[25] Ambrósio Mendes, when he freed all of his Indian slaves, provided each couple with two hoes, a scythe, and an axe, "so that they have with which to better their lives." This bequest, according to Mendes, would compensate the Indians "for them having served me."[26]

Paths to Freedom: The Law

Few Indians could count on the goodwill of their masters to guarantee their freedom and survival. If poor economic conditions softened the temperaments of some masters, it hardened others, who responded to the commercial crisis by intensifying the demands they made on their slaves. Consequently, many Indians found they needed to fight for their autonomy and freedom, making use of legal as well as illegal means. This meant that, even as running away became more common, so too did Indians increasingly turn to litigation as a path to freedom.

In the early eighteenth century, Indians became increasingly aware of the advantages offered by access to Crown justice, particularly with regard to the question of freedom. This was made possible, in large part, by administrative reforms that were put into effect beginning in the 1690s. This reform movement, though it achieved only partial success, was intended to subordinate the region to the authority of the Crown in the context of the gold strikes in the northern reaches of the captaincy, which would later become the separate captaincy of Minas Gerais. The most direct method of effecting this subordination was the Crown's interposition in relations between colonists and Indians. Though the Crown would not effectively abolish Indian slavery – "abolition" had been proclaimed innumerable times by that point – the increasing involvement of royal officialdom in the Indian question in São Paulo during these years did accelerate the process of its dissolution.[27]

Beginning in 1698, the new governor of Rio de Janeiro began to act energetically, particularly with respect to the mission villages, immediately appointing a representative for Indian affairs in São Paulo. The new advocate of the Indians, Isidoro Tinoco de Sá, produced surprising results – if his reports are to be believed – returning to the mission villages many Indians who had been held by the colonists as personal servants. At the time of his arrival in the town of São Paulo in 1698, he counted a mere 90 Indians in the four mission villages of the region, but only two years later he proudly reported that the villages were now home to 1,224 Indian residents. According to Sá, the colonists had responded quickly to the threat of fines and returned these Indians to the mission villages voluntarily.[28]

Such measures, however, created more problems than they solved. On the one hand, the mission villages, lacking adequate croplands and effective economic organization, could not sustain this population. On the other, the delicate question of Indian labor and freedom, which had supposedly been resolved by the royal decree of 1696, was reopened with new intensity, placing the colonists in an uncomfortable position, squeezed between their material interests and their loyalty to the Crown. However, the Paulistas' resentment of the encroachment of external authority on their carefully guarded affairs became the prevailing sentiment, earning São Paulo its reputation as an anti-absolutist bastion. Indeed, several of the settlers' actions during this period – an attack on the royally sanctioned salt monopoly at Santos and the attempted murder of a Crown magistrate, among other violent acts – by striking directly at royal authority, reinforced this reputation.[29] And when it came to the specific issue of the mission villages, the colonists feared that the Crown and the Jesuits had hatched a plot aimed at depriving them of their Indians.[30]

One direct result of the increasing reach of royal authority was greater access to Crown justice in disputes over the status of the Indians. For the first time, royal authorities opened a channel through which legislation concerning the freedom of the Indians could be invoked in the defense of their freedom. During the seventeenth century, attempts at making existing labor relations meet the conditions prescribed by law failed in the face of insuperable contradictions. The colonists, backed by local judicial authority, which rested with the municipal councils, forged the institutional contours of personal service as a matter of rights acquired in the past, that is, as stemming from "practice and custom." In a notable case from 1666 – a lawsuit over ownership of some captives – this right to property was given precedence over the Indians' right to freedom, in spite of exhaustive citation of legislation prohibiting the enslavement of the natives.[31]

This pattern began to change with the intromission of royal justice in the region, particularly with the arrival of the first Crown magistrate to be based in São Paulo, in the final years of the seventeenth century. From then on, the Indians themselves became frequent litigants, suing for their freedom based on the specific wording of the relevant legislation. By the letter of the law, after all, the enslavement of Indians was notoriously illegal.

An illuminating example of this process unfolded in Itu in the early eighteenth century. Here, in a township on the western edge of Paulista settlement, Micaela Bastarda had been manumitted in 1703 by Gonçalo de Pedrosa, who left her "free of all servitude and administration so that she may live as a free person with whomever she may like." Pedrosa's will, however, did not ensure Micaela's freedom and so in 1721 she sued the Carmelite prior, who forced her to work in the convent of São Luís while claiming that she was one of a number of Indians that her late master's widow had bequeathed to the friars. This case should have been beyond dispute (Pedrosa had predeceased his wife, and his will had thus freed Micaela before she could be passed on to any possible heirs), but the prior nevertheless argued in defense of the convent's interest that it was "practice and custom for more than 150 years [that colonists be] served by heathen, *mamalucos* and *bastardos*" and, what is more, "to pass the administration of some to others, from parents to children." In response, Micaela's legal representative argued that "practice and custom cannot have a place where there is law to the contrary and also against freedoms there is not nor could there be such a prescription much less an immemorial one." After many hearings, the ordinary judge Claudio Furquim de Abreu handed down a sentence favorable to Micaela, guaranteeing her freedom and forcing the Carmelites to pay back wages for the twelve years and seven months during which she was "unjustly and violently" exploited. The friars never paid the indemnity they owed the "miserable pauper," but after nearly twenty years of uncertainty, Micaela gained her freedom, while also opening a precedent for the other Indians held by the convent.[32]

In this context of decisions favorable to the complainants, Rosa Dias Moreira brought a suit against her master, Francisco Xavier de Almeida, of Jundiaí, alleging her enslavement was illegal because she was a descendant of "carijós." In a similar case, two "descendants of Carijós" sued José Pais on the same grounds.[33] By testifying to their Indian ancestry – consubstantiated in Carijó identity – these Indians sought to guarantee their status as free persons, which was legally established by the laws of the kingdom of Portugal. In some instances, they sought to back up their case by alleging poor treatment or unjust captivity in order to characterize their condition as equivalent to slavery.

As an alternative strategy, some slaves sought refuge in the mission villages of the region, then fought in court for the right to remain in these communities. For example, in 1723, the widow Maria Leme do Prado appeared before a judge to justify her rights of administration over the "mulata" Marta. Marta's mother, enslaved on an expedition to Guarulhos territory by João da Cunha some forty years earlier, had been sold to Pedro Fernandes Aragonês, Maria Leme's father. At the time of the suit, Marta was "fugitive" in the mission village of Conceição dos Guarulhos, alleging that she belonged there by virtue of her Guarulhos ancestry. After hearing testimony, the judge returned Marta to the custody of Maria Leme do Prado.[34]

In another case, with a different outcome, the Indians Vicente, José, Inácio, Joaquim, Romana (Joaquim's mother), and Marcela de Oliveira (his wife) presented a petition accusing the colonist Antonio Pedroso of holding them "with [the] rigorous treatment of slaves." Alleging that they were descendants "of the old inhabitants of the mission villages," these Indians obtained a favorable verdict that stated that they were to be restored to the village of Pinheiros. Despite this verdict, however, one of the men was pressed into service to fight the warlike Paiaguá of the upper Paraguay River basin and the elderly Romana was returned to Antonio Pedroso to serve him in exchange for a bond deposited against his use of her labor.[35]

Taken together, the litigation brought by "descendants of Carijós" delineates the process of disintegration of Indian slavery and illuminates the question of the ethnic identity of the local population. Litigants who received favorable sentences – most of them, at least – came to join the most numerous stratum of Paulista society, composed of smallholders and nominally free tenants (*agregados*), the precursors of the "*caipira* society" that would be studied so thoroughly in the twentieth century. By the same token, only a minority of manumitted Indians "reintegrated themselves" into the mission villages of the region as stipulated by the Indian policy of the early eighteenth century. Thus, the major trend in this process was an increase in the distance separating the local poor from their indigenous pasts and Indian identities.

Meanwhile, masters proved obstinate in defense of their privileges, seeking to retain their Indian slaves at all costs. For example, Francisco Dias and his wife Úrsula, Indians of the village of Escada, "free by birth," alleged that their daughter was being held by Marcos da Fonseca of Mogi das Cruzes, who treated the girl as if she were a slave. They asked the judge to restore the girl to their village, where she could enjoy the freedom that was hers by right. The case was investigated by the town captain of Mogi das Cruzes, who determined that Fonseca was treating the girl well and recommended that the case be dismissed.[36] Thus, there were circumstances in which the judicial system could serve the interests of masters rather than Indian litigants.

Indeed, the masters themselves increasingly turned to the law to resolve issues regarding Indian labor. The records of a lawsuit over a rural chapel provide interesting insight into the questions of Indian liberty and access to Indian labor during this period of transition, in which Indian slavery was a dying institution. On the face of it, the suit was a conflict over the administration of the chapel of Bonsucesso, founded and legated haphazardly by Francisco Cubas Preto in the 1670s. But what was truly at stake was control over the thirty-four Indians who remained attached to the chapel, a considerable labor force at that time, particularly in the poor *bairro* of São Miguel. In 1710, Francisco Cubas's last daughter, named Brígida Sobrinha, died. At that point, control over the chapel and its Indians lay in the hands of Amador Bueno da Veiga, the owner of a neighboring property. What emerges from the proceedings is that Amador Bueno, who was already rich in lands and Indians, had wanted to use the chapel's Indians, who had remained idle under the careless administration of the property by the last direct heiress. While the exact details remain somewhat obscure, it would seem that Amador Bueno, with Brígida Sobrinha's consent, had assumed management of the property, rebuilding the chapel and reorganizing its productive base.

With Brígida's death, however, administration of Bonsucesso passed to her niece, married to João dos Reis Cabral, who immediately secured an eviction order served to Amador Bueno da Veiga. Unsatisfied with eviction alone, Cabral also requested an indemnity for the use of the Indians' labor, calculated at 200 réis per day per Indian for the eighteen months in which Bueno had benefited from their service.

Obviously shocked with the prospect of having to pay more than 4,000 milréis for Indian labor that he had enjoyed free access to up to that point, Amador Bueno's first impulse was to recalculate the wage bill, deciding that 160 réis per day was fair, as "some pieces provide fewer services than others and are less useful." He then discounted forty days per year from the previous tally "because of the rains," as well as eighty-three Sundays and religious holidays, during which the Indians did not work. This brought him to a new sum that amounted to only half of the original one but which still seemed exorbitant, and so Bueno's attorney resorted to a complex legal argument intended to prove that the Indians did not work for Amador Bueno, but only for the chapel, which they were obligated to serve. In addition, he argued, Amador Bueno incurred losses, providing the Indians with food while they restored the chapel, rebuilt a bridge leading to the property, and cleared plots of land for their own sustenance. Citing the royal decree of 1696, the defense attorney added that "the service of the Indians belongs to the Indians themselves and that their administrators are to pay them." Contending that Amador Bueno had never been the administrator of the Indians, the attorney sought to show that the defendant owed nothing. Summing up, he alleged that "the labors rendered by said Indians were of no profit at all" to Amador Bueno, but rather were to the benefit of the chapel.[37]

In any case, even if he had profited from the labor of these Indians, Amador Bueno da Veiga could not have agreed to pay such a high wage bill, in spite of his wealth, for it would undermine the fundamental logic of the regime of personal service. For the Paulistas, Indian labor was incompatible with Indian freedom. If they could not avail themselves of Indian slaves, they would be forced to seek alternative sources of unfree labor or, still worse, to work the land on their own.

A Transition to African Slavery?

At first glance, one solution to the crisis of Indian slavery would be to replace the Indians with African slaves, a solution taken up by all of the wealthiest Paulistas in the early eighteenth century. According to some historians, the increased presence of African captives in São Paulo in the context of indigenous population decline indicates that a transition to African slavery was underway. To be sure, small numbers of black slaves, clearly distinguished from the Indians by the terms "heathen of Guinea," "pieces from Angola," or, most often, "*tapanhunos*" – a Tupi term used to designate an African slave – had been present in the captaincy from its earliest years, but they represented a tiny fraction of the overall labor force, made up almost entirely of Indian workers. Only in the final quarter of the seventeenth century and particularly after 1700 did larger numbers of African slaves begin to transform the lodges of Indian servants (*tijupares*) into Afro-Brazilian slave quarters (*senzalas*).

But to refer to a transition, at least in the sense of the replacement of Indian captives in agricultural work, would be premature: during this period it remained an incomplete process that would be completed only in the late eighteenth century, when the expansion of sugar cultivation revitalized the Paulista economy.[38] In the early decades of the century, high demand for slave labor in the mines suddenly raised the prices of African captives throughout Brazil. In São Paulo between 1695 and 1700, the price of an adult male slave jumped from 45$000 to 180$000, reaching 250$000 in 1710.[39] Few Paulistas possessed sufficient resources or had access to sources of credit that would allow them to import large numbers of African slaves. Therefore, the use of Africans in Paulista agriculture was limited to some of the newest units of commercial production that managed to overcome the difficulties imposed by the decline of Indian slavery, most of which were found in the rural *bairros* to the west of Santana de Parnaíba and to the north of the town of São Paulo.

In this sense, the expansion of African slavery in São Paulo in the early years of the eighteenth century more than anything else reflected important changes in the economic organization of the plateau, which were intrinsically linked to the emerging mining economy of Minas Gerais. At that point, African slavery assumed two distinct, though complementary forms. On the one hand, the trade in African slaves, as merchandise bound for the mines, contributed to São Paulo's transformation into a commercial entrepôt. On the other, some black slaves were introduced on the large rural estates of the region.

These two faces of African slavery are evident in the composition of slaveholdings during these years. The preference for adult males, most of them African, and the near-complete absence of children, is clear in the demographic profile of the holdings of slaves by merchants who did business in the mining region. On large agricultural properties, the profile was very different. On rural estates, the makeup of the African slave population corresponded to the pattern established for Indian slavery in the seventeenth century, with greater balance between the sexes, considerable numbers of children, a preference for slaves born in the colony, including *mestiços*, and high rates of intermarriage or informal unions, now involving partners of African and Indian origin (see Tables 13 and 14).

Table 13 *Composition of Captive African Population on Agricultural Properties, São Paulo and Santana de Parnaíba**

Owner (no. of Indians)	M	F	C	T	Date/Source
Domingos da Rocha (92)	13	10	1	24	1661 IE, cx. 6
Francisco de Camargo (58)	5	3	8	16	1672 INP, cx. 10
Marcellino de Camargo (124)	3	7	4	14	1684 IT, 21
Jerônimo Bueno (55)	1	10	0	11	1693 IT, 21
Pedro Vaz de Barros (47)	10	12	2	24	1697 IT, 24
Maria de Mendonça ("many")	24	15	13	52	1700 IPO, 14.563
Salvador Jorge Velho (81)	15	5	0	20	1708 IPO, 14.518
Maria Bueno (54)	6	7	12	25	1710 IPO, 13.909
João Pereira de Avelar (27)	14	7	3	24	1713 IPO, 14.151
Gaspar de Godoi Colaço (57)	12	4	5	21	1714 IPO, 14.091
Baltasar de Godoi Bicudo (52)	18	12	23	53	1719 IPO, 14.676
Amador Bueno da Veiga (92)	11	11	23	45	1720 IPO, 14.962
Total	132	103	94	329	

* M = adult men, F = adult women, C = children, T = total slaves of African origin.

Summing up, these two faces of slavery reflected important new developments in the Paulista economy involving a handful of wealthy merchants and rural producers. The first group was made up primarily of immigrants from Portugal, some of whom married into the local elite, to a certain extent easing potential conflicts between the two groups.[40] By introducing greater commercial capital and linking the region more closely to the Atlantic economy, the economic activities of these merchants represented a major break with the period before the discovery of gold. It was through the trade in African slaves, among the most sought-after commodities in the mining region, that the bases of Paulista society were transformed.

The second group – that of the rural producers – was made up of settlers who had prospered from the exploitation of Indian labor and had the resources that allowed them to import African slaves. At first glance, it

Table 14 *Composition of Captive African Population in Estates Involved in Mining or Mercantile Activity, São Paulo and Santana de Parnaíba**

Owner (no. of Indians)	M	F	C	T	Date/Source
Antonio da Rocha Pimentel (28)	19	5	0	24	1709 IPO, 13.919
Potencia Leite do Prado ("few")	29	15	3	47	1710 IPO, 14.853
Luzia Bueno (15)	17	1	0	18	1711 INP, cx. 24
Martinho Cordeiro (2)	10	3	0	13	1711 IPO, 14.900
Francisco B. de Brito (19)	22	4	5	31	1712 IPO, 14.448
Ana Proença (0)	11	1	1	13	1713 IPO, 14.217
Maria Lima do Prado (20)	15	3	3	21	1715 INP, cx. 26
João de Almeida Naves (15)	27	9	8	44	1715 IPO, 14.758
Pascoa do Rego (9)	12	2	1	15	1716 INP, cx. 26
João Francisco Duarte (11)	13	1	1	15	1716 IPO, 15.927
Isabel Barbosa da Silva (0)	24	7	2	33	1717 IPO, 14.068
Miguel Gonçalves Medeiros ("few")	17	4	11	32	1717 IPO, 14.340
Bento Amaral da Silva (21)	25	10	11	46	1719 IPO, 14.308
Domingos Dias da Silva (12)	30	16	8	54	1725 IPO, 15.086
Total	271	81	54	406	

* M = adult men, F = adult women, C = children, T = total slaves of African origin.

may seem that this transition was limited to simply inserting African captives into the existing structure of Indian slavery, which would indicate significant continuity, not only in terms of the organization of production, but also in the context of the internal commercial circuit that had prevailed through the preceding century. However, a thorough analysis reveals a profound shakeup of the economy and society of the plateau. Due to their close relationship with the market provided by the mines, the great estates of the region assumed characteristics that were clearly new at the dawn of the eighteenth century.

During this period the great rural estates began to specialize in the production of a few commodities to meet the needs of the growing market of the mining zones in the north of the captaincy. While in the seventeenth century the largest Paulista properties produced foodstuffs – especially wheat – for the coastal market, during the era of the gold boom Paulista agriculture contributed little to the market of the mining zones, in spite of massive inflation in the prices of corn and beans.[41] According to commercial records from the period, most transactions with the mining region involved sugar-cane brandy, slaves, and, notably, cattle.[42] This makes sense when one considers transport costs, which were the major obstacle between Paulista producers and the market of Minas Gerais. We have already shown how the settlers resolved the problem of transport in the seventeenth century, by mobilizing large numbers of Indian porters who journeyed to the coast burdened with goods. The gold mines, however, demanded a far longer voyage of up to two months, "with laden saddle animals and blacks," as a Paulista complained in 1700.[43] It was one thing to send an Indian to Santos carrying 30 kilograms of grain or beans, on a two-to-four-day trip; a journey of two months was another, one that would represent certain death for most porters.

Two options were left to the Paulistas. The first, as we have indicated, lay in the reorientation of production to goods of sufficiently high value to cover steep transport costs. The second was to establish agricultural properties closer to the mines. It seems likely that the latter option was the solution preferred by most Paulistas, as is shown in the values of tithes collected during the first half of the eighteenth century, which grew spectacularly in Minas do Ouro (Minas Gerais), while showing more modest growth in São Paulo. In 1710, when the tithe contract for the mining district was separated from that of the rest of the captaincy, the value of the tithe contract for São Paulo fell from 15:210$000 to a mere 3:934$000.[44] At mid-century, whereas the contract for São Paulo had increased threefold, reaching 10:600$000, the contract for Minas Gerais had jumped to 92:038$000.[45] These figures certainly reflect the enormous demographic growth of Minas Gerais, which was made a separate captaincy in 1720, but at the same time they demonstrate the feeble response of Paulista agriculture to the enormous market provided by the mines.

In fact, by the early eighteenth century, Paulista agriculture had suffered a reversal of fortune. Whereas São Paulo had once been the primary site of wheat production in Brazil, in 1724 Governor Rodrigo César de Meneses found it necessary to request shipments of flour from other captaincies because of a serious shortage in the region.[46] His successor was more explicit when it came to the failure of Paulista agriculture, blaming it on the diminished size of *sesmarias* granted by the Crown, which had been reduced in an effort to avoid the concentration of vast tracts of lands in few hands in Minas Gerais. According to the governor, the new *sesmarias* were unsuited for wheat production, as the primitive techniques of the colonists – slash and burn, or swidden, agriculture – constantly demanded new tracts of land, a situation made still worse by the tendency to plant small stands of cane for the production of sugar-cane brandy and by the ravages of the cattle that were squeezed onto these small properties.[47]

In the end, the opening of the mines affected the agrarian organization of the plateau in at least two important ways. First, due to prohibitive transport costs and the increasing scarcity of Indian labor, the leading producers who remained on the plateau reoriented their commercial production, transforming their wheat fields into pastures, planting sugar cane, and building stills. Second, intense migration of much of the Indian labor supply to the mining zone and the concentration of what remained on the largest properties relegated the vast majority of rural colonists to a marginal, poverty-stricken existence. Many men abandoned their modest properties to seek their fortunes, a few of them striking it rich in the distant mines of Minas Gerais, Mato Grosso, and Goiás. But for the families that remained, the era of the gold boom meant the deepening of rural poverty, a process underway since the rapid decline of Indian slavery that began in the mid-seventeenth century and accelerated thereafter.[48]

Ultimately, as Frei Gaspar and other chroniclers of local decline observed so well, the Paulista farmer of the eighteenth century was but a shadow of the large slaveowner who dominated the rural landscape of the previous century. Responding to the opportunities offered by the presence of abundant lands and Indians, no Portuguese settler moved to the interior with the intention of becoming a peasant; in the words of the discerning observer Bartolomeu Lopes de Carvalho, "it is certain that in those parts there has not been seen until today a servant who comes from Portugal with his master who does not soon aspire to be more than him..."[49] But an impoverished peasantry was what remained after the rapid destruction of so much land and so many Indians.

Notes

1. For a detailed description of the changes that occurred in the first half of the eighteenth century, Boxer's *Golden Age of Brazil* remains indispensable. As far as Paulista historiography is concerned, this is considered to have been a transitional period. See Alfredo Ellis Júnior, *Resumo da história de São Paulo* (São Paulo: Rothschild Loureiro, 1942) and, coauthored with Myriam Ellis, *A economia paulista no século XVIII: o ciclo do muar, o ciclo do acúcar* (São Paulo: Universidade de São Paulo, 1950), among other works. Sérgio Buarque de Holanda, *Caminhos e fronteiras*, treats the gold rush with a certain amount of caution, associating it with the simultaneous expansion of muleteering and riverine transport (*monções*), essential steps in the accumulation of capital for subsequent

agricultural expansion, thus providing a link between the frugal backwoodsman of the past and the rich planter of the future. In my view, both portrayals mischaracterize seventeenth-century Paulista society by denying the existence of commercial agriculture and ignoring the dynamics of Indian slavery.

2. For example, João Pedroso Xavier, one of those to strike gold at Sumidouro, settled about twenty Indians from the mining region on his estate in Parnaíba during the first decade of the eighteenth century (AESP-INP, cx. 24); see also "Coleção das notícias dos primeiros descobrimentos das minas na América" (Cód. Costa Mattoso), Biblioteca Municipal de São Paulo, fol. 14. Other documents on the discovery of gold deposits may be found in Afonso d'Escragnolle Taunay (ed.), *Relatos sertanistas* (São Paulo: Comissão do IV Centenário, 1953).
3. The Costa Mattoso codex, cited extensively by Boxer in *Golden Age of Brazil* in other contexts, contains valuable information on the Indians of what would become the captaincy of Minas Gerais, as well as of other regions of Portuguese America.
4. On the formation of a noble identity among the Paulistas, which was intrinsically linked to the origins and growth of *bandeirante* "mythology," see Katia Maria Abud, "O sangue intimorato e as nobilíssimas tradições (a construção de um símbolo paulista: o bandeirante)" (tese de doutorado, Universidade de São Paulo, 1985); see also Stuart B. Schwartz, "The Formation of a Colonial Identity in Brazil," in Nicholas Canny and Anthony Pagden (eds.), *Colonial Identity in the Atlantic World, 1500–1800* (Princeton University Press, 1987), 15–50. In this context, one must return to the well-trodden ground of Paulista historiography dealing with the role of interethnic mixture (*mestiçagem*) in the making of Paulista society and its elites. Two classic interpretations, radically different in their theoretical approaches and assumptions, are Alfredo Ellis Júnior, *Os primeiros troncos paulistas e o cruzamento euro-americano*, 2nd edn. (São Paulo: Nacional, 1976 [1936]), which – as Ellis himself confessed – was a re-edition of his *Raça de gigantes: a civilisação no planalto paulista. Estudo da evolução racial anthroposocial e psychicologica do paulista dos séculos XVI, XVII, XVIII e XIX, e das mesologias physica e social do planalto paulista* (São Paulo: Helios, 1926); and Holanda, *Caminhos e fronteiras*. Finally, the little-known book by Edmundo Zenha, *Mamelucos*, approaches the subject by way of a larger study of the enslavement of the Guarani.
5. Fonseca, *Vida de Belchior de Pontes*, 109–110.
6. Will of Antonio Nunes, IT, 38:19.
7. Will of Catarina de Mendonça, 1671, AESP-INP, cx. 12. The term *mulato*, in this context, refers to the son of an African father and an Indian mother.
8. Domingas Mamaluca v. Bernardo de Quadros, Itu, 1700, AESP-AC, cx. 2, doc. 28.
9. "Lançamento de um escripto de venda e troca," Apr. 17, 1722, and "Carta de liberdade a Maria Carijó," Sept. 30, 1722, AESP-Notas Sorocaba, cx. 6020-1.
10. While the focus here is on rural areas, it is important to keep in mind that a similar process was underway in the towns. For example, the will of Ana Bastarda offers a rare glimpse of a woman who fought to survive as a poor, single mother, facing a world that tended to to classify her as a slave: "I declare that I am a poor unmarried woman free and unbound and I was never married, the daughter of Eliador Eanes and Simoa [an Indian woman], and I have a son by the name of Mateus and a daughter by the name of Mariana; the son is of Inácio do Prado, his father having gotten him and taken him to his house, and the daughter, I ask for the love of God, that the Reverend Father Vicar

shelter her in his house in company of the lady, his sister, Leonor Gomes to teach her and indoctrinate in her the love and service of God and I also ask the Reverend Father Vicar, for the love of God, to agree to be my executor so that some small mercy before God may be found for my soul. . ." Will of Ana Bastarda, 1676, in AESP-AC, cx. 3, doc. 44. The document refers to her suit for the freedom of Mariana, who was being held as a slave by the municipal judge (*juíz ordinário*) Francisco de Godoi.

11. Of the 318 children born to Indian women and *bastardas* who were baptized in Santo Amaro in the late seventeenth century, 169 (53 percent) were listed with the descriptor "unknown father," while 139 (44 percent) were registered as the children of stable couples. See Table 8. AMDDLS, 04-02-23, Batizados, Santo Amaro, livro 1.
12. Will of Pedro Vaz de Barros, 1674, in inventory of Brás de Barros, AESP-INP, cx. 22.
13. While the question of the freedom of the Indians has been amply discussed in the historiography, especially in its juridical aspects, the issue of manumission has hardly been touched upon. A noteworthy exception, based on evidence from Maranhão, is David G. Sweet, "Francisca: Indian Slave," in David G. Sweet and Gary B. Nash (eds.), *Struggle and Survival in Colonial America* (Berkeley: University of California Press, 1981), 274–291.
14. Will of Ignez Pedroso [Ines Pedroso], 1632, IT, 8:365.
15. Petition of "a india Magdalena," June 18, 1634, IT, 9:9.
16. Will of Francisco Pinto Guedes, 1701, AESP-IPO, 13.998.
17. Letter of manumission, 1690, AESP-Notas Parnaíba.
18. Letter of manumission by José Ortiz de Camargo to Paulo, 1663, Cartório do Primeiro Ofício, Jundiaí, Notas, 1663, fol. 35.
19. "Reclamação de uma alforria," Mar. 1, 1681, AESP-Notas Parnaíba, 1680.
20. Letter of manumission, July 28, 1672, and writ revoking manumission, Jan. 11, 1681, Livros de Notas de Jundiaí, Cartório do Primeiro Ofício, Jundiaí.
21. Letter of manumission, Feb. 8, 1700, AESP-Notas Parnaíba, 1699.
22. Will of Sebastiana de Oliveira, 1713, AESP-INP, cx. 25.
23. Will of Gaspar Favacho, 1681, AESP-INP, cx. 16
24. Inventory of Maria de Lima Barbosa, 1715, AESP-INP, cx. 26.
25. Will of Angela de Siqueira, 1728, AESP-INP, cx. 32.
26. Will of Ambrósio Mendes, 1642, IT, 13:481.
27. Paes Leme, *Nobiliarquia paulistana*, 3:19, asserts that Indian slavery was extinguished throughout Brazil around 1732. This assertion is mistaken, as the event to which Paes Leme refers is the proclamation by Governor Sarzedas that demanded that all Indians be relocated to the mission villages so that adult male Indians could be used in the wars against the Paiaguá of the upper Paraguay River basin. This error was repeated by many authors.
28. Artur de Sá e Meneses to the Crown, May 5, 1700, AHU-Rio de Janeiro, doc. 2513.
29. These issues are discussed in greater detail in Monteiro, "Sal, justiça social e autoridade colonial."
30. Antonio Rodrigues, "Carta de missão," Jan. 25, 1700, ARSI Brasilia 10, fol. 1v.
31. João Pires Rodrigues v. João Rodrigues da Fonseca, 1666, AESP-AC, cx. 1.
32. Micaela Bastarda v. Prior do Carmo, 1721, AESP-AC 1700–1800, cx. 15, doc. 320; civil ruling in favor of Micaela Bastarda, 1724, AESP-AC, cx. 13, doc. 190; Domingos Lopes de Godoi v. Convento do Carmo, 1730, AESP-AC, cx. 25, doc. 428.

33. Listing of criminal petitions, various dates (eighteenth century), AESP, cxs. 437–479.
34. Justification of Maria Leme do Prado, 1723, AESP-AC, cx. 12.
35. Departamento do Arquivo do Estado de São Paulo, *Boletim do Departamento do Arquivo do Estado* 7 (1947): 37–38, 61.
36. Departamento do Arquivo do Estado de São Paulo, *Boletim do Departamento do Arquivo do Estado* 5 (1945): 17–18.
37. Francisco Cubas de Miranda v. Marta Miranda del Rei, 1721, AESP-AC, cx. 9, doc. 133.
38. Maria Theresa Schorer Petrone, *A lavoura canavieira em São Paulo* (São Paulo: Difusão Européia do Livro, 1968), remains the best work on the expansion of commercial agriculture in the late eighteenth century. See also Ellis Júnior and Ellis, *A economia paulista no século XVIII*.
39. The prices cited here are from estate inventories, which – together with parish registers – provide the most solid evidence of the growth of the African and Afro-American population of São Paulo. This material awaits a more systematic treatment. It is noteworthy that slave traders showed some enthusiasm regarding the prospect of supplying the market of the mining region through São Paulo, particularly once the Municipal Council of São Paulo petitioned the Overseas Council for permission to establish direct trade between Santos and Angola. However, the idea was opposed by the captains of the ships involved in the trade, who alleged that their ships would have to depart Santos with empty holds, because of the lack of worthwhile merchandise at the principal port of the captaincy of São Paulo. See AHU-SP, docs. 56 (Feb. 12, 1700) and 60 (1700).
40. Boxer, *Golden Age of Brazil*, provides abundant examples of conflicts between agriculturalists and merchants, as well as between Portuguese and Brazilian-born colonists, which became more intense during this period in various corners of the colony. While much of the historiography has focused on the struggle between Paulistas and Emboabas – the colonists from São Paulo who made the first strikes of gold and the newcomers drawn to Minas Gerais thereafter, respectively – the documentation features constant complaints of abuses by forestallers, monopolists, usurers, and royal officials from the opening of the mines onward, sometimes resulting in significant outbreaks of violence. As far as the assimilation of Portuguese immigrants in Paulista society is concerned, it reached the point by mid-century that a Crown magistrate urged the Overseas Council to suspend the privileges granted the Pires and Camargo families, who succeeded one another at the head of the Municipal Council, given the growth of the Portuguese-born population of the town of São Paulo. AHU-SP, doc. 1820, Jan. 20, 1749.
41. The best description of the inflation that struck the mining districts is in Antonil, *Cultura e opulência do Brasil*, esp. 139–143. See also Boxer, *Golden Age of Brazil*, 54–56 and 187ff.
42. There are two important studies of the provisioning of the mining zone: Mafalda P. Zemella, *O abastecimento da capitania de Minas Gerais no século XVIII*, 2nd edn. (São Paulo: Hucitec, 1990 [1951]), and Myriam Ellis, *Contribuição ao estudo do abastecimento das áreas mineradoras do Brasil no século XVIII* (Rio de Janeiro: Biblioteca Nacional, 1961). These two studies are based primarily on documentation regarding monopoly contracts and rights to passage. Beyond the official sphere, estate inventories provide

numerous examples of commercial relations with the mining zone, but these activities are best illustrated in the account book of Father Guilherme Pompeu de Almeida, published in the *Revista do Instituto Histórico e Geográfico de São Paulo* 58 (1960): 491–579, and in his 1710 will, filed in AESP-INP. Father Pompeu owned large estates in Parnaíba and Itu, with a labor force of approximately 300 Indian and African slaves. Upon his death in 1713, his properties passed to the Jesuit College of São Paulo, part of them becoming the immense estate of Araçariguama. The account book is analyzed along with unpublished and little-known documentation in Herbert Cahn, "Padre Guilherme Pompeu de Almeida e suas atividades comerciais, 1686–1713" (tese de doutorado, Universidade de São Paulo, 1967). In a curious attempt to hew to the conventions of Paulista historiography, Cahn asserts that Father Pompeu's acquisition of African slaves – like that of other Paulistas in this period – was a matter of conspicuous consumption rather than obtaining productive labor (see p. 9).

43. Pedro Taques de Almeida to Governor Lencastre, Mar. 20, 1700, Ajuda, cód. 51-IX-33, fol. 450. On conditions of travel and transport to the mining zone, see also Cód. Costa Mattoso, fol. 21.
44. Timoteo Correia de Gois to Conselho Ultramarino, Sept. 8, 1710, AHU-SP, doc. 83.
45. Lyra, "Os dízimos." For a more general discussion of tithes in Minas, see Manoel Cardozo, "Tithes in Colonial Minas Gerais," *Catholic Historical Review* 38/2 (July 1952): 175–182.
46. Governor Meneses to Governor Saldanha, Mar. 8, 1724, AHU-SP, doc. 371.
47. Governor Pimentel to Conselho Ultramarino, Apr. 18, 1730, AHU-SP, doc. 760.
48. The spread and scale of poverty resulting from the growth of mining are well explored in the interesting works of Mello e Souza, *Desclassificados do ouro*, and Volpato, *A conquista da terra no universo da pobreza*.
49. Bartolomeu Lopes de Carvalho, "Manifesto a sua magestade," n.d., Ajuda, cód. 51-IX-33.

Afterword

James Woodard and Barbara Weinstein

The success of *Negros da terra* is evidenced by its multiple printings and the crucial but unquantifiable consensus among historians of Brazil that it is a classic. In the shorter term, it was also reflected in other kinds of popular and scholarly recognition, in Brazil and in the United States. Within months of the book's release, Rio de Janeiro's leading newspaper named it one of the books of the year, an unusual distinction for a work of colonial history. A month later, the same newspaper published a long, insightful interview with the book's author, which further contributed to the book's circulation beyond the academy. In the United States, *Negros da terra* was the recipient of an honorable mention for the Howard F. Cline Prize in Latin American Ethnohistory, a rare commendation for a book on Brazilian history, and a singular one for a monograph published in Portuguese.

Rather than rest on his laurels, John redoubled his efforts to demonstrate the importance of indigenous peoples in Brazilian history across the centuries and to contribute to the larger Latin American historical corpus. Even as reviews of *Negros da terra* began to appear, he was at work on his "The Crises and Transformations of Invaded Societies: Coastal Brazil in the Sixteenth Century" for *The Cambridge History of the Native Peoples of the Americas* (1999), which also featured the collaboratively produced essay "Destruction, Resistance, and Transformation: Southern, Coastal, and Northern Brazil (1580–1890)," in which the imprint of *Negros da terra* remains apparent. Another project begun during those years was his contribution to the *Cambridge Economic History of Latin America* (2005–2006), which was to cover the region's labor systems from the Columbian encounter through the mid-nineteenth century. The result was a tour d'horizon of great erudition, in which John's remarkable personal modesty is also apparent. While many scholars would have approached his task as an opportunity to tout the importance of their own work, perhaps while copy-and-pasting from old publications, John demurred, introducing the first third of the essay, which would deal with forced native labor in colonial Latin America, "The main focus falls on sixteenth-century developments in the Caribbean, New Spain, and Peru; because of space limitations, this chapter does not discuss patterns of indigenous labor in other regions extending into the seventeenth and eighteenth centuries." In other words, Brazil, despite its now-evident importance as a site in the development of systems of indigenous slavery, would go unmentioned in a broader discussion of unfree, but non-slave forms of labor recruitment and regimentation in the areas of greatest Amerindian demographic density.

The approach of the year 2000, as the quincentennial of the first arrival in South America of a Portuguese fleet, however, provided ample opportunity for reflection on the encounter between Old World and New on Brazilian shores, including presentations and publications in Brazil, Europe, and the United States. A handful of these works became chapters in the postdoctoral thesis John presented in August 2001 to the committee that would award him the equivalent, at São Paulo state universities, of a full professorship. Titled "Tupis, Tapuias e historiadores: estudos de história indígena e do indigenismo" (Tupis, Tapuias, and Historians: Studies in Indigenous History and the History of the Study of Indigenous Peoples), the collection was as marked by tensions and transitions as *Negros da terra* had been. While its introductory framing found John lamenting what he saw as the paucity of serious historical work on Brazil's native peoples, study of which remained largely the province of anthropologists, the chapters that followed showed him moving into new thematic, chronological and geographic terrain. This expansion of his fields of interest and expertise included a turn from the traditions in social history that had characterized most of his work to that point toward the history of ideas, identity, and memory, as well as an increasing interest in the nineteenth century. In its final chapter, the thesis pointed to a new geographical orientation in his studies, though one that contained within it echoes of earlier interests and approaches.

Only the first of these tensions and transitions would be fully resolved, John pointing out to the Brazilian Studies section of the Conference on Latin American History in 2012, "the number of publications, masters' theses, and doctoral dissertations covering subjects linked to the history of Amerindian peoples [in Brazil] is on the rise." This profusion of original, university-produced scholarship, a complete reversal of the situation that existed when he began the work that became *Negros da terra*, led John to confess, "I find it hard to keep up with the bibliography," an implicit disavowal of his lament of ten years earlier. This remarkable set of developments, including the fact that less than two decades separated the contemporary flourishing of historical scholarship on Brazil's indigenous peoples from the conception of ethnohistory as a field in that country – in Manuela Carneiro da Cunha's *História dos índios no Brasil* and John's contribution thereto, followed two years later by *Negros da terra* – was in large part due to John's efforts, inspiration, and example. For beginning with his arrival at the University of Campinas in the mid-1990s, John began to devote vast energies to graduate training, serving on sixty doctoral committees in Brazil between 1995 and 2011 and directing eighteen doctoral dissertations between 2000 and 2012. The equivalent figures for masters-level committee service and advising were thirty-two and ten for the period 1995–2013, totals that on their own reflect a considerable effort on John's part, as well as on the part of his students, who produced works of real scholarly importance, many of them published as books, the Brazilian masters thesis in history not yet having become the vestigial practicum of the North American academy. At both the doctoral and masters level, one may note qualitative change as well as quantitative growth, as John's graduate training came to involve increasing numbers of students of history, as opposed to anthropology, the history department at Campinas in particular proving over time to be more welcoming than the University of São Paulo's had been when he visited as a graduate-student researcher. These shifts within the Brazilian academy coincided with John's continued engagement with his counterparts in the United States, in conference presentations and professional service, as a visiting professor at Harvard University and the University of Michigan, and through *Negros da terra*, his masterwork, which helped to inspire doctoral-level work on Brazil's indigenous peoples at institutions from Johns Hopkins University to the University of Texas at Austin. Not only in Brazil, but in the United States as well, the pessimism expressed in John's introduction to his 2001 thesis was mooted in the very short term.

The transitions implied in the thesis's turn to ideas, identity, and memory, together with John's advance into the nineteenth century, were not so neatly resolved. To be sure, neither was an outright rupture with his earlier scholarship. Already in *Negros da terra* one may note the beginnings of an argument about the way Portuguese colonists classified different indigenous groups according to their alleged aptitudes for conversion and civilized comportment, and how these ethnic classifications shaped strategies to secure and discipline labor. This subtext to John's earlier work came to the forefront in "Tupis, Tapuias e historiadores," several of its chapters elucidating the ways in which certain assumptions about indigenous peoples not only worked their way into intellectual debates, archival collections, and scholarly production, but also into the formulation and implementation of policy, with often grave consequences for Amerindian peoples. In other words, John's increased interest in representations did not preclude attention to material forces.

Indeed, as John's contribution to the *Cambridge Economic History of Latin America* suggests, he kept one foot in the materialist tradition he had been formed in and did not rule out the bringing together of old and at least some new, envisioning a labor history "to be written … in terms of the actions and strategies, triumphs and defeats of those who most matter." For John as a scholar and an advocate, of course, those who most mattered were the country's indigenous people. The pursuit of their history, as he described it in *The Cambridge History of the Native Peoples of the Americas*, had to register the impact and legacies of colonialism, but it must also involve "rethinking Indian history itself – that is, the history experienced and reflected upon by Brazil's native peoples." In part because of the massive weight of John's teaching responsibilities, that problem remained unresolved, though glimpses toward resolution may be found in two essays written after the works gathered in "Tupis, Tapuias e historiadores," the first a paper eventually published in the edited volume *New Approaches to Resistance in Brazil and Mexico* (2012), the second a contribution to a multivolume history of São Paulo across the ages, in its introduction and epilogue containing John's remarks on the contemporary presence of indigenous peoples in Brazil's largest metropolis.

The geographic transition signaled in the thesis's final chapter was toward Portuguese-ruled South Asia, to be considered alongside Brazil as a site of colonial-era inter-ethnic mixture (*mestiçagem*) that left indelible imprints on history, society, and culture. While the chapter contrasted the work of two twentieth-century authors, the Paulista Alfredo Ellis Júnior and the Goa-born descendent of Portuguese settlers Germano Correia, the incipient project of which it was a part aimed to take a considerably longer view, one that would examine Portuguese colonial policies alongside actual relations between settlers, natives, and clerics on the ground, as well as the emergence of new kinds of social classification and the forging of colonial and postcolonial mythologies in relation to real and imagined processes of *mestiçagem* and its absence. The transition signaled by John's turn to Goa was thus at least a triple return: superficially, to his earlier work on the racist pseudo-scholar Ellis Júnior, as he acknowledged in the chapter in the thesis; geographically as well as topically, to Portuguese India and to the subject of his undergraduate thesis at Colorado College, "Portuguese Colonization in the Tropics: Afonso de Albuquerque's Marriage Plan in Goa," which had been researched and written under the direction of Peter Blasenheim; temporally, to the early history of Portugal's world-spanning empire, colonial Goa to become the object of the same careful research and discerning analysis once given seventeenth-century São Paulo. At the heart of that dauntingly complex project, as John described it, was something akin to what drove the making of *Negros da terra*: "to recuperate a missing link in the history of Portuguese expansion, raising questions that have much to teach us about the Brazilian past."

John's recuperation of that missing link will not be made, for he was killed in an automobile accident in March 2013 as he drove home from the University of Campinas, leaving family, friends, and colleagues in Brazil and abroad stunned by their loss. Some of John's unfinished work will be taken up by his former students, but there is no way of recovering the entirety of what we have lost and what might have been. The quiet, easy way with students, the understated erudition, the knowing smile for the absurdities of academic life will be long remembered by those fortunate enough to have known him, together with the many other qualities that made him who he was. John's scholarship – especially *Negros da terra*, until now a missing link in the English-language historiography on Indian slavery in the Americas – will live on.

Bibliography

Almeida, Maria Regina Celestino de. "John Manuel Monteiro, 1956–2013: um legado inestimável para a historiografia." *Revista Brasileira de História* 65 (2013): 399–403.

Cunha, Manuela Carneiro da (ed.). *História dos índios no Brasil*. São Paulo: Companhia das Letras, 1992.

"O índio é tabu na história." *Jornal do Brasil*, January 28, 1995, section Idéias/Livros, 6.

Johnson, Elizabeth A. "Ora et Labora: Labor Transitions on Benedictine and Carmelite Properties in Colonial São Paulo." Ph.D. dissertation, Johns Hopkins University, 2008.

Langfur, Harold Lawrence. "The Forbidden Lands: Frontier Settlers, Slaves, and Indians in Minas Gerais, Brazil, 1760–1830." Ph.D. dissertation, University of Texas at Austin, 1999. (Revised version published as Hal Langfur, *The Forbidden Lands: Colonial Identity, Frontier Violence, and the Persistence of Brazil's Eastern Indians, 1750–1830*. Stanford University Press, 2006.)

Lara, Silvia Hunold, Stuart B. Schwartz, and Barbara Weinstein. "John Manuel Monteiro (1956–2013)." *Hispanic American Historical Review* 94/3 (August 2014): 487–491.

"Os livros de 1994." *Jornal do Brasil*, December 31, 1994, section Idéias/Livros, 3–4.

Metcalf, Alida C. Review of *Negros da terra*, by John Monteiro. *The Americas* 52/2 (October 1995): 247–248.

Monteiro, John. "Caçando com gato: raça, mestiçagem e identidade paulista na obra de Alfredo Ellis Júnior." *Novos Estudos CEBRAP* 38 (1994): 79–88.

"The Crises and Transformations of Invaded Societies: Coastal Brazil in the Sixteenth Century." In Frank Salomon and Stuart B. Schwartz (eds.), *The Cambridge History of the Native Peoples of the Americas*, vol. 3: *South America*, pt. 1, 973–1023.Cambridge University Press, 1999.

"Dos Campos de Piratininga ao Morro da Saudade: a presença indígena na história de São Paulo." In Paula Porta (ed.), *História da Cidade de São Paulo*, vol. 1, 21–67. São Paulo: Paz e Terra, 2004.

"Os guarani e a história do Brasil meridional, séculos XVI–XVII." In Manuela Carneiro da Cunha (ed.), *História dos índios no Brasil*, 475–498. São Paulo: Companhia das Letras, 1992.

"Labor Systems." In Victor Bulmer-Thomas, John Coatsworth, and Roberto Cortes-Conde (eds.), *Cambridge Economic History of Latin America*, vol. 1: *The Colonial Era and the Short Nineteenth Century*, 185–233. Cambridge University Press, 2005.

"Portuguese Colonization in the Tropics: Afonso de Albuquerque's Marriage Plan in Goa." Undergraduate honors thesis, Colorado College, 1978.

"Rethinking Amerindian Resistance and Persistence in Colonial Portuguese America." In John Gledhill and Patience A. Schell (eds.), *New Approaches to Resistance in Brazil and Mexico*, 25–43. Durham, NC: Duke University Press, 2012.

"Tupis, Tapuias e historiadores: estudos de história indígena e do indigenismo." Tese de livre-docência, Universidade Estadual de Campinas, 2001.

Untitled presentation to the Brazilian Studies Committee of the Conference on Latin American History. Chicago, January 6, 2012.

Peixoto, Fernanda. Review of *Negros da terra*, by John Monteiro. *Revista de Antropologia* 48/2 (1995): 241–243.

Thomaz, Omar Ribeiro. "Goa, os índios no Brasil e a obra de John Manuel Monteiro." *Novos Estudos CEBRAP* 97 (November 2013): 5–12.

Vainfas, Ronaldo. "Negros brasis." *Folha de São Paulo*, April 3, 1995, section Jornal de Resenhas, 13.

Wright, Robin M., with Manuela Carneiro da Cunha and the Núcleo de História Indígena e do Indigenismo. "Destruction, Resistance, and Transformation: Southern, Coastal, and Northern Brazil (1580–1890)." In Frank Salomon and Stuart B. Schwartz (eds.), *The Cambridge History of the Native Peoples of the Americas*, vol. 3: *South America*, pt. 2, 287–381. Cambridge University Press, 1999.

Bibliography

Archival Sources

Brazil

Guarulhos
Arquivo da Cúria Diocesana
Jundiaí
Arquivo da Cúria Diocesana
Cartório do Primeiro Ofício de Notas
Museu Histórico e Cultural
Mogi das Cruzes
Arquivo da Cúria Diocesana
Arquivo da Prefeitura
Rio de Janeiro
Arquivo da Cúria Metropolitana
Biblioteca Nacional
Instituto Histórico e Geográfico Brasileiro
São Paulo
Arquivo da Cúria Metropolitana
Arquivo do Estado de São Paulo
Arquivo Histórico Municipal Washington Luís
Biblioteca Municipal Mário de Andrade
Instituto de Estudos Brasileiros
Instituto Histórico e Geográfico de São Paulo
Museu do Ipiranga – Museu Paulista
Sorocaba
Arquivo da Cúria Diocesana
Taubaté
Museu de Taubaté

Italy

Rome
Archivum Romanum Societatis Iesu, Rome
Biblioteca Nazionale Centrale Vittorio Emanuele

Portugal

Évora
Biblioteca Pública Eborense
Lisbon
Arquivo Histórico Ultramarino
Biblioteca do Palácio da Ajuda
Biblioteca Nacional

Printed Documents and Contemporary Accounts

Abbeville, Claude d'. *História da missão dos padres capuchinhos na ilha do Maranhão e terras circunvizinhas* (1614). Translated by Sérgio Milliet. 2nd edn. Belo Horizonte: Itatiaia, 1975 (1945).

Actas da Camara da villa de S. Paulo. 7 vols. São Paulo: Archivo Municipal, 1914–1915.

Actas da Camara de Sto. André da Borda do Campo. São Paulo: Archivo Municipal, 1914.

Anchieta, José de. *Cartas: correspondência ativa e passiva*, ed. Hélio Abranches Viotti. São Paulo: Loyola, 1984.

"Informação dos casamentos dos indios do Brasil." *Revista Trimensal de Historia e Geografia, ou Jornal do Instituto Historico e Geographico Brasileiro* 8 (1846): 254–262.

Antonil, André João (pseudonym). *Cultura e opulência do Brasil.* Facs. edn. Recife: Universidade Federal de Pernambuco, 1969 (1711).

Bandeirantes no Paraguai, século XVII: documentos inéditos. São Paulo: Departamento de Cultura, 1949.

Benci, Jorge. *Economia cristã dos senhores no governo dos escravos: livro brasileiro de 1700*, ed. Serafim Leite. Porto: Livraria Apostolado da Imprensa, 1954.

Campos, Antonio Pires de. "Breve noticia que dá o capitão Antonio Pires de Campos do gentio barbaro que ha na derrota da viagem das Minas do Cuyabá e seu reconcavo." *Revista Trimensal do Instituto Historico, Geographico e Ethnographico do Brasil* 25 (1862): 437–449.

Cardim, Fernão. *Tratados da terra e gente do Brasil*, ed. Baptista Caetano, Capistrano de Abreu, and Rodolpho Garcia. 3rd edn. São Paulo: Nacional, 1978 (1925).

Cartas de datas de terra. 20 vols. São Paulo: Departamento de Cultura, 1937–1940.

Casal, Manuel Ayres de. *Corografia brazilica, ou, relação historico-geografica do reino do Brazil, composta e dedicada a Sua Magestade fidelissima por hum presbitero secular do gram priorado do Crato.* 2 vols. Rio de Janeiro: Impressão Regia, 1817.

Castro e Almeida, Eduardo de. *Inventario dos documentos relativos ao Brasil existentes no Archivo da Marinha e Ultramar de Lisboa.* 8 vols. Rio de Janeiro: Biblioteca Nacional, 1913–1936.

Charlevoix, Pierre-François-Xavier de. *Histoire du Paraguay.* 3 vols. Paris: Chez Didot, 1756.

Cleto, Marcellino Pereira. "Dissertação a respeito da capitania de S. Paulo, sua decadencia e modo de restabelece-la" (1782). *Annaes da Bibliotheca Nacional do Rio de Janeiro* 21 (1899): 193–254.

Cordeiro, José Pedro Leite (ed.). "Documentação sobre o capitão-mor Guilherme Pompeo de Almeida, morador que foi na vila de Parnaíba." *Revista do Instituto Histórico e Geográfico de São Paulo* 58 (1960): 491–579.

Cortesão, Jaime (ed.). *Pauliceae lusitana monumenta histórica.* 2 vols. Rio de Janeiro: Real Gabinete Português de Leitura, 1956–1961.

Cortesão, Jaime, and Hélio Viana (eds.). *Manuscritos da coleção de Angelis.* 7 vols. Rio de Janeiro: Biblioteca Nacional, 1951–1970.

Departamento do Arquivo do Estado de São Paulo. *Boletim do Departamento do Arquivo do Estado*. 8 vols. São Paulo: Arquivo do Estado, 1942–1948.

Documentos avulsos de interesse para a história e costumes de São Paulo. 5 vols. São Paulo: Arquivo do Estado, 1954.

Inventários e testamentos. 44 vols. São Paulo: Archivo/Arquivo do Estado, 1920–1977.

Publicação official de documentos interessantes para a historia e costumes de S. Paulo. 54 vols. São Paulo: Archivo do Estado, 1894–1932.

Sesmarias. 3 vols. in 5. São Paulo: Archivo/Arquivo do Estado, 1921–1940.

Documentos históricos. 110 vols. Rio de Janeiro: Biblioteca Nacional, 1928–1955.

Documentos para a história do açúcar. 3 vols. Rio de Janeiro: Instituto do Açúcar e do Alcool, 1954–1963.

"Excerpto de uma memoria manuscripta sobre a historia do Rio de Janeiro durante o governo de Salvador Correia de Sá e Benevides." *Revista Trimensal de Historia e Geografia, ou Jornal do Instituto Historico e Geographico Brasileiro* 3 (1841): 3–38.

Fonseca, Luiza da (ed.). "Índice abreviado dos documentos do século XVII do Arquivo Histórico Colonial de Lisboa." *Anais do Primeiro Congresso de História da Bahia* 2 (1950): 7–353.

Fonseca, Manuel da. *Vida do veneravel padre Belchior de Pontes, da Companhia de Jesus da provincia do Brasil*. Facs. edn. São Paulo: Melhoramentos, 1932 (1752).

Gandavo, Pero de Magalhães. *Tratado da Terra do Brasil: história da província de Santa Cruz* (1576), ed. Rodolpho Garcia. 2nd edn. Belo Horizonte: Itatiaia, 1980 [1924].

Knivet, Antony. "The Admirable Adventures and Strange Fortunes of Master Antonie Knivet." In *Hakluytus póstumas or Purchas his pilgrimes*, ed. Samuel Purchas, 16:177–289. Facs. edn. New York: AMS Press, 1965.

Leite, Serafim (ed.). *Monumenta brasiliae*. 5 vols. Rome: Monumenta Historica Societatis Iesu, 1956–1960. (Vols. 1–3 were also published in Brazil as *Cartas dos primeiros jesuítas do Brasil*. São Paulo: Comissão do IV Centenário, 1956–1957.)

(ed.). *Novas cartas jesuíticas*. São Paulo: Nacional, 1940.

Leme, Pedro Taques de Almeida Paes. *Historia da capitania de S. Vicente*. São Paulo: Melhoramentos, n.d.

Informações sobre as minas de São Paulo: a expulsão dos jesuítas do Colégio de São Paulo, ed. Afonso d'Escragnolle Taunay. São Paulo: Melhoramentos, 1946.

Nobiliarquia paulistana histórica e genealógica, ed. Afonso d'Escragnolle Taunay. 3 vols. 5th edn. Belo Horizonte: Itatiaia, 1980 (1926).

Léry, Jean de. *Viagem á terra do Brasil*, trans. Sérgio Milliet. 2nd edn. Belo Horizonte: Itatiaia, 1980 (1941).

Madre de Deus, Gaspar da. *Memórias para a história da capitania de São Vicente, hoje chamada São Paulo*. 2nd edn. Belo Horizonte: Itatiaia, 1975 (1797).

Madureira, Pedro de Moraes (attributed). "Expulsão dos jesuitas e causas que tiveram para ella os paulistas desde o anno de 1611 até o de 1640, em que os lançaram fóra de toda a capitania de São Paulo e S. Vicente." *Revista do Instituto Historico e Geographico de São Paulo* 3 (1898): 57–123.

Maldonado, Miguel Ayres, Jozé de Castilho Pinto, and others. "Descripção que faz o capitão Miguel Ayres Maldonado e o capitão Jozé de Castilho Pinto e seus companheiros dos trabalhos e fadigas das suas vidas, que tiveram nas conquistas da capitania do Rio de Janeiro e São Vicente, com a gentilidade e com os piratas n'esta costa" (1661). *Revista Trimensal do Instituto Historico e Geographico Brazileiro* 56, pt. 1 (1893): 345–400.

Mello, José Antônio Gonsalves de (ed.). *Fontes para a história do Brasil holandês*, vol. 1: *A economia açucareira*. Recife: Museu do Açúcar, 1981.

Mendonça, Antonio Manuel de Mello Castro e. "Memória econômica-política da capitania de São Paulo." *Anais do Museu Paulista* 15 (1961): 81–248.

Pereira, Estevam. "Descrezão da fazenda que o Collegio de Santo Antão tem no Brazil e de seus rendimentos, pelo Padre Estevam Pereira, S. J." (1635). *Annaes do Museu Paulista* 4 (1931): 773–794.

Pitta, Sebastião da Rocha. *História da América portuguesa*. 2nd edn. Belo Horizonte: Itatiaia, 1980 (1730).

"Processo das despesas feitas por Martim de Sá no Rio de Janeiro, 1628–33." *Anais da Biblioteca Nacional do Rio de Janeiro* 59 (1937): 5–186.

Registro geral da Câmara Municipal de São Paulo. 20 vols. São Paulo: Archivo Municipal, 1917–23.

Rendon, José Arouche de Toledo. "Memoria sobre as aldeas de indios da provincia de S. Paulo, segundo as observações feitas no ano de 1798." *Revista Trimensal de Historia e Geografia, ou Jornal do Instituto Historico e Geographico Brasileiro* 4 (1842): 295–317.

Ruiz (de Montoya), Antonio. "Primeira catechese dos indios selvagens feita pelos padres da Companhia de Jesus." *Annaes da Bibliotheca Nacional do Rio de Janeiro* 6 (1878–1879): 91–366.

Ruyer, Claudio. "Relación de la guerra y victoria alcanzada contra los portugueses del Brasil, año 1641 en 6 de abril." *Revista do Instituto Historico e Geographico de S. Paulo* 10 (1905): 529–553.

Schmidl, Ulrich. *Relato de la conquista del Río de la Plata y Paraguay, 1534–1554*, trans. Klaus Wagner. Madrid: Alianza Editorial, 1986.

Sousa, Afonso Botelho de S. Paio e. "Notícia da Conquista e descobrimento dos sertões do Tibagi." *Anais da Biblioteca Nacional do Rio de Janeiro* 76 (1956): 1–290.

Sousa, Gabriel Soares de. *Tratado descritivo do Brasil em 1587*, ed. Francisco Adolfo de Varnhagen. 4th edn. São Paulo: Nacional, 1971 (1851).

Sousa, Pero Lopes de. *Diário da navegação*, ed. Eugênio de Castro. São Paulo: Obelisco, 1964.

Staden, Hans. *The Captivity of Hans Stade* [sic] *of Hesse in A.D. 1547–1555, Among the Wild Tribes of Eastern Brazil*, trans. Albert Tootal with notes by Richard Burton. Facs. edn. New York: Burt Franklin, 1963 (1874).

Duas viagens ao Brasil, trans. Guiomar de Carvalho Franco. 2nd edn. Belo Horizonte: Itatiaia, 1974 (1942).

Taunay, Afonso [Affonso] d'Escragnolle (ed.). *Relatos monçoeiros*. São Paulo: Comissão do IV Centenário, 1953.

Relatos sertanistas. São Paulo: Comissão do IV Centenário, 1953.

Techo, Nicolás del. *Historia provinciæ Paraquariæ Societatis Jesv*. Liège: Joan. Mathiae Hovii, 1673.

"Termo de erecção da capella da freguezia de Nossa Senhora do Ó, anno de 1618, petição." *Revista do Instituto Historico e Geographico de São Paulo* 6 (1900–1901): 473–477.

Thevet, André. *As singularidades da França Antártica*, trans. Eugenio Amado. Belo Horizonte: Itatiaia, 1978.

Vasconcelos, Simão de. *Crônica da Companhia de Jesus*. 2 vols. 3rd edn. Petrópolis: Vozes, 1977 (1663).

Vida do p. Joam d'Almeida da Companhia de Iesu na provincia do Brazil. Lisbon: Officina Craesbeeckiana, 1658.

Vida do venerável padre José de Anchieta. 2 vols. Rio de Janeiro: Imprensa Nacional, 1943.

Vieira, Antonio. *Cartas*, ed. João Lúcio de Azevedo. 3 vols. Coimbra: Imprensa da Universidade, 1925–1928.

Vilhena, Luís dos Santos. *Recopilação de notícias da capitania de S. Paolo* [*sic*]. Salvador: Imprensa Official, 1935.

Books, Articles, and Theses

Abreu, Daisy Bizzocchi de Lacerda. *A terra e a lei: estudo de comportamentos sócio-econômicos em São Paulo nos séculos XVI e XVII*. São Paulo: Secretaria de Estado da Cultura, 1983.

Abreu, João Capistrano de. *Capítulos de história colonial e os caminhos antigos e o povoamento do Brasil*, ed. José Honório Rodrigues. Brasília: Universidade de Brasília, 1982.

Abud, Kátia Maria. "O sangue intimorato e as nobilíssimas tradições (A construção de um símbolo paulista: o bandeirante)." Tese de doutorado, Universidade de São Paulo, 1985.

Aguirra, João Baptista de Campos. "Relação das sesmarias concedidas na comarca da capital entre os anos de 1559 a 1820." *Revista do Instituto Historico e Geographico de São Paulo* 25 (1927): 493–567.

Alden, Dauril. "Black Robes Versus White Settlers: The Struggle for Freedom of the Indians in Colonial Brazil." In Howard H. Peckham and Charles Gibson (eds.), *Attitudes of Colonial Powers Toward the American Indian*, 19–46. Salt Lake City: University of Utah Press, 1969.

"Economic Aspects of the Expulsion of the Jesuits from Brazil: A Preliminary Report." In *Conflict and Continuity in Brazilian Society*, ed. Henry H. Keith and S. F. Edwards, 25–65. Columbia: University of South Carolina, 1969.

"Indian versus Black Slavery in the State of Maranhão during the Seventeenth and Eighteenth Centuries." *Bibliotheca Americana* 1/3 (1983): 91–142.

Alden, Dauril, and Joseph C. Miller "Out of Africa: The Slave Trade and the Transmission of Smallpox to Brazil, 1560–1830." *Journal of Interdisciplinary History* 18/2 (1987): 195–224.

Alencastro, Luiz Felipe de. "O aprendizado da colonização." *Economia e Sociedade* 1/1 (August 1992): 135–162.

Almeida, Aluísio de. "A fundação de Sorocaba." *Revista do Arquivo Municipal* 57 (May 1939): 197–202.

Almeida, Luiz Castanho de. "Bandeirantes no ocidente." *Revista do Instituto Histórico e Geográfico de São Paulo* 40 (1941): 343–381.

Alves Filho, Ivan. *Memorial dos Palmares*. Rio de Janeiro: Xenon, 1988.

Amaral, Amadeu. *O dialeto caipira: gramática, vocabulário*. 4th edn. São Paulo: Hucitec, 1982 (1920).

Amaral, Antonio Barreto de. *Dicionário da história de São Paulo*. São Paulo: Governo do Estado, 1980.

Amaral, Aracy. *A hispanidade em São Paulo: da casa rural à capela de Santo Antonio*. São Paulo: Perspectiva, 1983.

Arruda, Terezinha de Jesus, and Elizabeth Madureira Siqueira. "Mão-de-obra ao pé da obra: a presença do índio no processo produtivo do Brasil-Colônia." *Leopoldianum* 31 (1984): 43–56.

Ayrosa, Plínio. *Estudos tupinológicos*. São Paulo: Instituto de Estudos Brasileiros, 1967.

"Mameluco é termo árabe ou tupi?" *Revista do Arquivo Municipal* 1 (June 1934): 21–24.

"Os primitivos habitantes de São Paulo." Conferências do Clube Atlético Bandeirante 4. São Paulo: Clube Atlético Bandeirante, 1934.

Azevedo, Aroldo de. "Aldeias e aldeamentos de índios." *Boletim Paulista de Geografia* 33 (October 1959): 23–40.

Vilas e cidades do Brasil colonial: ensaio de geografia urbana retrospectiva. São Paulo: Universidade de São Paulo, 1956.

Azevedo, Victor de. *Manuel Preto, "O herói de Guairá."* São Paulo: Governo do Estado, 1983.

Barreiros, Eduardo Canabrava. *Roteiro das esmeraldas: a bandeira de Fernão Dias Pais*. Rio de Janeiro: José Olympio, 1979.

Barro, Máximo. *Nossa Senhora do Ó*. São Paulo: Departamento do Patrimônio Histórico, 1977.
Belotto, Heloísa Liberalli. "Trabalho indígena, regalismo e colonização no estado do Maranhão nos séculos XVII e XVIII." *Revista Brasileira de História* 4 (1982): 177–192.
Beozzo, José Oscar. *Leis e regimentos das missões: política indigenista no Brasil*. São Paulo: Loyola, 1983.
Boxer, Charles R. *The Golden Age of Brazil, 1695–1750: Growing Pains of a Colonial Society*. Berkeley: University of California Press, 1962.
Portuguese Society in the Tropics: The Municipal Councils of Goa, Macau, Bahia, and Luanda, 1510–1800. Madison: University of Wisconsin Press, 1965.
Race Relations in the Portuguese Colonial Empire, 1415–1825. Oxford University Press, 1963.
Salvador de Sá and the Struggle for Brazil and Angola, 1602–1686. London: Athlone, 1952.
Brandão, Carlos Rodrigues. *Os caipiras de São Paulo*. São Paulo: Brasiliense, 1983.
Bruno, Ernani Silva. *Viagem ao país dos paulistas*. Rio de Janeiro: José Olympio, 1966.
Cahn, Herbert. "Padre Guilherme Pompeu de Almeida e suas atividades comerciais, 1686–1713." Tese de doutorado, Universidade de São Paulo, 1967.
Camargo, Paulo Florêncio da Silveira. *História de Santana de Parnaíba*. São Paulo: Conselho Estadual de Cultura, 1971.
Canabrava, Alice P. *O comércio português no Rio da Prata, 1580–1640*. 2nd edn. Belo Horizonte: Itatiaia, 1984 (1944).
"Uma economia de decadência: os níveis de riqueza na capitania de São Paulo, 1765–1767." *Revista Brasileira de Economia* 26/4 (October–December 1972): 95–123.
Cardozo, Manoel. "Dom Rodrigo de Castel-Blanco and the Brazilian El Dorado, 1673–1682." *The Americas* 1/2 (October 1944): 131–159.
"Tithes in Colonial Minas Gerais." *Catholic Historical Review* 38/2 (July 1952): 175–182.
Cardozo, Ramón Indalecio. *El Guairá: historia de la antigua provincia, 1554–1676*. Asunción: El Arte, 1970.
Casal, Manuel Ayres do. *Corografia brasílica*. 2nd edn. 2 vols. Rio de Janeiro: José Olympio, 1945 (1817).
Castro, Eduardo Viveiros de. "Bibliografia etnológica básica tupi-guarani." *Revista de Antropologia* 27–28 (1984–1985): 7–24.
César, José Vicente. "Situação legal do índio durante o período colonial, 1500–1822." *América Indígena* 45/2 (1985): 391–425.
Clastres, Hélène. *Terra sem mal: o profetismo tupi-guarani*, trans. Renato Janine Ribeiro. São Paulo: Brasiliense, 1978.
Clastres, Pierre. *Arqueologia da violência: ensaios de antropologia política*, trans. Carlos Eugênio Marcondes de Moura. São Paulo: Brasiliense, 1982.
A sociedade contra o estado: pesquisas de antropologia política, trans. Théo Santiago. Rio de Janeiro: Francisco Alves, 1978.
Cordeiro, José Pedro Leite. *O Engenho de São Jorge dos Erasmos*. São Paulo: Nacional, 1945.
"Sobre a fundação de Jundiaí." *Revista do Instituto Histórico e Geográfico de São Paulo* 57 (1959): 41 50.
Cortesão, Jaime. "A maior bandeira do maior bandeirante." *Revista de História* 22 (1961): 3–27.
Raposo Tavares e a formação territorial do Brasil. Rio de Janeiro: Imprensa Nacional, 1958.
Craton, Michael. "From Caribs to Black Caribs: The Amerindian Roots of Servile Resistance in the Caribbean." In Gary Y. Okihiro (ed.), *In Resistance: Studies in African, Caribbean, and Afro-American History*, 96–116. Amherst: University of Massachusetts Press, 1986.
Cunha, Manuela Carneiro da, *Antropologia do Brasil: mito, história, etnicidade*. São Paulo: Brasiliense, 1986.

Os direitos do índio: ensaios e documentos. São Paulo: Brasiliense, 1987.
(ed.). *História dos índios no Brasil*. São Paulo: Companhia das Letras, 1992.
Cunha, Manuela Carneiro da, and Eduardo B. Viveiros de Castro. "Vingança e temporalidade: os Tupinambá." *Journal de la Societé des Américanistes* 79 (1987): 191–208.
Cushner, Nicholas P. *Jesuit Ranches and the Agrarian Development of Colonial Argentina, 1650–1767*. Albany: State University of New York Press, 1983.
Dantas, Beatriz G., José Augusto L. Sampaio, and Maria Rosário G. de Carvalho. "Os povos indígenas no Nordeste brasileiro: um esboço histórico." In Cunha (ed.), *História dos índios no Brasil*, 431–456.
Davidoff, Carlos Henrique. *Bandeirantismo: verso e reverso*. São Paulo: Brasiliense, 1992.
Dean, Warren. "Ecological and Economic Relationships in Frontier History: São Paulo, Brazil." In George Wolfskill and Stanley Palmer (eds.), *Essays on Frontiers in World History*, 71–100. College Station: Texas A&M University Press, 1981.
"The Indigenous Population of the São Paulo–Rio de Janeiro Coast: Trade, Aldeamento, Slavery, and Extinction." *Revista de História* 117 (1984): 3–26.
Derby, Orville. "As bandeiras paulistas de 1601 a 1604." *Revista do Instituto Historico e Geographico de São Paulo* 8 (1903): 399–423.
Dias, Maria Odila Leite da Silva. *Quotidiano e poder em São Paulo no século XIX*. São Paulo: Brasiliense, 1984.
Dickason, Olive P. *The Myth of the Savage and the Beginnings of French Colonialism in the Americas*. Edmonton: University of Alberta Press, 1984.
Dollar, Charles M. and Richard Jensen. *Historian's Guide to Statistics: Quantitative Analysis and Historical Research*. New York: Holt, Rinehart and Winston, 1971.
Ellis, Myriam. "As bandeiras na expansão geográfica do Brasil." In Sérgio Buarque de Holanda (ed.), *História geral da civilização brasileira*, t. 1: *A época colonial*, vol. 1, 273–296. São Paulo: Difusão Européia do Livro, 1960.
Contribuição ao estudo do abastecimento das áreas mineradoras do Brasil no século XVIII. Rio de Janeiro: Biblioteca Nacional, 1961.
(as Myriam Ellis Austregésilo). "Pesquisas sobre a existência do ouro e da prata no planalto paulista nos séculos XVI e XVII." *Revista de História* 1 (1950): 51–71.
"A presença de Raposo Tavares na expansão paulista." *Revista do Instituto de Estudos Brasileiros* 9 (1970): 23–61.
Ellis Júnior, Alfredo. *O bandeirismo paulista e o recuo do meridiano*. 2nd edn. São Paulo: Nacional, 1934 (1923).
Os primeiros troncos paulistas e o cruzamento euro-americano. 2nd edn. São Paulo: Nacional, 1976 (1936).
"A queda do bandeirismo de apresamento." *Revista de História* 1 (1950): 301–308.
Raça de gigantes: a civilisação no planalto paulista. Estudo da evolução racial anthroposocial e psychicologica do paulista dos séculos XVI, XVII, XVIII e XIX, e das mesologias physica e social do planalto paulista. São Paulo: Helios, 1926.
Resumo da história de São Paulo. São Paulo: Rothschild, Loureiro, 1942.
Ellis Júnior, Alfredo, and Myriam Ellis. *A economia paulista no século XVIII: o ciclo do muar, o ciclo do açúcar*. São Paulo: Universidade de São Paulo, 1950.
Ennes, Ernesto. *As guerras nos Palmares: subsídios para a sua história*. São Paulo: Nacional, 1938.
Farage, Nádia. *As muralhas dos sertões: os povos indígenas do Rio Branco e a colonização*. Rio de Janeiro: Paz e Terra, 1991.
Fausto, Carlos. "Fragmentos de história e cultura tupinambá: da etnologia como instrumento crítico do conhecimento etno-histórico." In Cunha (ed.), *História dos índios no Brasil*, 381–396.
"O ritual antropofágico." *Ciência Hoje*, 86 (1992): 88–89.

Fernandes, Florestan. *A função social da guerra na sociedade tupinambá*. 2nd edn. São Paulo: Pioneira, 1970 (1952).

A investigação etnológica no Brasil e outros ensaios. Petrópolis: Vozes, 1975.

Mudanças sociais no Brasil: aspectos do desenvolvimento da sociedade brasileira. 2nd edn. São Paulo: Difusão Européia do Livro, 1979 (1960).

A organização social dos Tupinambá. São Paulo: Instituto Progresso Editorial, 1949 (2nd edn., São Paulo: Difusão Européia do Livro, 1963).

Ferreira, Manoel Rodrigues. *As bandeiras do Paraupava*. São Paulo: Prefeitura Municipal, 1979.

Ferry, Robert J. "Encomienda, African slavery, and Agriculture in Seventeenth-Century Caracas." *Hispanic American Historical Review* 61/4 (November 1981): 609–635.

Fina, Wilson Maia. *O chão de Piratininga*. São Paulo: Anhambi, 1965.

Forsyth, Donald W. "Beginnings of Brazilian Anthropology: Jesuits and Tupinambá Cannibalism." *Journal of Anthropological Research* 39/2 (1983): 147–178.

Franco, Francisco de Assis Carvalho. *Os Camargos de São Paulo: noticia sobre os representantes dessa linhagem, na capitania vicentina, nos seculos XVI e XVII*. São Paulo: Editora S.P.S., 1937.

Dicionário de bandeirantes e sertanistas do Brasil. São Paulo: Comissão do IV Centenário, 1954.

História das minas de São Paulo: administradores gerais e provedores, séculos XVI–XVII. São Paulo: Conselho Estadual de Cultura, 1964.

Freitas, Affonso A. de. *Os Guayanás de Piratininga*. São Paulo: Laemmert, 1910.

French, John. "Riqueza, poder e mão-de-obra numa economia de subsistência: São Paulo, 1596–1625." *Revista do Arquivo Municipal* 195 (January–December 1982): 79–107.

Fukui, Lia Freitas Garcia. *Sertão e bairro rural: parentesco e família entre sitiantes tradicionais*. São Paulo: Ática, 1979.

Gadelha, Regina A. Fonseca. *As missões jesuíticas do Itatim: um estudo das estruturas sócio-econômicas do Paraguai, séculos XVI e XVII*. Rio de Janeiro: Paz e Terra, 1980.

Gallois, Dominique T. *Migração, guerra e comércio: os Waiãpi na Guiana*. São Paulo: Faculdade de Filosofia, Letras e Ciências Humanas da Universidade de São Paulo, 1986.

Gama, José Mário. "O patrimônio da Companhia de Jesus da capitania de São Paulo: da formação ao confisco, 1550–1775." Dissertação de mestrado, Universidade de São Paulo, 1982.

Gambini, Roberto. *O espelho índio: os jesuítas e a destruição da alma indígena*. Rio de Janeiro: Espaço e Tempo, 1988.

Garavaglia, Juan Carlos. "Um modo de produção subsidiária: a organização econômica das comunidades guaranizadas durante os séculos XVII–XVIII na formação Alto Peruano-Rio Platense." In Philomena Gebran (ed.), *Conceito de modo de produção*, 247–275. Rio de Janeiro: Paz e Terra, 1978.

Genovese, Eugene. *Roll, Jordan, Roll: The World the Slaves Made*. New York: Pantheon, 1974.

Giucci, Guillermo, "A colonização acidental." *Ciência Hoje* 86 (1992): 19–23.

Gomes, Mércio Pereira. *Os índios e o Brasil: ensaio sobre um holocausto e sobre uma nova possibilidade de convivência*. Petrópolis: Vozes, 1988.

Gorender, Jacob. *O escravismo colonial*. 4th edn. São Paulo: Ática, 1985 (1978).

Grinberg, Isaac. *Gaspar Vaz, fundador de Mogi das Cruzes*. São Paulo: by the author, 1980.

Haubert, Maxime. *Índios e jesuítas no tempo das missões: séculos XVII–XVIII*, trans. Marina Appenzeller. São Paulo: Companhia das Letras, 1990.

Helms, Mary W. "Miskito Slaving and Culture Contact: Ethnicity and Opportunity in an Expanding Population." *Journal of Anthropological Research* 39/2 (1983): 179–197.

Hemming, John. *Red Gold: The Conquest of the Brazilian Indians, 1500–1760*. Cambridge, MA: Harvard University Press, 1978.

Henretta, James. *The Evolution of American Society, 1700–1815*. Lexington MA: D. C. Heath, 1973.

Holanda, Sérgio Buarque de. *Caminhos e fronteiras*. Rio de Janeiro: José Olympio, 1957.

"Expansão paulista em fins de século XVI e princípios do XVII." *Boletim do Instituto de Administração* 29 (1948): 3–23.

O extremo oeste. São Paulo: Brasiliense, 1986.

"A fábrica de ferro de Santo Amaro." *Digesto Econômico*, January–February 1948, 78–81.

Monções. 3rd edn. São Paulo: Brasiliense, 1990 (1945).

"Movimentos da população em São Paulo no século XVIII." *Revista do Instituto de Estudos Brasileiros* 1 (1966): 55–111.

(ed.). *História geral da civilização brasileira*, t. 1: *Época colonial*. 2 vols. São Paulo: Difusão Européia do Livro, 1960.

Höner, Urs. *Die Versklavung der brasilianischen Indianer: der Arbeitsmarkt in portugiesisch Amerika im XVI. Jahrhundert*. Zurich: Atlantis Verlag, 1980.

Hoornaert, Eduardo (ed.). *História da Igreja no Brasil: ensaio de interpretação a partir do povo*. 2 vols. Petrópolis: Vozes, 1977–1980.

Ianni, Octávio (ed.). *Florestan Fernandes: sociologia*. São Paulo: Ática, 1986.

Ihering, Hermann von. "Os indios patos e o nome da Lagoa dos Patos." *Revista do Museu Paulista* 7 (1907): 31–45.

Jaeger, Luiz Gonzaga. *As invasões bandeirantes no Rio Grande do Sul, 1635–41*. Porto Alegre: Ginásio Estadual Anchieta, 1940.

Johnson, Harold B. "The Donatory Captaincy in Perspective: Portuguese Background of the Settlement of Brazil." *Hispanic American Historical Review* 52/2 (May 1972): 203–214.

José, Oiliam. *Indígenas de Minas Gerais: aspectos sociais, políticos e etnológicos*. Belo Horizonte: Movimento-Perspectiva, 1965.

Joyner, Charles W. *Down by the Riverside: A South Carolina Slave Community*. Urbana: University of Illinois Press, 1984.

Kern, Arno Alvarez. *Missões: uma utopia política*. Porto Alegre: Mercado Aberto, 1982.

Kiemen, Mathias. *The Indian Policy of Portugal in the Amazon Region, 1614–1693*. Washington, DC: Catholic University Press, 1954.

Kracke, Waud H. *Force and Persuasion: Leadership in an Amazonian Community*. University of Chicago Press, 1978.

Kuznesof, Elizabeth Anne. *Household Economy and Urban Development: São Paulo, 1765–1836*. Boulder, CO: Westview Press, 1986.

"The Role of the Merchants in the Economic Development of São Paulo, 1765–1836." *Hispanic American Historical Review* 60/4 (November 1980): 571–592.

Laga, Carl. "O engenho dos Erasmos em São Vicente: resultado de pesquisas em arquivos belgas." *Estudos Históricos* 1 (1963): 113–143.

Lamego, Alberto. *A terra goytacá á luz de documentos inéditos*. 7 vols. Brussels: L'Édition d'art; Niterói: Governo do Estado, 1913–1943.

Lapa, José Roberto do Amaral (ed.). *Modos de produção e realidade brasileira*. Petrópolis: Vozes, 1980.

Leite, Francisco Rodrigues. "Preços em São Paulo seiscentista." *Anais do Museu Paulista* 17 (1963): 41–120.

Leite, Serafim. *História da Companhia de Jesus no Brasil*. 10 vols. Lisbon: Portugalia, 1938–50.

"Os jesuitas e os indios Maromomis na capitania de São Vicente." *Revista do Instituto Historico e Geographico de São Paulo* 32 (1935): 253–257.

Novas páginas de história do Brasil. São Paulo: Nacional, 1965.

Páginas de história do Brasil. São Paulo: Nacional, 1965.

Leme, Luiz Gonzaga da Silva. *Genealogia paulistana*. 9 vols. São Paulo: Duprat, 1903–1905.

Leonzo, Nanci. "As companhias de ordenanças na capitania de São Paulo, das origens ao governo do Morgado de Matheus." *Coleção Museu Paulista. Série de História* 6 (1977): 123–239.

Lévi-Strauss, Claude. "Guerra e comércio entre os índios da América do Sul." *Revista do Arquivo Municipal* 87 (December 1942): 131–146.

Levy, Maria Bárbara. *História financeira do Brasil colonial*. Rio de Janeiro: Instituto Brasileiro de Mercados de Capitais, 1979.

Lima, João Francisco Tidei. "A ocupação da terra e a destruição dos índios na região de Bauru." Dissertação de mestrado, Universidade de São Paulo, 1978.

Lima, Ruy Cirne. *Pequena história territorial do Brasil: sesmarias e terras devolutas*. 2nd edn. Porto Alegre: Livraria Sulina, 1954 (1935).

Lindoso, Dirceu. *A utopia armada: rebeliões de pobres nas matas do Tombo Real, 1832–1850*. Rio de Janeiro: Paz e Terra, 1984.

Linhares, Maria Yedda, and Francisco Carlos Teixeira da Silva. *História da agricultura brasileira: combates e controvérsias*. São Paulo: Brasiliense, 1981.

Lombardi, Mary. "The Frontier in Brazilian History: An Historiographical Essay." *Pacific Historical Review* 44/4 (November 1975): 437–57.

Lugon, Clovis. *A república comunista-cristã dos Guaranis, 1610–1768*, trans. Álvaro Cabral. Rio de Janeiro: Paz e Terra, 1968.

Luna, Francisco Vidal. *Minas Gerais, escravos e senhores: análise da estrutura populacional e econômica de alguns centros mineratórios, 1718–1804*. São Paulo: Instituto de Pesquisas Econômicas, 1981.

Luna, Luiz. *Resistência do índio à dominação do Brasil*. Rio de Janeiro: Leitura, 1965.

Lyra, Maria de Lourdes Viana. "Os dízimos reais na capitania de São Paulo: contribuição á história tributária do Brasil colonial, 1640–1750." Dissertação de mestrado, Universidade de São Paulo, 1971.

Machado, José de Alcântara. *Vida e morte do bandeirante*. 3rd edn. São Paulo: Martins, 1943 (1929).

Machado, Maria Helena P.T. *Crime e escravidão: trabalho, luta e resistência nas lavouras paulistas, 1830–1888*. São Paulo: Brasiliense, 1987.

MacNicoll, Murray Graeme. "Seventeenth-Century Maranhão: Beckman's Revolt." *Estudos Ibero-Americanos* 4/1 (July 1978): 129–140.

Maffei, Lucy de Abreu, and Arlinda Rocha Nogueira. "O ouro na capitania de São Vicente nos séculos XVI e XVII." *Anais do Museu Paulista* 20 (1966): 7–136.

Main, Gloria L. "Inequality in Early America: The Evidence from Probate Records of Massachusetts and Maryland." *Journal of Interdisciplinary History* 7/4 (1977): 559–581.

Makino, Miyoko. "Jundiaí: povoamento e desenvolvimento, 1655–1854." Dissertação de mestrado, Universidade de São Paulo, 1981.

Malheiro, Agostinho Marques Perdigão. *A escravidão no Brasil: ensaio histórico, jurídico, social*. 2 vols. 3rd edn. Petrópolis: Vozes, 1976 (1866–1867).

Marchant, Alexander. *From Barter to Slavery: The Economic Relations of Portuguese and Indians in the Settlement of Brazil, 1500–1580*. Baltimore: Johns Hopkins University Press, 1942.

Marcílio, Maria Luíza. *Caiçara: terra e população*. São Paulo: Edições Paulinas/CEDHAL, 1986.

A cidade de São Paulo: povoamento e população, 1750–1850. São Paulo: Pioneira, 1973.

"Crescimento demográfico e evolução agrária paulista, 1700–1836." Tese de livre-docência, Universidade de São Paulo, 1974.

Marks, Shula, and Anthony Atmore (eds.). *Economy and Society in Pre-Industrial South Africa*. London: Longmans, 1980.

Marques, Manuel Eufrásio de Azevedo. *Apontamentos históricos, geográficos, biográficos, estatísticos e noticiosos da província de São Paulo.* 2 vols. 3rd edn. Belo Horizonte: Itatiaia, 1980 (1879).

Mazzuia, Mário. *Jundiaí e sua história*. Jundiaí: Prefeitura Municipal, 1979.

Melià, Bartomeu. *El Guaraní conquistado y reducido*. 2nd edn. Asunción: Universidad Católica, 1988 (1986).

Mesgravis, Laima. *A Santa Casa de Misericórdia de São Paulo, 1599?-1884: contribuição ao estudo da assistência social no Brasil*. São Paulo: Conselho Estadual de Cultura, 1976.

Metcalf, Alida C. *Family and Frontier in Colonial Brazil: Santana de Parnaíba, 1580–1822*. Berkeley: University of California Press, 1992.

"Fathers and Sons: The Politics of Inheritance in a Colonial Brazilian Township." *Hispanic American Historical Review* 66/3 (August 1986): 455–484.

Métraux, Alfred. "The Guaraní." In Julian H. Steward (ed.), *Handbook of South American Indians*, 7 vols., vol. 3: *The Tropical Forest Tribes*, 69–94. Washington, DC: Smithsonian Institution, 1946–1950.

A religião dos Tupinambás e suas relações com a das demais tribos tupi-guaranis, trans. Estêvão Pinto. 2nd edn. São Paulo: Nacional, 1979 (1950).

Miller, Joseph C. "Capitalism and Slaving: The Financial and Commercial Organization of the Angolan Slave Trade, according to the Accounts of Antonio Coelho Guerreiro (1684–1692)." *International Journal of African Historical Studies* 17/1 (1984): 1–56.

Milliet, Sérgio. *Roteiro do café e outros ensaios*. 2nd edn. São Paulo: Hucitec, 1982 (1939).

Mintz, Sidney. "Slavery and the Rise of Peasantries." *Historical Reflections/Réflexions Historiques* 6 (1979): 213–242.

Monteiro, John M. "Celeiro do Brasil: escravidão indígena e a agricultura paulista no século XVII." *História* 7 (1988): 1–12.

"Distribuição da riqueza e as origens da pobreza rural em São Paulo no século XVII." *Estudos Econômicos* 19/1 (1989): 109–130.

"Escravidão indígena e despovoamento: São Paulo e Maranhão no século XVII." In Jill Dias (ed.), *Brasil nas vésperas do mundo moderno*, 137–167. Lisbon: Comissão dos Descobrimentos Portugueses, 1992.

"A escravidão indígena e o problema da identidade étnica em São Paulo colonial." *Ciências Sociais Hoje* (1990): 237–252.

"Os escravos índios de São Paulo no século XVII: alguns aspectos demográficos." *Revista da Sociedade Brasileira de Pesquisa Histórica* 5 (1989–1990): 11–18.

"From Indian to Slave: Forced Native Labour and Colonial Society in São Paulo during the Seventeenth Century." *Slavery & Abolition* 9/2 (1988): 105–127.

"Os Guarani e a história do Brasil meridional, séculos XVI–XVII." In Cunha (ed.), *História dos índios no Brasil*, 475–498.

"Sal e justiça social em São Paulo colonial: o caso Bartolomeu Fernandes de Faria." Paper presented to the IX Reunião Anual da Sociedade Brasileira de Pesquisa Histórica, Rio de Janeiro, 1989.

"São Paulo in the Seventeenth Century: Economy and Society." Ph.D. dissertation, University of Chicago, 1985.

"Tupis, Tapuias e história de São Paulo: revisitando a velha questão guaianá." *Novos Estudos CEBRAP* 34 (1992): 125–135.

"Vida e morte do índio: São Paulo colonial." In Monteiro et al., *Índios no estado de São Paulo*, 21–44. São Paulo: Comissão Pró-Índio de São Paulo, 1984.

Monteiro, John M., Lúcia Helena Rangel, Mara L. Manzoni Luz, Marco Antonio Barbosa, Maria Inês Ladeira, and Silvia Helena Simões Borelli. *Índios no estado de São Paulo: resistência e transfiguração*. São Paulo: Comissão Pró-Índio de São Paulo, 1984.

Moraes, Rubens Borba de, and William Berrien (eds.). *Manual bibliográfico de estudos brasileiros*. Rio de Janeiro: Souza, 1949.
Mörner, Magnus. *The Political and Economic Activities of the Jesuits in the La Plata Region: The Habsburg Era*. Stockholm: Institute of Ibero-American Studies, 1953.
Morse, Richard M. *From Community to Metropolis: A Biography of São Paulo*. Gainesville: University of Florida Press, 1958.
"Some Themes in Brazilian History." *South Atlantic Quarterly* 61/1 (1962): 159–182.
(ed.). *The Bandeirantes: The Historical Role of the Brazilian Pathfinders*. New York: Knopf, 1965.
Moscoso, Francisco. *Tribu y clase en el Caribe antiguo*. San Pedro de Macoris, Dominican Republic: Universidad Central del Este, 1986.
Mott, Luiz R. B. "Os índios e a pecuária nas fazendas de gado do Piauí colonial." *Revista de Antropologia* 22 (1979): 61–78.
Nazzari, Muriel. *Disappearance of the Dowry: Women, Families, and Social Change in São Paulo, Brazil, 1600–1900*. Stanford University Press, 1991.
"Dotes paulistas: composição e transformações, 1600–1870." *Revista Brasileira de História* 17 (1988–1989): 87–100.
"Transition Toward Slavery: Changing Legal Practice regarding Indians in Seventeenth-Century São Paulo." *The Americas* 49/2 (October 1992): 131–155.
Necker, Louis. *Indiens guarani et chamanes franciscains: les premières réductions du Paraguay, 1580–1600*. Paris: Anthropos, 1979.
Neme, Mário. *Apossamento do solo e evolução da propriedade rural na zona de Piracicaba*. São Paulo: Museu Paulista, 1974.
"Dados para a história dos índios Caiapó." *Anais do Museu Paulista* 23 (1969): 101–147.
Notas de revisão da história de São Paulo: século XVI. São Paulo: Anhambi, 1959.
Neves, Luis Felipe Baêta. *O combate dos soldados de Cristo na Terra dos Papagaios: colonialismo e repressão cultural*. Rio de Janeiro: Forense-Universitária, 1978.
Newson, Linda A. *The Cost of Conquest: Indian Decline in Honduras under Spanish Rule*. Boulder, CO: Westview Press, 1986.
Nimuendajú, Curt. *Mapa etno-histórico do Brasil e regiões adjacentes*. Rio de Janeiro: Instituto Brasileiro de Geografia e Estatística, 1981.
Nordenskiöld, Erland. "The Guarani Invasion of the Inca Empire in the Sixteenth Century: An Historical Indian Migration." *Geographical Review* 4/2 (August 1917): 103–121.
Novais, Fernando. *Estrutura e dinâmica do antigo sistema colonial*. 5th edn. São Paulo: Brasiliense, 1986 (1974).
Oliveira, José Joaquim Machado de. "Os Cayapós." *Revista Trimensal do Instituto Historico, Geographico e Ethnographico do Brasil* 24 (1861): 491–524.
"Noticia raciocinada sobre as aldêas de indios da provincia de S. Paulo, desde o seu começo até à actualidade." *Revista Trimensal de Historia e Geografia, ou Jornal do Instituto Historico e Geographico Brasileiro* 8 (1846): 204–254.
Quadro histórico da província de São Paulo até o ano de 1822. 3rd edn. São Paulo: Governo do Estado, 1978 (1864).
Overton, Mark. "Estimating Crop Yields from Probate Inventories: An Example from East Anglia, 1585–1735." *Journal of Economic History* 39/2 (June 1979): 363–78.
Pastells, Pablo. *Historia de la Compañia de Jesus en la provincia del Paraguay*. 8 vols. Madrid: Victoriano Suárez, 1912–1949.
Perrone-Moisés, Beatriz. "A guerra justa em Portugal no século XVI." *Revista da Sociedade Brasileira de Pesquisa Histórica* 5 (1989–1990): 5–10.
"Índios livres e índios escravos: os princípios da legislação indigenista do período colonial (séculos XVI a XVIII)." In Cunha (ed.), *História dos Índios no Brasil*, 115–132.

"Legislação indígena colonial: inventário e índice." Dissertação de mestrado, Universidade Estadual de Campinas, 1990.
Petrone, Maria Theresa Schorer. *A lavoura canavieira em São Paulo*. São Paulo: Difusão Européia do Livro, 1968.
Petrone, Pasquale. "Os aldeamentos paulistas e sua função na valorização da região paulista." Tese de livre-docência, Universidade de São Paulo, 1964.
Pinto, Luiz de Aguiar da Costa. *Lutas de famílias no Brasil: introdução ao seu estudo*. 2nd edn. São Paulo: Nacional, 1980 (1949).
Porto, Aurélio. *História das missões orientais do Uruguai*. Rio de Janeiro: Imprensa Nacional, 1943.
Prado Júnior, Caio. *Formação do Brasil contemporâneo: colônia*. 14th edn. São Paulo: Brasiliense, 1976 (1942).
História econômica do Brasil. 17th edn. São Paulo: Brasiliense, 1974 (1945).
Prado, João Fernando de Almeida. *Os primeiros povoadores do Brasil*. São Paulo: Nacional, 1935.
São Vicente e as capitanias do sul, as origens, 1501–1531: história da formação da sociedade brasileira. São Paulo: Nacional, 1961.
Prado, Paulo. *Retrato do Brasil: ensaio sobre a tristeza brasileira*. 7th edn. Rio de Janeiro: José Olympio, 1972 (1928).
Prestage, Edgar. *D. Francisco Manuel de Mello, esboço biographico*. Coimbra: Imprensa da Universidade, 1914.
Price, David. "Nambiquara leadership." *American Ethnologist* 8/4 (November 1981): 686–708.
Queiroz, Maria Isaura Pereira de. *Bairros rurais paulistas: dinâmica das relações bairro rural-cidade*. São Paulo: Duas Cidades, 1973.
Quintiliano, Aylton. *A guerra dos Tamoios*. Rio de Janeiro: Reper, 1965.
Radell, David R. "The Indian Slave Trade and Population of Nicaragua during the Sixteenth Century." In William M. Denevan (ed.), *The Native Population of the Americas in 1492*, 67–76. Madison: University of Wisconsin Press, 1976.
Ramos, Alcida Rita. *Hierarquia e simbiose: relações intertribais no Brasil*. São Paulo: Hucitec, 1980.
Sociedades indígenas. São Paulo: Ática, 1986.
Reis, Paulo Pereira dos. *O indígena do Vale do Paraíba*. São Paulo: Governo do Estado, 1979.
Ribeiro, Berta. *O índio na história do Brasil*. São Paulo: Global, 1983.
Ribeiro, J. C. Gomes. "Os indigenas primitivos de S. Paulo (Guayanazes, Tapuias ou Tupis?)." *Revista do Instituto Historico e Geographico de São Paulo* 13 (1908): 181–195.
Ribeiro, Joaquim. *Folclore dos bandeirantes*. Rio de Janeiro: José Olympio, 1946.
Ricardo, Cassiano. *Marcha para oeste: a influência da "bandeira" na formação social e política do Brasil*. 3rd edn. 2 vols. Rio de Janeiro: José Olympio, 1959 (1940).
"O negro no bandeirismo paulista." *Revista do Arquivo Municipal* 47 (May 1938): 5–46.
Russell-Wood, A. J. R. "Local Government in Portuguese America: A Study in Cultural Divergence." *Comparative Studies in Society and History* 16/2 (March 1974): 187–231.
"Women and Society in Colonial Brazil." *Journal of Latin American Studies* 9/1 (May 1977): 1–34.
Salvador, José Gonçalves. *Os cristãos novos e o comércio do Atlântico meridional, com enfoque nas capitanias do Sul, 1530–1680*. São Paulo: Pioneira, 1978.
Os cristãos-novos: povoamento e conquista do solo brasileiro, 1530–1680. São Paulo: Pioneira, 1976.
Samara, Eni de Mesquita. *A família brasileira*. São Paulo: Brasiliense, 1983.
Sampaio, Theodoro. "Os Guayanãs na capitania de S. Vicente." *Revista do Instituto Historico e Geographico de São Paulo* 8 (1903): 159–169.

Santos, Corcino Medeiros dos. *Economia e sociedade do Rio Grande do Sul*. São Paulo: Nacional, 1984.

Scatamacchia, Maria Cristina Mineiro. "Tentativa da caracterização da tradição tupi-guarani." Dissertação de mestrado, Universidade de São Paulo: 1981.

Schaden, Egon. *Aspectos fundamentais da cultura guarani*. São Paulo: Universidade de São Paulo, 1974.

"Os primitivos habitantes do território paulista." *Revista de História* 18 (1954): 385–406.

Schwartz, Stuart B. "The Formation of a Colonial Identity in Brazil." In Nicholas Canny and Anthony Pagden (eds.), *Colonial Identity in the Atlantic World, 1500–1800*, 15–50. Princeton University Press, 1987.

"Indian Labor and New World Plantations: European Demands and Indian Responses in Northeastern Brazil." *American Historical Review* 83/1 (February 1978): 43–79.

"Patterns of Slaveholding in the Americas: New Evidence from Brazil." *American Historical Review* 87/1 (February 1982): 55–86.

Sovereignty and Society in Colonial Brazil: The High Court of Bahia and its Judges, 1609–1750. Berkeley: University of California Press, 1973.

Sugar Plantations in the Formation of Brazilian Society: Bahia, 1550–1835. Cambridge University Press, 1985.

(ed.). *A Governor and his Image in Baroque Brazil: The Funereal Eulogy of Afonso Furtado de Castro do Rio de Mendonça*. Minneapolis: University of Minnesota Press, 1979.

Serrano, Antonio. *Etnografía da la antigua provincia del Uruguay*. Paraná: Melchior, 1936.

Serrão, Joel (ed.). *Dicionário de história portuguesa*. 5 vols. Lisbon and Porto, various edns.

Service, Elman R. *Spanish–Guarani Relations in Early Colonial Paraguay*. Ann Arbor: University of Michigan Press, 1954.

Sherman, William L. *Forced Native Labor in Sixteenth-Century Central America*. Lincoln: University of Nebraska Press, 1979.

Silva, Duarte Leopoldo e. *Notas de história ecclesiástica*, vol. 3: *Baruery-Parnahyba*. São Paulo: Augusto Siqueira, 1916.

Silva, Janice Theodoro da. *São Paulo, 1554–1880: discurso ideológico e organização espacial*. São Paulo: Moderna, 1984.

Silveira, Waldomiro Franco da. *História de Atibaia*. São Paulo: by the author, 1950.

Simonsen, Roberto. *História econômica do Brasil, 1500–1820*. 8th edn. São Paulo: Nacional, 1978 (1937).

Siqueira, Elizabeth Madureira. "O segmento indígena: uma tentativa de recuperação histórica." *Leopoldianum* 33 (1985): 129–141.

Slenes, Robert W. "The Demography and Economics of Brazilian Slavery 1850–1888." Ph.D. dissertation, Stanford University, 1976.

Sousa, Washington Luís Pereira de. *Capitania de São Paulo, governo de Rodrigo Cesar de Meneses*. 2nd edn. São Paulo: Nacional, 1938 (1904).

Souza, Antonio Candido de Mello e. *Os parceiros do Rio Bonito*. 5th edn. São Paulo: Duas Cidades, 1979 (1964).

Souza, Laura de Mello e. *Desclassificados do ouro: a pobreza mineira no século XVIII*. Rio de Janeiro: Graal, 1982.

O diabo e a Terra de Santa Cruz: feitiçaria e religiosidade popular no Brasil colonial. São Paulo: Companhia das Letras, 1986.

Stern, Steve J. *Peru's Indian Peoples and the Challenge of Spanish Conquest: Huamanga to 1640*. Madison: University of Wisconsin Press, 1982.

(ed.). *Resistance, Rebellion, and Consciousness in the Andean Peasant World, 18th to 20th Centuries*. Madison: University of Wisconsin Press, 1987.

Steward, Julian H. (ed.). *Handbook of South American Indians*. 7 vols. Washington, DC: Smithsonian Institution, 1946–1950.

Susnik, Branislava. *Dispersión Tupi-Guaraní prehistórica: ensayo analítico.* Asunción: Museo Etnográfico Andrés Barbero, 1975.

El indio colonial del Paraguay, vol. 1: *El Guaraní colonial.* Asunción: Museo Etnográfico Andrés Barbero, 1965.

Sweet, David G. "Black Robes and 'Black Destiny': Jesuit Views of African slavery in Seventeenth-Century Latin America." *Revista de Historia de América* 86 (July–December 1978): 87–133.

"Francisca: Indian Slave." In David G. Sweet and Gary B. Nash (eds.), *Struggle and Survival in Colonial America*, 274–291. Berkeley: University of California Press, 1981.

"A Rich Realm of Nature Destroyed: The Middle Amazon Valley, 1640–1750." Ph.D. dissertation, University of Wisconsin, 1974.

Taunay, Afonso d'Escragnolle. "A fortuna do padre Pompeu, 1656–1713." *Revista do Arquivo Municipal* 19 (January 1936): 41–50.

"A guerra dos barbaros." *Revista do Arquivo Municipal* 22 (April 1936): 7–331.

Historia geral das bandeiras paulistas. 11 vols. São Paulo: H. L. Canton, 1924–1950.

Historia seiscentista da villa de S. Paulo: escripta á vista de avultada documentação inedita dos archivos brasileiros e extrangeiros. 4 vols. São Paulo: H. L. Canton, 1926–1929.

Non ducor, duco: noticias de S. Paulo, 1565–1820. São Paulo: H. L. Canton, 1924.

Piratininga: aspectos sociaes de S. Paulo seiscentista. São Paulo: H. L. Canton, 1923.

"O preço da vida em S. Paulo em fins do seculo XVII e em meiados do século XVIII." *Annaes do Museu Paulista* 3 (1927): 389–405.

Sob El Rey Nosso Senhor: aspectos da vida setecentista brasileira sobretudo, em São Paulo. São Paulo: Diário Official, 1923.

Trigaes paulistanos dos seculos XVI e XVII. São Paulo: Secretaria da Agricultura, Industria e Commercio, 1929.

Teschauer, Carlos. *Historia do Rio Grande do Sul, dos dous primeiros seculos.* 3 vols. Porto Alegre: Livraria Selbach, 1918–1922.

Thomas, Georg. *A política indigenista dos portugueses no Brasil, 1500–1640.* São Paulo: Loyola, 1982.

Toral, André Amaral de. "Os índios negros ou os Carijó de Goiás: a história dos Avá-Canoeiro." *Revista de Antropologia* 27–28 (1984–1985): 287–325.

Varnhagen, Francisco Adolfo [Adolpho] de. *História geral do Brasil.* 7th edn. 5 vols. Belo Horizonte: Itatiaia, 1981 (1854–1857).

Os indios bravos e o sr. Lisboa. Lima: Imprensa Liberal, 1867.

Vianna Filho, Luis. "O trabalho do engenho e a reação do índio: estabelecimento da escravatura africana." *Congresso do mundo português: publicações*, vol. 10, 11–29. Lisbon: Comissão Executiva dos Centenários, 1940.

Viotti, Hélio Abranches. "A aldeia de Maniçoba e a fundação de Itu." *Revista do Instituto Histórico e Geográfico de São Paulo* 71 (1974): 389–401.

Volpato, Luiza Rios Ricci. *A conquista da terra no universo da pobreza: formação da fronteira oeste do Brasil, 1719–1819.* São Paulo: Hucitec, 1987.

Zemella, Mafalda. *O abastecimento da capitania de Minas Gerais no século XVIII.* 2nd edn. São Paulo: Hucitec, 1990 (1951).

Zenha, Edmundo. *Mamelucos.* São Paulo: Revista dos Tribunais, 1970.

O município no Brasil, 1552–1700. São Paulo: Progresso, 1948.

Index

Other Books in the Series (continued from page ii)

96. *Warfare and Shamanism in Amazonia*, Carlos Fausto
95. *Rebellion on the Amazon: The Cabanagem, Race, and Popular Culture in the North of Brazil, 1798–1840*, Mark Harris
94. *A History of the Khipu*, Galen Brokaw
93. *Politics, Markets, and Mexico's "London Debt," 1823–1887*, Richard J. Salvucci
92. *The Political Economy of Argentina in the Twentieth Century*, Roberto Cortés Conde
91. *Bankruptcy of Empire: Mexican Silver and the Wars Between Spain, Britain, and France, 1760–1810*, Carlos Marichal
90. *Shadows of Empire: The Indian Nobility of Cusco, 1750–1825*, David T. Garrett
89. *Chile: The Making of a Republic, 1830–1865: Politics and Ideas*, Simon Collier
88. *Deference and Defiance in Monterrey: Workers, Paternalism, and Revolution in Mexico, 1890–1950*, Michael Snodgrass
87. *Andrés Bello: Scholarship and Nation-Building in Nineteenth-Century Latin America*, Ivan Jaksic
86. *Between Revolution and the Ballot Box: The Origins of the Argentine Radical Party in the 1890s*, Paula Alonso
85. *Slavery and the Demographic and Economic History of Minas Gerais, Brazil, 1720–1888*, Laird W. Bergad
84. *The Independence of Spanish America*, Jaime E. Rodríguez
83. *The Rise of Capitalism on the Pampas: The Estancias of Buenos Aires, 1785–1870*, Samuel Amaral
82. *A History of Chile, 1808–2002*, Second Edition, Simon Collier and William F. Sater
81. *The Revolutionary Mission: American Enterprise in Latin America, 1900–1945*, Thomas F. O'Brien
80. *The Kingdom of Quito, 1690–1830: The State and Regional Development*, Kenneth J. Andrien
79. *The Cuban Slave Market, 1790–1880*, Laird W. Bergad, Fe Iglesias García, and María del Carmen Barcia
78. *Business Interest Groups in Nineteenth-Century Brazil*, Eugene Ridings
77. *The Economic History of Latin America since Independence*, Second Edition, Victor Bulmer-Thomas
76. *Power and Violence in the Colonial City: Oruro from the Mining Renaissance to the Rebellion of Tupac Amaru (1740–1782)*, Oscar Cornblit
75. *Colombia before Independence: Economy, Society and Politics under Bourbon Rule*, Anthony McFarlane

74. *Politics and Urban Growth in Buenos Aires, 1910–1942*, Richard J. Walter
73. *The Central Republic in Mexico, 1835–1846: "Hombres de Bien" in the Age of Santa Anna*, Michael P. Costeloe
72. *Negotiating Democracy: Politicians and Generals in Uruguay*, Charles Guy Gillespie
71. *Native Society and Disease in Colonial Ecuador*, Suzanne Austin Alchon
70. *The Politics of Memory: Native Historical Interpretation in the Colombian Andes*, Joanne Rappaport
69. *Power and the Ruling Classes in Northeast Brazil: Juazeiro and Petrolina in Transition*, Ronald H. Chilcote
68. *House and Street: The Domestic World of Servants and Masters in Nineteenth-Century Rio de Janeiro*, Sandra Lauderdale Graham
67. *The Demography of Inequality in Brazil*, Charles H. Wood and José Alberto Magno de Carvalho
66. *The Politics of Coalition Rule in Colombia*, Jonathan Hartlyn
65. *South America and the First World War: The Impact of the War on Brazil, Argentina, Peru and Chile*, Bill Albert
64. *Resistance and Integration: Peronism and the Argentine Working Class, 1946–1976*, Daniel James
63. *The Political Economy of Central America since 1920*, Victor Bulmer-Thomas
62. *A Tropical Belle Epoque: Elite Culture and Society in Turn-of-the-Century Rio de Janeiro*, Jeffrey D. Needell
61. *Ambivalent Conquests: Maya and Spaniard in Yucatan, 1517–1570*, Second Edition, Inga Clendinnen
60. *Latin America and the Comintern, 1919–1943*, Manuel Caballero
59. *Roots of Insurgency: Mexican Regions, 1750–1824*, Brian R. Hamnett
58. *The Agrarian Question and the Peasant Movement in Colombia: Struggles of the National Peasant Association, 1967–1981*, Leon Zamosc
57. *Catholic Colonialism: A Parish History of Guatemala, 1524–1821*, Adriaan C. van Oss
56. *Pre-Revolutionary Caracas: Politics, Economy, and Society 1777–1811*, P. Michael McKinley
55. *The Mexican Revolution, Volume 2: Counter-Revolution and Reconstruction*, Alan Knight
54. *The Mexican Revolution, Volume 1: Porfirians, Liberals, and Peasants*, Alan Knight
53. *The Province of Buenos Aires and Argentine Politics, 1912–1943*, Richard J. Walter
52. *Sugar Plantations in the Formation of Brazilian Society: Bahia, 1550–1835*, Stuart B. Schwartz

51. *Tobacco on the Periphery: A Case Study in Cuban Labour History, 1860–1958*, Jean Stubbs
50. *Housing, the State, and the Poor: Policy and Practice in Three Latin American Cities*, Alan Gilbert and Peter M. Ward
49. *Unions and Politics in Mexico: The Case of the Automobile Industry*, Ian Roxborough
48. *Miners, Peasants and Entrepreneurs: Regional Development in the Central Highlands of Peru*, Norman Long and Bryan Roberts
47. *Capitalist Development and the Peasant Economy in Peru*, Adolfo Figueroa
46. *Early Latin America: A History of Colonial Spanish America and Brazil*, James Lockhart and Stuart B. Schwartz
45. *Brazil's State-Owned Enterprises: A Case Study of the State as Entrepreneur*, Thomas J. Trebat
44. *Law and Politics in Aztec Texcoco*, Jerome A. Offner
43. *Juan Vicente Gómez and the Oil Companies in Venezuela, 1908–1935*, B. S. McBeth
42. *Revolution from Without: Yucatán, Mexico, and the United States, 1880–1924*, Gilbert M. Joseph
41. *Demographic Collapse: Indian Peru, 1520–1620*, Noble David Cook
40. *Oil and Politics in Latin America: Nationalist Movements and State Companies*, George Philip
39. *The Struggle for Land: A Political Economy of the Pioneer Frontier in Brazil from 1930 to the Present Day*, J. Foweraker
38. *Caudillo and Peasant in the Mexican Revolution*, ed. D. A. Brading
37. *Odious Commerce: Britain, Spain and the Abolition of the Cuban Slave Trade*, David Murray
36. *Coffee in Colombia, 1850–1970: An Economic, Social and Political History*, Marco Palacios
35. *A Socioeconomic History of Argentina, 1776–1860*, Jonathan C. Brown
34. *From Dessalines to Duvalier: Race, Colour and National Independence in Haiti*, David Nicholls
33. *Modernization in a Mexican Ejido: A Study in Economic Adaptation*, Billie R. DeWalt
32. *Haciendas and Ranchos in the Mexican Bajío, Léon, 1700–1860*, D. A. Brading
31. *Foreign Immigrants in Early Bourbon Mexico, 1700–1760*, Charles F. Nunn
30. *The Merchants of Buenos Aires, 1778–1810: Family and Commerce*, Susan Migden Socolow
29. *Drought and Irrigation in North-East Brazil*, Anthony L. Hall
28. *Coronelismo: The Municipality and Representative Government in Brazil*, Victor Nunes Leal

27. *A History of the Bolivian Labour Movement, 1848–1971*, Guillermo Lora
26. *Land and Labour in Latin America: Essays on the Development of Agrarian Capitalism in the Nineteenth and Twentieth Centuries*, ed. Kenneth Duncan and Ian Rutledge
25. *Allende's Chile: The Political Economy of the Rise and Fall of the Unidad Popular*, Stefan de Vylder
24. *The Cristero Rebellion: The Mexican People Between Church and State, 1926–1929*, Jean A. Meyer
23. *The African Experience in Spanish America: 1502 to the Present Day*, Leslie B. Rout, Jr.
22. *Letters and People of the Spanish Indies: Sixteenth Century*, ed. James Lockhart and Enrique Otte
21. *Chilean Rural Society from the Spanish Conquest to 1930*, Arnold J. Bauer
20. *Studies in the Colonial History of Spanish America*, Mario Góngora
19. *Politics in Argentina, 1890–1930: The Rise and Fall of Radicalism*, David Rock
18. *Politics, Economics and Society in Argentina in the Revolutionary Period*, Tulio Halperín Donghi
17. *Marriage, Class and Colour in Nineteenth-Century Cuba: A Study of Racial Attitudes and Sexual Values in a Slave Society*, Verena Stolcke
16. *Conflicts and Conspiracies: Brazil and Portugal, 1750–1808*, Kenneth Maxwell
15. *Silver Mining and Society in Colonial Mexico: Zacatecas, 1546–1700*, P. J. Bakewell
14. *A Guide to the Historical Geography of New Spain*, Peter Gerhard
13. *Bolivia: Land, Location and Politics Since 1825*, J. Valerie Fifer, Malcolm Deas, Clifford Smith, and John Street
12. *Politics and Trade in Southern Mexico, 1750–1821*, Brian R. Hamnett
11. *Alienation of Church Wealth in Mexico: Social and Economic Aspects of the Liberal Revolution, 1856–1875*, Jan Bazant
10. *Miners and Merchants in Bourbon Mexico, 1763–1810*, D. A. Brading
9. *An Economic History of Colombia, 1845–1930*, W. P. McGreevey
8. *Economic Development of Latin America: Historical Background and Contemporary Problems*, Celso Furtado and Suzette Macedo
7. *Regional Economic Development: The River Basin Approach in Mexico*, David Barkin and Timothy King
6. *The Abolition of the Brazilian Slave Trade: Britain, Brazil and the Slave Trade Question, 1807–1869*, Leslie Bethell
5. *Parties and Political Change in Bolivia, 1880–1952*, Herbert S. Klein

4. *Britain and the Onset of Modernization in Brazil, 1850–1914*, Richard Graham
3. *The Mexican Revolution, 1910–1914: The Diplomacy of Anglo-American Conflict*, P. A. R. Calvert
2. *Church Wealth in Mexico: A Study of the "Juzgado de Capellanias" in the Archbishopric of Mexico 1800–1856*, Michael P. Costeloe
1. *Ideas and Politics of Chilean Independence, 1808–1833*, Simon Collier